𝔖𝔱𝔞𝔫𝔡𝔞𝔯𝔡 𝔏𝔦𝔟𝔯𝔞𝔯𝔶 𝔈𝔡𝔦𝔱𝔦𝔬𝔫

THE HISTORICAL WRITINGS

OF

JOHN FISKE

ILLUSTRATED WITH MANY PHOTOGRAVURES,

MAPS, CHARTS, FACSIMILES, ETC.

IN TWELVE VOLUMES

VOLUME II

Americus Vespucius

THE DISCOVERY OF AMERICA

WITH SOME ACCOUNT OF ANCIENT AMERICA AND THE SPANISH CONQUEST

BY

JOHN FISKE

IN THREE VOLUMES. VOLUME II

Then I unbar the doors; my paths lead out
The exodus of nations; I disperse
Men to all shores that front the hoary main.
I too have arts and sorceries;
Illusion dwells forever with the wave.
I make some coast alluring, some lone isle
To distant men, who must go there or die
EMERSON

The Riverside Press

BOSTON AND NEW YORK
HOUGHTON, MIFFLIN AND COMPANY
The Riverside Press, Cambridge

4435

CONTENTS

V

V

CONTENTS

CONTENTS

vii

CONTENTS

CONTENTS

VI

THE FINDING OF STRANGE COASTS

CONTENTS

CONTENTS

VII

MUNDUS NOVUS

CONTENTS

CONTENTS

CONTENTS

CONTENTS

XV

CONTENTS

xvi

CONTENTS

CONTENTS

CONTENTS

LIST OF ILLUSTRATIONS

LIST OF ILLUSTRATIONS

LIST OF ILLUSTRATIONS

LIST OF ILLUSTRATIONS

LIST OF ILLUSTRATIONS

From original in the Lenox Collection, New York Public Library. This map was discovered at Munich in 1885, and was supposed by Dr. Wieser and Henry Stevens to be the long lost globe of Johann Schöner, made in 1523. Later research, however, by Baron Nordenskiöld and Henry Harrisse, has proved that it cannot be the work of Schöner, and that its authorship is unknown.

XXV

THE
DISCOVERY OF AMERICA

V

THE SEARCH FOR THE INDIES

WESTWARD OR SPANISH ROUTE

OUR information concerning the life of
Columbus before 1492 is far from being
as satisfactory as one could wish. Unquestionably he is to be deemed fortunate in
having had for his biographers two such men
as his friend Las Casas, one of the noblest char-
acters and most faithful historians of that or
any age, and his own son Ferdinand Columbus,
a most accomplished scholar and bib- Sources of
liographer. The later years of Ferdi- information
concerning
nand's life were devoted, with loving the life of
care, to the preparation of a biogra- Columbus :
Las Casas
phy of his father; and his book — and Ferdinand Colum-
which unfortunately survives only in bus
the Italian translation of Alfonso Ulloa,[1] pub-

[1] *Historie del S. D. Fernando Colombo ; Nelle quali s'*
ha particolare, & vera relatione della vita, & de' fatti dell'

lished in Venice in 1571 — is of priceless value. As Washington Irving long ago wrote, it is "an invaluable document, entitled to great faith, and is the corner-stone of the history of the American continent."[1] After Ferdinand's death, in 1539, his papers seem to have passed into the hands of Las Casas, who, from 1552 to 1561, in the seclusion of the college of San Gregorio at Valladolid, was engaged in writing his great "History of the Indies."[2] Ferdinand's superb library, one of the finest in Europe, was bequeathed to the cathedral at Seville.[3] It con-

---

Ammiraglio D. Christoforo Colombo, suo padre : Et dello scoprimento, ch' egli fece dell' Indie Occidentali, dette Monde-Nvovo, hora possedute dal Sereniss. Re Catolico : Nuouamente di lingua Spagnuola tradotte nell' Italiana dal S. Alfonso Vlloa. Con privilegio. IN VENETIA, M D LXXI. *Appresso Francesco de' Franceschi Sanese.* The principal reprints are those of Milan, 1614 ; Venice, 1676 and 1678 ; London, 1867. I always cite it as *Vita dell' Ammiraglio.*

[1] Irving's *Life of Columbus*, New York, 1868, vol. iii. p. 375. My references, unless otherwise specified, are to this, the "Geoffrey Crayon," edition.

[2] Las Casas, *Historia de las Indias, ahora por primera vez dada á luz por el Marqués de la Fuensanta del Valle y D. José Sancho Rayon,* Madrid, 1875, 5 vols. 8vo.

[3] " Fu questo D. Ernando di non minor valore del padre, ma di molte più lettere et scienze dotato che quelle non fu ; et il quale lasciò alla Chiesa maggiore di Siviglia, dove hoggi si vede honorevolmente sepolto, una, non sola numerosissima, ma richissi ma libraria, et piena di molti libri in ogni facoltà et scienza rarissimi : laquale da coloro che l' han veduta, vien

tained some twenty thousand volumes in print
and manuscript, four fifths of which, through
shameful neglect or vandalism, have perished or
been scattered. Four thousand volumes, however, are still preserved, and this library (known
as the " Biblioteca Colombina ") is full
of interest for the historian. Book- The Biblio-
buying was to Ferdinand Columbus teca Colombina at Seville
one of the most important occupations in life.
His books were not only carefully numbered,
but on the last leaf of each one he wrote a mem-
orandum of the time and place of its purchase
and the sum of money paid for it.[1] This habit
of Ferdinand's has furnished us with clues to
the solution of some interesting questions. Besides this, he was much given to making marginal notes and comments, which are sometimes
of immense value, and, more than all, there are
still to be seen in this library a few books that
belonged to Christopher Columbus himself,
with very important notes in his own handwriting and in that of his brother Bartholomew.
Las Casas was familiar with this grand collection

stimata delle più rare cose di tutta Europa." Moleto's pre-
fatory letter to *Vita dell' Ammiraglio*, April 25, 1571.

[1] For example, " *Manuel de la Sancta Fe católica*, Sevilla,
1495, in-4. Costó en Toledo 34 maravedis, año 1511, 9
de Octubre, No. 3004." " *Tragicomedia de Calisto y Mel-
ibea*, Sevilla, 1502, in-4. Muchas figuras. Costó en Roma
25 cuatrines, por Junio de 1515. No. 2417," etc. See
Harrisse, *Fernand Colomb*, Paris, 1872, p. 13.

3

in the days of its completeness, he was well acquainted with all the members of the Columbus family, and he had evidently read the manuscript sources of Ferdinand's book ; for a comparison with Ulloa's version shows that considerable portions of the original Spanish text — or of the documents upon which it rested — are preserved in the work of Las Casas.[1] The citation and adoption of Ferdinand's statements by the latter writer, who was able independently to verify them, is therefore in most cases equivalent to corroboration, and the two writers together form an authority of the weightiest kind, and not lightly to be questioned or set aside.

Besides these books of most fundamental importance, we have valuable accounts of some parts of the life of Columbus by his friend Andres Bernaldez, the curate of Los Palacios near Seville.[2] Peter Martyr, of Anghiera, by Lago Maggiore, was

Bernaldez and Peter Martyr

[1] " L' autorita di Las Casas è d' una suprema e vitale importanza tanto nella storia di Cristoforo Colombo, come nell' esame delle *Historie* di Fernando suo figlio. . . . E dal confronto tra questi due scrittori emergerà una omogeneità sì perfetta, che si potrebbe coi termini del frate domenicano ritrovare o rifare per due terzi il testo originale spagnuolo delle *Historie* di Fernando Colombo.'' Peragallo, *L' autenticità delle Historie di Fernando Colombo*, Genoa, 1884, p. 23.

[2] *Historia de los Reyes Católicos D. Fernando y Dª Isabel. Crónica inédita del siglo XV, escrita por el Bachiller Andrés*

4

an intimate friend of Columbus, and gives a good account of his voyages, besides mentioning him in sundry epistles.[1] Columbus himself, moreover, was such a voluminous writer that his contemporaries laughed about it. " God grant," says Zuñiga in a letter to the Marquis de Pescara, " God grant that Gutierrez may never come short for paper, for he writes more than Ptolemy, more than Columbus, the man who discovered the Indies." [2] These writings are in great part lost, though doubt- *Letters of* less a good many things will yet be *Columbus* brought to light in Spain by persistent rummaging. We have, however, from sixty to seventy letters and reports by Columbus, of which twenty-three at least are in his own handwriting; and all these have been published.[3]

Nevertheless, while these contemporary materials give us abundant information concerning the great discoverer, from the year 1492

Bernaldez, cura que fué de Los Palacios, Granada, 1856, 2 vols. small 4to. It is a book of very high authority.

[1] De orbe novo Decades, Alcalá, 1516 ; Opus epistolarum, Compluti (Alcalá), 1530 ; Harrisse, Bibliotheca Americana Vetustissima, Nos. 88, 160.

[2] " A Gutierrez vuestro solicitador, ruego à Dios que nunca le falte papel, porque escribe mas que Tolomeo y que Colon, el que halló las Indias." Rivadeneyra, Curiosidades bibliográficas, p. 59, apud Harrisse, Christophe Colomb, tom. i. p. 1.

[3] Harrisse, loc. cit., in 1884, gives the number at sixty-four.

until his death, it is quite otherwise with his earlier years, especially before his arrival in Spain in 1484. His own allusions to these earlier years are sometimes hard to interpret; [1] and as for his son Ferdinand, that writer confesses,

Defects in Ferdinand's information

with characteristic and winning frankness, that his information is imperfect, inasmuch as filial respect had deterred him from closely interrogating his father on such points, or, to tell the plain truth, being still very young when his father died, he had not then come to recognize their importance. [2] This does not seem strange when we reflect that Ferdinand must have seen very little of his father until in 1502, at the age of fourteen, he accompanied him on that last difficult and disastrous voyage, in which the sick and harassed old man could have had but little time or strength for aught but

---

[1] Sometimes from a slip of memory or carelessness of phrasing, on Columbus's part, sometimes from our lacking the clue, sometimes from an error in numerals, common enough at all times.

[2] " Ora, l' Ammiraglio avendo cognizione delle dette scienze, cominciò ad attendere al mare, e a fare alcuni viaggi in levante e in ponente ; de' quali, e di molte altre cose di quei primi dì io non ho piena notizia ; perciocchè egli venne a morte a tempo che io non aveva tanto ardire, o pratica, per la riverenza filiale, che io ardissi di richiederlo di cotali cose ; o, per parlare più veramente, allora mi ritrovava io, come giovane, molto lontano da cotal pensiero." *Vita dell' Ammiraglio*, cap. iv.

the work in hand. It is not strange that when,
a quarter of a century later, the son set about his
literary task, he should now and then have got
a date wrong, or have narrated some incidents in
a confused manner, or have admitted some gos-
siping stories, the falsehood of which can now
plainly be detected. Such blemishes, which
occur chiefly in the earlier part of Ferdinand's
book, do not essentially detract from its high
authority.[1] The limits which bounded the son's

[1] Twenty years ago M. Harrisse published in Spanish and
French a critical essay maintaining that the *Vita dell' Ammiraglio* was not written by Ferdinand Columbus, but probably
by the famous scholar Perez de Oliva, professor in the university of Salamanca, who died in 1530 (*D. Fernando Colon,
historiador de su padre*, Seville, 1871 ; *Fernand Colomb : sa
vie, ses œuvres*, Paris, 1872). The Spanish manuscript of
the book had quite a career. As already observed, it is clear
that Las Casas used it, probably between 1552 and 1561.
From Ferdinand's nephew, Luis Columbus, it seems to have
passed in 1568 into the hands of Baliano di Fornari, a prominent
citizen of Genoa, who sent it to Venice with the intention
of having it edited and published with Latin and Italian versions. All that ever appeared, however, was the Italian version made by Ulloa and published in 1571. Harrisse supposes that the Spanish manuscript, written by Oliva, was
taken to Genoa by some adventurer and palmed off upon
Baliano di Foranri as the work of Ferdinand Columbus. But
inasmuch as Harrisse also supposes that Oliva probably wrote
the book (about 1525) at Seville, under Ferdinand's eyes and
with documents furnished by him, it becomes a question, in
such case, how far was Oliva anything more than an amanu-
ensis to Ferdinand ? and there seems really to be precious little

accurate knowledge seem also to have bounded that of such friends as Bernaldez, who did not become acquainted with Columbus until after his arrival in Spain.

In recent years elaborate researches have been made, by Henry Harrisse and others, in the ar-
Researches chives of Genoa, Savona, Seville, and
of Henry other places with which Columbus
Harrisse was connected, in the hope of supplementing this imperfect information concerning his earlier years.[1] A number of data have thus

wool after so much loud crying. If the manuscript was actually written " sous les yeux de Fernand et avec documents fournis par lui," most of the arguments alleged to prove that it could not have emanated from the son of Columbus fall to the ground. It becomes simply a question whether Ulloa may have here and there tampered with the text, or made additions of his own. To some extent he seems to have done so, but wherever the Italian version is corroborated by the Spanish extracts in Las Casas, we are on solid ground, for Las Casas died five years before the Italian version was published. M. Harrisse does not seem as yet to have convinced many scholars. His arguments have been justly, if somewhat severely, characterized by my old friend, the lamented Henry Stevens (*Historical Collections*, London, 1881, vol. i. No. 1379), and have been elaborately refuted by M. d'Avezac, *Le livre de Ferdinand Colomb : revue critique des allegations proposées contre son authenticité*, Paris, 1873 ; and by Prospero Peragallo, *L' autenticità delle Historie di Fernando Colombo*, Genoa, 1884. See also Fabié, *Vida de Fray Bartolomé de Las Casas*, Madrid, 1869, tom. i. pp. 360–372.

[1] See Harrisse, *Christophe Colomb*, Paris, 1884, 2 vols.,

been obtained, which, while clearing up the subject most remarkably in some directions, have been made to mystify and embroil it in others. There is scarcely a date or a fact relating to Columbus before 1492 but has been made the subject of hot dispute ; and some pretty wholesale reconstructions of his biography have been attempted.[1] The general impression, however, which the discussions of the past twenty years have left upon my mind, is that the more violent hypotheses are not likely to be sustained, and that the newly ascertained facts do not call for any very radical interference with the traditional lines upon which the life of Columbus has heretofore been written.[2] At any rate there

a work of immense research, absolutely indispensable to every student of the subject, though here and there somewhat over-ingenious and hypercritical, and in general unduly biased by the author's private crotchet about the work of Ferdinand.

[1] One of the most radical of these reconstructions may be found in the essay by M. d'Avezac, "Canevas chronologique de la vie de Christophe Colomb," in *Bulletin de la Société de Géographie*, Paris, 1872, 6ᵉ série, tom. iv. pp. 5–59.

[2] Washington Irving's *Life of Columbus*, says Harrisse, "is a history written with judgment and impartiality, which leaves far behind it all descriptions of the discovery of the New World published before or since." *Christophe Colomb*, tom. i. p. 136. Irving was the first to make use of the superb work of Navarrete, *Coleccion de los viages y descubrimientos que hicieron por mar los Españoles desde fines del siglo XV.*, Madrid, 1825–37, 5 vols. 4to. Next followed Alexander

sentence but one he adds that " now for forty
years I have been in this business and have
Columbus's gone to every place where there is
letter of Sep- any navigation up to the present
tember, 1501 time." [1] The expression " very ten-
der age" agrees with Ferdinand's statement
that his father was fourteen years old when he
first took to the sea.[2] Since $1446 + 14 + 40 =$
1500, it is argued that Columbus was probably
born about 1446; some sticklers for extreme
precision say 1447. But now there were eight
years spent by Columbus in Spain, from 1484
to 1492, without any voyages at all; they were
years, as he forcibly says "dragged out in dis-
putations."[3] Did he mean to include those
eight years in his forty spent upon the sea?
Navarrete thinks he did not. When he wrote
under excitement, as in this letter, his language
was apt to be loose, and it is fair to construe it
according to the general probabilities of the case.
This addition of eight years brings his statement
substantially into harmony with that of Bernaldez, which it really will not do to set aside

[1] " Serenissimi principi, di età molto tenera io entrai in
mare navigando, et vi ho continovato fin' hoggi : . . . et
hoggimai passano quaranta anni che io uso per tutte quelle
parti che fin hoggi si navigano." *Vita dell' Ammiraglio*,
cap. iv.

[2] *Op. cit.* cap. iv. *ad fin.*

[3] " Traido en disputas," Navarrete, *Coleccion*, tom. ii.
p. 254.

lightly. Moreover, in the original text of the letter, since published by Navarrete, Columbus appears to say, "now for *more than* forty years," so that the agreement with Bernaldez becomes practically complete.[1] The good curate spoke from direct personal acquaintance, and his phrases "seventy years" and "a good old age" are borne out by the royal decree of February 23, 1505, permitting Columbus to ride on a mule, instead of a horse, by reason of his old age (*ancianidad*) and infirmities.[2] Such a phrase applies much better

The balance of probability is in favour of 1436

---

[1] "Muy altos Reyes, de muy pequeña edad entré en la mar navegando, é lo he continuado fasta hoy. . . . Yá pasan de cuarenta años que yo voy en este uso : todo lo que hoy se navega, todo lo he andado." Navarrete, *Coleccion*, tom. ii. p. 262. Observe the lame phrase "pasan de cuarenta ;" what business has that " de " in such a place without " mas " before it ? " Pasan mas de cuarenta," *i. e.* " more than forty ;" writing in haste and excitement, Columbus left out a little word ; or shall we blame the proof-reader ? Avezac himself translates it " il y a plus de quarante ans," and so does Eugène Müller, in his French version of Ferdinand's book, *Histoire de la vie de Christophe Colomb*, Paris, 1879, p. 15.

[2] That was the golden age of sumptuary laws. Because Alfonso XI. of Castile (1312–1350), when he tried to impress horses for the army, found it hard to get as many as he wanted, he took it into his head that his subjects were raising too many mules and not enough horses. So he tried to remedy the evil by a wholesale decree prohibiting all Castilians from riding upon mules ! In practice this precious de-

to a man of sixty-nine than to a man of fifty-nine. On the whole, I think that Washington Irving showed good sense in accepting the statement of the curate of Los Palacios as decisive, dating as it does the birth of Columbus at 1436, "a little more or less."

With regard to the place where the great discoverer was born there ought to be no dispute, since we have his own most explicit and unmistakable word for it, as I shall presently show. Nevertheless there has been no end of dispute. He has been claimed by as many places as Homer,[1] but the only real question is whether

cree, like other villainous prohibitory laws that try to prevent honest people from doing what they have a perfect right to do, proved so vexatious and ineffective withal that it had to be perpetually fussed with and tinkered. One year you could ride a mule and the next year you could n't. In 1492, as we shall see, Columbus immortalized one of these patient beasts by riding it a few miles from Granada. But in 1494 Ferdinand and Isabella decreed that nobody except women, children, and clergymen could ride on mules, — " dont la marche est beaucoup plus douce que celle des chevaux " (Humboldt, *Examen critique*, tom. iii. p. 338). This edict remained in force in 1505, so that the Discoverer of the New World, the inaugurator of the greatest historic event since the birth of Christ, could not choose an easy-going animal for the comfort of his weary old weather-shaken bones without the bother of getting a special edict to fit his case. *Eheu, quam parva sapientia regitur mundus!*

[1] " Nous avons démontré l'inanité des théories qui le font naître à Pradello, à Cuccaro, à Cogoleto, à Savona, à

he was born in the city of Genoa or in some neighbouring village within the boundaries of the Genoese republic. It is easy to understand how doubt has arisen on this point, if we trace the changes of residence of his family. The grandfather of Columbus seems to have been Giovanni Colombo, of Terrarossa, an inland hamlet some twenty miles east by north from Genoa. Giovanni's son, Domenico Colombo, was probably born at Terrarossa, and moved thence with his father, somewhere between 1430 and 1445, to Quinto al Mare, four miles east of

Nervi, à Albissola, à Bogliasco, à Cosseria, à Finale, à Oneglia, voire même en Angleterre ou dans l'isle de Corse." Harrisse, tom. i. p. 217. In Cogoleto, about sixteen miles west of Genoa on the Corniche road, the visitor is shown a house where Columbus is said first to have seen the light. Upon its front is a quaint inscription in which the discoverer is compared to the dove (*Colomba*) which, when sent by Noah from the ark, discovered dry land amid the waters: —

Con generoso ardir dall' Arca all' onde
Ubbidiente il vol Colomba prende,
Corre, s' aggira, terren scopre, e fronde
D' olivo in segno, al gran Noè ne rende.
L' imita in ciò Colombo, ne' s' asconde,
E da sua patria il mar solcando fende ;
Terreno al fin scoprendo diede fondo,
Offerendo all' Ispano un Nuovo Mondo.

This house is or has been mentioned in Baedeker's *Northern Italy* as the probable birthplace, along with Peschel's absurd date 1456. It is pretty certain that Columbus was *not* born in that house or in Cogoleto. See Harrisse, tom. i. pp. 148–155.

Genoa on the coast. All the family seem to have been weavers. Before 1445, but how many years before is not known, Domenico married Susanna Fontanarossa, who belonged to a family of weavers, probably of Quezzi, four miles northeast of Genoa. Between 1448 and 1451 Domenico, with his wife and three children, moved into the city of Genoa, where he became the owner of a house and was duly qualified as a citizen. In 1471 Domenico moved to Savona, thirty miles west on the Corniche road, where he set up a weaving establishment and also kept a tavern. He had then five children, Cristoforo, Giovanni, Bartolommeo, Giacomo, and a daughter. Domenico lived in Savona till 1484. At that time his wife and his son Giovanni were dead, Giacomo was an apprentice, learning the weaver's trade, Christopher and Bartholomew had long been domiciled in Portugal, the daughter had married a cheese merchant in Genoa, and to that city Domenico returned in the autumn of 1484, and lived there until his death, at a great age, in 1499 or 1500. He was always in pecuniary difficulties, and died poor and in debt, though his sons seem to have sent him from Portugal and Spain such money as they could spare.[1]

The family of Domenico Colombo, and its changes of residence

The reader will observe that Christopher and

[1] Harrisse, tom. i. pp. 166–216.

his two next brothers were born before the family went to live in the city of Genoa. It has hence been plausibly inferred that they were born either in Quinto or in Terrarossa; more likely the latter, since both Christopher and Bartholomew, as well as their father, were called, and sometimes signed themselves, Columbus of Terrarossa.[1] In this opinion the most indefatigable modern investigator, Harrisse, agrees with Las Casas.[2] Nevertheless, in a solemn legal instrument executed February 22, 1498, establishing a *mayorazgo*, or right of succession to his estates and emoluments in the Indies, Columbus expressly declares that he was born in the city of Genoa: " I enjoin it upon my son, the said Don Diego, or whoever may inherit the said *mayorazgo*, always to keep and maintain in the City of Genoa one person of our lineage, because from thence I came and in it I was born." [3] I do not see how such a definite and

Christopher tells us that he was born in the city of Genoa

---

[1] Harrisse, tom. i. p. 188; *Vita dell' Ammiraglio*, cap. xi.

[2] " Fué este varon escogido de nacion genovés, de algun lugar de la provincia de Génova; cual fuese, donde nació ó qué nombre tuvo el tal lugar, no consta la verdad dello más de que se solia llamar ántes que llegase al estado que llegó, Cristobal Colombo de Terra-rubia y lo mismo su hermano Bartolomé Colon." Las Casas, *Historia de las Indias*, tom. i. p. 42; cf. Harrisse, tom. i. pp. 217–222.

[3] " Mando al dicho D. Diego, mi hijo, ó á la persona que

17

positive statement, occurring in such a document, can be doubted or explained away. It seems clear that the son was born while the parents were dwelling either at Terrarossa or at Quinto, but what is to hinder our supposing that the event might have happened when the mother was in the city on some errand or visit? The fact that Christopher and his brother were often styled " of Terrarossa " does not prove that they were born in that hamlet. A family moving thence to Quinto and to Genoa would stand in much need of some such distinctive epithet, because the name Colombo was extremely common in that part of Italy; insomuch that the modern historian, who prowls among the archives of those towns, must have a care lest he get hold of the wrong person, and thus open a fresh and prolific source of confusion. This has happened more than once.

On the whole, then, it seems most probable that the Discoverer of America was born in the city of Genoa in 1436, or not much later. Of his childhood we know next to nothing. Las Casas tells us that he studied at the University of Pavia and acquired a good knowledge of

heredare el dicho mayorazgo, que tenga y sostenga siempre en la *Ciudad de Génova* una persona de nuestro linage . . . pues que della salí *y en ella nací* " [italics mine]. Navarrete, *Coleccion,* tom. ii. p. 232.

Latin.[1] This has been doubted, as incompatible with the statement of Columbus that he began a seafaring life at the age of fourteen. Christopher's early years It is clear, however, that the earlier years of Columbus, before his departure for Portugal, were not all spent in seafaring. Somewhere, if not at Pavia, he not only learned Latin, but found time to study geography, with a little astronomy and mathematics, and to become an expert draughtsman. He seems to have gone to and fro upon the Mediterranean in merchant voyages, now and then taking a hand in sharp scrimmages with Mussulman pirates.[2] In the intervals of this adventurous life he was probably to be found in Genoa, earning his bread by making maps and charts, for which there was a great and growing demand. About 1470, having become noted for his skill in such work, he followed his younger brother Bartholomew to Lisbon,[3] whither Prince Henry's undertakings

[1] Las Casas, *Historia*, tom. i. p. 46.

[2] The reader must beware, however, of some of the stories of adventure attaching to this part of his life, even where they are confirmed by Las Casas. They evidently rest upon hearsay, and the incidents are so confused that it is almost impossible to extract the kernel of truth.

[3] The date 1470 rests upon a letter of Columbus to King Ferdinand of Aragon in May, 1505. He says that God must have directed him into the service of Spain by a kind of miracle, since he had already been in Portugal, whose king was more interested than any other sovereign in making discover-

had attracted able navigators and learned geographers until that city had come to be the chief ies, and yet God closed his eyes, his ears, and all his senses to such a degree that *in fourteen years* Columbus could not prevail upon him to lend aid to his scheme. " Dije milagrosamente porque fui á aportar á Portugal, adonde el Rey de allí entendia en el descubrir mas que otro : él le atajó la vista, oido y todos los sentidos, que en catorce años no le pude hacer entender lo que yo dije." Las Casas, *op. cit.* tom. iii. p. 187 ; Navarrete, tom. iii. p. 528. Now it is known that Columbus finally left Portugal late in 1484, or very early in 1485, so that fourteen years would carry us back to before 1471 for the first arrival of Columbus in that country. M. Harrisse (*op. cit.* tom. i. p. 263) is unnecessarily troubled by the fact that the same person was not king of Portugal during the whole of that period. Alfonso V. (brother of Henry the Navigator) died in 1481, and was succeeded by his son John II. ; but during a considerable part of the time between 1475 and 1481 the royal authority was exercised by the latter. Both kings were more interested in making discoveries than any other European sovereigns. Which king did Columbus mean ? Obviously his words were used loosely ; he was too much preoccupied to be careful about trifles ; he probably had John in his mind, and did not bother himself about Alfonso ; King Ferdinand, to whom he was writing, did not need to have such points minutely specified, and could understand an elliptical statement ; and the fact stated by Columbus was simply that during a residence of fourteen years in Portugal he had not been able to enlist even that enterprising government in behalf of his novel scheme.

In the town archives of Savona we find Christopher Columbus witnessing a document March 20, 1472, endorsing a kind of promissory note for his father August 26, 1472, and joining with his mother and his next brother Giovanni, August 7, 1473, in relinquishing all claims to the house in

centre of nautical science in Europe. Las Casas
assures us that Bartholomew was quite equal to

Genoa sold by his father Domenico by deed of that date. It
will be remembered that Domenico had moved from Genoa
to Savona in 1471. From these documents (which are all
printed in his *Christophe Colomb*, tom. ii. pp. 419, 420,
424–426) M. Harrisse concludes that Christopher cannot
have gone to Portugal until after August 7, 1473. Probably
not, so far as to be domiciled there ; but inasmuch as he had
long been a sailor, why should he not have been in Portugal,
or upon the African coast in a Portuguese ship, in 1470 and
1471, and nevertheless have been with his parents in Savona
in 1472 and part of 1473 ? His own statement " fourteen
years " is not to be set aside on such slight grounds as this.
Furthermore, from the fact that Bartholomew's name is not
signed to the deed of August 7, 1473, M. Harrisse infers
that he was then a minor ; *i. e.* under five and twenty. But
it seems to me more likely that Bartholomew was already
domiciled at Lisbon, since we are expressly told by two good
contemporary authorities — both of them Genoese writers
withal — that he moved to Libson and began making maps
there at an earlier date than Christopher. See Antonio Gallo,
*De navigatione Columbi per inaccessum antea Oceanum Com-
mentariolus*, apud Muratori, tom. xxiii. col. 301–304 ; Giustiniani, *Psalterium*, Milan, 1516 (annotation to Psalm xix.) ;
Harrisse, *Bibliotheca Americana Vetustissima*, No. 88. To
these statements M. Harrisse objects that he finds (in Belloro,
Notizie, p. 8) mention of a document dated Savona, June 16,
1480, in which Domenico Colombo gives a power of attorney
to his son Bartholomew to act for him in some matter. The
document itself, however, is not forthcoming, and the notice
cited by M. Harrisse really affords no ground for the assumption that Bartholomew was in 1480 domiciled at Savona or at
Genoa.

Christopher as a sailor, and surpassed him in the art of making maps and globes, as well as in the beauty of his handwriting.[1] In Portugal, as before in Italy, the work of the brothers Columbus was an alternation of map-making on land and adventure on the sea. We have Christopher's own word for it that he sailed with more than one of those Portuguese expeditions down the African coast;[2] and I think it not altogether unlikely that he may have been with Santarem and Escobar in their famous voyage of 1471.

Christopher and Bartholomew at Lisbon

He had not been long in Portugal before he found a wife. We have already met the able Italian navigator, Bartholomew Perestrelo, who was sent by Prince Henry to the island of Porto Santo with Zarco and Vaz, about 1425. In recognition of eminent services Prince Henry afterwards, in 1446, appointed him governor of Porto Santo. Perestrelo died in 1457, leaving a widow (his second

Philippa Moñiz de Perestrelo

[1] Las Casas, *op. cit.* tom. i. p. 224 ; tom. ii. p. 80. He possessed many maps and documents by both the brothers.

[2] "Spesse volte navigando da Lisbona a Guinea," etc. *Vita dell' Ammiraglio,* cap. iv. The original authority is Columbus's marginal note in his copy of the *Imago Mundi* of Alliacus, now preserved in the Colombina at Seville : "Nota quod sepius navigando ex Ulixbona ad austrum in Guineam, notavi cum diligentia viam," etc. Compare the allusions to Guinea in his letters, Navarrete, *Coleccion,* tom. i. pp. 55, 71, 101.

wife, Isabella Moñiz) and a charming daughter Philippa,[1] whom Columbus is said to have first met at a religious service in the chapel of the convent of All Saints at Lisbon. From the accounts of his personal appearance, given by Las Casas and others who knew him, we can well understand how Columbus should have won the heart of this lady, so far above him at that time in social position. He was a man of noble and commanding presence, tall and power-fully built, with fair ruddy complexion and keen blue-gray eyes that easily kindled ; while his waving white hair must have been quite picturesque. His manner was at once courteous and cordial and his conversation charming, so that strangers were quickly won, and in friends who knew him well he inspired strong affection and respect.[2] There was an indefinable air of authority about him, as befitted a man of great heart and lofty thoughts.[3] Out of those kindling eyes looked a grand and po-

Personal appearance of Columbus

---

[1] There are some vexed questions concerning this lady and the connections between the Moñiz and Perestrelo families, for which see Harrisse, tom. i. pp. 267-292.

[2] Las Casas, *Historia*, tom. i. p. 43. He describes Bartholomew as not unlike his brother, but not so tall, less affable in manner, and more stern in disposition, *id.* tom. ii. p. 80.

[3] "Christoval Colon . . . persona de gran corazon y altos pensamientos." Mariana, *Historia de España*, tom. viii. p. 341.

etic soul, touched with that divine spark of religious enthusiasm which makes true genius.

The acquaintance between Columbus and Philippa Moñiz de Perestrelo was not long in ripening into affection, for they were married in 1473. As there was a small estate at Porto Santo, Columbus went home thither with his bride to live for a while in quiet and seclusion. Such repose we may believe to have been favourable to meditation, and on that little island, three hundred miles out on the mysterious ocean, we are told that the great scheme of sailing westward to the Indies first took shape in the mind of Columbus.[1] His father-in-law Perestrelo had left a quantity of sailing charts and nautical notes, and these Columbus diligently studied, while ships on their way to and from Guinea every now and then stopped at the island, and one can easily imagine the eager discussions that must have been held over the great commercial

His marriage, and life upon the island of Porto Santo

[1] Upon that island his eldest son Diego was born. This whole story of the life upon Porto Santo and its relation to the genesis of Columbus's scheme is told very explicitly by Las Casas, who says that it was told to him by Diego Columbus at Barcelona in 1519, when they were waiting upon Charles V., just elected Emperor and about to start for Aachen to be crowned. And yet there are modern critics who are disposed to deny the whole story. (See Harrisse, tom. i. p. 298.) The grounds for doubt are, however, extremely trivial when confronted with Las Casas, *Historia*, tom. i. p. 54.

problem of the age, — how far south that African coast extended and whether there was any likelihood of ever finding an end to it.

How long Columbus lived upon Porto Santo is not known, but he seems to have gone from time to time back to Lisbon, and at length to have made his home — or in the case of such a rover we might better say his headquarters — in that city. We come now to a document of supreme importance for our narrative. Paolo del Pozzo dei Toscanelli, born at Florence in 1397, was one of the most famous astronomers and cosmographers of his time, a man to whom it was natural that questions involving the size and shape of the earth should be referred. To him Alfonso V. of Portugal made application, through a gentleman of the royal household, Fernando Martinez, who happened to be an old friend of Toscanelli. What Alfonso wanted to know was whether there could be a shorter oceanic route to the Indies than that which his captains were seeking by following the African coast; if so, he begged that Toscanelli would explain the nature and direction of such a route. The Florentine astronomer replied with the letter presently to be quoted in full, dated June 25, 1474; and along with the letter he sent to the king a sailing chart, exhibiting his conception of the Atlantic Ocean, with Europe on the

Alfonso V. asks advice of the great astronomer Toscanelli

of your intimacy and favour with your most noble and illustrious king. I have formerly spoken with you about a shorter route to the places of Spices by ocean navigation than that which you are pursuing by Guinea. The most gracious king now desires from me some statement, or rather an exhibition to the eye, so that even slightly educated persons can grasp and comprehend that route. Although I am well aware that this can be proved from the spherical shape of the earth, nevertheless, in order to make the point clearer and to facilitate the enterprise, I have decided to exhibit that route by means of a sailing chart. I therefore send to his majesty a chart made by my own hands,[1] upon which are laid down your

Toscanelli's copy of his former letter to Martinez —enclosed in his first letter to Columbus

of it upon the fly-leaves of one of his books. These same fly-leaves contain extracts from Josephus and St. Augustine. The reader will rightly infer from my translation that the astronomer's Latin was somewhat rugged and lacking in literary grace. Apparently he was anxious to jot down quickly what he had to say, and get back to his work.

[1] A sketch of this most memorable of maps is given opposite. Columbus carried it with him upon his first voyage, and shaped his course in accordance with it. Las Casas afterwards had it in his possession (*Hist. de las Indias*, tom. i. pp. 96, 279). It has since been lost, that is to say, it may still be in existence, but nobody knows where. But it has been so well described that the work of restoring its general outlines is not difficult and has several times been done. The sketch here given is taken from Winsor (*Narr. and Crit. Hist.*, ii. 103),

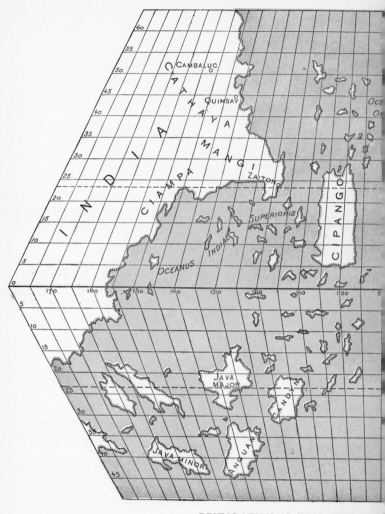

RESTORATION OF TOSCANELLI'S M

Used by Columbus in his first

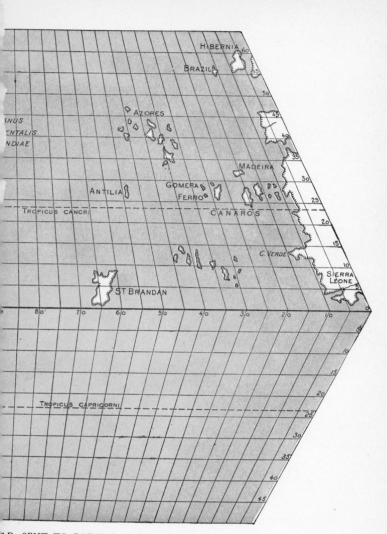

HIBERNIA

BRAZIL

60

55

50

45

40

35

30

25

20

15

10

5

AZORES

CANUS

ENTALIS

NDIAE

MADEIRA

ANTILIA

GOMERA

FERRO

CANAROS

TROPICUS CANCRI

C. VERDE

SIERRA
LEONE

ST BRANDAN

8o'   7o   6o   5o   4o   3o   2o   1o

5

10

15

20

25

30

35

40

45

TROPICUS CAPRICORNI

AP, SENT TO PORTUGAL IN 1474

voyage across the Atlantic

coasts, and the islands from which you must begin to shape your course steadily westward, and the places at which you are bound to arrive, and how far from the pole or from the equator you ought to keep away, and through how much space or through how many miles you are to arrive at places most fertile in all sorts of spices and gems; and do not wonder at my calling *west* the parts where the spices are, whereas they are commonly called *east*, because to persons sailing persistently westward those parts will be found by courses on the under side of the earth. For if [you go] by land and by routes on this upper side, they will always be found in the east. The straight lines drawn lengthwise upon the map indicate distance from east to west, while the transverse lines show distances from south to north. I have drawn upon the map various places upon which you may come, for the better information of the navigators in case of their arriving, whether through accident of wind or what not, at some different place from what they had expected; but partly in order that they may show the inhabitants that they have some knowledge of their country, which is sure to be a pleasant thing. It is

who takes it from *Das Ausland*, 1867, p. 5. Another restoration may be found in St. Martin's *Atlas*, pl. ix. This map was the source of the western part of Martin Behaim's globe, as given below, p. 106.

said that none but merchants dwell in the islands.[1] For so great there is the number of navigators with their merchandise that in all the rest of the world there are not so many as in one very splendid port called Zaiton.[2] For they say that a hundred great ships of pepper unload in that port every year, besides other ships bringing other spices. That country is very populous and very rich, with a multitude of provinces and kingdoms and cities without number, under one sovereign who is called the Great Khan, which name signifies King of Kings, whose residence is for the most part in the province of Cathay. His predecessors two hundred years ago desired an alliance with Christendom; they sent to the Pope and asked for a number of persons learned in the faith, that they might be enlightened; but those who were sent, having encountered obstacles on the way, returned.[3] Even in the time of Eugenius [4] there came one to Eugenius and made a declaration concerning their great good-will toward Christians, and I had a long talk with him about many things,

[1] All the description that follows is taken by Toscanelli from the book of Marco Polo.

[2] On modern maps usually called Chang-chow, about 100 miles S. W. from Fou-chow.

[3] I have given an account of this mission, above, vol. i. p. 324.

[4] Eugenius IV., Pope from 1431 to 1447.

about the great size of their royal palaces and the remarkable length and breadth of their rivers, and the multitude of cities on the banks of the rivers, such that on one river there are about two hundred cities, with marble bridges very long and wide and everywhere adorned with columns. This country is worth seeking by the Latins, not only because great treasures may be obtained from it, — gold, silver, and all sorts of jewels and spices, — but on account of its learned men, philosophers, and skilled astrologers, and [in order that we may see] with what arts and devices so powerful and splendid a province is governed, and also [how] they conduct their wars. This for some sort of answer to his request, so far as haste and my occupations have allowed, ready in future to make further response to his royal majesty as much as he may wish. Given at Florence 25th June, 1474.'

"From[1] the city of Lisbon due west there are 26 spaces marked on the map, each of which contains 250 miles, as far as the very great and splendid city of Quinsay.[2] For it is a hundred miles in circumfer-

Conclusion of Toscanelli's first letter to Columbus

[1] This paragraph is evidently the conclusion of the letter to Columbus, and not a part of the letter to Martinez, which has just ended with the date. In *Vita dell' Ammiraglio* the two letters are mixed together.

[2] On modern maps Hang-chow. After 1127 that city was for some time the capital of China, and Marco Polo's name *Quinsay* represents the Chinese word *King-sse* or "capital,"

31

ence and has ten bridges, and its name means City of Heaven, and many wonderful things are told about it and about the multitude of its arts and revenues. This space is almost a third part of the whole sphere. That city is in the province of Mangi, or near the province of Cathay in which land is the royal residence. But from the island of Antilia, which you know, to the very splendid island of Cipango[1] there are ten spaces. For that island abounds in gold, pearls, and precious stones, and they cover the temples and palaces

now generally applied to Peking. Marco Polo calls it the finest and noblest city in the world. It appears that he does not overstate the circumference of its walls at 100 Chinese miles or *li*, equivalent to about 30 English miles. It has greatly diminished since Polo's time, while other cities have grown. Toscanelli was perhaps afraid to repeat Polo's figure as to the number of stone bridges ; Polo says there were 12,000 of them, high enough for ships to pass under ! We thus see how his Venetian fellow-citizens came to nickname him " Messer Marco Milione." As Colonel Yule says, " I believe we must not bring Marco to book for the literal accuracy of his statements as to the bridges ; but all travellers have noticed the number and elegance of the bridges of cut stone in this part of China." *Marco Polo*, vol. ii. p. 144.

[1] For Cipango, or Japan, see Yule's *Marco Polo*, vol. ii. pp. 195–207. The venerable astronomer's style of composition is amusing. He sets out to demonstrate to Columbus that the part of the voyage to be accomplished through new and unfamiliar stretches of the Atlantic is not great ; but he is so full of the glories of Cathay and Cipango that he keeps reverting to that subject, to the manifest detriment of his exposition. His argument, however, is perfectly clear.

with solid gold. So through the unknown parts of the route the stretches of sea to be traversed are not great. Many things might perhaps have been stated more clearly, but one who duly considers what I have said will be able to work out the rest for himself. Farewell, most esteemed one."

Some time after the receipt of this letter Columbus wrote again to Toscanelli, apparently sending him either some charts of his own, or some notes, or something bearing upon the subject in hand. No such letter is preserved, but Toscanelli replied as follows : —

"Paul, the physicist, to Christopher Columbus greeting.[1] I have received your letters, with the things which you sent me, for which I thank you very much. I regard as noble and grand your project of sailing from east to west according to the indications furnished by the map which I sent you, and which would appear still more plainly upon a sphere. I am much pleased to see that I have been well understood, and that the voyage has become not only possible but certain,[2] fraught with honour as it must be, and inestimable gain, and most lofty fame among all Chris-

Toscanelli's second letter to Columbus

---

[1] The original of this letter is not forthcoming. I translate from *Vita dell' Ammiraglio*, cap. viii.

[2] Yet poor old Toscanelli did not live to see it accomplished ; he died in 1482, before Columbus left Portugal.

tian people. You cannot take in all that it means except by actual experience, or without such copious and accurate information as I have had from eminent and learned men who have come from those places to the Roman court, and from merchants who have traded a long time in those parts, persons whose word is to be believed (*persone di grande autorità*). When that voyage shall be accomplished, it will be a voyage to powerful kingdoms, and to cities and provinces most wealthy and noble, abounding in all sorts of things most desired by us; I mean, with all kinds of spices and jewels in great abundance. It will also be advantageous for those kings and princes who are eager to have dealings and make alliances with the Christians of our countries, and to learn from the erudite men of these parts,[1] as well in religion as in all other branches of knowledge. For these reasons, and many others that might be mentioned, I do not wonder that you, who are of great courage, and the whole Portuguese nation, which has always had men distinguished in all

[1] That is, of Europe, and especially of Italy. Toscanelli again refers to Kublai Khan's message to the Pope which — more or less mixed up with the vague notions about Prester John — had evidently left a deep impression upon the European mind. In translating the above sentence I have somewhat retrenched its excessive verbiage without affecting the meaning.

such enterprises, are now inflamed with desire[1] to execute the said voyage."

These letters are intensely interesting, especially the one to Martinez, which reveals the fact that as early as 1474 the notion that a westward route to the Indies would be shorter than the southward route had somehow been suggested to Alfonso V.; and had, moreover, sufficiently arrested his attention to lead him to make inquiries of the most eminent astronomer within reach. Who could have suggested this notion to the king of Portugal? Was it Columbus, the trained mariner and map-maker, who might lately have been pondering the theories of Ptolemy and Mela as affected by the voyage of Santarem and Escobar, and whose connection with the Moñiz and Perestrelo families would now doubtless facilitate his access to the court? On some accounts this may seem probable, especially if we bear in mind Columbus's own statement implying that his appeals to the Crown dated almost from the beginning of his fourteen years in Portugal.

Who first suggested the feasibleness of a westward route? Was it Columbus?

All the circumstances, however, seem to be equally consistent with the hypothesis that the first suggestion of the westward route may have

[1] In including the " whole Portuguese nation " as feeling this desire, the good astronomer's enthusiasm again runs away with him.

come from Toscanelli himself, through the medium of the canon Martinez, who had for so

Perhaps it
was Tosca-
nelli many years been a member of King
Alfonso's household. The words at
the beginning of the letter lend some
probability to this view: "I have formerly
spoken with you about a shorter route to the
places of Spices by ocean navigation than that
which you are pursuing by Guinea." It was
accordingly earlier than 1474 — how much earlier does not appear — that such discussions
between Toscanelli and Martinez must probably
have come to the ears of King Alfonso; and
now, very likely owing to the voyage of Santarem and Escobar, that monarch began to think
it worth while to seek for further information,
"an exhibition to the eye," so that mariners
not learned in astronomy like Toscanelli might
"grasp and comprehend" the shorter route
suggested. It is altogether probable that the
Florentine astronomer, who was seventy-seven
years old when he wrote this letter, had already
for a long time entertained the idea of a westward route; and a man in whom the subject
aroused so much enthusiasm could hardly have
been reticent about it. It is not likely that Martinez was the only person to whom he des-
canted [1] upon the glory and riches to be found

[1] Luigi Pulci, in his famous romantic poem published in
1481, has a couple of striking stanzas in which Astarotte says

by sailing "straight to Cathay," and there were many channels through which Columbus might have got some inkling of his views, even before going to Portugal.

However this may have been, the letter clearly to Rinaldo that the time is at hand when Hercules shall blush to see how far beyond his Pillars the ships shall soon go forth to find another hemisphere, for although the earth is as round as a wheel, yet the water at any given point is a plane, and inasmuch as all things tend to a common centre so that by a divine mystery the earth is suspended in equilibrium among the stars, just so there is an antipodal world with cities and castles unknown to men of olden time, and the sun in hastening westwards descends to shine upon those peoples who are awaiting him below the horizon: —

> Sappi che questa opinione è vana
> Perchè più oltre navicar si puote,
> Però che l' acqua in ogni parte è piana,
> Benchè la terra abbi forma di ruote ;
> Era più grossa allor la gente umana,
> Tal che potrebbe arrossirne le gote
> Ercule ancor, d' aver posti que' segni,
> Perchè più oltre passeranno i legni.
>
> E puossi andar giù nell' altro emisperio,
> Però che al centro ogni cosa reprime :
> Sicchè la terra per divin misterio
> Sospesa sta fra le stelle sublime,
> E laggiù son città, castella, e imperio ;
> Ma nol cognobbon quelle gente prime.
> Vedì che il sol di camminar s' affretta,
> Dove io dico che laggiù s' aspetta.
>
> Pulci, *Morgante Maggiore*, xxv. 229, 230.

This prophecy of western discovery combines with the astronomical knowledge here shown, to remind us that the Florentine Pulci was a fellow-townsman and most likely an acquaintance of Toscanelli.

proves that at that most interesting period, in or about 1474, Columbus was already meditating upon the westward route.[1] Whether he owed

---

[1] It was formerly assumed, without hesitation, that the letter from Toscanelli to Columbus was written and sent in 1474. The reader will observe, however, that while the enclosed letter to Martinez is dated June 25, 1474, the letter to Columbus, in which it was enclosed, has no date. But according to the text as given in *Vita dell' Ammiraglio*, cap. viii., this would make no difference, for the letter to Columbus was sent only a few days later than the original letter to Martinez : " I send you a copy of another letter, which I wrote a few days ago (*alquanti giorni fa*) to a friend of mine, a gentleman of the household of the king of Portugal before the wars of Castile, in reply to another," etc. This friend, Martinez, had evidently been a gentleman of the household of Alfonso V. since before the civil wars of Castile, which in 1474 had been going on intermittently for nine years under the feeble Henry IV., who did not die until December 12, 1474. Toscanelli apparently means to say " a friend of mine who has for ten years or more been a gentleman of the royal household," etc. ; only instead of mentioning the number of years, he alludes less precisely (as most people, and perhaps especially old people, are apt to do) to the most notable, mentionable, and glaring fact in the history of the Peninsula for that decade, — namely, the civil wars of Castile. As if an American writer in 1864 had said, " a friend of mine, who has been secretary to A. B. since before the war," instead of saying " for four years or more." This is the only reasonable interpretation of the phrase as it stands above, and it was long ago suggested by Humboldt (*Examen critique*, tom. i. p. 225). Italian and Spanish writers of that day, however, were lavish with their commas and sprinkled them in pretty much at haphazard. In this case Ferdinand's translator, Ulloa,

the idea to Toscanelli, or not, is a question of
no great importance so far as con- The idea was
cerns his own originality ; for the idea suggested by the globular
was already in the air. The origi- form of the earth ;
nality of Columbus did not consist in
his conceiving the possibility of reaching the

sprinkled in one comma too many, and it fell just in front of
the clause "before the wars of Castile ; " so that Toscanelli's
sentence was made to read as follows : "I send you a copy
of another letter, which I wrote a few days ago to a friend
of mine, a gentleman of the household of the king of Portugal, before the wars of Castile, in reply to another," etc.
Now this unhappy comma, coming after the word "Portugal," has caused ream after ream of good paper to be inked
up in discussion, for it has led some critics to understand the
sentence as follows : "I send you a copy of another letter,
which I wrote a few days ago, before the wars of Castile, to
a friend of mine," etc. This reading brought things to a
pretty pass. Evidently a letter dated June 25, 1474, could
not have been written before the civil wars of Castile, which
began in 1465. It was therefore assumed that the phrase
must refer to the "War of Succession" between Castile and
Portugal (in some ways an outgrowth from the civil wars of
Castile) which began in May, 1475, and ended in September, 1479. M. d'Avezac thinks that the letter to Columbus
must have been written after the latter date, or more than five
years later than the enclosed letter. M. Harrisse is somewhat
less exacting, and is willing to admit that it may have been
written at any time after this war had fairly begun, — say in
the summer of 1475, not more than a year or so later than
the enclosed letter. Still he is disposed on some accounts to
put the date as late as 1482. The phrase *alquanti giorni fa*
will not allow either of these interpretations. It means "a
few days ago," and cannot possibly mean a year ago, still

shores of Cathay by sailing west, but in his conceiving it in such distinct and practical shape as

less five years ago. The Spanish retranslator from Ulloa ren-
ders it exactly *algunos dias há* (Navarrete, *Coleccion*, tom. ii.
p. 7), and Humboldt (*loc. cit.*) has it *il y a quelques jours.*
If we could be sure that the expression is a correct rendering
of the lost Latin original, we might feel sure that the letter to
Columbus must have been written as early as the beginning
of August, 1474. But now the great work of Las Casas, after
lying in manuscript for 314 years, has at length been published in 1875. Las Casas gives a Spanish version of the Toscanelli letters (*Historia de las Indias*, tom. i. pp. 92–97),
which is unquestionably older than Ulloa's Italian version,
though perhaps not necessarily more accurate. The phrase in
Las Casas is not *algunos dias há*, but *há dias*, *i. e.* not "a
few days ago," but "some time ago." Just which expression Toscanelli used cannot be determined unless somebody
is fortunate enough to discover the lost Latin original. The
phrase in Las Casas admits much more latitude of meaning
than the other. I should suppose that *há dias* might refer to
an event a year or two old, which would admit of the interpretation considered admissible by M. Harrisse. I should
hardly suppose that it could refer to an event five or six years
old ; if Toscanelli had been referring in 1479 or 1480 to a
letter written in 1474, his phrase would probably have appeared in Spanish as *algunos años há*, *i. e.* "a few years ago,"
not as *há dias*. M. d'Avezac's hypothesis seems to me not
only inconsistent with the phrase *há dias*, but otherwise improbable. The frightful anarchy in Castile, which began in
1465 with the attempt to depose Henry IV. and alter the
succession, was in great measure a series of ravaging campaigns
and raids, now more general, now more local, and can hardly
be said to have come to an end before Henry's death in 1474.
The war which began with the invasion of Castile by Alfonso

to be ready to make the adventure in his own person. As a matter of theory the possibility of such a voyage could not fail to be suggested by the globular form of the earth; and ever since the days of Aristotle that had been generally admitted by men learned in physical science. Aristotle proved, from the different altitudes of the pole-star in different places, that the earth must necessarily be a globe. Moreover, says Aristotle, "some stars are seen in Egypt or at Cyprus, but are not seen in the countries to the north of these; and the stars that in the north are visible while they make a complete circuit, there undergo a setting. So that from this it is manifest, not only that the

V. of Portugal, in May, 1475, was simply a later phase of the same series of conflicts, growing out of disputed claims to the Crown and rivalries among great barons, in many respects similar to the contemporary anarchy in England called the Wars of the Roses. It is not likely that Toscanelli, writing at any time between 1475 and 1480, and speaking of the "wars of Castile" in the plural, could have had 1474 in his mind as a date previous to those wars; to his mind it would have rightly appeared as a date in the midst of them. In any case, therefore, his reference must be to a time before 1465, and Humboldt's interpretation is in all probability correct. The letter from Toscanelli to Columbus was probably written within a year or two after June 25, 1474.

On account of the vast importance of the Toscanelli letters, and because the early texts are found in books which the reader is not likely to have at hand, I have given them entire in the Appendix at the end of this work.

form of the earth is round, but also that it is part of not a very large sphere ; for otherwise the difference would not be so obvious to persons making so small a change of place. Wherefore we may judge that *those persons who connect the region in the neighbourhood of the Pillars of Hercules with that towards India, and who assert that in this way the sea is* ONE, do not assert things very improbable." [1]   It thus appears that more than eighteen centuries before Columbus took counsel of Toscanelli, " those persons " to whom Aristotle alludes were discussing, as a matter of theory, this same subject.   Eratosthenes held that it would be easy enough to sail from Spain to India on the same parallel were it not for the vast extent

and was as old as Aristotle

[1] Ὥστε τὰ ὑπὲρ τῆς κεφαλῆς ἄστρα μεγάλην ἔχειν τὴν μεταβολήν, καὶ μὴ ταῦτα φαίνεσθαι πρὸς ἄρκτον τε καὶ μεσημβρίαν μεταβαίνουσιν· ἔνιοι γὰρ ἐν Αἰγύπτῳ μὲν ἀστέρες ὁρῶνται, καὶ περὶ Κύπρον· ἐν τοῖς πρὸς ἄρκτον δὲ χωρίους οὐχ ὁρῶνται καὶ τὰ διὰ παντὸς ἐν τοῖς πρὸς ἄρκτον φαινόμενα τῶν ἄστρων, ἐν ἐκείνοις τοῖς τόποις ποιεῖται δύσιν. Ὥστ' οὐ μόνον ἐκ τούτων δῆλον περιφερὲς ὂν τὸ σχῆμα τῆς γῆς, ἀλλὰ καὶ σφαίρας οὐ μεγάλης. Οὐ γὰρ ἂν οὕτω ταχὺ ἐπίδηλον ἐποίει μεθιστεμένοις οὕτω βραχύ. Διὸ τοὺς ὑπολαμβάνοντας συνάπτειν τὸν περὶ τὰς Ἡρακλείους στήλας τόπον τῷ περὶ τὴν Ἰνδικήν, καὶ τοῦτον τὸν τρόπον εἶναι τὴν Θάλατταν μίαν, μὴ λίαν ὑπολαμβάνειν ἄπιστα δοκεῖν. Aristotle, *De Cælo*, ii. 14. He goes on to say that " those persons " allege the existence of elephants alike in Mauretania and in India in proof of their theory.

of the Atlantic Ocean.[1] On the other hand,
Seneca maintained that the distance was probably not so very great, and that with favouring
winds a ship might make the voyage in a few
days.[2] In one of his tragedies Seneca has a striking passage [3] which has been repeatedly quoted
as referring to the discovery of America, and is
certainly one of the most notable instances of
prophecy on record. There will come a time, he
says, in the later years, when Ocean   Opinions of
shall loosen the bonds by which we   ancient
have been confined, when an im-   writers
mense land shall lie revealed, and Tethys shall

---

[1] Ὥστ' εἰ μὴ τὸ μέγεθος τοῦ Ἀτλαντικοῦ πελάγους ἐκώλυε,
κἂν πλεῖν ἡμᾶς ἐκ τῆς Ἰβηρίας εἰς τὴν Ἰνδικὴν διά τοῦ αὐτοῦ
παραλλήλου.   Strabo, i. 4, § 6.

[2] "Quantum enim est, quod ab ultimis litoribus Hispaniæ
usque ad Indos jacet? Paucissimorum dierum spatium, si na-
vem suus ventus implevit." Seneca, *Nat. Quæst.*, i. præf.
§ 11.

> [3] Venient annis sæcula seris,
> Quibus Oceanus vincula rerum
> Laxet, et ingens pateat tellus,
> Tethysque novos detegat orbes,
> Nec sit terris ultima Thule.
>
> Seneca, *Medea*, 376.

In the copy of Seneca's tragedies, published at Venice in
1510, bought at Valladolid by Ferdinand Columbus in March,
1518, for 4 reals (plus 2 reals for binding), and now to be
seen at the Biblioteca Colombina, there is a marginal note attached to these verses : " hæc prophetia expleta ē per patrē
meu3 cristoforū colō almirātē anno 1492."

43

disclose new worlds, and Thule will no longer
be the most remote of countries. In Strabo
there is a passage, less commonly noticed, which
hits the truth — as we know it to-day — even
more closely. Having argued that the total
length of the Inhabited World is only about a
third part of the circumference of the earth in
the temperate zone, he suggests it as possible,
or even probable, that within this space there
may be another Inhabited World, or even more
than one ; but such places would be inhabited
by different races of men, with whom the geographer, whose task it is to describe the *known*
world, has no concern.[1] Nothing could better
illustrate the philosophical character of Strabo's
mind. In such speculations, so far as his means
of verification went, he was situated somewhat
as we are to-day with regard to the probable
inhabitants of Venus or Mars.

Early in the Christian era we are told by an
eminent Greek astronomer that the doctrine of

[1] Καλοῦμεν γὰρ οἰκουμένην ἣν οἰκοῦμεν καὶ γνωρίζομεν·
ἐνδέκεται δὲ καὶ ἐν τῇ αὐτῇ εὐκράτῳ ζώνῃ καὶ δύο οἰκουμένας
εἶναι ἢ καὶ πλείους. Strabo, i. 4, § 6 ; καὶ γὰρ εἰ οὕτως ἔχει,
οὐχ ὑπὸ τούτων γε οἰκεῖται τῶν παρ' ἡμῖν · ἀλλ' ἐκείνην ἄλλην
οἰκουμένην θετέον · ὅπερ ἐστὶ πιθανόν. Ἡμῖν δὲ τὸ
ἐν αὐτῇ ταῦτα λεκτέον. Id. ii. 5, § 13. This has always
seemed to me one of the most remarkable anticipations of
modern truth in all ancient literature. Mr. Bunbury thinks
it may have suggested the famous verses of Seneca just quoted.
History of Ancient Geography, vol. ii. p. 224.

the earth's sphericity was accepted by all competent persons except the Epicureans.[1] Among the Fathers of the Church there was some difference of opinion; while in general they denied the existence of human beings beyond the limits of their Œcumene, or Inhabited World, this denial did not necessarily involve disbelief in the globular figure of the earth.[2] The views of the great mass of people, and of the more ignorant of the clergy, down to the time of Columbus, were probably well represented in the book of Cosmas Indicopleustes already cited.[3] Nevertheless among the more enlightened clergy the views of the ancient astronomers were never quite forgotten, and in the great revival of intellectual life in the thirteenth century the doctrine of the earth's sphericity was again brought prominently into the foreground. We find Dante basing upon it the cosmical theory elaborated in his immortal poem.[4] In 1267 Roger Bacon

Opinions of Christian writers

Roger Bacon

---

[1] Οἱ δὲ ἡμέτεροι [*i. e.* the Stoics] καὶ ἀπὸ μαθημάτων πάντες, καὶ οἱ πλείους τῶν ἀπὸ τοῦ Σωκρατικοῦ διδασκαλείου σφαιρικὸν εἶναι τὸ σχῆμα τῆς γῆς διεβεβαιώσαντο. Cleomedes, i. 8 ; cf. Lucretius, *De Rerum Nat.*, i. 1052–1082 ; Stobæus, *Eclog.* i. 19 ; Plutarch, *De facie in Orbe Luna*, cap. vii.

[2] See Augustine, *De civitate Dei*, xvi. 9 ; Lactantius, *Inst. Div.*, iii. 23 ; Jerome, *Comm. in Ezechiel*, i. 6 ; Whewell's *History of the Inductive Sciences*, vol. i. p. 196.

[3] See above, vol. i. p. 306.

[4] For an account of the cosmography of the Divine Com-

— stimulated, no doubt, by the reports of the ocean east of Cathay — collected passages from ancient writers to prove that the distance from Spain to the eastern shores of Asia could not be very great. Bacon's argument and citations were copied in an extremely curious book, the " Imago Mundi," published in 1410 by the Cardinal Pierre d'Ailly, Bishop of Cambrai, better known by the Latinized form of his name as Petrus Alliacus. This treatise, which throughout the fifteenth century enjoyed a great reputation, was a favourite book with Columbus, and his copy of it, covered with marginal annotations in his own handwriting, is still preserved among the priceless treasures of the Biblioteca Colombina.[1] He

The "Imago Mundi" of Petrus Alliacus

edy, illustrated with interesting diagrams, see Artaud de Montor, *Histoire de Dante Alighieri*, Paris, 1841.

[1] It was first printed without indication of place or date, but probably the place was Paris and the date somewhere from 1483 to 1490. Manuscript copies were very common, and Columbus probably knew the book long before that time. There is a good account of it in Humboldt's *Examen critique*, tom. i. pp. 61–76, 96–108. Humboldt thinks that such knowledge as Columbus had of the opinions of ancient writers was chiefly if not wholly obtained from Alliacus. It is doubtful if Columbus had any direct acquaintance with the works of Roger Bacon, but he knew the *Liber Cosmographicus* of Albertus Magnus and the *Speculum Naturale* of Vincent de Beauvais (both about 1250), and drew encouragement from them. He also knew the book of Mandeville, first printed in French at Lyons in 1480, and a Latin translation of Marco

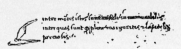

inter motes istos se inestimabilis in maximo caldis
inter ques sunt gipliones margarites τ lapides
preciosis.

refertā Crisā τ Argirem au
m solus nunc carentem. ba
illustrantes Jndos. Terra
tū meāt fruges vice byemis
τs homines. elephantes in
Ebenuz quoq̃ ligno. τ plu
ꝰ preciosos plurimos Jbi
cbones τ griffes ac immēso
Jndia valde magna ē. Haz
ota est tertia pars babitabi
ipse dicat Europaz esse ma
Dico igit̃ ꝙ frons Jndie
propter regionem Patha
uz maris magnū descendēs
ram inferiorem seu Africaz
us Jndie descendit a tropi
ub montem Maleū. τ regi
nunc Arym vocatur Hā
st Syene. vna sub solsti
io de qua nunc est sermo
ci in medio habitationis
occidēte septētrione τ meri
monis ponētis Vierusalē
t falutem in medio terre
re babitabilis vt ostendūt
mi sicut supradictum est
uilibꝰ Jndie. Ca. xvi.
ndia in cĩuitate. Sed ex
mirabiliū varietate. Hā
Pigmei duox cubitox
pariūt octauo senescunt.
ramen serpentūm qui ibi
acrobii xii. cubitox lōgi
lasꝙ et ungues pferunt
to in igne amore alter al

trapobania bꝫ gēms vt elephã
rosa vt argūre auro et argēto
tlē y.

india multas vregꝫ vt perumꝰ
aromaticas vt lapus ꝗciosos
plurimos vt mōꝫ aurei // ipā
τ tertia ꝑs buitabilis

frōs indie descendit vsꝗ ad
Eꝑcū raꝗ corni

ambit brachiū maris inꝫ
indiā vt ispaniā //

duplex ū sūnt vna sub
solstio alia sub eqꝗnoꝗ

falsitas ponitꝫ hierusalē
i medio terre

boūig duorū cubitox ꝗb̃ buē τ ꝗl
gruis / Heroaūo pūt d sinostrāt
piꝑ albū
agarobii· 12· cubitox lõgi ꝑforāt
ꝙ griffꝫ

ANNOTATIONS BY COLUMBUS

found in it strong confirmation of his views, and it is not impossible that the reading of it may have first put such ideas into his head. Such a point, however, can hardly be determined. As I have already observed, these ideas were in the air. What Columbus did was not to originate them, but to incarnate them in facts and breathe into them the breath of life. It was one thing to suggest, as a theoretical possibility, that Cathay might be reached by sailing westward ; and it was quite another thing to prove that the enterprise was feasible with the ships and instruments then at command.

The principal consideration, of course, was the distance to be traversed ; and here Columbus was helped by an error which he shared with many geographers of his day. He somewhat underestimated the size of the earth, and at the same time greatly overestimated the length of Asia. The first astronomer to calculate, by scientific methods, the circumference of our planet at the equator was Eratosthenes (B. C. 276–196), and he came — all things considered — fairly near the truth; he made it 25,200 geographical miles (of ten stadia), or about one seventh too great. The true figure is 21,600 geographical miles, equivalent to 24,899 English statute

Ancient estimates of the size of the globe and the length of the Œcumene

Polo, published in 1485, a copy of which, with marginal MS. notes, is now in the Colombina.

miles.[1] Curiously enough, Posidonius, in re-
vising this calculation a century later, reduced the
figure to 18,000 miles, or about one seventh too
small. The circumference in the latitude of Gibraltar he estimated at 14,000 miles; the length
of the Œcumene, or Inhabited World, he called
7000; the distance across the Atlantic from the
Spanish strand to the eastern shores of Asia was
the other 7000. The error of Posidonius was partially rectified by Ptolemy, who made the equatorial circumference 20,400 geographical miles,
and the length of a degree 56.6 miles.[2] This
estimate, in which the error was less than one
sixteenth, prevailed until modern times. Ptolemy also supposed the Inhabited World to extend over about half the circumference of the
temperate zone, but the other half he imagined
as consisting largely of bad lands, quagmires,
and land-locked seas, instead of a vast and open
ocean.[3]

[1] See Herschel's *Outlines of Astronomy*, p. 140. For an
account of the method employed by Eratosthenes, see Delambre, *Histoire de l'astronomie ancienne*, tom. i. pp. 86–91 ;
Lewis, *Astronomy of the Ancients*, p. 198.

[2] See Bunbury's *History of Ancient Geography*, vol. ii. pp.
95–97, 546–579 ; Müller and Donaldson, *History of Greek
Literature*, vol. iii. p. 268.

[3] Strabo, in arguing against this theory of bad lands, etc.,
as obstacles to ocean navigation — a theory which seems to be at
least as old as Hipparchus — has a passage which finely expresses
the loneliness of the sea : Οἴτε γὰρ περιπλεῖν ἐπιχειρή-

Ptolemy's opinion as to the length of the Inhabited World was considerably modified in the minds of those writers who toward the end of the Middle Ages had been strongly impressed by the book of Marco Polo. Among these persons was Toscanelli. This excellent astronomer calculated the earth's equatorial circumference at almost exactly the true figure ; his error was less than 124 English miles in excess. The circumference in the latitude of Lisbon he made 26×250×3= 19,500 miles.[1] Two thirds of this figure, or 13,000 miles, he allowed for the length of the Œcumene, from Lisbon eastward to Quinsay (i. e. Hang-chow), leaving 6500 for the westward voyage from Lisbon to Quinsay. Thus Toscanelli elongated Asia by nearly the whole width of the Pacific Ocean. His Quinsay would come about 130° W., a few hundred miles west of the mouth of the Columbia River. Zaiton (i. e. Chang-chow), the easternmost city in Tosca-

(marginal note) Toscanelli's calculation of the size of the earth,

σαντες, εἶτα ἀναστρέψαντες, οὐχ ὑπὸ ἠπείρου τινὸς ἀντιπι-πτούσης καὶ κωλυούσης, τὸν ἐπέκεινα πλοῦν ἀνακρουσθῆναι φα-σὶν, ἀλλὰ ὑπὸ ἀπορίας καὶ ἐρημίας, οὐδὲν ἧττον τῆς θαλάττης ἐχούσης τὸν πόρον (lib. i. cap. i. § 8). When one thinks of this ἀπορία and ἐρημία, one fancies oneself far out on the Atlantic, alone in an open boat on a cloudy night, bewildered and hopeless.

[1] See above, p. 31. Toscanelli's mile was nearly equivalent to the English statute mile. See the very important note in Winsor, *Narr. and Crit. Hist.*, vol. i. p. 51.

nelli's China, would come not far from the tip
end of Lower California. Thus the eastern
coast of Cipango, about a thousand miles east
from Zaiton, would fall in the Gulf of Mexico
somewhere near the ninety-third meridian, and
that island, being over a thousand miles in length

and of the   north and south, would fill up the
position of   space between the parallel of New
Cipango   Orleans and that of the city of Guatemala. The westward voyage from the Canaries
to Cipango, according to Toscanelli, would be
rather more than 3250 miles, but at a third of
the distance out he placed the imaginary island
of "Antilia," with which he seems to have supposed Portuguese sailors to be familiar.[1] "So
through the unknown parts of the route," said
the venerable astronomer, "the stretches of
sea to be traversed are not great," — not much
more than 2000 English miles, not so long as
the voyage from Lisbon to the Guinea coast.

While Columbus attached great importance

[1] The reader will also notice upon Toscanelli's map the
islands of Brazil and St. Brandan. For an account of all these
fabulous islands see Winsor, *Narr. and Crit. Hist.*, vol. i.
pp. 46–51. The name of "Antilia" survives in the name
"Antilles," applied since about 1502 to the West India Islands. All the islands west of Toscanelli's ninetieth meridian
belong in the Pacific. He drew them from his understanding
of the descriptions of Marco Polo, Friar Odoric, and other
travellers. These were the islands supposed, rightly, though
vaguely, to abound in spices.

to these calculations and carried Toscanelli's map with him upon his first voyage, he improved somewhat upon the estimates of distance, and thus made his case still more hopeful. Columbus was not enough of an astronomer to adopt Toscanelli's improved measurement of the size of the earth. He accepted Ptolemy's figure of 20,400 geographical miles for the equatorial girth,[1] which would make the

Columbus's opinion of the size of the globe, the length of the Œcumene, and the width of the Atlantic Ocean

---

[1] Columbus was confirmed in this opinion by the book of the Arabian astronomer Alfragan, written about A. D. 950, a Latin translation of which appeared in 1447. There is a concise summary of it in Delambre, *Histoire de l'astronomie du Moyen Age*, pp. 63–73. Columbus proceeded throughout on the assumption that the length of a degree at the equator is 56.6 geographical miles, instead of the correct figure 60. This would oblige him to reduce all Toscanelli's figures by about six per cent., to begin with. Upon this point we have the highest authority, that of Columbus himself, in an autograph marginal note in his copy of the *Imago Mundi*, where he expresses himself most explicitly : " Nota quod sepius navigando ex Ulixbona ad Austrum in Guineam, notavi cum diligentia viam, ut solitum naucleris et malineriis, et preteria accepi altitudinem solis cum quadrante et aliis instrumentis plures vices, et inveni concordare cum Alfragano, videlicet respondere quemlibet gradum milliariis 56⅔. Quare ad hanc mensuram fidem adhibendam. Tunc igitur possumus dicere quod circuitus Terræ sub aræ equinoctiali est 20,400 milliariorum. Similiter que id invenit magister Josephus phisicus et astrologus et alii plures missi specialiter ad hoc per serenissimum regem Portugaliæ," etc. ; *anglicè,* " Observe that in sailing often from Lisbon southward to Guinea, I carefully marked

circumference in the latitude of the Canaries about 18,000; and Columbus, on the strength of sundry passages from ancient authors which he found in Alliacus (cribbed from Roger Bacon), concluded that six sevenths of this circumference must be occupied by the Œcumene, including Cipango, so that in order to reach that wonderful island he would only have to sail over one seventh, or not much more than 2500 miles from the Canaries.[1] An authority upon

the course, according to the custom of skippers and mariners, and moreover I took the sun's altitude several times with a quadrant and other instruments, and in agreement with Alfragan I found that each degree [*i. e.* of longitude, measured on a great circle] answers to 56⅔ miles. So that one may rely upon this measure. We may therefore say that the equatorial circumference of the earth is 20,400 miles. A similar result was obtained by Master Joseph, the physicist [or, perhaps, physician] and astronomer, and several others sent for this special purpose by the most gracious king of Portugal." — Master Joseph was physician to John II. of Portugal, and was associated with Martin Behaim in the invention of an improved astrolabe which greatly facilitated ocean navigation. — The exact agreement with Ptolemy's figures shows that by a mile Columbus meant a geographical mile, equivalent to ten Greek stadia.

[1] One seventh of 18,000 is 2571 geographical miles, equivalent to 2963 English miles. The actual length of Columbus's first voyage, from last sight of land in the Canaries to first sight of land in the Bahamas, was according to his own dead reckoning about 3230 geographical miles. See his journal in Navarrete, *Coleccion*, tom. i. pp. 6–20.

I give here in parallel columns the passage from Bacon and

which he placed great reliance in this connection was the fourth book of Esdras, which although not a canonical part of the Bible was approved by holy men, and which expressly asserted that six parts of the

The fourth book of Esdras

the one from Alliacus upon which Columbus placed so much reliance. In the Middle Ages there was a generous tolerance of much that we have since learned to stigmatize as plagiarism.

From Roger Bacon, *Opus Majus* (A. D. 1267), London, 1733, ed. Jebb, p. 183: " Sed Aristoteles vult in fine secundi Cœli et Mundi quod plus [terræ] habitetur quam quarta pars. Et Averroes hoc confirmat. Dicit Aristoteles quod mare parvum est inter finem Hispaniæ a parte occidentis et inter principium Indiæ a parte orientis. Et Seneca, libro quinto Naturalium, dicit quod mare hoc est navigabile in paucissimis diebus si ventus sit conveniens. Et Plinius docet in Naturalibus quod navigatum est a sinu Arabico usque ad Gades: unde refert quendam fugisse a rege suo præ timore et intravit sinum Maris Rubri . . . qui circiter spatium navigationis annualis distat a Mari Indico:

From Petrus Alliacus, *De imagine Mundi* (A. D. 1410), Paris, cir. 1490, cap. viii. fol. 13 b : " Summus Aristoteles dicit quod mare parvum est inter finem Hispaniæ a parte occidentis et inter principium Indiæ a parte orientis, et vult quod plus habitetur quam quarta pars, et Averroes hoc confirmat. Insuper Seneca, libro quinto Naturalium, dicit quod mare est navigabile in paucis diebus si ventus sit conveniens. Et Plinius docet in Naturalibus, libro secundo, quod navigatum est a sinu Arabico usque ad Gades Herculis non multum magno tempore,

earth (*i. e.* of the length of the Œcumene, or north temperate zone) are inhabited and only

. . . ex quo patet principium Indiæ in oriente multum a nobis distare et ab Hispania, postquam tantum distat a principio Arabiæ versus Indiam. A fine Hispaniæ sub terra tam parvum mare est quod non potest cooperire tres quartas terræ. Et hoc per auctoritatem alterius considerationis probatur. Nam Esdras dicit quarto libro, quod sex partes terræ sunt habitatæ et septima est cooperta aquis. Et ne aliquis impediat hanc auctoritatem, dicens quod liber ille est apocryphus et ignotæ auctoritatis, dicendum est quod sancti habuerunt illum librum in usu et confirmant veritates sacras per illum librum."

unde concludunt aliqui, quod mare non est tantum quod possit cooperire tres quartas terræ. Accedit ad hoc auctoritas Esdræ libro suo quarto, dicentis quod sex partes terræ sunt habitatæ et septima est cooperta aquis,

cujus libri auctoritatem sancti habuerunt in reverentia."

Columbus must either have carried the book of Alliacus with him on his voyages, or else have read his favourite passages until he knew them by heart, as may be seen from the following passage of a letter, written from Hispaniola in 1498 to Ferdinand and Isabella (Navarrete, tom. i. p. 261) : " El Aristotel dice que este mundo es pequeño y es el agua muy poca, y que facilmente se puede pasar de España à las Indias, y esto confirma el Avenryz [Averroes], y le alega el cardenal Pedro de Aliaco, autorizando este decir y aquel de Seneca, el qual conforma con estos. . . . À esto trae una autoridad de Esdras del tercero libro suyo, adonde dice que de siete

the seventh part covered with water. From the general habit of Columbus's mind it may be inferred that it was chiefly upon this scriptural authority that he based his confident expectation of finding land soon after accomplishing seven hundred leagues from the Canaries. Was it not as good as written in the Bible that land was to be found there?

Thus did Columbus arrive at his decisive conclusion, estimating the distance across the Sea of Darkness to Japan at something less than the figure which actually expresses the distance to the West Indies. Many a hopeful enterprise has been ruined by errors in figuring, but this wrong calculation was certainly a great help to Columbus. When we consider how difficult he found it to obtain men and ships for a voyage supposed to be not *Fortunate mixture of truth and error* more than 2500 miles in this new and untried partes del mundo las seis son descubiertas y la una es cubierta de agua, la cual autoridad es aprobada por Santos, los cuales dan autoridad al 3° é 4° libro de Esdras, ansí come es S. Agustin é S. Ambrosio en su *exámeron*," etc. — " Singular period," exclaims Humboldt, " when a mixture of testimonies from Aristotle and Averroes, Esdras and Seneca, on the small extent of the ocean compared with the magnitude of continental land, afforded to monarchs guarantees for the safety and expediency of costly enterprises ! " *Cosmos*, tr. Sabine, vol. ii. p. 250. The passages cited in this note may be found in Humboldt, *Examen critique*, tom. i. pp. 65–69. Another interesting passage from *Imago Mundi*, cap. xv., is quoted on p. 78 of the same work.

direction, we must admit that his chances would have been poor indeed if he had proposed to sail westward on the Sea of Darkness for nearly 12,000 miles, the real distance from the Canaries to Japan. It was a case where the littleness of the knowledge was not a dangerous but a helpful thing. If instead of the somewhat faulty astronomy of Ptolemy and the very hazy notions prevalent about " the Indies," the correct astronomy of Toscanelli had prevailed and had been joined to an accurate knowledge of eastern Asia, Columbus would surely never have conceived his great scheme, and the discovery of America would probably have waited to be made by accident.[1] The whole point of his scheme lay in its promise of a shorter route to the Indies than that which the Portuguese were seeking by way of Guinea. Unless it was probable that it could furnish such a shorter route, there was no reason for such an extraordinary enterprise.

The whole point and purport of Columbus's scheme

The years between 1474 and 1480 were not favourable for new maritime ventures on the part of the Portuguese government. The war with Castile absorbed the energies of Alfonso V. as well as his money, and he was badly beaten into the bargain. About this time Columbus was writing a treatise on " the five hab-

[1] See below, p. 323.

itable zones," intended to refute the old notions about regions so fiery or so frozen as to be inaccessible to man. As this book is lost we know little or nothing of its views and speculations, but it appears that in writing it Columbus utilized sundry observations made by himself in long voyages into the torrid and arctic zones. He spent some time at the fortress of San Jorge de la Mina, on the Gold Coast, and made a study of that equinoctial climate.[1] This could not have been earlier than 1482, the year in which the fortress was built. Five years before this he seems to have gone far in the opposite direction. In a fragment of a letter or diary, preserved by his son and by Las Casas, he says : " In the month of February, 1477, I sailed a hundred leagues beyond the island of Thule, [to ?] an island of which the south part is in latitude 73°, not 63°, as some say ; and it [*i. e.* Thule] does not lie within Ptolemy's western boundary, but much farther west. And to this island, which is as big as England, the English go with their wares, especially from Bristol. When I was there the sea was not frozen. In some places the tide rose and fell twenty-six fathoms. It is true that the Thule mentioned by Ptolemy lies where he says

Columbus's speculations on climate

His voyage to Guinea

His voyage into the Arctic Ocean, 1477

[1] *Vita dell' Ammiraglio,* cap. iv. ; Las Casas, *Historia,* tom. i. p. 49.

it does, and this by the moderns is called Frislanda." [1]

Taken as it stands this passage is so bewildering that we can hardly suppose it to have come
in just this shape from the pen of Columbus.
It looks as if it had been abridged from some
diary of his by some person unfamiliar with the
Arctic seas; and I have ventured to insert in
brackets a little preposition which may perhaps
help to straighten out the meaning. By Thule

[1] "Io navigai l' anno M CCCC LXXVII nel mese di Febraio
oltra Tile isola cento leghe, la cui parte Australe è lontana dall'
Equinottiale settantatrè gradi, e non sessantatrè, come alcuni
vogliono; nè giace dentro della linea, che include l' Occidente
di Tolomeo, ma è molto più Occidentale. Et a questa isola,
che è tanto grande, come l' Inghilterra, vanno gl' Inglesi con
le loro mercatantie, specialmente quelli di Bristol. Et al
tempo che io vi andai, non era congelato il mare, quantunque
vi fossero si grosse maree, che in alcuni luoghi ascendeva ven-
tisei braccia, e discendeva altretanti in altezza. È bene il vero,
che Tile, quella, di cui Tolomeo fa mentione, giace dove egli
dice; & questa da' moderni è chiamata Frislanda." *Vita
dell' Ammiraglio*, cap. iv. In the original edition of 1571,
there are no quotation-marks; and in some modern editions,
where these are supplied, the quotation is wrongly made to
end just before the last sentence, so as to make it appear like
a gloss of Ferdinand's. This is, however, impossible. Ferdinand died in 1539, and the Zeno narrative of Frislanda was
not published till 1558, so that the only source from which
that name could have come into his book was his father's document. The genuineness of the passage is proved by its re-
currence, almost word for word, in Las Casas, *Historia*, tom.
i. p. 48.

Columbus doubtless means Iceland, which lies between latitudes 64° and 67°, and it looks as if he meant to say that he ran beyond it as far as the little island, just a hundred leagues from Iceland and in latitude 71°, since discovered by Jan Mayen in 1611. The rest of the paragraph is more intelligible. It is true that Iceland lies thirty degrees farther west than Ptolemy placed Thule; and that for a century before the discovery of the Newfoundland fisheries the English did much fishing in the waters about Iceland, and carried wares thither, especially from Bristol.[1] There can be no doubt that by Frislanda Columbus means the Færoe Islands,[2] which do lie in the latitude though not in the longitude mentioned by Ptolemy. As for the voyage into the Jan Mayen waters in February, it would be dangerous but by no means impossible.[3] In another letter Columbus mentions visiting England, apparently in connection with this voyage,[4] and it is highly probable that he went in an English ship from Bristol.

He may have reached Jan Mayen Island,

and stopped at Iceland

[1] See Thorold Rogers, *The Economic Interpretation of History*, London, 1888, pp. 103, 319.

[2] See above, vol. i. p. 272.

[3] See the graphic description of a voyage in these waters in March, 1882, in Nansen's *The First Crossing of Greenland*, London, 1890, vol. i. pp. 149–152.

[4] " E vidi tutto il Levante, e tutto il Ponente, che si dice

The object of Columbus in making these long voyages to the equator and into the polar circle was, as he tells us, to gather observations upon climate. From the circumstance of his having made a stop at some point in Iceland, it was conjectured by Finn Magnusson that Columbus might have learned something about Vinland which served to guide him to his own enterprise or to encourage him in it. Starting from this suggestion, it has been argued[1] that Columbus must have read the geographical appendix to Adam of Bremen's " Ecclesiastical History ; " that he must have understood, as we now do, the reference therein made to Vinland ; that he made his voyage to Iceland in order to obtain further information; that he there not only heard about Vinland and other localities mentioned in the sagas, but also mentally placed them about where they were placed in 1837 by Professor Rafn; that, among other things, he thus obtained a correct knowledge of the width of the Atlantic Ocean in latitude 28° N. ; and that during fifteen subsequent years of weary endeavour to obtain ships and men for his westward voyage, he sedulously re-

The hypothesis that Columbus "must have" heard and understood the story of the Vinland voyages

per andare verso il Settentrione, cioè l' Inghilterra, e ho camminato per la Guinea." *Vita dell' Ammiraglio,* cap. iv.

[1] See Anderson's *America not discovered by Columbus,* Chicago, 1874; 3d ed. enlarged, Chicago, 1883.

frained from using the most convincing argument at his command, — namely, that land of continental dimensions had actually been found (though by a very different route) in the direction which he indicated.

I have already given an explanation of the process by which Columbus arrived at the firm belief that by sailing not more than about 2500 geographical miles due west from the Canaries he should reach the coast of Japan. Every step of that explanation is sustained by documentary evidence, and as his belief is thus completely accounted for, the hypothesis that he may have based it upon information obtained in Iceland is, to say the least, superfluous. We do not need it in order to explain his actions, and accordingly his actions do not afford a presumption in favour of it. There is otherwise no reason, of course, for refusing to admit that he might have obtained information in Iceland, were there any evidence that he did. But not a scrap of such evidence has ever been produced. Every step in the Scandinavian hypothesis is a pure assumption.

That hypothesis has no evidence in its favour

First it is assumed that Columbus *must* have read the appendix to Adam of Bremen's history. But really, while it is not impossible that he should have read that document, it is, on the whole, improbable. The appendix was first printed in Lindenbrog's edition, published at

Leyden, in 1595. The eminent Norwegian historian, Gustav Storm, finds that in the six-

teenth century just six MSS. of Adam's works can now be traced. Of these, two were preserved in Denmark, two in Hamburg, one had *perhaps* already wandered southward to

Leyden, and one as far as Vienna. Dr. Storm, therefore, feels sure that Columbus never saw

Adam's mention of Vinland, and pithily adds that "had Columbus known it, it would not have been able to show him the way to the West

Indies, but perhaps to the North Pole."[1] From the account of this mention and its context, which I have already given,[2] it is in the highest degree improbable that if Columbus had read the passage he could have understood it as bearing upon his own problem. There is, therefore, no ground for the assumption that Columbus went to Iceland in order to make inquiries about Vinland.

It may be argued that even if he did not go for such a purpose, nevertheless when once there

[1] " Det er derfor sikkert, at Columbus ikke, som nogle har formodet, kan have kjendt Adam af Bremens Beretning om Vinland ; vi kan gjerne tilføie, at havde Columbus kjendt den, vilde den ikke have kunnet vise ham Vei til Vesten (Indien), men kanske til Nordpolen." *Aarbøger for Nordisk Oldkyndighed*, 1887, ii. 2, p. 301.

[2] See above, vol. i. p. 242.

he could hardly have failed incidentally to get the information. This, however, is not at all clear. Observe that our sole authority for the journey to Iceland is the passage above quoted at second-hand from Columbus himself; and there is nothing in it to show whether he staid a few hours or several weeks ashore, or met with any one likely to be possessed of the knowledge in question. The absence of any reference to Vinland in the Zeno narrative is an indication that the memory of it had faded away before 1400, and it was not distinctly and generally revived until the time of Torfæus in 1705.[1]

It is doubtful if Columbus would have stumbled upon the story in Iceland

[1] In 1689 the Swedish writer, Ole Rudbeck, could not understand Adam of Bremen's allusion to Vinland. The passage is instructive. Rudbeck declares that in speaking of a wine-growing country near to the Arctic Ocean, Adam must have been misled by some poetical or figurative phrase ; he was deceived either by his trust in the Danes, or by his own credulity, for he manifestly refers to *Finland*, for which the form *Vinland* does not once occur in Sturleson, etc. : " Ne tamen poetis solis hoc loquendi genus in suis regionum laudationibus familiare fuisse quis existimet, sacras adeat literas quæ Palæstinæ fæcunditatem appellatione *fluentorum lactis* & *mellis* designant. Tale aliquid, sine omne dubio, Adamo Bremensi quondam persuaserat insulam esse in ultimo septentrione sitam, mari glaciali vicinam, vini feracem, & ea propter fide tamen Danorum, *Vinlandiam* dictam prout ipse . . . fateri non dubitat. Sed deceptum eum hac sive Danorum fide, sive credulitate sua planum facit affine isti vocabulum *Finlandiæ* provinciæ ad Regnum nostrum pertinentis, pro quo apud Snorrodem & in

But to hear about Vinland was one thing, to be guided by it to Japan was quite another affair. It was not the mention of timber and peltries and Skrælings that would fire the imagination of Columbus; his dreams were of stately cities with busy wharves where ships were laden with silks and jewels, and of Oriental magnates decked out with "barbaric pearl and gold," dwelling in pavilions of marble and jasper amid flowery gardens in "a summer fanned with spice." The mention of Vinland was no more likely to excite Columbus's attention than that of St. Brandan's Isle or other places supposed to lie in the western ocean. He was after higher game.

If he had heard it, he would probably have classed it with such tales as that of St. Brandan's Isle

To suppose that Columbus, even had he got hold of the Saga of Eric the Red and conned it from beginning to end, with a learned interpreter at his elbow, could have gained from it a knowledge of the width of the Atlantic Ocean, is simply preposterous. It would be impossible to extract any such knowledge from that document to-day without the aid of our modern maps. The most diligent critical study of all the

He could not have obtained from such a source his opinion of the width of the ocean

Hist. Regum non semel occurrit *Vinlandiæ* nomen, cujus promontorium ad ultimum septentrionem & usque ad mare glaciale sese extendit." Rudbeck, *Atland eller Manheim,* Upsala, cir. 1689, p. 291.

Icelandic sources of information, with all the resources of modern scholarship, enables us with some confidence to place Vinland somewhere between Cape Breton and Point Judith, that is to say, somewhere between two points distant from each other more than four degrees in latitude and more than eleven degrees in longitude! When we have got thus far, knowing as we do that the coast in question belongs to the same continental system as the West Indies, we can look at our map and pick up our pair of compasses and measure the width of the ocean at the twenty-eighth parallel. But it is not the mediæval document, but our modern map that guides us to this knowledge. And yet it is innocently assumed that Columbus, without any knowledge or suspicion of the existence of America, and from such vague data concerning voyages made five hundred years before his time, by men who had no means of reckoning latitude and longitude, could have obtained his figure of 2500 miles for the voyage from the Canaries to Japan![1] The fallacy here is that which

[1] The source of such a confusion of ideas is probably the ridiculous map in Rafn's *Antiquitates Americanæ*, upon which North America is represented in all the accuracy of outline attainable by modern maps, and then the Icelandic names are put on where Rafn thought they ought to go, *i. e.* Markland upon Nova Scotia, Vinland upon New England, etc. Any person using such a map is liable to forget that it cannot possibly represent the crude notions of locality to which the

could see with his mind's eye solid land beyond the Sea of Darkness while they could not. To them the ocean, like the sky, had nothing beyond, unless it might be the supernatural world.[1] For while the argument from the earth's rotundity was intelligible enough, there were few to whom, as to Toscanelli, it was a living truth. Even of those who admitted, in theory, that Cathay lay to the west of Europe, most deemed the distance untraversable. Inductive proof of the existence of accessible land to the west was thus what Columbus chiefly needed, and what he sought every opportunity to find and produce; but it was not easy to find anything more substantial than sailors' vague mention of driftwood of foreign aspect or other outlandish jetsam washed up on the Portuguese strand.[2] What a

[1] See below, p. 76, note.

[2] For example, the pilot Martin Vicenti told Columbus that 1200 miles west of Cape St. Vincent he had picked up from the sea a piece of carved wood evidently not carved with iron tools. Pedro Correa, who had married Columbus's wife's sister, had seen upon Porto Santo a similar piece of carving that had drifted from the west. Huge reeds sometimes floated ashore upon those islands, and had not Ptolemy mentioned enormous reeds as growing in eastern Asia? Pine-trees of strange species were driven by west winds upon the coast of Fayal, and two corpses of men of an unknown race had been washed ashore upon the neighbouring island of Flores. Certain sailors, on a voyage from the Azores to Ireland, had caught glimpses of land on the west, and believed it to be the coast of "Tartary;" etc., etc. See *Vita dell' Ammiraglio*,

godsend it would have been for Columbus if he could have had the Vinland business to hurl at the heads of his adversaries ! If he could have said, " Five hundred years ago some Icelanders coasted westward in the polar regions, and then coasted southward until they reached a country beyond the ocean and about opposite to France or Portugal ; therefore that country must be Asia, and I can reach it by striking boldly across the ocean, which will obviously be shorter than going down by Guinea," — if he could have said this, he would have had precisely the un-answerable argument for lack of which his case was waiting and suffering. In persuading men to furnish hard cash for his commercial enter-prise, as Colonel Higginson so neatly says, " an ounce of Vinland would have been worth a pound of cosmography." [1] We may be sure that the silence of Columbus about the Norse voy-ages proves that he knew nothing about them or quite failed to see their bearings upon his own undertaking. It seems to me absolutely decisive.

Furthermore, this silence is in harmony with the fact that in none of his four voyages across the Atlantic did Columbus betray any conscious-ness that there was anything for him to gain

cap. ix. Since he cited these sailors, why did he not cite the Northmen also, if he knew what they had done ?

[1] *Larger History of the United States,* p. 54.

by steering toward the northwest. If he could correctly have conceived the position of Vinland he surely would not have conceived it as south of the fortieth parallel. On his first voyage he steered due west in latitude 28° because Toscanelli placed Japan opposite the Canaries. When at length some doubts began to arise and he altered his course, as we shall hereafter see, the change was toward the southwest. His first two voyages did not reveal to him the golden cities for which he was looking, and when on his third and fourth voyages he tried a different course it was farther toward the equator, not farther away from it, that he turned his prows. Not the slightest trace of a thought of Vinland appears in anything that he did.

No trace of a thought of Vinland appears in the voyages of Columbus

Finally it may be asked, if the memory of Vinland was such a living thing in Iceland in 1477 that a visitor would be likely to be told about it, why was it not sufficiently alive in 1493 to call forth a protest from the North? When the Pope, as we shall presently see, was proclaiming to the world that the Spanish Crown was entitled to all heathen lands and islands already discovered or to be discovered in the ocean west of the Azores, why did not some zealous Scandinavian at once jump up and cry out, " Look here, old Columbus, *we* discovered that western route, you

Why did not Norway or Iceland utter a protest in 1493 ?

know! Stop thief!" Why was it necessary to wait more than a hundred years longer before the affair of Vinland was mentioned in this connection?

Simply because it was not until the seventeenth century that the knowledge of North American geography had reached such a stage of completeness as to suggest to anybody the true significance of the old voyages from Greenland. That significance could not have been understood by Leif and Thorfinn themselves, or by the compilers of Hauks-bók and Flateyarbók, or by any human being, until about the time of Henry Hudson. Not earlier than that time should we expect to find it mentioned, and it is just then, in 1610, that we do find it mentioned by Arngrim Jonsson, who calls Vinland "an island of *America*, in the region of Greenland, perhaps the modern Estotilandia." [1] This is the earliest glimmering of

The idea of Vinland was not associated with the idea of America until the seventeenth century

[1] " Terram veró Landa Rolfoni quæsitam existimarem esse Vinlandiam olim Islandis sic dictam ; de qua alibi insulam nempe Americæ e regione Gronlandiæ, quæ fortè hodie Estotilandia," etc. *Crymogæa*, Hamburg, 1610, p. 120.

Abraham Ortelius in 1606 speaks of the Northmen coming to America, but bases his opinion upon the Zeno narrative (published in 1558) and upon the sound of the name *Norumbega*, and apparently knows nothing of Vinland : " Iosephus Acosta in his booke *De Natura noui orbis* indeuors by many reasons to proue, that this part of *America* was origi-

an association of the idea of Vinland with that of America.

The genesis of the grand scheme of Columbus has now been set forth, I believe, with sufficient fulness. The cardinal facts are 1, that the
need for some such scheme was suggested in 1471, by the discovery that the Guinea coast extended south of the equator; 2, that by 1474 advice had been sought from Toscanelli by the king of Portugal, and not very long after 1474 by Columbus; 3, that upon Toscanelli's letters and map, amended by the Ptolemaic estimate of the earth's size

nally inhabited by certaine Indians, forced thither by tempestuous weather ouer the South sea which now they call Mare del Zur. But to me it seemes more probable, out of the historie of the two Zeni, gentlemen of Venice, . . . that this New World many ages past was entred upon by some islanders of *Europe*, as namely of *Grœnland*, Island, and Frisland ; being much neerer thereunto than the Indians, nor disioyned thence . . . by an Ocean so huge, and to the Indians so vnnauigable. Also, what else may we coniecture to be signified by this *Norumbega* [the name of a North region of *America*] but that from *Norway*, signifying a North land, some Colonie in times past hath hither beene transplanted ? " *Theatre of the Whole World*, London, 1606, p. 5. These passages are quoted and discussed by Reeves, *The Finding of Wineland the Good*, pp. 95, 96. The supposed connection of *Norumbega* with *Norway* is very doubtful. Possibly Stephanius, in his map of 1570 (Torfæus, *Gronlandia antiqua*, 1706), may have had reference to Labrador or the north of Newfoundland.

and by the authority of passages quoted in the book of Alliacus (one of which was a verse from the Apocrypha), Columbus based his firm conviction of the feasibleness of the western route. How or by whom the suggestion of that route was first made — whether by Columbus himself or by Toscanelli or by Fernando Martinez or, as Antonio Gallo declares, by Bartholomew Columbus,[1] or by some person in Portugal whose name we know not — it would be difficult to decide. Neither can we fix the date when Columbus first sought aid for his scheme from the Portuguese government. There seems to be no good reason why he should not have been talking about it before 1474; but the affair did not come to any kind of a climax until after his return from Guinea, some time after 1482 and certainly not later than 1484. It was on some accounts a favourable time. The war with Castile was out of the way, and Martin Behaim had just invented an improved astrolabe which made it ever so much easier to find and keep one's latitude at sea. It was in 1484 that Portuguese discoveries took a fresh start after a ten years' lull, and Diego Cam, with the learned Behaim and his bran-new astrolabe on board, was about to sail a thousand miles farther south than white

<small>Martin Behaim's improved astrolabe</small>

[1] Gallo, *De navigatione Columbi,* apud Muratori, *Rerum Italicarum Scriptores,* tom. xxiii. col. 302.

men had ever gone before. About this time the scheme of Columbus was formally referred by King John II. to the junto of learned cosmographers from whom the Crown had been wont to seek advice. The project was condemned as "visionary," [1] as indeed it was, — the outcome of vision that saw farther than those men could see. But the king, who had some of his uncle Prince Henry's love for bold enterprises, was more hospitably inclined toward the ideas of Columbus, and he summoned a council of the most learned men in the kingdom to discuss the question. [2] In this council the new scheme found some defenders, while others correctly urged that Columbus must be wrong in supposing Asia to extend so far to the east, and it must be a much longer voyage than he supposed to Cipango and Cathay. [3] Others argued that the late war had

Negotiations of Columbus with John II. of Portugal

[1] Lafuente, *Historia de España*, tom. ix. p. 428.

[2] Vasconcellos, *Vida del rey Don Juan II.*, lib. iv. ; La Clède, *Histoire de Portugal*, lib. xiii.

[3] The Portuguese have never been able to forgive Columbus for discovering a new world for Spain, and their chagrin sometimes vents itself in amusing ways. After all, says Cordeiro, Columbus was no such great man as some people think, for he did not discover what he promised to discover ; and, moreover, the Portuguese geographers were right in condemning his scheme, because it really is not so far by sea from Lisbon around Africa to Hindustan as from Lisbon by any practicable route westward to Japan ! See Luciano Cordeiro, *De*

impoverished the country, and that the enterprises on the African coast were all that the treasury could afford. Here the demands of Columbus were of themselves an obstacle to his success. He never at any time held himself cheap,[1] and the rewards and honours for which he insisted on stipulating were greater than the king of Portugal felt inclined to bestow upon a plain Genoese mariner. It was felt that if the enterprise should prove a failure, as very likely

la part prise par les Portogais dans la découverte d'Amérique, Lisbon, 1876, pp. 23, 24, 29, 30. Well, I don't know that there is any answer to be made to this argument. Logic is logic, says the wise Autocrat : —

> " End of the wonderful one-hoss shay,
>   Logic is logic, that 's all I say."

Cordeiro's book is elaborately criticised in the learned work of Prospero Peragallo, *Cristoforo Colombo in Portogallo: studi critici*, Genoa, 1882.

[1] " Perciocchè essendo l'Ammiraglio di generosi ed alti pensieri, volle capitolare con suo grande onore e vantaggio, per lasciar la memoria sua, e la grandezza della sua casa, conforme alla grandezza delle sue opere e de' suoi meriti." *Vita dell' Ammiraglio*, cap. xi. The jealous Portuguese historian speaks in a somewhat different tone from the affectionate son : " Veó requerer á el rey Dom João que le desse algums navios pera ir á descobrir a ilha de Gypango [*sic*] per esta mar occidental. . . . El rey, porque via ser este Christovão Colom homem falador e glorioso em mostrar suas habilidades, e mas fantastico et de imaginacão com sua ilha de Cypango, que certo no que dezia : davalhe pouco credito." Barros, *Decada primeira da Asia*, Lisbon, 1752, liv. iii. cap. xi. fol. 56.

it would, the less heartily the government should have committed itself to it beforehand, the less it would expose itself to ridicule. King John was not in general disposed toward unfair and dishonest dealings, but on this occasion, after much parley, he was persuaded to sanction a proceeding quite unworthy of him. Having obtained Columbus's sailing plans, he sent out a ship secretly, to carry some goods to the Cape Verde Islands, and then to try the experiment of the westward voyage. If there should turn out to be anything profitable in the scheme, this would be safer and more frugal than to meet the exorbitant demands of this ambitious foreigner. So it was done; but the pilots, having no grand idea to urge them forward, lost heart before the stupendous expanse of waters that confronted them, and beat an ignominious retreat to Lisbon; whereupon Columbus, having been informed of the trick,[1] departed in high

A shabby trick

Columbus leaves Portugal,

---

[1] It has been urged in the king's defence that "such a proceeding was not an instance of bad faith or perfidy (!) but rather of the policy customary at that time, which consisted in distrusting everything that was foreign, and in promoting by whatever means the national glory." Yes, indeed, whether the means were fair or foul. Of course it was a common enough policy, but it was lying and cheating all the same. "Não foi sem duvida por mà fè ou perfidia que tacitamente se mandon armar hum navio à cujo capitao se confiou o plano que Colombo havia proposto, e cuja execução se lhe encarre-

dudgeon, to lay his proposals before the Crown of Castile. He seems to have gone rather suddenly, leaving his wife, who died shortly after, and one or two children who must also have died, for he tells us that he never saw them again. But his son Diego, aged perhaps four or five years, he took with him as far as the town of Huelva, near the little port of Palos in Andalusia, where he left him with one of his wife's sisters, who had married a man of that town named Muliar.[1] This arrival in Spain was prob-

gou ; mas sim por seguir a politica naquelle tempo usada, que toda consistia em olhar com desconfiança para tudo o que era estrangeiro, e en promover por todos os modos a gloria nacional. O capitão nomeado para a empreza, como não tivesse nem o espirito, nem a convicção de Colombo, depois de huma curta viagem nos mares do Oeste, fez-se na volta da terra ; e arribou à Lisboa descontente e desanimado." Campe, *Historia do descobrimento da America*, Paris, 1836, tom. i. p. 13. The frightened sailors protested that YOU MIGHT AS WELL EXPECT TO FIND LAND IN THE SKY AS IN THAT WASTE OF WATERS ! See Las Casas, *Hist. de las Indias*, tom. i. p. 221. Las Casas calls the king's conduct by its right name, *dobladura*, "trickery."

[1] It has generally been supposed, on the authority of *Vita dell' Ammiraglio*, cap. xi., that his wife had lately died ; but an autograph letter of Columbus, in the possession of his lineal descendant and representative, the present Duke of Veraguas, proves that this is a mistake. In this letter Columbus says expressly that when he left Portugal he left wife and children, and never saw them again. (Navarrete, *Coleccion*, tom. ii. doc. cxxxvii. p. 255.) As Las Casas, who knew Diego so well, also supposed his mother to have died before his father

ably late in the autumn of 1484, and Columbus seems to have entered into the service of Ferdi-

and enters the service of the Spanish sovereigns, 1486

nand and Isabella January 20, 1486. What he was doing in the interval of rather more than a year is not known. There is a very doubtful tradition that he tried to interest the republic of Genoa in his enterprise,[1] and a still more doubtful rumour that he afterwards made proposals to the Venetian senate.[2] If these things ever happened, there was

left Portugal, it is most likely that she died soon afterwards. Ferdinand Columbus says that Diego was left in charge of some friars at the convent of La Rábida near Palos (*loc. cit.*) ; Las Casas is not quite so sure ; he thinks Diego was left with some friend of his father at Palos, or perhaps (*por ventura*) at La Rábida. (*Historia*, tom. i. p. 227.) These mistakes were easy to make, for both La Rábida and Huelva were close by Palos, and we know that Diego's aunt Muliar was living at Huelva. (Las Casas, *op. cit.* tom. i. p. 241 ; Harrisse, tom. i. pp. 279, 356, 391 ; tom. ii. p. 229.) It is pretty clear that Columbus never visited La Rábida before the autumn of 1491 (see below, p. 93). My own notion is that Columbus may have left his wife with an infant and perhaps one older child, relieving her of the care of Diego by taking him to his aunt, and intending as soon as practicable to reunite the family. He clearly did not know at the outset whether he should stay in Spain or not.

[1] It rests upon an improbable statement of Ramusio, who places the event as early as 1470. The first Genoese writer to allude to it is Casoni, *Annali della Republica di Genova*, Genoa, 1708, pp. 26–31. Such testimony is of small value.

[2] First mentioned in 1800 by Marin, *Storia del commercio de' Veneziani*, Venice, 1798–1808, tom. vii. p. 236.

time enough for them in this year, and they can hardly be assigned to any later period. In 1486 we find Columbus at Cordova, where the sovereigns were holding court. He was unable to effect anything until he had gained the ear of Isabella's finance minister Alonso de Quintanilla, who had a mind hospitable to large ideas. The two sovereigns had scarcely time to attend to such things, for there was a third king in Spain, the Moor at Granada, whom there now seemed a fair prospect of driving to Africa, and thus ending the struggle that had lasted with few intermissions for nearly eight centuries. The final war with Granada had been going on since the end of 1481, and considering how it weighed upon the minds of Ferdinand and Isabella it is rather remarkable that cosmography got any hearing at all. The affair was referred to the queen's confessor Fernando de Talavera, whose first impression was that if what Columbus said was true, it was very strange that other geographers should have failed to know all about it long ago. Ideas of evolution had not yet begun to exist in those days, and it was thought that what the ancients did not know was not worth knowing. Toward the end of 1486 the Spanish sovereigns were at Salamanca, and Talavera referred the question to a junto of learned men, including professors of

The junto at Salamanca

79

the famous university.[1] There was no lack of taunt and ridicule, and a whole arsenal of texts from Scripture and the Fathers were discharged at Columbus, but it is noticeable that quite a number were inclined to think that his scheme might be worth trying, and that some of his most firmly convinced supporters were priests. No decision had been reached when the sovereigns started on the Malaga campaign in the spring of 1487.

After the surrender of Malaga in August, 1487, Columbus visited the court in that city. For a year or more after that time silken chains seem to have bound him to Cordova. He had formed a connection with a lady of noble family, Beatriz Enriquez de Arana, who gave birth to his son Ferdinand on the 15th of August, 1488.[2]

Birth of Ferdinand Columbus, Aug. 15, 1488

---

[1] The description usually given of this conference rests upon the authority of Remesal, *Historia de la prouincia de Chyapa*, Madrid, 1619, lib. ii. cap. vii. p. 52. Las Casas merely says that the question was referred to certain persons at the court, *Hist. de las Indias*, tom. i. p. 228. It is probably not true that the project of Columbus was officially condemned by the university of Salamanca as a corporate body. See Camara, *Religion y Ciencia*, Valladolid, 1880, p. 261.

[2] Some historians, unwilling to admit any blemishes in the character of Columbus, have supposed that this union was sanctioned by marriage, but this is not probable. He seems to have been tenderly attached to Beatriz, who survived him many years. See Harrisse, tom. ii. pp. 353–357.

Shortly after this event, Columbus made a visit to Lisbon, in all probability for the purpose of meeting his brother Bartholomew, who had returned in the last week of December, 1487, in the Dias expedition, with the proud news of the discovery of the Cape of Good Hope,[1]

Bartholomew Columbus returns from the Cape of Good Hope Dec., 1487

---

[1] The authority for Bartholomew Columbus having sailed to the Cape of Good Hope with Dias is a manuscript note of his own in Christopher's copy of the *Imago Mundi*: "Nota quod hoc anno de 88 [it should be 87] in mense decembri appulit in Ulixbona Bartholomeus Didacus capitaneus trium carabelarum quem miserat serenissimus rex Portugalie in Guineam ad tentandum terram. Et renunciavit ipse serenissimo regi prout navigaverat ultra jam navigata leuchas 600, videlicet 450 ad austrum et 150 ad aquilonem usque montem per ipsum nominatum *Cabo de boa esperança* quem in Agesimba estimamus. Qui quidem in eo loco invenit se distare per astrolabium ultra lineam equinoctialem gradus 35. Quem viagium pictavit et scripsit de leucha in leucham in una carta navigationis ut oculi visum ostenderet ipso serenissimo regi. In quibus omnibus interfui." M. Varnhagen has examined this note and thinks it is in the handwriting of Christopher Columbus (*Bulletin de Géographie*, janvier, 1858, tom. xv. p. 71); and M. d'Avezac (*Canevas chronologique*, p. 58), accepting this opinion, thinks that the words *in quibus omnibus interfui*, "in all of which I took part," only mean that Christopher was present in Lisbon when the expedition returned, and heard the whole story! With all possible respect for such great scholars as MM. d'Avezac and Varnhagen, I submit that the opinion of Las Casas, who first called attention to this note, must be much better than theirs on such a point as the handwriting of the two brothers. When Las Casas found the note he wondered whether it was meant for Bartholomew or Chris-

which was rightly believed to be the extremity of Africa ; and we can well understand how

topher, *i. e.* wondered which of the two was meant to be described as having "taken part ; " but at all events, says Las Casas, the handwriting is Bartholomé's : " Estas palabras escritas de la mano de Bartolomé Colon, no sé si las escribió de sí ó de su letra por su hermano Cristóbal Colon." Under these circumstances it seems idle to suppose that Las Casas could have been mistaken about the handwriting ; he evidently put his mind on that point, and in the next breath he goes on to say, " la letra yo conozco ser de Bartolomé Colon, porque tuve muchas suyas," *i. e.* " I know it is Bartholomew's writing, for I have had many letters of his ; " and again " estas palabras . . . de la misma letra y ma no de Bartolomé Colon, la cual muy bien conocí y agora tengo hartas cartas y letras suyas, tratando deste viaje," *i. e.* " these words . . . from the very writing and hand of Bartholomew Columbus, which I knew very well, and I have to-day many charts and letters of his, treating of this voyage." (*Hist. de las Indias*, tom. i. pp. 213, 214.) This last sentence makes Las Casas an independent witness to Bartholomew's presence in the expedition, a matter about which he was not likely to be mistaken. What puzzled him was the question, not whether Bartholomew went, but whether Christopher could have gone also, " pudo ser tambien que se hallase Cristóbal Colon." Now Christopher certainly did not go on that voyage. The expedition started in August, 1486, and returned to Lisbon in December, 1487, after an absence of sixteen months and seventeen days, " auendo dezaseis meses et dezasete dias que erão partidos delle." (Barros, *Decada primeira da Asia*, Lisbon, 1752, tom. i. fol. 42, 44.) The account-book of the treasury of Castile shows that sums of money were paid to Christopher at Seville, May 5, July 3, August 27, and October 15, 1487 ; so that he could not have

Christopher, on seeing the success of Prince Henry's method of reaching the Indies so nearly vindicated, must have become more impatient than ever to prove the superiority of his own method. It was probably not long after Bartholomew's return that Christopher determined to go and see him, for he applied to King John II. for a kind of safe-conduct, which was duly granted March 20, 1488. This document[1] guarantees Christopher against arrest or arraignment or detention on any charge civil or criminal whatever, during his stay in Portugal, and commands all magistrates in that kingdom to

gone with Dias (see Harrisse, tom. ii. p. 191). Neither could Christopher have been in Lisbon in December, 1487, when the little fleet returned, for his safe-conduct from King John is dated March 20, 1488. It was not until the autumn of 1488 that Columbus made this visit to Portugal, and M. d'Avezac has got the return of the fleet a year too late. Bartholomew's note followed a custom which made 1488 begin at Christmas, 1487.

In reading a later chapter of Las Casas for another purpose (tom. i. p. 227), I come again upon this point. He rightly concludes that Christopher could not have gone with Dias, and again declares most positively that the handwriting of the note was Bartholomew's and not Christopher's.

This footnote affords a good illustration of the kind of difficulties that surround such a subject as the life of Columbus, and the ease with which an excess of ingenuity may discover mare's nests.

[1] It may be found in Navarrete, *Coleccion de viages*, tom. ii. pp. 5, 6.

respect it. From this it would seem probable that in the eagerness of his geographical speculations he had neglected his business affairs and left debts behind him in Portugal for which he was liable to be arrested. The king's readiness to grant the desired privilege seems to indicate that he may have cherished a hope of regaining the services of this accomplished chart-maker and mariner. Christopher did not avail himself of the privilege until late in the summer,[1] and it is only fair to suppose that he waited for the birth of his child and some assurance of its mother's safety. On meeting Bartholomew he evidently set him to work forthwith in making overtures to the courts of England and France. It was natural enough that Bartholomew should first set out for Bristol, where old shipmates and acquaintances were sure to be found. It appears that on the way he was captured by pirates, and thus some delay was occasioned before he arrived in London and showed the king a map, probably similar to Toscanelli's and embellished with quaint Latin verses. An entry on this map informs us that it was made by Bartholomew Columbus in London, February 10, 1488, which I think should be read

Christopher visits Bartholomew at Lisbon, cir. Sept., 1488;

and sends him to England

Bartholomew, after mishaps, reaches England cir. Feb., 1490;

[1] The account-book of the treasury shows that on June 16 he was still in Spain. See Harrisse, tom. i. p. 355.

1489 or even 1490, so we may suppose it to have been about that time or perhaps later that he approached the throne.[1] Henry VII. was intelli-

---

[1] The entry, as given by Las Casas, is " Pro authore, seu pictore, || Gennua cui patria est, nomen cui Bartolomeus || Columbus de terra rubea, opus edidit istud || Londonijs : anno domini millesimo quatercentessimo octiesque uno || Atque insuper anno octavo : decimaque die mensis Februarii. || Laudes Christo cantentur abunde." *Historia*, tom. i. p. 225. Now since Bartholomew Columbus was a fairly educated man, writing this note in England on a map made for the eyes of the king of England, I suppose he used the old English style which made the year begin at the vernal equinox instead of Christmas, so that his February, 1488, means the next month but one after December, 1488, *i. e.* what in our new style becomes February, 1489. Bartholomew returned to Lisbon from Africa in the last week of December, 1487, and it is not likely that his plans could have been matured and himself settled down in London in less than seven weeks. The logical relation of the events, too, shows plainly that Christopher's visit to Lisbon was for the purpose of consulting his brother and getting first-hand information about the greatest voyage the world had ever seen. In the early weeks of 1488 Christopher sends his request for a safe-conduct, gets it March 20, waits till his child is born, August 15, and then presently goes. Bartholomew may have sailed by the first of October for England, where (according to this reading of his date) we actually find him four months later. What happened to him in this interval ? Here we come to the story of the pirates. M. Harrisse, who never loses an opportunity for throwing discredit upon the *Vita dell' Ammiraglio*, has failed to make the correction of date which I have here suggested. He puts Bartholomew in London in February, 1488, and is thus unable to assign any reason for Christopher's visit to Lis-

gent enough to see the bearings of Bartholomew's arguments, and at the same time, as a

bon. He also finds that in the forty-six days between Christmas, 1487, and February 10, 1488, there is hardly room
enough for any delay due to so grave a cause as capture by
pirates. (*Christophe Colomb*, vol. ii. p. 192.) He therefore
concludes that the statement in the *Vita dell' Ammiraglio*,
cap. xi., is unworthy of credit, and it is upon an accumulation of small difficulties like this that he bases his opinion that
Ferdinand Columbus cannot have written that book. But Las
Casas also gives the story of the pirates, and adds the information
that they were "Easterlings," though he cannot say of what
nation, *i. e.* whether Dutch, German, or perhaps Danes. He
says that Bartholomew was stripped of his money and fell sick,
and after his recovery was obliged to earn money by map-
making before he could get to England. (*Historia*, tom. i.
p. 225.) Could all this have happened within the four
months which I have allowed between October, 1488, and
February, 1489? Voyages before the invention of steam-
boats were of very uncertain duration. John Adams in 1784
was fifty-four days in getting from London to Amsterdam (see
my *Critical Period of American History*, ch. iv.). But with
favourable weather a Portuguese caravel in 1488 ought to have
run from Lisbon to Bristol in fourteen days or less, so that in
four months there would be time enough for quite a chapter
of accidents. Las Casas, however, says it was *a long time*
before Bartholomew was able to reach England : " Esto
fué causa que enfermase y viniese á mucha pobreza, y estu-
viese mucho tempo sin poder llegar á Inglaterra, hasta tanto
que quiso Dios sanarle ; y reformado algo, por su industria y
trabajos de sus manos, haciendo cartas de marear, llegó á
Inglaterra, y, pasados un dia y otros, hobo de alcanzar que
le oyese Enrique VII." It is impossible, I think, to read
this passage without feeling that at least a year must have been

good man of business, he was likely to be cautious about investing money in remote or doubt-

consumed; and I do not think we are entitled to disregard the words of Las Casas in such a matter. But how shall we get the time?

Is it possible that Las Casas made a slight mistake in deciphering the date on Bartholomew's map? Either that mariner did not give the map to Henry VII., or the king gave it back, or more likely it was made in duplicate. At any rate Las Casas had it, along with his many other Columbus documents, and for aught we know it may still be tumbling about somewhere in the Spanish archives. It was so badly written (*de muy mala é corrupta letra*), apparently in abbreviations (*sin ortografía*), that Las Casas says he found extreme difficulty in making it out. Now let us observe that date, which is given in fantastic style, apparently because the inscription is in a rude doggerel, and the writer seems to have wished to keep his " verses " tolerably even. (They don't scan much better than Walt Whitman's.) As it stands, the date reads *anno domini millesimo quatercentessimo octiesque uno atque insuper anno actavo, i. e.* " in the year of our Lord the thousandth, four hundredth, AND EIGHT-TIMES-ONE, and thereafter the eighth year." What business has this cardinal number *octiesque uno* in a row of ordinals? If it were translatable, which it is not, it would give us 1000 + 400 + 8 + 8 = 1416, an absurd date. The most obvious way to make the passage readable is to insert the ordinal *octogesimo primo* instead of the incongruous *octiesque uno;* then it will read " in the year of our Lord the one-thousand-four-hundred-and-eighty-first, and thereafter the eighth year," that is to say 1489. Now translate old style into new style, and February, 1489, becomes February, 1490, which I believe to be the correct date. This allows sixteen months for Bartholomew's mishaps; it justifies the statement in which Las Casas confirms Ferdinand Columbus;

ful enterprises. What arguments were used we do not know, but the spring of 1492 had arrived before any decisive answer had been given. Meanwhile Bartholomew had made his way to France, and found a powerful protector in a certain Madame de Bourbon,[1] while he made maps for people at the court and waited to see if there were any chances of getting help from Charles VIII.

and goes thence to France before 1492

As for Christopher Columbus, we find him back in Spain again, in May, 1489, attending court at Cordova. In the following autumn there was much suffering in Spain from floods and famine,[2] and the sovereigns were too busy with the Moorish war to give ear to Columbus. It

and it harmonizes with the statement of Lord Bacon : " For Christopherus Columbus, refused by the king of Portugal (who would not embrace at once both east and west), employed his brother Bartholomew Columbus unto King Henry to negotiate for his discovery. And it so fortuned that he was taken by pirates at sea ; by which accidental impediment he was long ere he came to the king ; so long that before he had obtained a capitulation with the king for his brother the enterprise was achieved, and so the West Indies by Providence were then reserved for the crown of Castilia." *Historie of the Raygne of K. Henry the Seventh,* Bacon's *Works,* Boston, 1860, vol. xi. p. 296. Lord Bacon may have taken the statement from Ferdinand's biography ; but it probably agreed with English traditions, and ought not to be slighted in this connection.

[1] One of the sisters of Charles VIII. See Harrisse, tom. ii. p. 194.

[2] Bernaldez, *Reyes Católicos,* cap. xci.

was no time for new undertakings, and the
weary suitor began to think seriously of going
in person to the French court. First, however,
he thought it worth while to make an attempt
to get private capital enlisted in his enterprise,
and in the Spain of that day such private capital meant a largess from some wealthy grandee.
Accordingly, about Christmas of 1489, after the
Beza campaign, in which Columbus is said to
have fought with distinguished valour,[1] he seems
to have applied to the most powerful nobleman in
Spain, the Duke of Medina-Sidonia, but without
success. But at the hands of Luis de la
Cerda, Duke of Medina-Celi, he met
with more encouragement than he had
as yet found in any quarter. That nobleman entertained Columbus most

The Duke of
Medina-Celi
proposes to
furnish the
ships for
Columbus,

hospitably at his castle at Puerto de Santa Maria
for nearly two years, until the autumn of 1491.
He became convinced that the scheme of Columbus was feasible, and decided to fit up two
or three caravels at his own expense, if necessary, but first he thought it proper to ask the
queen's consent, and to offer her another chance
to take part in the enterprise.[2] Isabella was

[1] Zuñiga, *Anales de Sevilla,* lib. xii. p. 404.
[2] See the letter of March 19, 1493, from the Duke of Medina-Celi to the Grand Cardinal of Spain (from the archives
of Simancas) in Navarrete, *Coleccion de viages,* tom. ii.
p. 20.

probably unwilling to have the duke come in for a large share of the profits in case the venture should prove successful. She refused the royal license, saying that she had not quite made up her mind whether to take up the affair or not, but if she should decide to do so she would be glad to have the duke take part in it.[1] Meanwhile she referred the question to Alonso de Quintanilla, comptroller of the treasury of Castile. This was in the spring of 1491, when the whole country was in a buzz of excitement with the preparations for the siege of Granada. The baffled Columbus visited the sovereigns in camp, but could not get them to attend to him, and early in the autumn, thoroughly disgusted and sick at heart, he made up his mind to shake the dust of Castile from his feet and see what could be done in France. In October or November he went to Huelva, apparently to get his son Diego, who

but Isabella withholds her consent

Columbus makes up his mind to get his family together and go to France, Oct., 1491

[1] This promise was never fulfilled. When Columbus returned in triumph, arriving March 6, 1493, at Lisbon, and March 15 at Palos, the Duke of Medina-Celi wrote the letter just cited, recalling the queen's promise and asking to be allowed to send to the Indies once each year an expedition on his own account ; for, he says, if he had not kept Columbus with him in 1490 and 1491 he would have gone to France, and Castile would have lost the prize. There was some force in this, but Isabella does not appear to have heeded the request.

had been left there, in charge of his aunt. It was probably his intention to take all the family he had — Beatriz and her infant son Ferdinand, of whom he was extremely fond, as well as Diego — and find a new home in either France or England, besides ascertaining what had become of his brother Bartholomew, from whom he had not heard a word since the latter left Portugal for England.[1]

But now at length events took a favourable turn. Fate had grown tired of fighting against such indomitable perseverance. For some years now the stately figure of Columbus had been a familiar sight in the streets of Seville and Cordova, and as he passed along, with his white hair streaming in the breeze, and countenance aglow with intensity of purpose or haggard with disappointment at some fresh rebuff, the ragged urchins of the pavement tapped their foreheads and smiled with mingled wonder and amusement at this madman. Seventeen years had elapsed since the letter from Toscanelli to Martinez, and all that was mortal of the Florentine astronomer had long since been laid in the grave. For Columbus himself old age was not far away, yet he seemed no nearer the fulfilment of his grand purpose than when he had first set it forth to the king of Portugal. We can well imagine that

[1] This theory of the situation is fully sustained by Las Casas, tom. i. p. 241.

when he started from Huelva, with his little son Diego, now some eleven or twelve years old, again to begin renewing his suit in a strange country, his thoughts must have been sombre enough. For some reason or other — tradition says to ask for some bread and water for his boy — he stopped at the Franciscan monastery of La Rábida, about half a league from Palos.

He stops at La Rábida, and meets the prior Juan Perez

The prior, Juan Perez, who had never seen Columbus before, became greatly interested in him and listened with earnest attention to his story. This worthy monk, who before 1478 had been Isabella's father confessor, had a mind hospitable to new ideas. He sent for Garcia Fernandez, a physician of Palos, who was somewhat versed in cosmography, and for Martin Alonso Pinzon, a well to do ship-owner and trained mariner of that town, and in the quiet of the monastery a conference was held in which Columbus carried conviction to the minds of these new friends. Pinzon declared himself ready to embark in the enterprise in person. The venerable

Perez writes to the queen,

prior forthwith sent a letter to the queen, and received a very prompt reply summoning him to attend her in the camp before Granada. The result of the interview was that within a few days Perez returned to the convent with a purse of 20,000 maravedis (equivalent to about 1180 dollars of the present day), out of

Convent of La Rabida

which Columbus bought a new suit of clothes and about the first of December he set out for the camp in company with Juan Perez, leaving the boy Diego in charge of the priest Martin Sanchez and a certain Rodriguez Cabejudo, upon whose sworn testimony, together with that of the physician Garcia Fernandez, some years afterward, several of these facts are related.[1]

<small>and Columbus is summoned back to court</small>

---

[1] My account of these proceedings at La Rábida differs in some particulars from any heretofore given, and I think gets the events into an order of sequence that is at once more logical and more in harmony with the sources of information than any other. The error of Ferdinand Columbus — a very easy one to commit, and not in the least damaging to his general character as biographer — lay in confusing his father's two real visits (in 1484 and 1491) to Huelva with two visits (one imaginary in 1484 and one real in 1491) to La Rábida, which was close by, between Huelva and Palos. The visits were all the more likely to get mixed up in recollection because in each case their object was little Diego and in each case he was left in charge of somebody in that neighbourhood. The confusion has been helped by another for which Ferdinand is not responsible, viz. : the friar Juan Perez has been confounded with another friar Antonio de Marchena, who Columbus says was the only person who from the time of his first arrival in Spain had always befriended him and never mocked at him. These worthy friars twain have been made into one (*e. g.* " the prior of the convent, Juan Perez de Marchena," Irving's *Columbus*, vol. i. p. 128), and it has often been supposed that Marchena's acquaintance began with Columbus at La Rábida in 1484, and that Diego was left at the convent at that time. But some modern sources of information have served at first

At once upon the arrival of Columbus in the camp before Granada, his case was argued then

to bemuddle, and then when more carefully sifted, to clear up the story. In 1508 Diego Columbus brought suit against the Spanish Crown to vindicate his claim to certain territories discovered by his father, and there was a long investigation in which many witnesses were summoned and past events were busily raked over the coals. Among these witnesses were Rodriguez Cabejudo and the physician Garcia Fernandez, who gave from personal recollection a very lucid account of the affairs at La Rábida. These proceedings are printed in Navarrete, *Coleccion de viages*, tom. iii. pp. 238–591. More recently the publication of the great book of Las Casas has furnished some very significant clues, and the elaborate researches of M. Harrisse have furnished others. (See Las Casas, lib. i. cap. xxix., xxxi.; Harrisse, tom. i. pp. 341–372; tom. ii. pp. 237–251; cf. Peragallo, *L' autenticità*, etc., pp. 117–134.) — It now seems clear that Marchena, whom Columbus knew from his first arrival in Spain, was not associated with La Rábida. At that time Columbus left Diego, a mere infant, with his wife's sister at Huelva. Seven years later, intending to leave Spain forever, he went to Huelva and took Diego, then a small boy. On his way from Huelva to the Seville road, and thence to Cordova (where he would have been joined by Beatriz and Ferdinand), he happened to pass by La Rábida, where up to that time he was evidently unknown, and to attract the attention of the prior Juan Perez, and the wheel of fortune suddenly and unexpectedly turned. As Columbus's next start was not for France, but for Granada, his boy was left in charge of two trustworthy persons. On May 8, 1492, the little Diego was appointed page to Don John, heir-apparent to the thrones of Castile and Aragon, with a stipend of 9400 maravedis. On February 19,

and there before an assembly of learned men and was received more hospitably than formerly, at Salamanca. Several eminent pre- The junto before Granada, Dec., 1491 lates had come to think favourably of his project or to deem it at least worth a trial. Among these were the royal confessors, Deza and Talavera, the latter having changed his mind, and especially Mendoza, Archbishop of Toledo, who now threw his vast influence decisively in favour of Columbus.[1] The treasurers of the two kingdoms, moreover, Quintanilla for Castile and Luis de Santangel for Aragon, were among his most enthusiastic supporters; and the result of the conference was the queen's promise to take up the matter in earnest as soon as the Moor should have surrendered Granada.

1498, after the death of that young prince, Diego became page to Queen Isabella.

[1] In popular allusions to Columbus it is quite common to assume or imply that he encountered nothing but opposition from the clergy. For example, the account in Draper's *Conflict between Science and Religion*, p. 161, can hardly be otherwise understood by the reader. But observe that Marchena, who never mocked at Columbus, Juan Perez, who gave the favourable turn to his affairs, the great prelates Deza and Mendoza, and the two treasurers Santangel and Quintanilla, were every one of them priests ! Without cordial support from the clergy no such enterprise as that of Columbus could have been undertaken, in Spain at least. It is quite right that we should be free-thinkers ; and it is also desirable that we should have some respect for facts.

Columbus had not long to wait for that great event, which came on the 2d of January, 1492,

Surrender of Granada, Jan. 2, 1492

and was hailed with rejoicings throughout Europe as in some sort a compensation for the loss of Constantinople. It must have been with a manifold sense of triumph that Columbus saw the banner of Spain unfurled to the breeze from the highest tower of the Alhambra. But at this critical moment in his fortunes the same obstacle was encountered that long before had broken off his negotiations with the king of Portugal. With pride and self-confidence not an inch abated by all these years of trial, he demanded such honours and substantial rewards as seemed extravagant to the queen, and Talavera advised her not to grant them. Columbus insisted upon being appointed admiral of the ocean and viceroy of such

Columbus negotiates with the queen

heathen countries as he might discover, besides having for his own use and behoof one eighth part of such revenues and profits as might accrue from the expedition. In principle this sort of remuneration did not differ from that which the Crown of Portugal had been wont to award to its eminent discoverers ;[1] but in amount it was liable to

---

[1] Our Scandinavian friends are fond of pointing to this demand of Columbus as an indication that he secretly expected to "discover America," and not merely to find the way to Asia. But how about Ferdinand and Isabella, who finally

prove indefinitely great, enough perhaps to raise to princely power and rank this foreign adventurer. Could he not be satisfied with something less? But Columbus was as inexorable as the Sibyl with her books, and would hear of no abatement in his price. For this " great constancy and loftiness of soul," [1] Las Casas warmly commends his friend Columbus. A querulous critic might call it unreasonable obstinacy. But in truth the good man seems to have entertained another grand scheme of his own, to which he wished to make his maritime venture contribute. It was natural that his feelings toward Turks

granted what was demanded, and their ministers who drew up the agreement, to say nothing of the clerks who engrossed it ? What did they all understand by " discovering islands and continents in the ocean " ? Were they all in this precious Vinland secret ? If so, it was pretty well kept. But in truth there was nothing singular in these stipulations. Portugal paid for discovery in just this way by granting governorships over islands like the Azores, or long stretches of continent like Guinea, along with a share of the revenues yielded by such places. See, for example, the cases of Gonzalo Cabral, Fernando Gomez, and others in Major, *Prince Henry the Navigator*, pp. 238, 321, and elsewhere. In their search for the Indies the Portuguese were continually finding new lands, and it was likely to be the same with the western route, which was supposed (see Catalan, Toscanelli, and Behaim maps) to lead among spice islands innumerable, and to Asiatic kingdoms whose heathen people had no rights of sovereignty that Christian monarchs felt bound to respect.

[1] Las Casas, *op. cit.* tom. i. p. 243.

should have been no more amiable than those of Hannibal toward the Romans. It was the Turks who had ruined the commerce of his native Genoa, in his youth he had more than once crossed swords with their corsairs, and now he looked forward to the time when he might play the part of a second Godfrey de Bouillon and deliver Jerusalem from the miscreant followers of Mahound.[1] Vast resources would be needed for such work, and from Cipango with its gold-roofed temples, and the nameless and numberless isles of spices that crowded the Cathayan seas, he hoped to obtain them. Long brooding over his cherished projects, in which chimeras were thus mixed with anticipations of scientific truth, had imparted to his character a tinge of religious fanaticism. He had come to regard himself as a man with a mission to fulfil, as God's chosen instrument for enlarging the bounds of Christendom and achieving triumphs of untold magnificence for its banners. In this mood he was apt to address kings with an air of equality that ill comported with his humble origin and slender means ; and on the present occasion, if Talavera felt his old doubts and suspicions reviving, and

His terms are considered exorbitant

[1] See his letter of February, 1502, to Pope Alexander VI. in Navarrete, tom. ii. p. 280 ; and cf. Helps, *Spanish Conquest in America*, vol. i. p. 96 ; Roselly de Lorgues, *Christophe Colomb*, p. 394.

was more than half inclined to set Columbus down as a mere vender of crotchets, one can hardly wonder.

The negotiations were broken off, and the indomitable enthusiast once more prepared to go to France. He had actually started on his mule one fine winter day, when Luis de Santangel rushed into the queen's room and spoke to her with all the passionate and somewhat reproachful energy of one who felt that a golden opportunity was slipping away forever. His arguments were warmly seconded by Quintanilla, who had followed him into the room, as well as by the queen's bosom friend Beatriz de Bobadilla, Marchioness of Moya, who happened to be sitting on the sofa and was a devoted admirer of Columbus. An impulse seized Isabella. A courier was sent on a fleet horse, and overtook Columbus as he was jogging quietly over the bridge of Pinos, about six miles out from Granada. The matter was reconsidered and an arrangement was soon made. It was agreed : —

Interposition of Luis de Santangel

" 1. That Columbus should have, for himself, during his life, and for his heirs and successors forever, the office of admiral in all the islands and continents which he might discover or acquire in the ocean, with similar honours and prerogatives to

Agreement between Columbus and the sovereigns

those enjoyed by the high admiral of Castile in
his district.

" 2. That he should be viceroy and governor-
general over all the said lands and continents ;
with the privilege of nominating three candidates
for the government of each island or province,
one of whom should be selected by the sov-
creigns.

" 3. That he should be entitled to reserve
for himself one tenth of all pearls, precious
stones, gold, silver, spices, and all other articles
and merchandises, in whatever manner found,
bought, bartered, or gained within his admiralty,
the costs being first deducted.

" 4. That he, or his lieutenant, should be the
sole judge in all causes and disputes arising out
of traffic between those countries and Spain,
provided the high admiral of Castile had similar
jurisdiction in his district.

" 5. That he might then, and at all after
times, contribute an eighth part of the expense
in fitting out vessels to sail on this enterprise,
and receive an eighth part of the profits." [1]

Columbus was not long in finding friends to

[1] I cite this version from Irving's *Columbus*, vol. i. p. 142,
making a slight amendment in the rendering ; the original text
is in Navarrete, tom. ii. p. 7. A few days later the title of
" Don " was granted to Columbus and made hereditary in
his family along with the offices of viceroy and governor-
general.

Queen Isabella

D. ISABEL 1.º

advance or promise on his account an eighth part of the sum immediately required. A considerable amount was assessed upon the town of Palos in punishment for certain misdeeds or delinquencies on the part of its people or some of them. Castile assumed the rest of the burden, though Santangel may have advanced a million maravedis out of the treasury of Aragon, or out of the funds of the *Hermandad*,[1] or perhaps more likely on his own account.[2] In any case it was

[1] A police organization formed in 1476 for suppressing highway robbery.

[2] It is not easy to give an accurate account of the cost of this most epoch-making voyage in all history. Conflicting statements by different authorities combine with the fluctuating values of different kinds of money to puzzle and mislead us. According to M. Harrisse 1,000,000 maravedis would be equivalent to 295,175 francs, or about 59,000 gold dollars of United States money at present values. Las Casas (tom. i. p. 256) says that the eighth part, raised by Columbus, was 500,000 maravedis (29,500 dollars). Account-books preserved in the archives of Simancas show that the sums paid from the treasury of Castile amounted to 1,140,000 maravedis (67,500 dollars). Assuming the statement of Las Casas to be correct, the amounts contributed would perhaps have been as follows : —

Queen Isabella, from Castile treasury . .	$67,500
Queen Isabella, loan from Santangel . . .	59,000
Columbus	29,500
Other sources, including contribution levied upon the town of Palos	80,000
Total	$236,000

This total seems to me altogether too large for probability,

a loan to the treasury of Castile simply. It was always distinctly understood that Ferdinand as king of Aragon had no share in the enterprise,

and so does the last item, which is simply put at the figure necessary to make the total eight times 29,500. I am inclined to suspect that Las Casas (with whom arithmetic was not always a strong point) may have got his figures wrong. The amount of Santangel's loan also depends upon the statement of Las Casas, and we do not know whether he took it from a document or from hearsay. Nor do we know whether it should be added to, or included in, the first item. More likely, I think, the latter. The only item that we know with documentary certainty is the first, so that our statement becomes modified as follows : —

Queen Isabella, from Castile treasury	. .	$67,500
Queen Isabella, loan from Santangel.	. .	?
Columbus		?
Town of Palos	rent of two fully equipped caravels for two months, etc.	
Total		?

(Cf. Harrisse, tom. i. pp. 391–404.) Unsatisfactory, but certain as far as it goes. Alas, how often historical statements are thus reduced to meagreness, after the hypothetical or ill-supported part has been sifted out ! The story that the Pinzon brothers advanced to Columbus his portion is told by Las Casas, but he very shrewdly doubts it. The famous story that Isabella pledged her crown jewels (*Vita dell' Ammiraglio*, cap. xiv.) has also been doubted, but perhaps on insufficient grounds, by M. Harrisse. It is confirmed by Las Casas (tom. i. p. 249). According to one account she pledged them to Santangel in security for his loan, — which seems not altogether improbable. See Pizarro y Orellana, *Varones ilustres del Nuevo Mundo*, Madrid, 1639, p. 10.

and that the Spanish Indies were an appurtenance to the Crown of Castile. The agreement was signed April 17, 1492, and with tears of joy Columbus vowed to devote every maravedi that should come to him to the rescue of the Holy Sepulchre.

When he reached Palos in May, with royal orders for ships and men, there had *Dismay at* like to have been a riot. Terrible *Palos* dismay was felt at the prospect of launching out for such a voyage upon the Sea of Darkness. Groans and curses greeted the announcement of the forced contribution. But Martin Pinzon and his brothers were active in supporting the Crown officials, and the work went on. To induce men to enlist, debts were forgiven and civil actions suspended. Criminals were released from jail on condition of serving. Three caravels were impressed into the service of the Crown for a time unlimited ; and the rent and maintenance of two of these vessels for two *The three fa-* months was to be paid by the town. *mous cara-* The largest caravel, called the Santa *Santa Maria* Maria or Capitana, belonged to Juan de La Cosa, a Biscayan mariner whose name was soon to become famous.[1] He now commanded her, with another consummate sailor, Sancho Ruiz, for his pilot. This single-decked craft, about ninety feet in length by twenty feet breadth of

[1] Navarrete, *Biblioteca maritima*, tom. ii. pp. 208, 209.

beam, was the admiral's flag-ship. The second caravel, called the Pinta, a much swifter vessel,

The Pinta

was commanded by Martin Pinzon. She belonged to two citizens of Palos, Gomez Rascon and Cristobal Quintero, who were now in her crew, sulky and ready for mischief. The third and smallest caravel,

The Niña

the Niña (" Baby "), had for her commander Vicente Yañez Pinzon, the youngest of the brothers, now about thirty years of age. Neither the Pinta nor the Niña was decked amidships. On board the three caravels were just ninety persons.[1] And so they set sail from Palos on Friday, August 3, 1492, half an hour before sunrise, and by sunset had run due south five and forty geographical miles, when they shifted their course a couple of points to starboard and stood for the Canaries.

No thought of Vinland is betrayed in these proceedings. Columbus was aiming at the northern end of Cipango (Japan). Upon Toscanelli's map, which he carried with him, the great island of Cipango extends from 5° to about 28° north latitude. He evidently aimed at the northern end of Cipango as being directly on the route to Zaiton (Chang-chow) and other

[1] The accounts of the armament are well summed up and discussed in Harrisse, tom. i. pp. 405–408. Eighty-seven names, out of the ninety, have been recovered, and the list is given in vol. iii. Appendix C.

MARTIN BEHAIM'S GLOBE, 1492, REDU

MERCATOR'S PROJECTION (See page 344)

Chinese cities mentioned by Marco Polo. Accordingly he began by running down to the Canaries, in order that he might sail thence due west on the 28th parallel without shifting his course by a single point until he should see the coast of Japan looming up before him.[1] On this preliminary run signs of mischief began already to show themselves. The Pinta's rudder was broken and unshipped, and Columbus suspected her two angry and chafing owners of having done it on purpose, in order that they and their vessel might be left behind. The Canaries at this juncture merited the name of Fortunate Islands; fortunately they, alone among African islands, were Spanish, so that Columbus could stop there and make repairs. While this was going on the sailors were scared out of their wits by an eruption of Teneriffe, which they deemed an omen of evil, and it was also reported that some Portuguese caravels were hovering in those waters, with intent to capture Columbus and carry him off to Lisbon.

At length, on the 6th of September, they set sail from Gomera, but were becalmed and had made only thirty miles by the night of the 8th. The breeze then freshened, and when next

They go to the Canaries and are delayed there

---

[1] "Para de allí tomar mi derrota, y navegar tanto que yo llegase á las Indias," he says in his journal, Navarrete, *Coleccion de viages*, tom. i. p. 3.

day the shores of Ferro, the last of the Canaries, sank from sight on the eastern horizon, Columbus starts for Japan, Sept. 6, 1492 many of the sailors loudly lamented their unseemly fate, and cried and sobbed like children. Columbus well understood the difficulty of dealing with these men. He provided against one chief source of discontent by keeping two different reckonings, a true one for himself and a false one for his officers and crews. He was shrewd enough not to overdo it and awaken distrust. Thus after a twenty-four hours' run of 180 miles on September 10, he reported it as 144 miles; next day the run was 120 miles and he announced it as 108, and so on. But for this prudent if somewhat questionable device, it is not unlikely that the first week of October would have witnessed a mutiny in which Columbus would have been either thrown overboard or forced to turn back.

The weather was delicious, and but for the bugaboos that worried those poor sailors it would have been a most pleasant voyage. Chief among the imaginary terrors were three which deserve especial mention. At nightfall on September 13 the ships had crossed the magnetic line of no variation, and Columbus was astonished to Deflection of the needle see that the compass-needle, instead of pointing a little to the right of the pole-star, began to sway toward the left, and next day this deviation increased. It was impossible to hide such a fact from the sharp eyes of the pilots, and all were seized with alarm at the suspicion that this witch instrument was beginning to play them some foul trick in punishment of their temerity; but Columbus was ready with an ingenious astronomical explanation, and their faith in the profundity of his knowledge prevailed over their terrors.

The second alarm came on September 16, when they struck into vast meadows of floating seaweeds and grasses, abounding in tunny fish and crabs. They had now come more than 800 miles from Ferro and were entering the wonderful Sargasso Sea, that region of the Atlantic six times as large as France, where vast tangles of vegetation grow upon the surface of water that is more than 2000 fathoms deep, and furnish sustenance for an untold wealth of fishy life.[1] To the eye of the mariner

The Sargasso Sea

---

[1] The situation of this Sargasso region in mid-ocean seems to be determined by its character as a quiet neutral ground between the great ocean-currents that flow past it on every side. Sargasso plants are found elsewhere upon the surface of the waves, but nowhere else do they congregate as here. There are reasons for supposing that in ancient times this region extended nearer to the African coast. Skylax (*Periplus*, cap. 109) says that beyond Kerne, at the mouth of Rio d' Ouro the sea cannot be navigated on account of the mud and seaweed. Sataspes, on his return to Persia, B. C. 470, told King Xerxes that his voyage failed because his ship stopped or was stuck fast. (Herodotus, iv. 43.) Festus Avienus mentions

the Sargasso Sea presents somewhat the appearance of an endless green prairie, but modern

vast quantities of seaweed in the ocean west of the Pillars of
Hercules : —

> Exsuperat autem gurgitem fucus frequens
> Atque impeditur æstus ex uligine . . .
> Sic nulla late flabra propellunt ratem,
> Sic segnis humor æquoris pigri stupet.
> Adjicit et illud, plurimum inter gurgites
> Exstare fucum, et sæpe virgulti vice
> Retinere puppim, etc.

Avienus, *Ora Maritima*, 108, 117.

See also Aristotle, *Meteorol.*, ii. 1, 14 ; Pseudo-Aristotle,
De Mirab. Auscult., p. 106 ; Theophrastus, *Historia plan-
tarum*, iv. 7 ; Jornandes, *De rebus Geticis*, apud Muratori,
tom. i. p. 191 ; according to Strabo (iii. 2, § 7) tunny fish
were caught in abundance in the ocean west of Spain, and
were highly valued for the table on account of their fatness,
which was due to submarine vegetables on which they fed.
Possibly the reports of these Sargasso meadows may have
had some share in suggesting to Plato his notion of a huge
submerged island Atlantis (*Timæus*, 25 ; *Kritias*, 108 ; cf.
the notion of a viscous sea in Plutarch, *De facie in Orbe
Lunæ*, 26). Plato's fancy has furnished a theme for much
wild speculation. See, for example, Bailly, *Lettres sur l'At-
lantide de Platon*, Paris, 1779. The belief that there can
ever have been such an island in that part of the Atlantic is
disposed of by the fact that the ocean there is nowhere less
than two miles in depth. See the beautiful map of the Atlantic sea-bottom in Alexander Agassiz's *Three Cruises of the
Blake*, Boston, 1888, vol. i. p. 108, and compare chap. vi.
of that noble work, on "The Permanence of Continents and
of Oceanic Basins ;" see also Wallace's *Island Life*, chap.
vi. It was formerly supposed that the Sargasso plants grow on
the sea-bottom, and becoming detached rise to the surface
(Peter Martyr, *De rebus oceanicis*, dec. iii. lib. v. p. 53 ;

ships plough through it with ease and so did the caravels of Columbus at first. After two or three days, however, the wind being light, their progress was somewhat impeded. It was not strange that the crews were frightened at such a sight. It seemed uncanny and weird, and revived ancient fancies about mysterious impassable seas and overbold mariners whose ships had been stuck fast in them. The more practical spirits were afraid of running aground upon submerged shoals, but all were somewhat reassured on this point when it was found that their longest plummet-lines failed to find bottom.

On September 22 the journal reports "no more grass." They were in clear water again, and more than 1400 geographical miles from the Canaries. A third source of alarm had already begun to disturb the sailors. They were discovering much more than they had bargained

Humboldt, *Personal Narrative*, book i. chap. i.) ; but it is now known that they are simply rooted in the surface water itself. " L'accumulation de ces plantes marines est l'exemple le plus frappant de plantes congénères réunies sur le même point. Ni les forêts colossales de l'Himalaya, ni les graminées qui s'étendent à perte de vue dans les savanes américaines ou les steppes sibériens ne rivalisent avec ces prairies océaniques. Jamais sur un espace aussi étendu, ne se rencontrent de telles masses de plantes semblables. Quand on a vu la mer des Sargasses, on n'oublie point un pareil spectacle." Paul Gaffarel, " La Mer des Sargasses," *Bulletin de Géographie*, Paris, 1872, 6e série, tom. iv. p. 622.

for. They were in the belt of the trade-winds, and as the gentle but unfailing breeze wafted them steadily westward, doubts began to arise as to whether it would ever be possible to return. Fortunately soon after this question began to be discussed, the wind, jealous of its character for capriciousness even there, veered into the southwest.

The trade-wind

By September 25 the admiral's chief difficulty had come to be the impatience of his crews at not finding land. On that day there was a mirage, or some such illusion, which Columbus and all hands supposed to be a coast in front of them, and hymns of praise were sung, but at dawn next day they were cruelly undeceived. Flights of strange birds and other signs of land kept raising hopes which were presently dashed again, and the men passed through alternately hot and cold fits of exultation and dejection. Such mockery seemed to show that they were entering a realm of enchantment. Somebody, perhaps one of the released jail-birds, hinted that if a stealthy thrust should happen some night to push the admiral overboard, it could be plausibly said that he had slipped and fallen while star-gazing. His situation grew daily more perilous, and the fact that he was an Italian commanding Spaniards did not help him. Perhaps what saved him was their vague belief in his superior knowledge;

Impatience of the crews

they may have felt that they should need him in going back.

By October 4 there were ominous symptoms of mutiny, and the anxiety of Columbus was evinced in the extent of his bold understatement

Martin Behaim's Atlantic Ocean (with outline of American continent superimposed).

of that day's run, — 138 miles instead of the true figure 189. For some days his pilots had been begging him to change his course ; perhaps they had passed between islands. Anything for a change! On the 7th at sunrise, they had come 2724 geographical miles from the Canaries, which was farther than the admiral's estimate of the

Change of course from W. to W. S. W.

distance to Cipango; but according to his false statement of the runs, it appeared that they had come scarcely 2200 miles. This leads one to suspect that in stating the length of the voyage, as he had so often done, at 700 leagues, he may have purposely made it out somewhat shorter than he really believed it to be. But now after coming more than 2500 miles he began to fear that he might be sailing past Cipango on the north, and so he shifted his course two points to larboard, or west-southwest. If a secret knowledge of Vinland had been his guiding-star he surely would not have turned his helm that way; but a glance at the Toscanelli map shows what was in his mind. Numerous flights of small birds confirmed his belief that land at the southwest was not far off. The change of direction was probably fortunate. If he had persisted in keeping on the parallel, 720 miles would have brought him to the coast of Florida, a little south of Cape Malabar. After the change he had but 505 miles of water before him, and the temper of the sailors was growing more dangerous with every mile,[1] —

[1] The often-repeated story that a day or two before the end of the voyage Columbus capitulated with his crew, promising to turn back if land were not seen within three days, rests upon the single and relatively inferior authority of Oviedo. It is not mentioned by Las Casas or Bernaldez or Peter Martyr or Ferdinand Columbus, and it is discredited by the

until October 11, when the signs of land became unmistakable, and the wildest excitement prevailed. A reward of 10,000 maravedis had been promised to the person who should first discover land, and ninety pair of eyes were strained that night with looking. About ten o'clock the admiral, standing on the tower-like poop of his vessel, saw a distant light moving as if somebody were running along the shore with a torch. This interpretation was doubted, but a few hours later a sailor on the Pinta saw land distinctly, and soon it was visible to all, a long low coast about five miles distant. This was at two in the morning of Friday, October 12,[1] — just ten weeks since they had sailed from Palos, just thirty-three days since they had lost sight of the coast of Ferro. The sails were now taken in, and the ships lay to, awaiting the dawn.

Land ahead !
Oct. 12
(N. S. 21),
1492

At daybreak the boats were lowered and Columbus, with a large part of his company, went ashore. Upon every side were trees of unknown kinds, and the landscape seemed exceedingly

tone of the admiral's journal, which shows as unconquerable determination on the last day of the voyage as on any previous day. Cf. Irving, vol. i. p. 187.

[1] Applying the Gregorian Calendar, or "new style," it becomes the 21st. The four hundredth anniversary will properly fall on October 21, 1892.

beautiful. Confident that they must have attained the object for which they had set sail,
The crews go ashore the crews were wild with exultation. Their heads were dazed with fancies of princely fortunes close at hand. The officers embraced Columbus or kissed his hands, while the sailors threw themselves at his feet, craving pardon and favour.

These proceedings were watched with unutterable amazement and awe by a multitude of
The astonished natives men, women, and children of cinnamon hue, different from any kind of people the Spaniards had ever seen. All were stark naked and most of them were more or less greased and painted. They thought that the ships were sea-monsters and the white men supernatural creatures descended from the sky.[1] At first they fled in terror as these formidable beings came ashore, but presently, as they found themselves unmolested, curiosity began to overcome fear, and they slowly approached the Spaniards, stopping at every few paces to prostrate themselves in adoration. After a time, as the Spaniards received them with encouraging

---

[1] This is a common notion among barbarians. "The Polynesians imagine that the sky descends at the horizon and encloses the earth. Hence they call foreigners *papalangi*, or 'heaven-bursters,' as having broken in from another world outside." Max Müller, *Chips from a German Workshop*, vol. ii. p. 268.

nods and smiles, they waxed bold enough to come close to the visitors and pass their hands over them, doubtless to make sure that all this marvel was a reality and not a mere vision. Experiences in Africa had revealed the eagerness of barbarians to trade off their possessions for trinkets, and now the Spaniards began exchanging glass beads and hawks' bells for cotton yarn, tame parrots, and small gold ornaments. Some sort of conversation in dumb show went on, and Columbus naturally interpreted everything in such wise as to fit his theories. Whether the natives understood him or not when he asked them where they got their gold, at any rate they pointed to the south, and thus confirmed Columbus in his suspicion that he had come to some island a little to the north of the opulent Cipango. He soon found that it was a small island, and he understood the name of Guanahani: where was it? it to be Guanahani. He took formal possession of it for Castile, just as the discoverers of the Cape Verde Islands and the Guinea coasts had taken possession of those places for Portugal; and he gave it a Christian name, San Salvador. That name has since the seventeenth century been given to Cat Island, but perhaps in pursuance of a false theory of map-makers; it is not proved that Cat Island is the Guanahani of Columbus. All that can positively be asserted of Guanahani is that it was one of the

115

Bahamas; there has been endless discussion as to which one, and the question is not easy to settle. Perhaps the theory of Captain Gustavus Fox, of the United States navy, is on the whole best supported. Captain Fox maintains that the true Guanahani was the little island now known as Samana or Atwood's Cay.[1] The problem well illustrates the difficulty in identifying any route from even a good description of landmarks, without the help of persistent proper names, especially after the lapse of time has somewhat altered the landmarks. From this point of view it is a very interesting problem and has its lessons for us; otherwise it is of no importance.

A cruise of ten days among the Bahamas, with visits to four of the islands, satisfied Columbus that he was in the ocean just east of Cathay, for Marco Polo had described it as studded with thousands of spice-bearing islands, and the Catalan map shows that some of these were supposed to be inhabited by naked savages. To be sure, he could not find any spices or valuable drugs, but the air was full of fragrance and the trees and herbs were strange in aspect and might mean

Groping for Cipango and the route to Quinsay

[1] "An Attempt to solve the Problem of the First Landing Place of Columbus in the New World," in *United States Coast and Geodetic Survey — Report for 1880 — Appendix* 18, Washington, 1882.

anything; so for a while he was ready to take the spices on trust. Upon inquiries about gold the natives always pointed to the south, apparently meaning Cipango; and in that direction Columbus steered on the 25th of October, intending to stay in that wealthy island long enough to obtain all needful information concerning its arts and commerce. Thence a sail of less than ten days would bring him to the Chinese coast, along which he might comfortably cruise northwesterly as far as Quinsay and deliver to the Great Khan a friendly letter with which Ferdinand and Isabella had provided him. Alas, poor Columbus — unconscious prince of discoverers — groping here in Cuban waters for the way to a city on the other side of the globe and to a sovereign whose race had more than a century since been driven from the throne and expelled from the very soil of Cathay! Could anything be more pathetic, or better illustrate the profound irony with which our universe seems to be governed?

On reaching Cuba the admiral was charmed with the marvellous beauty of the landscape, — a point in which he seems to have been unusually sensitive. He found pearl oysters along the shore, and although no splendid cities as yet appeared, he did not doubt that he had reached Cipango. But his attempts at talking

Columbus reaches Cuba, and sends envoys to find a certain Asiatic prince with the amazed natives only served to darken counsel. He understood them to say that Cuba was part of the Asiatic continent, and that there was a king in the neighbourhood who was at war with the Great Khan! So he sent two messengers to seek this refractory potentate, — one of them a converted Jew acquainted with Arabic, a language sometimes heard far eastward in Asia, as Columbus must have known. These envoys found pleasant villages, with large houses, surrounded with fields of such unknown vegetables as maize, potatoes, and tobacco; they saw men and women smoking cigars,[1] and little dreamed that in that fragrant and soothing herb there was a richer source of revenue than the spices of the East. They passed acres of growing cotton and saw in the houses piles of yarn waiting to be woven into rude cloth or twisted into nets for hammocks. But they found neither cities nor kings, neither gold nor spices, and after a tedious quest returned, somewhat disappointed, to the coast.

[1] The first recorded mention of tobacco is in Columbus's diary for November 20, 1492 : " Hallaron los dos cristianos por el camino mucha gente que atravesaba á sus pueblos, mugeres y hombres con un tizon en la mano, yerbas para tomar sus sahumerios que acostumbraban," *i. e.* " the two Christians met on the road a great many people going to their villages, men and women with brands in their hands, made of herbs for taking their customary smoke." Navarrete, tom. i. p. 51.

Columbus seems now to have become perplexed, and to have vacillated somewhat in his purposes. If this was the continent of Asia it was nearer than he had supposed, and how far mistaken he had been in his calculations no one could tell. But where was Cipango? He gathered Columbus turns eastward; Pinzon deserts him from the natives that there was a great island to the southeast, abounding in gold, and so he turned his prows in that direction. On the 20th of November he was deserted by Martin Pinzon, whose ship could always outsail the others. It seems to have been Pinzon's design to get home in advance with such a story as would enable him to claim for himself an undue share of credit for the discovery of the Indies. This was the earliest instance of a kind of treachery such as too often marred the story of Spanish exploration and conquest in the New World.

For a fortnight after Pinzon's desertion Columbus crept slowly eastward along the coast of Cuba, now and then landing to examine the country and its products; and it seemed to him that besides pearls and mastic and aloes he found in the rivers indications of gold. When he reached the cape at the end of the island he named it Alpha and Omega, as being the extremity of Asia, — Omega from the Portuguese point of view, Alpha from his own. On the 6th of December he landed upon the northwestern

coast of the island of Hayti, which he called
Española, Hispaniola, or "Spanish land."[1]

Columbus
arrives at
Hayti and
thinks it must
be Japan

Here, as the natives seemed to tell
him of a region to the southward and
quite inland which abounded in gold,
and which they called Cibao, the admiral at once caught upon the apparent similar-
ity of sounds and fancied that Cibao must be
Cipango, and that at length he had arrived upon
that island of marvels. It was much nearer the
Asiatic mainland (*i. e.* Cuba) than he had supposed, but then, it was beginning to appear that
in any case somebody's geography must be
wrong. Columbus was enchanted with the scen-
ery. "The land is elevated," he says, "with
many mountains and peaks . . . most beautiful, of a thousand varied forms, accessible, and
full of trees of endless varieties, so tall that they
seem to touch the sky; and I have been told
that they never lose their foliage. The nightin-
gale [*i. e.* some kind of thrush] and other small
birds of a thousand kinds were singing in the
month of November [December] when I was
there."[2] Before he had done much toward

[1] Not "Little Spain," as the form of the word, so much
like a diminutive, might seem to indicate. It is simply the
feminine of *Español*, "Spanish," sc. *tierra* or *isla*. Columbus
believed that the island was larger than Spain. See his letter
to Gabriel Sanchez, in Harrisse, tom. i. p. 428.

[2] Columbus to Santangel, February 15, 1493 (Navarrete,
tom. i. p. 168).

exploring this paradise, a sudden and grave mishap quite altered his plans. On Christmas morning, between midnight and dawn, owing to careless disobedience of orders on the part of the helmsman, the flag-ship struck upon a sand-bank near the present site of Port au Paix. All attempts to get her afloat were unavailing, and the waves soon beat her to pieces.

Wreck of the Santa Maria, Dec. 25, 1492

This catastrophe brought home, with startling force, to the mind of Columbus, the fact that the news of his discovery of land was not yet known in Europe. As for the Pinta and her insubordinate commander, none could say whether they would ever be seen again or whether their speedy arrival in Spain might not portend more harm than good to Columbus. His armament was now reduced to the little undecked Niña alone, such a craft as we should deem about fit for a summer excursion on Long Island Sound. What if his party should all perish, or be stranded helpless on these strange coasts, before any news of their success should reach the ears of friends in Europe! Then the name of Columbus would serve as a by-word for foolhardiness, and his mysterious fate would simply deter other expeditions from following in the same course. Obviously the first necessity of the situation was to return to Spain immediately and

Columbus decides to go back to Spain

report what had already been done. Then it would be easy enough to get ships and men for a second voyage.

This decision led to the founding of an embryo colony upon Hispaniola. There was not room enough for all the party to go in the Niña, and quite a number begged to be left behind, because they found life upon the island lazy and the natives, especially the women, seemed well disposed toward them. So a blockhouse was built out of the wrecked ship's timbers and armed with her guns, and in commemoration of that eventful Christmas it was called Fort Nativity (*La Navidad*). Here forty men were left behind, with provisions enough for a whole year, and on January 4, 1493, the rest of the party went on board the Niña and set sail for Spain. Two days later in following the northern coast of Hispaniola they encountered the Pinta, whose commander had been delayed by trading with the natives and by finding some gold. Pinzon tried to explain his sudden disappearance by alleging that stress of weather had parted him from his comrades, but his excuses were felt to be lame and improbable. However it may have been with his excuses, there was no doubt as to the lameness of his foremast; it had been too badly sprung to

Building of the blockhouse, La Navidad

Meeting with Pinzon

carry much sail, so that the Pinta could not again run away from her consort.

On this return voyage the admiral, finding the trade-winds dead against him, took a north-easterly course until he had passed the thirty-seventh parallel and then headed straight toward Spain. On the 12th of February a storm was brewing, and during the next four days it raged with such terrific vio- lence that it is a wonder how those two frail caravels ever came out of it. They were separated this time not to meet again upon the sea. Expecting in all likelihood to be engulfed in the waves with his tiny craft, Co-lumbus sealed and directed to Ferdinand and Isabella two brief reports of his discovery, writ-ten upon parchment. Each of these he wrapped in a cloth and enclosed in the middle of a large cake of wax, which was then securely shut up in a barrel. One of the barrels was flung into the sea, the other remained standing on the little quarter-deck to await the fate of the caravel. The anxiety was not lessened by the sight of land on the 15th, for it was impossible to ap-proach it so as to go ashore, and there was much danger of being dashed to pieces.

At length on the 18th, the storm having abated, the ship's boat went ashore and found that it was the island of St. Mary, one of the

Terrible storm in mid-ocean, Feb., 1493

Azores. It is worthy of note that such skilful sailors as the Niña's captain, Vicente Yañez Pinzon, and the pilot Ruiz were so confused in their reckoning as to suppose themselves near the Madeiras, whereas Columbus had correctly maintained that they were approaching the Azores, — a good instance of his consummate judgment in nautical questions.[1] From the Portuguese governor of the island this Spanish company met with a very ungracious reception. A party of sailors whom Columbus sent ashore to a small chapel of the Virgin, to give thanks for their deliverance from shipwreck, were seized and held as prisoners for five days. It afterwards appeared that this was done in pursuance of general instructions from the king of Portugal to the governors of his various islands. If Columbus had gone ashore he would probably have been arrested himself. As it was, he took such a high tone and threatened to such good purpose that the governor of St. Mary was fain to give up his prisoners for fear of bringing on another war between Portugal and Castile.

Cold reception at the Azores

Having at length got away from this unfriendly island, as the Niña was making her way toward Cape St. Vincent and within 400 miles of it, she was seized by another fierce tempest and driven upon the coast of Portugal,

[1] Las Casas, tom. i. pp. 443, 449.

where Columbus and his crew were glad of a chance to run into the river Tagus for shelter. The news of his voyage and his discoveries aroused intense excitement in Lisbon. Astonishment was mingled with chagrin at the thought that the opportunity for all this glory and profit had first been offered to Portugal and foolishly lost. The king even now tried to persuade himself that Columbus had somehow or other been trespassing upon the vast and vague undiscovered dominions granted to the Crown of Portugal by Pope Eugenius IV. Some of the king's counsellors are said to have urged him to have Columbus assassinated; it would be easy enough to provoke such a high-spirited man into a quarrel and then run him through the body.[1] To clearer heads, however, the imprudence of such a course was manifest. It was already impossible to keep the news of the discovery from reaching Spain, and Portugal could not afford to go to war with her stronger neighbour. In fact, even had John II. been base enough to resort to assassination, which seems quite incompati-

Columbus is driven ashore in Portugal, where the king is advised to have him assassinated;

but to offend Spain so grossly would be dangerous

[1] This story rests upon the explicit statement of a contemporary Portuguese historian of high authority, Garcia de Resende, *Chronica del Rey Dom João II.*, Lisbon, 1622, cap. clxiv. (written about 1516); see also Vasconcellos, *Vida del Rey Don Juan II.*, Madrid, 1639, lib. vi.

ble with the general character of Lope de Vega's "perfect prince," Columbus was now too important a personage to be safely interfered with. So he was invited to court and made much of. On the 13th of March he set sail again and arrived in the harbour of Palos at noon of the 15th. His little caravel was promptly recognized by the people, and as her story flew from mouth to mouth all the business of the town was at an end for that day.[1]

Towards evening, while the bells were ringing and the streets brilliant with torches, another vessel entered the harbour and dropped anchor. She was none other than the Pinta! The storm had driven her to Bayonne, whence Martin Pinzon instantly despatched a message to Ferdinand and Isabella, making great claims for himself and asking permission to wait upon them with a full account of the discovery. As soon as practicable he made his way to Palos, but when on arriving he saw the Niña already anchored in the harbour his guilty heart failed

Columbus and Pinzon at Palos; death of Pinzon

---

[1] "When they learnt that she returned in triumph from the discovery of a world, the whole community broke forth into transports of joy." Irving's *Columbus*, vol. i. p. 318. This is projecting our present knowledge into the past. We now know that Columbus had discovered a new world. He did not so much as suspect that he had done anything of the sort; neither did the people of Palos.

him. He took advantage of the general hub-
bub to slink ashore as quickly and quietly as
possible, and did not dare to show himself until
after the admiral had left for Seville. The
news from Columbus reached the sovereigns
before they had time to reply to the message
of Pinzon; so when their answer came to him
it was cold and stern and forbade him to appear
in their presence. Pinzon was worn out with
the hardships of the homeward voyage, and this
crushing reproof was more than he could bear.
His sudden death, a few days afterward, was
generally attributed to chagrin.[1]

From Seville the admiral was summoned to
attend court at Barcelona, where he was received
with triumphal honours. He was directed to
seat himself in the presence of the
sovereigns, a courtesy usually reserved
for royal personages.[2] Intense interest
was felt in his specimens of stuffed
birds and small mammals, his live parrots, his collection of herbs which he supposed

Columbus is received by the sovereigns at Barcelona, April, 1493

[1] Charlevoix, *Histoire de l'isle Espagnole, ou de St. Do-
mingue*, Paris, 1730, liv. ii.; Muñoz, *Historia de las Indias
ó Nuevo Mundo*. Madrid, 1793, lib. iv. § 14.

[2] He was also allowed to quarter the royal arms with his
own, "which consisted of a group of golden islands amid
azure billows. To these were afterwards added five anchors,
with the celebrated motto, well known as being carved on his
sepulchre." Prescott's *Ferdinand and Isabella*, part i. chap.
vii. This statement about the motto is erroneous. See below,

to have medicinal virtues, his few pearls and
trinkets of gold, and especially his six painted
and bedizened barbarians, the survivors of ten
with whom he had started from Hispaniola.
Since in the vague terminology of that time the
remote and scarcely known parts of Asia were
called the Indies, and since the islands and
coasts just discovered were Indies, of course
these red men must be Indians. So Columbus had already named them in his first letter
written from the Niña, off the Azores, sent
by special messenger from Palos, and now in
April, 1493, printed at Barcelona, containing
the particulars of his discovery, — a letter ap-
propriately addressed to the worthy Santangel,
but for whose timely intervention he might have
ridden many a weary league on that mule of his
to no good purpose.[1] It was generally assumed

p. 210. Considering the splendour of the reception given to
Columbus, and the great interest felt in his achievement, Mr.
Prescott is surprised at finding no mention of this occasion in
the local annals of Barcelona, or in the royal archives of Aragon. He conjectures, with some probability, that the cause
of the omission may have been what an American would call
" sectional " jealousy. This Cathay and Cipango business
was an affair of Castile's, and, as such, quite beneath the
notice of patriotic Aragonese archivists ! That is the way history has too often been treated. With most people it is only
a kind of ancestor worship.

[1] The unique copy of this first edition of this Spanish letter
is a small folio of two leaves, or four pages. It was announced

Eñor porque se que aureis plazer dela grand victoria que nuestro señor me
ha dado en mi viaje vos escriuo esta por la ql sabreys como en xxxiij dias pase
a las indias con la armada q los illustrissimos Rey e Reyna nros señores me dieron
donde yo falle muy muchas islas pobladas con gente sin numero: y dellas todas
he tomado possession por sus altezas con pregon y vandera real estendida y non me fue
contradicho Ala primera q yo falle puse nombre sant saluador a conmemoracion de su alta mages
tat el qual marauillosamente todo esto ha andado los indios la llaman guanahani. Ala seguda
puse nombre la isla de santa maria de concepcion ala tercera ferrandina ala quarta la isla bella
ala quinta la Isla Juana e asi a cada vna nombre nueuo Quando yo llegue ala Juana seg
ui io la costa della al poniente y la falle tan grande q pense que seria tierra firme la prouincia de
catayo y como no falle asi villas y lugaares en la costa dela mar saluo pequeñas poblaciones
con la gente delas qles no podia hauer fabla por que luego fuyan todos: andaua yo a de
lante por el dicho camino pensando de no errar grandes Ciudades o villas y al cabo de muchas
leguas visto q no hauia inouacio i que la costa me leuaua al setetrion de adode mi voluntad
era contraria porq el yuierno era ya encarnado yo tenia propossito de hazer del al austro y tan bie
el vieto medio adelate determine de no aguardar otro tiepo y bolui atras fasta vn señalado puerto
to de adode ebie dos hobres por la tierra para saber si hauia Rey o grades Ciudades adoui
no tres iornadas y hallazo infinitas poblaciones pequeñas i gete si numero mas no cosa de reg

ridad có muchas oraciones solénes a nuestra sancta fe: y assi pues por los bienes téporales se nidad có muchas oraciones solénes por el tanto en s alcamiento que hauran en tornando se tantos pueblos a nuestra sancta fe: y assi pues por los bienes téporales q no solamēte a la españa mas a todos los christianos ternan aqui refrigerio y ganancia esto segun el fecho a si embreue fecha en la calauera sobre las yslas de canaria a xv de febrero año Mil. cccclxxxxiij.

Fara lo que mandareys   El Almirāte

Anima que venia dentro en la Carta.

Despues desta escripto y estádo en mar de. Castilla salio tanto victo có migo.sul y suestte que me ha fecho descargar los nauios po cōr aqui en este puerto delisbona oy que fue la mayor marauilla del mundo adōde acorde escriuir a sus altezas. en todas las ynsias se siempre halla do y los téporal como en mayo adōde yo fuy en xxxiiij dias y volui en xxviij saluo questas tormē tas me ha detenido xiij dias corriendo por esta mar: dizen aqua todos los hōbres dela mar.q ja mas ouo tan mal yuierno ni tantas perdidas de naues fecha a quatorze dias de marzo?

ESTA Carta embio Colom Al'Escriuano De raciō
De las Islas Halladas en Las Indias: Cōtenida
A Otra De Sus Altezas

without question that the admiral's theory of
his discovery must be correct, that the coast
of Cuba must be the eastern extremity of China,
that the coast of Hispaniola must be the northern extremity of Cipango, and that a direct
route — much shorter than that which Portugal
had so long been seeking — had now been found
to those lands of illimitable wealth described by
Marco Polo.[1] To be sure Columbus had not as

for sale in Quaritch's Catalogue, April 16, 1891, No. 111,
p. 47, for £1750. Evidently most book-lovers will have
to content themselves with the facsimile published in London,
1891, price two guineas. A unique copy of a Spanish reprint
in small quarto, made in 1493, is preserved in the Ambrosian Library at Milan. In 1889 Messrs. Ellis & Elvey, of
London, published a facsimile *alleged* to have been made from
an edition of about the same date as the Ambrosian quarto ;
but there are good reasons for believing that these highly respectable publishers have been imposed upon. It is a time just
now when fictitious literary discoveries of this sort may command a high price, and the dealer in early Americana must
keep his eyes open. See Quaritch's note, *op. cit.* p. 49 ; and
Justin Winsor's letter in *The Nation*, April 9, 1891, vol. lii.
p. 298.

[1] " The lands, therefore, which Columbus had visited were
called the West Indies ; and as he seemed to have entered
upon a vast region of unexplored countries, existing in a state
of nature, the whole received the comprehensive appellation
of the New World." Irving's *Columbus*, vol. i. p. 333.
These are very grave errors, again involving the projection of
our modern knowledge into the past. The lands which Columbus had visited were called simply the Indies ; it was not
until long after his death, and after the crossing of the Pacific

yet seen the evidences of this Oriental splendour, and had been puzzled at not finding them,
but he felt confident that he had come very near
them and would come full upon them in a second voyage. There was nobody who knew
enough to refute these opinions,[1] and really why
should not this great geographer, who had accomplished so much already which
people had scouted as impossible,—
why should he not know what he was
about? It was easy enough now to
get men and money for the second
voyage. When the admiral sailed from Cadiz
on September 25, 1493, it was with seventeen
ships carrying 1500 men. Their dreams were
of the marble palaces of Quinsay, of isles of

General ex-
citement at
the news that
a way to the
Indies had
been found

Ocean, that they were distinguished from the East Indies.
The *New World* was not at first a " comprehensive appellation " for the countries discovered by Columbus ; it was at
first applied to one particular region never visited by him,
viz. to that portion of the southeastern coast of South America first explored by Vespucius. See below, pp. 359, 360.

[1] Peter Martyr, however, seems to have entertained some
vague doubts, inasmuch as this assumed nearness of the China
coast on the west implied a greater eastward extension of the
Asiatic continent than seemed to him probable : " Insulas
reperit plures ; has esse, de quibus fit apud cosmographos
mentio extra oceanum orientalem, adjacentes Indiæ arbitran-
tur. Nec inficior ego penitus, *quamvis sphæræ magnitudo
aliter sentire videatur ;* neque enim desunt qui parvo tractu
a finibus Hispaniæ distare littus Indicum putent." *Opus
Epist.,* No. 135. The italicizing is mine.

Finita la storia della inuentione delle nuoue insule di Channaria in
diane tracte duna pistola di Xpofano cholonbo e per messer Giuliano
dati tradurra di latino in uersi uulgari a laude dela celestial chortee a
cõsolatione della xpiana religione e a preghiera del magnifico chaua
liere messer Giouan filippo de ligntamine domestico familiare dello il
lustrissimo Re di Spagna xpianissimo a .xv. de guigno M.cccc.xcui.
Rome.

Esle libreo cossa en Rome vn quatreri por altbre de tiz Fēti R?   7

THE DATI–COLUMBUS LETTER IN ITALIAN, 1493

First page and colophon

spices, and the treasures of Prester John. The sovereigns wept for joy as they thought that such untold riches were vouchsafed them by the special decree of Heaven, as a reward for having overcome the Moor at Granada and banished the Jews from Spain.[1] Columbus shared these views and regarded himself as a special instrument for executing the divine decrees. He renewed his vow to rescue the Holy Sepulchre, promising within the next seven years to equip at his own expense a crusading army of 50,000 foot and 4000 horse; within five years thereafter he would follow this with a second army of like dimensions.

Thus nobody had the faintest suspicion of what had been done. In the famous letter to Santangel there is of course not a word about a New World. The grandeur of the achievement was quite beyond the ken of the generation that witnessed it. For we have since come to learn that in 1492 the contact between the eastern and the western halves of our planet was first really begun, and the two streams of human life which had flowed on for countless ages apart

This voyage was an event without any parallel in history

---

[1] This abominable piece of wickedness, driving 200,000 of Spain's best citizens from their homes and their native land, was accomplished in pursuance of an edict signed March 30, 1492. There is a brief account of it in Prescott's *Ferdinand and Isabella*, part i. chap. vi.

were thenceforth to mingle together. The first voyage of Columbus is thus a unique event in the history of mankind. Nothing like it was ever done before, and nothing like it can ever be done again. No worlds are left for a future Columbus to conquer. The era of which this great Italian mariner was the most illustrious representative has closed forever.

VI

THE FINDING OF STRANGE COASTS

BUT that era did not close with Columbus, nor did he live long enough to complete the Discovery of America. Our practice of affixing specific dates to great events is on many accounts indispensable, but it is sometimes misleading. Such an event as the discovery of a pair of vast continents does not take place within a single year. When we speak of America as discovered in 1492, we do not mean that the moment Columbus landed on two or three islands of the West Indies, a full outline map of the western hemisphere from Labrador and Alaska to Cape Horn suddenly sprang into existence — like Pallas from the forehead of Zeus — in the minds of European men. Yet people are perpetually using arguments which have neither force nor meaning save upon the tacit assumption that somehow or other some such sort of thing must have happened. This grotesque fallacy lies at the bottom of the tradition which has caused so many foolish things to be said about that gallant

133

mariner, Americus Vespucius. In geographical discussions the tendency to overlook the fact that Columbus and his immediate successors did not sail with the latest edition of Black's General Atlas in their cabins is almost inveterate; it keeps revealing itself in all sorts of queer statements, and probably there is no cure for it except in familiarity with the long series of perplexed and struggling maps made in the sixteenth century. Properly regarded, the Discovery of America was not a single event, but a very gradual process. It was not like a case of special creation, for it was a case of evolution, and the voyage of 1492 was simply the most decisive and epoch-marking incident in that evolution. Columbus himself, after all his four eventful voyages across the Sea of Darkness, died in the belief that he had simply discovered the best and straightest route to the eastern shores of Asia. Yet from his first experiences in Cuba down to his latest voyage upon the coasts of Honduras and Veragua, he was more or less puzzled at finding things so different from what he had anticipated. If he had really known anything with accuracy about the eastern coast of Asia, he would doubtless soon have detected his fundamental error, but no European in his day had any such knowledge. In his four voyages Columbus was finding what he supposed to be parts of Asia, what we now know to have been parts of America, but what were really to him and his contemporaries neither more nor less than Strange Coasts. We have now to consider briefly his further experiences upon these strange coasts.

The second voyage of Columbus was begun in a very different mood and under very different auspices from either his former or his two subsequent voyages. On his first departure from Palos, in 1492, all save a few devoted friends regarded him as a madman rushing upon his doom; and outside the Spanish peninsula the expedition seems to have attracted no notice. But on the second start, in 1493, all hands supposed that they were going straight to golden Cathay and to boundless riches. It was not now with groans but with pæans that they flocked on board the ships; and the occasion was observed, with more or less interest, by some people in other countries of Europe, — as in Italy, and for the moment in France and England.

At the same time with his letter to Santangel, the admiral had despatched another account, substantially the same,[1] to Gabriel Sanchez,[2] another officer of the royal treasury. Several copies of a Latin translation of this letter were published at Rome, at Paris,

The letter to Sanchez

---

[1] "Un duplicata de cette relation," Harrisse, *Christophe Colomb*, tom. i. p. 419.

[2] Often called Raphael Sanchez.

and elsewhere, in the course of the year 1493.[1]
The story which it contained was at once paraphrased in Italian verse by Giuliano Dati, one

[1] The following epigram was added to the first Latin edition of the latter by Corbaria, Bishop of Monte-Peloso : —

Ad Invictissimum Regem Hispaniarum :

Iam nulla Hispanis tellus addenda triumphis,
    Atque parum tantis viribus orbis erat.
Nunc longe eois regio deprensa sub undis,
    Auctura est titulos Betice magne tuos.
Unde repertori incrita referenda Columbo
    Gratia, sed summo est maior habenda deo,
Qui vincenda parat noua regna tibique sibique
    Teque simul fortem prestat et esse pium.

These lines are thus paraphrased by M. Harrisse : —

To the Invincible King of the Spains :

Less wide the world than the renown of Spain,
To swell her triumphs no new lands remain.
Rejoice, Iberia ! see thy fame increased !
Another world Columbus from the East
And the mid-ocean summons to thy sway !
Give thanks to him — but loftier homage pay
To God Supreme, who gives its realms to thee !
Greatest of monarchs, first of servants be !

Bibliotheca Americana Vetustissima, p. 13.

The following is a literal version : " Already there is no
land to be added to the triumphs of Spain, and the earth was
too small for such great deeds. Now a far country under the
eastern waves has been discovered, and will be an addition to
thy titles, O great Bætica ! wherefore thanks are due to the
illustrious discoverer Columbus ; but greater thanks to the supreme God, who is making ready new realms to be conquered
for thee and for Himself, and vouchsafes to thee to be at once
strong and pious." It will be observed that nothing is said
about " another world."

An elaborate account of these earliest and excessively rare
editions is given by M. Harrisse, *loc. cit.*

of the most popular poets of the age, and perhaps in the autumn of 1493 the amazing news
that the Indies had been found by sailing west[1]
was sung by street urchins in Florence. We are

[1] Or, as Mr. Major carelessly puts it, " the astounding
news of the discovery of a new world." (*Select Letters of
Columbus*, p. vi.) Mr. Major knows very well that no such
" news " was possible for many a year after 1493 ; his remark is, of course, a mere slip of the pen, but if we are ever
going to straighten out the tangle of misconceptions with which
this subject is commonly surrounded, we must be careful in our
choice of words. — As a fair specimen of the chap-book style
of Dati's stanzas, we may cite the fourteenth : —

> Hor vo tornar almio primo tractato
> dellisole trovate incognite a te
> in q̄sto anno presente q̄sto e stato
> nel millequatrocento novatātre,
> uno che xp̄ofan colōbo chiamato,
> che e stato in corte der prefecto Re
> ha molte volte questa stimolato,
> el Re ch'cerchi acrescere il suo stato.

M. Harrisse gives the following version : —

> Back to my theme, O Listener, turn with me
> And hear of islands all unknown to thee !
> Islands whereof the grand discovery
> Chanced in this year of fourteen ninety-three.
> One Christopher Colombo, whose resort
> Was ever in the King Fernando's court,
> Bent himself still to rouse and stimulate
> The King to swell the borders of his State.

Bibliotheca Americana Vetustissima, p. 29.

The entire poem of sixty-eight stanzas is given in Major, *op.
cit.* pp. lxxiii–xc. It was published at Florence, Oct. 26,
1493, and was called " the story of the discovery [not of a
new world, but] of the new Indian islands of Canary !"
(*Storia della inventione delle nuove isole dicanaria indiane.*)

also informed, in an ill-vouched but not improbable clause in Ramusio, that not far from that same time the news was heard with admiration in London, where it was pronounced " a thing more divine than human to sail by the West unto the East, where spices grow, by a way that was never known before ; " [1] and it seems altogether likely that it was this news that prompted the expedition of John Cabot, hereafter to be mentioned.[2]

The references to the discovery are very scanty, however, until after the year 1500, and extremely vague withal. For example, Bernardino de Carvajal, the Spanish ambassador at the papal court, delivered an oration in Rome on June 19, 1493, in which he said: " And Christ placed under their [Ferdinand and Isa-

Earliest refer-
ences to the
discovery

bella's] rule the Fortunate [Canary] islands, the fertility of which has been ascertained to be wonderful. And he has lately disclosed some other unknown ones towards the Indies which may be considered among the most precious things on earth ; and it is believed that they will be gained over to Christ by the emissaries of the king." [3] Outside of the Romance countries we find one German

[1] *Raccolta di Navigazioni*, etc., Venice, 1550, tom. i. fol. 414.

[2] See below, pp. 214–230.

[3] Harrisse, *Bibliotheca Americana Vetustissima*, p. 35.

version of the first letter of Columbus, published at Strasburg, in 1497,[1] and a brief allusion to the discovery in Sebastian Brandt's famous allegorical poem, "Das Narrenschiff," the first edition of which appeared in 1494.[2] The earliest distinct reference to Columbus in the English language is to be found in a translation of this poem, "The Shyppe of Fooles," by Henry Watson, published in London by Wynkyn de Worde in 1509. The purpose of Brandt's allegory was to satirize the follies committed by all sorts and conditions of men. In the chapter, "Of hym that

Earliest reference in English

---

[1] Harrisse, *Bibliotheca Americana Vetustissima*, p. 50.

[2]   Auch hat man sydt in Portigall
       Und in Hyspanyen uberall
       Golt-inseln funden, und nacket lůt
       Von den man vor wust sagen nůt.

   Harrisse, *Bibl. Amer. Vet.* ; *Additions*, p. 4.

Or, in more modern German : —

       Wie man auch jüngst von Portugal
       Und Hispanien aus schier überall
       Goldinseln fand und nakte Leute,
       Von denen man erst weiss seit heute.

   Das Narrenschiff, ed. Simrock, Berlin, 1872, p. 161.

In the Latin version of 1497, now in the National Library at Paris, it goes somewhat differently : —

       Antea quę fuerat priscis incognita tellus :
       Exposita est oculis & manifesta patet.
       Hesperię occiduę rex Ferdinandus : in alto
       Aequore nunc gentes repperit innumeras.

   Harrisse, *op. cit.* ; *Additions*, p. 7.

It will be observed that these foreign references are so ungallant, and so incorrect, as to give all the credit to Ferdinand, while poor Isabella is not mentioned !

wyll wryte and enquere of all regyons," it is
said: "There was one that knewe that in y°
ysles of Spayne was enhabitantes. Wherefore
he asked men of Kynge Ferdynandus & wente
& founde them, the whiche lyved as beestes." [1]
Until after the middle of the sixteenth century
no English chronicler mentions either Columbus
or the Cabots, nor is there anywhere an indication that the significance of the discoveries in
the western ocean was at all understood.[2]

North of the Alps and Pyrenees the interest
in what was going on at the Spanish court in
1493 was probably confined to very few people.
As for Venice and Genoa we have no adequate
means of knowing how they felt about the
matter, — a fact which in itself is significant.
The interest was centred in Spain and Portugal. There it was intense and awakened fierce
heart-burnings. Though John II. had not given
his consent to the proposal for murdering Columbus, he appears to have seriously entertained

Portuguese the thought of sending a small fleet
claim to the across the Atlantic as soon as possi-
Indies ble, to take possession of some point
in Cathay or Cipango and then dispute the
claims of the Spaniards.[3] Such a summary pro-

[1] Harrisse, *op. cit.*; *Additions*, p. 45.

[2] Harrisse, *Jean et Sébastien Cabot*, Paris, 1882, p. 15.

[3] Vasconcellos, *Vida del Rey Don Juan II.*, Madrid,
1639, lib. vi.

ceeding might perhaps be defended on the
ground that the grant from Pope Eugenius V.
to the Crown of Portugal expressly included
"the Indies." In the treaty of 1479, moreover,
Spain had promised not to interfere with the
discoveries and possessions of the Portuguese.

But whatever King John may have intended,
Ferdinand and Isabella were too quick for him.
No sooner had Columbus arrived at Barcelona
than an embassy was despatched to Rome, asking for a grant of the Indies just discovered by
that navigator in the service of Castile. The
notorious Rodrigo Borgia, who had lately been
placed in the apostolic chair as Alexander VI.,
was a native of Valencia in the kingdom of Aragon, and would not be likely to refuse such a
request through any excess of regard for Portugal. As between the two rival powers the
pontiff's arrangement was made in a Bulls of Pope
spirit of even-handed justice. On the Alexander
3d of May, 1493, he issued a bull VI.
conferring upon the Spanish sovereigns all lands
already discovered or thereafter to be discovered in the western ocean, with jurisdiction and
privileges in all respects similar to those formerly bestowed upon the Crown of Portugal.
This grant was made by the Pope "out of our
pure liberality, certain knowledge, and plenitude
of apostolic power," and by virtue of "the authority of Omnipotent God granted to us in

St. Peter, and of the Vicarship of Jesus Christ which we administer upon the earth." [1] It was a substantial reward for the monarchs who had completed the overthrow of Mahometan rule in Spain, and it afforded them opportunities for further good work in converting the heathen inhabitants of the islands and mainland of Asia.[2]

On the following day Alexander issued a second bull in order to prevent any occasion for quarrel between Spain and Portugal.[3] He de-

[1] " De nostra mera liberalitate, et ex certa scientia, ac de apostolicæ potestatis plenitudine." . . . " auctoritate omnipotentis Dei nobis in beato Petro concessa, ac vicariatus Jesu Christi qua fungimur in terris." The same language is used in the second bull. Mr. Prescott (*Ferdinand and Isabella*, part i. chap. vii.) translates *certa scientia* " infallible knowledge," but in order to avoid any complications with modern theories concerning papal infallibility, I prefer to use a less technical word.

[2] A year or two later the sovereigns were further rewarded with the decorative title of " Most Catholic." See Zurita, *Historia del Rey Hernando*, Saragossa, 1580, lib. ii. cap. xl. ; Peter Martyr, *Epist.* clvii.

[3] The complete text of this bull, with Richard Eden's translation, is given at the end of this work ; see below, Appendix B. The official text is in *Magnum Bullarium Romanum*, ed. Cherubini, Lyons, 1655, tom. i. p. 466. The original document received by Ferdinand and Isabella is preserved in the Archives of the Indies at Seville ; it is printed entire in Navarrete, *Coleccion de viages*, tom. ii. No. 18. Another copy, less complete, may be found in Raynaldus, *Annales ecclesiastici*, Lucca, 1754, tom. xi. p. 214, No.

creed that all lands discovered or to be discovered to the west of a meridian one hundred

19–22 ; and another in Leibnitz, *Codex Diplomaticus*, tom. i.
part i. p. 471. It is often called the Bull "Inter Cetera,"
from its opening words.

The origin of the Pope's claim to apostolic authority for
giving away kingdoms is closely connected with the fictitious
"Donation of Constantine," an edict probably fabricated in
Rome about the middle of the eighth century. The title of
the old Latin text is *Edictum domini Constantini Imp.*, apud
Pseudo-Isidorus, *Decretalia*. Constantine's transfer of the
seat of empire from the Tiber to the Bosphorus tended greatly
to increase the dignity and power of the papacy, and I presume that the fabrication of this edict, four centuries afterward,
was the expression of a sincere belief that the first Christian
emperor *meant* to leave the temporal supremacy over Italy in
the hands of the Roman See. The edict purported to be such
a donation from Constantine to Pope Sylvester I., but the extent and character of the donation was stated with such vague-
ness as to allow a wide latitude of interpretation. Its genuineness was repeatedly called in question, but belief in it seems
to have grown in strength until after the thirteenth century.
Leo IX., who was a strong believer in its genuineness, granted
in 1054 to the Normans their conquests in Sicily and Cala-
bria, to be held as a fief of the Roman See. (Muratori, *Annali
d' Italia*, tom. vi. part ii. p. 245.) It was next used to sus-
tain the papal claim to suzerainty over the island of Corsica.
A century later John of Salisbury maintained the right of the
Pope to dispose " of all *islands* on which Christ, the Sun of
righteousness, hath shined," and in conformity with this opinion Pope Adrian IV. (Nicholas Breakspeare, an Englishman)
authorized in 1164 King Henry II. of England to invade and
conquer Ireland. (See Adrian IV., *Epist.* 76, apud Migne,
Patrologia, tom. clxxxviii.) Dr. Lanigan, in treating of this

leagues west of the Azores and Cape Verde Islands should belong to the Spaniards. Inasmuch

matter, is more an Irishman than a papist, and derides " this
nonsense of the Pope's being the head-owner of all Christian
islands." (*Ecclesiastical History of Ireland*, vol. iv. p. 159.)
— Gregory VII., in working up to the doctrine that all
Christian kingdoms should be held as fiefs under St. Peter (Ba-
ronius, *Annales*, tom. xvii. p. 430 ; cf. Villemain, *Histoire
de Grégoire VII.*, Paris, 1873, tom. ii. pp. 59–61), does
not seem to have appealed to the Donation. Perhaps he was
shrewd enough to foresee the kind of objection afterwards
raised by the Albigensians, who pithily declared that if the
suzerainty of the popes was derived from the Donation, then
they were successors of Constantine and not of St. Peter.
(Moneta Cremonensis, *Adversus Catharos et Waldenses*, ed.
Ricchini, Rome, 1743, v. 2.) But Innocent IV. summarily
disposed of this argument at the Council of Lyons in 1245,
when he deposed the Emperor Frederick II. and King Sancho II. of Portugal, — saying that Christ himself had bestowed temporal as well as spiritual headship upon St. Peter
and his successors, so that Constantine only gave up to the
church what belonged to it already. The opposite or Ghibel-
line theory was eloquently set forth by Dante, in his treatise
De Monarchia ; he held that inasmuch as the Empire existed
before the church, it could not be derived from it. Dante
elsewhere expressed his abhorrence of the Donation : —

> Ahi Constantin, di quanto mal fu matre,
> Non la tua conversion, ma quella dote
> Che da te prese il primo ricco patre !
>
> *Inferno*, xix. 115.

Similar sentiments were expressed by many of the most popular poets from the twelfth century to the sixteenth. Walther
von der Vogelweide was sure that if the first Christian emperor could have foreseen the evils destined to flow from his
Donation, he would have withheld it : —

as between the westernmost of the Azores and
the easternmost of the Cape Verde group the

> Solte ich den pfaffen raten an den triuwen min,
> So spræche ir haut den armen zuo : se, daz ist din,
> Ir zunge sünge, unde lieze mengem man daz sin,
> Gedæhten daz ouch si dur Got wæren almuosenære.
> Do gab ir erste teil der Kuenik Konstantin,
> Het er gewest, daz da von uebel kuenftik wære,
> So het er wol underkomen des riches swære,
> Wan daz si do waren kiusche, und uebermuete lære.
>
> Hagen, *Minnesinger-Sammlung*, Leipsic, 1838, bd. i. p. 270.

Ariosto, in a passage rollicking with satire, makes his itinerant
paladin find the " stinking " Donation in the course of his
journey upon the moon : —

> Di varii fiori ad un gran monte passa,
> Ch' ebber già buono odore, or puzzan forte,
> Questo erá il dono, se però dir lece,
> Che Constantino al buon Silvestro fece.
>
> *Orlando Furioso*, xxxiv. 80.

The Donation was finally proved to be a forgery by Lau-
rentius Valla in 1440, in his *De falso credita et ementita
Constantini donatione declamatio* (afterward spread far and
wide by Ulrich von Hutten), and independently by the noble
Reginald Pecock, Bishop of Chichester, in his *Repressor*, written about 1447. — During the preceding century the theory
of Gregory VII. and Innocent IV. had been carried to its
uttermost extreme by the Franciscan monk Alvaro Pelayo, in
his *De Planctu Ecclesiæ*, written at Avignon during the " Baby-
lonish Captivity," about 1350 (printed at Venice in 1560),
and by Agostino Trionfi, in his *Summa de potestate ecclesias-
tica*, Augsburg, 1473, an excessively rare book, of which there
is a copy in the British Museum. These writers maintained
that the popes were suzerains of the whole earth and had absolute power to dispose not only of all Christian kingdoms, but
also of all heathen lands and powers. It was upon this theory
that Eugenius IV. seems to have acted with reference to Portu-

difference in longitude is not far from ten degrees, this description must be allowed to be

gal and Alexander VI. with reference to Spain. Of course
there was never a time when such claims for the papacy were
not denied by a large party within the church. The Spanish
sovereigns in appealing to Alexander VI. took care to hint that
some of their advisers regarded them as already entitled to
enjoy the fruits of their discoveries, even before obtaining the
papal permission, but they did not choose to act upon that
opinion (Herrera, decad. i. lib. ii. cap. 4). The kings of
Portugal were less reserved in their submission. In *Valasci
Ferdinandi ad Innocentium octauum de obedientia oratio,* a
small quarto printed at Rome about 1488, John II. did homage to the Pope for the countries just discovered by Bartholomew Dias. His successor Emanuel did the same after the
voyages of Gama and Vespucius. In a small quarto, *Obedientia potentissimi Emanuelis Lusitaniæ regis &c. per claris-
simum juris consultum Dieghum Pacettū oratorem ad Iuliū
Pont. Max.*, Rome, 1505, all the newly found lands are
laid at the feet of Julius II. in a passage that ends with words
worth noting : " Accipe tandem orbem ipsum terrarum, Deus
enim noster es," *i. e.* " Accept in fine the earth itself, for
thou art our God." Similar homage was rendered to Leo X.
in 1513, on account of Albuquerque's conquests in Asia. —
We may suspect that if the papacy had retained, at the end
of the fifteenth century, anything like the overshadowing
power which it possessed at the end of the twelfth, the kings
of Portugal would not have been quite so unstinted in their
homage. As it came to be less of a reality and more of a
flourish of words, it cost less to offer it. Among some modern
Catholics I have observed a disposition to imagine that in the
famous bull of partition Alexander VI. acted not as supreme
pontiff but merely as an arbiter, in the modern sense, between
the Crowns of Spain and Portugal ; but such an interpretation

somewhat vague, especially in a document emanating from " certain knowledge ; " [1] and it
left open a source of future disputes which
one would suppose the " plenitude of apostolic
power " might have been worthily employed
in closing. The meridian 25° W., however,
would have satisfied the conditions, and the
equitable intent of the arrangement is manifest.
The Portuguese were left free to pursue their
course of discovery and conquest along the

is hardly compatible with Alexander's own words. An
arbiter, as such, does not make awards by virtue of " the
authority of Omnipotent God granted to us in St. Peter, and
of the Vicarship of Jesus Christ which we administer upon
the earth."

Since writing this note my attention has been called to Dr.
Ignaz von Döllinger's *Fables respecting the Popes of the Middle
Ages*, London, 1871 ; and I find in it a chapter on the Donation of Constantine, in which the subject is treated with a
wealth of learning. Some of my brief references are there
discussed at considerable length. To the references to Dante
there is added a still more striking passage, where Constantine
is admitted into Heaven *in spite of* his Donation (*Paradiso*,
xx. 55).

[1] The language of the bull is even more vague than my
version in the text. His Holiness describes the lands to be
given to the Spaniards as lying " to the west and south " (versus occidentem et meridiem) of his dividing meridian. Land
to the south of a meridian would be in a queer position! Probably it was meant to say that the Spaniards, once west of the
papal meridian, might go south as well as north. For the king
of Portugal had suggested that they ought to confine themselves
to northern waters.

a special Indian custom-house was set up at Cadiz. There was to be another custom-house upon the island of Hispaniola (supposed to be Japan), and a minute registry was to be kept of all ships and their crews and cargoes, going out or coming in. Nobody was to be allowed to go to the Indies for any purpose whatever without a license formally obtained. Careful regulations were made for hampering trade and making everything as vexatious as possible for traders, according to the ordinary wisdom of governments in such matters. All expenses were to be borne and all profits received by the Crown of Castile, saving the rights formerly guaranteed to Columbus. The cost of the present expedition was partly defrayed with stolen money, the plunder wrung from the worthy and industrious Jews who had been driven from their homes by the infernal edict of the year before. Extensive "requisitions" were also made; in other words, when the sovereigns wanted a ship or a barrel of gunpowder they seized it, and impressed it into the good work of converting the heathen. To superintend this missionary work, a Franciscan monk [1] was se-

---

[1] Irving calls him a Benedictine, but he is addressed as "fratri ordinis Minorum" in the bull clothing him with apostolic authority in the Indies, June 25, 1493. See Raynaldus, *Annales ecclesiastici*, tom. xi. p. 216. I cannot imagine what M. Harrisse means by calling him "religieux de

lected who had lately distinguished himself as
a diplomatist in the dispute with France over
the border province of Rousillon.

Friar Boyle

This person was a native of Cata-
lonia, and his name was Bernardo Boyle, which
strongly suggests an Irish origin. Alexander
VI. appointed him his apostolic vicar for the
Indies,[1] and he seems to have been the first
clergyman to perform mass on the western shores
of the Atlantic. To assist the vicar, the six Indians brought over by Columbus were baptized
at Barcelona, with the king and queen for their
godfather and godmother. It was hoped that
they would prove useful as missionaries, and
when one of them presently died he was said
to be the first Indian ever admitted to heaven.[2]

The three summer months were occupied in
fitting out the little fleet. There were fourteen
caravels, and three larger store-ships known as
carracks. Horses, mules, and other cattle were
put on board,[3] as well as vines and sugar-canes,
and the seeds of several European cereals, for
it was intended to establish a permanent colony
upon Hispaniola. In the course of this work

Saint-Vincent de Paule " (*Christophe Colomb*, tom. ii. p.
55.) Vincent de Paul was not born till 1576.

[1] Not for " the New World," as Irving carelessly has it
in his *Columbus,* vol. i. p. 346. No such phrase had been
thought of in 1493, or until long afterward.

[2] Herrera, *Hist. de las Indias,* decad. i. lib. ii. cap. 5.

[3] *Vita dell' Ammiraglio,* cap. xliv.

some slight matters of disagreement came up between Columbus and Fonseca, and the question having been referred to the sovereigns, Fonseca was mildly snubbed and told that he must in all respects be guided by the admiral's wishes. From that time forth this ungodly prelate nourished a deadly hatred toward Columbus, and never lost an opportunity for whispering evil things about him. The worst of the grievous afflictions that afterward beset the great discoverer must be ascribed to the secret machinations of this wretch.

At last the armament was ready. People were so eager to embark that it was felt necessary to restrain them. It was not intended to have more than 1200, but about 1500 in all contrived to go, so that some of the caravels must have been overcrowded. The character of the company was very different from that of the year before. Those who went in the first voyage were chiefly common sailors. Now there were many aristocratic young men, hot-blooded and feather-headed hidalgos whom the surrender of Granada had left without an occupation. Most distinguished

Notable persons who embarked on the second voyage

among these was Alonso de Ojeda, a dare-devil of unrivalled muscular strength, full of energy and fanfaronade, and not without generous qualities, but with very little soundness of judgment or character. Other notable personages in this expedition were Columbus's youngest brother Giacomo (henceforth called Diego), who had come from Genoa at the first news of the admiral's triumphant return ; the monk Antonio de Marchena,[1] whom historians have so long confounded with the prior Juan Perez ; an Aragonese gentleman named Pedro Margarite, a favourite of the king and destined to work sad mischief ; Juan Ponce de Leon, who afterwards gave its name to Florida ; Francisco de Las Casas, father of the great apostle and historian of the Indies ; and, last but not least, the pilot Juan de La Cosa, now charged with the work of chart-making, in which he was an acknowledged master.[2]

The pomp and bustle of the departure from Cadiz, September 25, 1493, at which the admiral's two sons, Diego and Ferdinand, were present, must have been one of the earliest recollections of the younger boy, then just five years of age.[3] Again Columbus stopped at the

[1] He went as astronomer, from which we may perhaps suppose that scientific considerations had made him one of the earliest and most steadfast upholders of Columbus's views.

[2] See Harrisse, *Christophe Colomb*, tom. ii. pp. 55, 56 ; Las Casas, *Hist. de las Indias*, tom. i. p. 498 ; Fabié, *Vida de Las Casas*, Madrid, 1879, tom. i. p. 11 ; Oviedo, *Hist. de las Indias*, tom. i. p. 467 ; Navarrete, *Coleccion de viages*, tom. ii. pp. 143–149.

[3] " E con questo preparamento il mercoledé ai 25 del mese di settembre dell' anno 1493 un' ora avanti il levar del sole,

Canary Islands, this time to take on board goats and sheep, pigs and fowls, for he had been struck by the absence of all such animals on the coasts which he had visited.[1] Seeds of melons, oranges, and lemons were also taken. On the 7th of October the ships weighed anchor, heading a trifle to the south of west, and after a pleasant and uneventful voyage they sighted land on the 3d of November.[2] It turned out to be a small mountainous island, and as it was discovered on Sunday they called it Dominica. In a fortnight's cruise in these Caribbean waters they discovered and named several islands, such as Marigalante, Guadaloupe, Antigua, and others, and at length reached Porto Rico. The inhabitants of these islands were ferocious cannibals, very different from the natives encountered on the former voyage. There were skirmishes in which a few Spaniards were killed

Cruise among the cannibal islands

essendovi io e mio fratel presenti, l' Ammiraglio levò le ancore," etc. *Vita dell' Ammiraglio*, cap. xliv.

[1] Eight sows were bought for 70 maravedis apiece, and " destas ocho puercas se han multiplicado todos los puercos que, hasta hoy, ha habido y hay en todas estas Indias," etc. Las Casas, *Historia*, tom. ii. p. 3.

[2] The relation of this second voyage by Dr. Chanca may be found in Navarrete, tom. i. pp. 198–241 ; an interesting relation in Italian by Simone Verde, a Florentine merchant then living in Valladolid, is published in Harrisse, *Christophe Colomb*, tom. ii. pp. 68–78. The narrative of the curate of Los Palacios is of especial value for this voyage.

with poisoned arrows. On Guadaloupe the natives lived in square houses made of saplings in-
tertwined with reeds, and on the rude porticoes
attached to these houses some of the wooden
pieces were carved so as to look like serpents.
In some of these houses human limbs were hanging from the roof, cured with smoke, like ham;
and fresh pieces of human flesh were found stew-
ing in earthen kettles, along with the flesh of
parrots. Now at length, said Peter Martyr, was
proved the truth of the stories of Polyphemus
and the Læstrygonians, and the reader must look
out lest his hair stand on end.[1] These western
Læstrygonians were known as Caribbees, Cari-
bales, or Canibales, and have thus furnished an
epithet which we have since learned to apply to
man-eaters the world over.

It was late at night on the 27th of November
that Columbus arrived in the harbour of La
Navidad and fired a salute to arouse the attention of the party that had been left there the
year before. There was no reply and the silence
seemed fraught with evil omen. On going ashore
next morning and exploring the neighbourhood,

---

[1] Martyr, *Epist.* cxlvii. *ad Pomponium Lætum;* cf. *Odys-
sey,* x. 119; Thucyd. vi. 2. — Irving (vol. i. p. 385) finds
it hard to believe these stories, but the prevalence of canni-
balism, not only in these islands, but throughout a very
large part of aboriginal America, has been superabundantly
proved.

the Spaniards came upon sights of dismal significance. The fortress was pulled to pieces and partly burnt, the chests of provisions were broken open and emptied, tools and fragments of European clothing were found in the houses of the natives, and finally eleven corpses, identifiable as those of white men, were found buried near the fort. Not one of the forty men who had been left behind in that place ever turned up to tell the tale. The little colony of La Navidad had been wiped out of existence. From the Indians, however, Columbus gathered bits of information that made a sufficiently probable story. It was a typical instance of the beginnings of colonization in wild countries. In such instances human nature has shown considerable uniformity. Insubordination and deadly feuds among themselves had combined with reckless outrages upon the natives to imperil the existence of this little party of rough sailors. The cause to which Horace ascribes so many direful wars, both before and since the days of fairest Helen, seems to have been the principal cause on this occasion. At length a fierce chieftain named Caonabo, from the region of Xaragua, had attacked the Spaniards in overwhelming force, knocked their blockhouse about their heads, and butchered all that were left of them.

This was a gloomy welcome to the land of

promise. There was nothing to be done but to build new fortifications and found a town. The site chosen for this new settlement, _{Building of} which was named Isabella, was at a _{Isabella} good harbour about thirty miles east of Monte Christi. It was chosen because Columbus understood from the natives that it was not far from there to the gold-bearing mountains of Cibao, a name which still seemed to signify Cipango. Quite a neat little town was presently built, with church, market-place, public granary, and dwelling-houses, the whole encompassed with a stone wall. An exploring party led by Ojeda into the mountains of Cibao found gold dust and pieces of gold ore in the beds of the brooks, and returned elated with this discovery. Twelve of the ships were now sent back to Spain for further supplies and reinforcements, and specimens of _{Exploration} the gold were sent as an earnest of what _{of Cibao} was likely to be found. At length, in March, 1494, Columbus set forth, with 400 armed men, to explore the Cibao country. The march was full of interest. It is upon this occasion that we first find mention of the frantic terror manifested by Indians at the sight of horses. At first they supposed the horse and his rider to be a kind of centaur, and when the rider dismounted this separation of one creature into two overwhelmed them with supernatural terror. Even when they had begun to get over this notion they were in dread of being eaten by the horses.[1] These natives lived in houses grouped into villages, and had carved wooden idols and rude estufas for their tutelar divinities. It was ascertained that different tribes tried to steal each other's idols and even fought for the possession of valuable objects of " medicine." [2] Columbus observed and reported the customs of these people with some minuteness. There was nothing that agreed with Marco Polo's descriptions of Cipango, but so far as concerned the discovery of gold mines, the indications were such as to leave little doubt of the success of this reconnaissance. The admiral now arranged his forces so as to hold the inland regions just visited and gave the general command to Margarite, who was to continue the work of exploration. He left his brother, Diego Columbus, in charge of the colony, and taking three caravels set sail from Isabella on the 24th of April, on a cruise of discovery in these Asiatic waters.

A brief westward sail brought the little squadron into the Windward Passage and in sight of Cape Mayzi, which Columbus on his first voyage had named Cape Alpha and Omega as being

[1] For an instance of 400 hostile Indians fleeing before a single armed horseman, see *Vita dell' Ammiraglio*, cap. lii.; Las Casas, *Hist.*, tom. ii. p. 46.

[2] Compare the Fisherman's story of Drogio, above, vol. i. pp. 282–287.

the easternmost point on the Chinese coast. He
believed that if he were to sail to the right of
this cape he should have the continent Cape Alpha
on his port side for a thousand miles and Omega
and more, as far as Quinsay and Cambaluc (Peking). If he had sailed in this direction and had
succeeded in keeping to the east of Florida, he
would have kept a continent on his port side,
and a thousand miles would have taken him a
long way toward that Vinland which our Scandinavian friends would fondly have us believe
was his secret guiding-star, and the geographical position of which they suppose him to have
known with such astounding accuracy. But on
this as on other occasions, if the admiral had
ever received any information about Vinland,
it must be owned that he treated it very cava-
lierly, for he chose the course to the left of Cape
Mayzi. His decision is intelligible if we bear in
mind that he had not yet circumnavigated Hayti
and was not yet cured of his belief that its northern shore was the shore of the great Cipango.
At the same time he had seen enough on his
first voyage to convince him that the relative
positions of Cipango and the mainland of Cathay
were not correctly laid down upon the Toscanelli map. He had already inspected two or
three hundred miles of the coast to the right of
Cape Mayzi without finding traces of civilization ; and whenever inquiries were made about

gold or powerful kingdoms the natives invariably pointed to the south or southwest. Columbus, therefore, decided to try his luck in this direction. He passed to the left of Cape Mayzi and followed the southern coast of Cuba.

By the 3d of May the natives were pointing so persistently to the south and off to sea that Discovery of he changed his course in that direction Jamaica and soon came upon the northern coast of the island which we still know by its native name Jamaica. Here he found Indians more intelligent and more warlike than any he had as yet seen. He was especially struck with the elegance of their canoes, some of them nearly a hundred feet in length, carved and hollowed from the trunks of tall trees. We may already observe that different tribes of Indians comported themselves very differently at the first sight of white men. While the natives of some of the islands prostrated themselves in adoration of these sky-creatures, or behaved with a timorous politeness which the Spaniards mistook for gentleness of disposition, in other places the red men showed fight at once, acting upon the brute impulse to drive away strangers. In both cases, of course, dread of the unknown was the prompting impulse, though so differently manifested. As the Spaniards went ashore upon Jamaica, the Indians greeted them with a shower of javelins and for a few moments stood up against

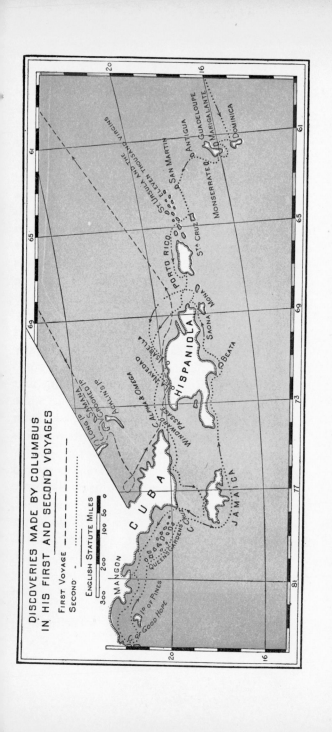

DISCOVERIES MADE BY COLUMBUS
IN HIS FIRST AND SECOND VOYAGES

First Voyage — — —
Second " ....

ENGLISH STATUTE MILES
300   200   100 50   0

the deadly fire of the cross-bows, but when they turned to flee, a single bloodhound, let loose upon them, scattered them in wildest panic.[1]

Finding no evidences of civilization upon this beautiful island, Columbus turned northward and struck the Cuban coast again at the point which still bears the name he gave it, Cape Cruz. Between the general contour of this end of Cuba and that of the eastern extremity of Cathay upon the Tosca-nelli map there is a curious resemblance, save that the direction is in the one case more east and west and in the other more north and south. Columbus passed no cities like Zaiton, nor cities of any sort, but when he struck into the smiling archipelago which he called the Queen's Gardens, now known as Cayos de las Doce Leguas, he felt sure that he was among Marco Polo's seven thousand spice islands. On the 3d of June, at some point on the Cuban coast, probably near Trinidad, the crops of several doves were opened and spices found in them. None of the natives here had ever heard of an end to Cuba, and they believed it was endless.[2]

Coasting the south side of Cuba

---

[1] Bernaldez, *Reyes Católicos*, cap. cxxv. Domesticated dogs were found generally in aboriginal America, but they were very paltry curs compared to these fierce hounds, one of which could handle an unarmed man as easily as a terrier handles a rat.

[2] As a Greek would have said, ἤπειρος, a continent.

The next country to the west of themselves was named Mangon, and it was inhabited by people with tails which they carefully hid by wearing loose robes of cloth. This information seemed decisive to Columbus. Evidently this Mangon was Mangi, the province in which was the city of Zaiton, the province just south of Cathay. And as for the tailed men, the book of Mandeville had a story of some naked savages in eastern Asia who spoke of their more civilized neighbours as wearing clothes in order to cover up some bodily peculiarity or defect. Could there be any doubt that the Spanish caravels had come at length to the coast of opulent Mangi?[1]

[1] Bernaldez, *Reyes Católicos*, cap. cxxvii. Mr. Irving, in citing these same incidents from Bernaldez, could not quite rid himself of the feeling that there was something strange or peculiar in the admiral's method of interpreting such information : " Animated by one of the pleasing illusions of his ardent imagination, Columbus pursued his voyage, with a prosperous breeze, along the supposed continent of Asia." (*Life of Columbus*, vol. i. p. 493.) This lends a false colour to the picture, which the general reader is pretty sure to make still falser. To suppose the southern coast of Cuba to be the southern coast of Toscanelli's Mangi required no illusion of an " ardent imagination." It was simply a plain common-sense conclusion reached by sober reasoning from such data as were then accessible (*i. e.* the Toscanelli map, amended by information such as was understood to be given by the natives) ; it was more probable than any other theory of the situation likely to be devised from those data ; and

Under the influence of this belief, when a few days later they landed in search of fresh water, and a certain archer, on the lookout for game, caught distant glimpses of a flock of tall white cranes feeding in an everglade, he fled to his comrades with the story that he had seen a party of men clad in long white tunics, and all The "people agreed that these must be the people of Mangon" of Mangon.[1] Columbus sent a small company ashore to find them. It is needless to add that the search was fruitless, but footprints of alligators, interpreted as footprints of griffins guarding hoarded gold,[2] frightened the men back to

it seems fanciful to us to-day only because knowledge acquired since the time of Columbus has shown us how far from correct it was. Modern historians abound in unconscious turns of expression — as in this quotation from Irving — which project modern knowledge back into the past, and thus destroy the historical perspective. I shall mention several other instances from Irving, and the reader must not suppose that this is any indication of captiousness on my part toward a writer for whom my only feeling is that of sincerest love and veneration.

[1] These tropical birds are called *soldados*, or "soldiers," because their stately attitudes remind one of sentinels on duty. The whole town of Angostura, in Venezuela, was one day frightened out of its wits by the sudden appearance of a flock of these cranes on the summit of a neighbouring hill. They were mistaken for a war-party of Indians. Humboldt, *Voyage aux régions équinoxiales du Nouveau Continent*, tom. ii. p. 314.

[2] See above, vol. i. p. 331, note.

their ships. From the natives, with whom the
Spaniards could converse only by signs, they
seemed to learn that they were going toward the
realm of Prester John;[1] and in such wise did
they creep along the coast to the point, some
fifty miles west of Broa Bay, where it begins to
trend decidedly to the southwest. Before they
had reached Point Mangles, a hundred miles
farther on, inasmuch as they found this southwesterly trend persistent, the proof that they
were upon the coast of the Asiatic continent
began to seem complete. Columbus thought
that they had passed the point (lat. 23°, long.
145° on Toscanelli's map) where the coast of
Asia began to trend steadily toward the southwest.[2] By pursuing this coast he felt sure that

[1] For these events, see Bernaldez, *Reyes Católicos*, cap.
cxxiii.; F. Columbus, *Vita dell' Ammiraglio*, cap. lvi. ;
Muñoz, *Historia del Nuevo Mundo*, lib. v. § 16 ; Humboldt,
Examen critique, tom. iv. pp. 237–263 ; Irving's *Columbus*,
vol. i. pp. 491–504.

[2] That is to say, he thought he had passed the coast of
Mangi (southern China) and reached the beginning of the coast
of Champa (Cochin China ; see Yule's *Marco Polo*, vol. ii.
p. 213). The name Champa, coming to European writers
through an Italian source, was written Ciampa and Ciamba.
See its position on the Behaim and Toscanelli maps, and
also on Ruysch's map, 1508, below, 346. Peter Martyr says that Columbus was sure that he had reached the
coast of Gangetic (*i. e.* what we call Farther) India : "Indiæ
Gangetidis continentem eam (Cubæ) plagam esse contendit
Colonus." *Epist.* xciii. *ad Bernardinum*. Of course Co-

he would eventually reach the peninsula (Malacca) which Ptolemy, who knew of it only by vague hearsay, called the Golden Chersonese.[1] An immense idea now flitted through the mind of Columbus. If he could reach and double that peninsula he could then find his way to the mouth of the Ganges River; thence he might cross the Indian Ocean, pass the Cape of Good Hope (for Dias had surely shown that the way was open), and return that way to Spain after circumnavigating the globe! But fate had reserved this achievement for another man of great heart and lofty thoughts, a quarter of a century later, who should indeed accomplish what Columbus dreamed, but only after crossing another Sea of Darkness, the most stupendous body of water on our globe, the mere existence of which until after Columbus had died no European ever suspected.[2] If Columbus had now sailed about a hundred miles farther, he

The Golden Chersonese

lumbus understood that this region, while agreeing well enough with Toscanelli's latitude, was far from agreeing with his longitude. But from the moment when he turned eastward on his first voyage he seems to have made up his mind that Toscanelli's longitudes needed serious amendment. Indeed, he had always used different measurements from Toscanelli.

[1] For an account of Ptolemy's almost purely hypothetical and curiously distorted notions about southeastern Asia, see Bunbury's *History of Ancient Geography*, vol. ii. pp. 604–608.

[2] See below, pp. 438–449.

would have found the end of Cuba, and might perhaps have skirted the northern shore of Yucatan and come upon the barbaric splendours of Uxmal and Campeche. The excitement which such news would have caused in Spain might perhaps have changed all the rest of his life and saved him from the worst of his troubles. But the crews were now unwilling to go farther, and the admiral realized that it would be impossible to undertake such a voyage as he had in mind with no more than their present outfit. So it was decided to return to Hispaniola.

Upon consultation with La Cosa and others, it was unanimously agreed that they were upon the coast of the continent of Asia. The evidence seemed conclusive. From Cape Mayzi (Alpha and Omega) they had observed, upon their own reckoning, 335 leagues, or about 1000 geographical miles, of continuous coast running steadily in nearly the same direction.[1] Clearly it was too long for the coast of an island; and then there was the name Mangon = Mangi. The only puzzling circumstance was that they did not find any of Marco Polo's cities. They kept getting scraps of information which seemed to refer to gorgeous kingdoms, but these were

[1] The length of Cuba from Cape Mayzi to Cape San Antonio is about 700 English miles. But in following the sinuosities of the coast, and including tacks, the estimate of these pilots was probably not far from correct.

always in the dim distance. Still there was no doubt that they had discovered the coast of a continent, and of course such a continent could be nothing else but Asia!

Such unanimity of opinion might seem to leave nothing to be desired. But Columbus had already met with cavillers. Before he started on this cruise from Isabella, some impatient hidalgos, disgusted at finding much to do and little to get, had begun to hint that the admiral was a humbug, and that his " Indies " were no such great affair after all. In order to silence these ill-natured critics, he sent his notary, accompanied by four witnesses, to every person in those three caravels, to get a sworn statement. If anybody had a grain of doubt about this coast being the coast of Asia, so that you could go ashore there and walk on dry land all the way to Spain if so disposed, let him declare his doubts once for all, so that they might now be duly considered. No one expressed any doubts. All declared, under oath, their firm belief. It was then agreed that if any of the number should thereafter deny or contradict this sworn statement, he should have his tongue slit;[1] and if an officer, he should be further

A solemn expression of opinion

---

[1] " É cortada la lengua ; " " y le cortarian la lengua." Irving understands it to mean cutting off the tongue. But in those days of symbolism slitting the tip of that unruly member was a recognized punishment for serious lying.

punished with a fine of 10,000 maravedis, or if a sailor, with a hundred lashes. These proceedings were embodied in a formal document, dated June 12, 1494, which is still to be seen in the Archives of the Indies at Seville.[1]

Having disposed of this solemn matter, the three caravels turned eastward, touching at the Isle of Pines and coasting back along the south side of Cuba. The headland where the admiral first became convinced of the significance of the curvature of the coast, he named Cape of Good Hope,[2] believing it to be much nearer the goal which all were seeking than the other cape of that name, discovered by Dias seven years before.

It will be remembered that the admiral, upon his first voyage, had carried home with him Vicissitudes of theory two theories, — first, that in the Cuban coast he had already discovered that of the continent of Asia; secondly, that Hispaniola was Cipango. The first theory seemed to be confirmed by further experience; the second was now to receive a serious shock. Leaving Cape Cruz the caravels stood over to Jamaica, leisurely explored the southern side of that island, and as soon as adverse winds would let them, kept on eastward till land appeared on the port bow. Nobody recognized it until an

---

[1] It is printed in full in Navarrete, tom. ii. pp. 143–149.
[2] It is given upon La Cosa's map ; see below, 228.

Indian chief who had learned some Spanish hailed them from the shore and told them it was Hispaniola. They then followed that southern coast its whole length, discovering the tiny islands, Beata, Saona, and Mona. Here Columbus, overcome by long-sustained fatigue and excitement, suddenly fell into a death-like lethargy, and in this sad condition was carried all the way to Isabella, and to his own house, where he was put to bed. Hispaniola had thus been circumnavigated, and either it was not Cipango or else that wonderland must be a much smaller affair than Toscanelli and Martin Behaim had depicted it.[1] There was something truly mysterious about these Strange Coasts!

When Columbus, after many days, recovered consciousness, he found his brother Bartholomew standing by his bedside. It was six years since they had last parted company at Lisbon whence the younger brother started for England, while the elder returned to Spain. The news of Christopher's return from his first voyage found Bartholomew in Paris, whence he started as soon as he could for Seville, but did not arrive there until just after the second expedition had started. Presently the sovereigns sent him with three

Arrival of Bartholomew Columbus

[1] Hispaniola continued, however, for many years to be commonly identified with Cipango. See note D on Ruysch's map, 1508, below, p. 346.

ships to Hispaniola, to carry supplies to the colony; and there he arrived while the admiral was exploring the coast of Cuba. The meeting of the two brothers was a great relief to both. The affection between them was very strong, and each was a support for the other. The admiral at once proceeded to appoint Bartholomew to the office of Adelantado, which in this instance was equivalent to making him governor of Hispaniola under himself, the Viceroy of the Indies. In making this appointment Columbus seems to have exceeded the authority granted him by the second article of his agreement of April, 1492, with the sovereigns;[1] but they mended the matter in 1497 by themselves investing Bartholomew with the office and dignity of Adelantado.[2]

Columbus was in need of all the aid he could summon, for, during his absence, the island had

Mutiny in Hispaniola; desertion of Boyle and Margarite

become a pandemonium. His brother Diego, a man of refined and studious habits, who afterwards became a priest, was too mild in disposition to govern the hotheads who had come to Hispaniola to get rich without labour. They would not submit to the rule of this foreigner. Instead of doing honest work they roamed about the island, abusing the Indians and slaying one another in silly

[1] See above, p. 99.
[2] Las Casas, *Hist. de las Indias*, tom. ii. p. 80.

quarrels. Chief among the offenders was King Ferdinand's favourite, the commander Margarite ; and he was aided and abetted by Friar Boyle. Some time after Bartholomew's arrival, these two men of Aragon gathered about them a party of malcontents and, seizing the ships which had brought that mariner, sailed away to Spain. Making their way to court, they sought pardon for thus deserting the colony, saying that duty to their sovereigns demanded that they should bring home a report of what was going on in the Indies. They decried the value of Columbus's discoveries, and reminded the king that Hispaniola was taking money out of the treasury much faster than it was putting it in ; an argument well calculated to influence Ferdinand that summer, for he was getting ready to go to war with France over the Naples affair. Then the two recreants poured forth a stream of accusations against the brothers Columbus, the general purport of which was that they were gross tyrants not fit to be trusted with the command of Spaniards.

No marked effect seems to have been produced by these first complaints, but when Margarite and Boyle were once within reach of Fonseca, we need not wonder that mischief was soon brewing. It was unfortunate for Columbus that his work of exploration was hampered by the necessity of founding a colony and governing a parcel of unruly men let loose in the wilderness, far away from the powerful restraints of civilized society. Such work required undivided attention and extraordinary talent for command. It does not appear that Columbus was lacking in such talent. On the contrary both he and his brother Bartholomew seem to have possessed it in a high degree. But the situation was desperately bad when the spirit of mutiny was fomented by deadly enemies at court. I do not find adequate justification for the charges of tyranny brought against Columbus. The veracity and fairness of the history of Las Casas are beyond question ; in his divinely beautiful spirit one sees now and then a trace of tenderness even for Fonseca, whose conduct toward him was always as mean and malignant as toward Columbus. One gets from Las Casas the impression that the admiral's high temper was usually kept under firm control, and that he showed far less severity than most men would have done under similar provocation. Bartholomew was made of sterner stuff, but his whole career presents no instance of wanton cruelty ; toward both white men and Indians his conduct was distinguished by clemency and moderation. Under the government of these brothers a few scoundrels were hanged in Hispaniola. Many more ought to have been.

The government of Columbus was not tyrannical

Of the attempt of Columbus to collect tribute from the native population, and its consequences in developing the system of *repartimientos* out of which grew Indian slavery, I shall treat in a future chapter.[1] That attempt, which was ill advised and ill managed, was part of a plan for checking wanton depredations and regulating the relations between the Spaniards and the Indians. The colonists behaved so badly toward the red men that the chieftain Caonabo, who had destroyed La Navidad the year before, now formed a scheme[2] for a general alliance among the native tribes, hoping with sufficient numbers to overwhelm and exterminate the strangers, in spite of their solid-hoofed monsters and death-dealing thunderbolts. This scheme was revealed to Columbus, soon after his return from the coast of Cuba, by the chieftain Guacanagari, who was an enemy to Caonabo and courted the friendship of the Spaniards. Alonso de Ojeda, by a daring stratagem, captured Caonabo and brought him to Columbus, who treated him kindly but kept him a prisoner until it should be convenient to send him to Spain. But this chieftain's scheme was nevertheless put in operation through the

(margin note: Troubles with the Indians)

[1] See below, vol. iii. pp. 255, 256.

[2] The first of a series of such schemes in American history, including those of Sassacus, Philip, Pontiac, and to some extent Tecumseh.

influence of his principal wife Anacaona. An Indian war broke out; roaming bands of Spaniards were ambushed and massacred; and there was fighting in the field, where the natives — assailed by firearms and cross-bows, horses and bloodhounds — were woefully defeated.

Thus in the difficult task of controlling mutinous white men and defending the colony against infuriated red men Columbus spent the first twelvemonth after his return from Cuba. In October, 1495, there arrived in the harbour of Isabella four caravels laden with welcome supplies. In one of these ships came Juan Aguado, sent by the sovereigns to gather information respecting the troubles of the colony. This appointment was doubtless made in a friendly spirit, for Columbus had formerly recommended Aguado to favour. But the arrival of such a person created a hope, which quickly grew into a belief, that the sovereigns were preparing to deprive Columbus of the government of the island; and, as Irving neatly says, "it was a time of jubilee for offenders; every culprit started up into an accuser." All the ills of the colony, many of them inevitable in such an enterprise, many of them due to the shiftlessness and folly, the cruelty and lust of idle swash-bucklers, were now laid at the door of Columbus. Aguado was presently won over by the malcontents, so that

Mission of Aguado

Discovery of gold mines

by the time he was ready to return to Spain, early in 1496, Columbus felt it desirable to go along with him and make his own explanations to the sovereigns. Fortunately for his purposes, just before he started, some rich gold mines were discovered on the south side of the island, in the neighbourhood of the Hayna and Ozema rivers. Moreover there were sundry pits in these mines, which looked like excavations and seemed to indicate that in former times there had been digging done.[1] This discovery confirmed the admiral in a new theory, which he was beginning to form. If it should turn out that Hispaniola was not Cipango, as the last voyage seemed to suggest, perhaps it might prove to be Ophir![2] Probably these ancient excavations were made by King Solomon's men when they came here to get gold for the temple at Jerusalem! If so, one might expect to find silver, ivory, red sandal-wood, apes, and peacocks at no great distance. Just where Ophir was situated no one could exactly tell,[3] but the things that were carried thence to Jerusalem certainly came from " the Indies."

Speculations about Ophir

---

[1] The Indians then living upon the island did not dig, but scraped up the small pieces of gold that were more or less abundant in the beds of shallow streams.

[2] Peter Martyr, *De Rebus Oceanicis*, dec. i. lib. iv.

[3] The original Ophir may be inferred, from *Genesis* x. 29, to have been situated where, as Milton says, —

175

Columbus conceived it as probably lying north-eastward of the Golden Chersonese (Malacca) and as identical with the island of Hispaniola.

The discovery of these mines led to the transfer of the headquarters of the colony to the mouth of the Ozema River, where, in the summer of 1496, Bartholomew Columbus made a settlement which became the city of San Domingo.[1] Meanwhile Aguado and the admiral sailed for Spain early in March, in two caravels overloaded with more than two hundred homesick passengers. In choosing his course Columbus did not show so much sagacity as on his first return voyage. Instead of working northward till clear of the belt of trade-winds, he kept straight to the east, and so spent a month in beating and tacking before getting out of the Caribbean Sea. Scarcity of food was imminent, and it be-

Founding of San Domingo, 1496

The return voyage

> " northeast winds blow
> Sabæan odours from the spicy shore
> Of Araby the Blest,"

but the name seems to have become applied indiscriminately to the remote countries reached by ships that sailed past that coast ; chiefly, no doubt, to Hindustan. See Lassen, *Indische Alterthumskunde*, bd. i. p. 538.

[1] Bartholomew's town was built on the left side of the river, and was called New Isabella. In 1504 it was destroyed by a hurricane, and rebuilt on the right bank in its present situation. It was then named San Domingo after the patron saint of Domenico, the father of Columbus.

came necessary to stop at Guadaloupe and make a quantity of cassava bread.[1] It was well that this was done, for as the ships worked slowly across the Atlantic, struggling against perpetual head-winds, the provisions were at length exhausted, and by the first week in June the famine was such that Columbus had some difficulty in preventing the crews from eating their Indian captives, of whom there were thirty or more on board.[2]

At length, on the 11th of June, the haggard and starving company arrived at Cadiz, and Columbus, while awaiting orders from the sovereigns, stayed at the house of his good friend Bernaldez, the curate of Los Palacios.[3] After a month he attended court at Burgos, and was kindly received. No allusion was made to the complaints against him, and the sovereigns promised to furnish ships for a third voyage of discovery. For the moment, however, other things

[1] While the Spaniards were on this island they encountered a party of tall and powerful women armed with bows and arrows; so that Columbus supposed it must be the Asiatic island of Amazons mentioned by Marco Polo. See Yule's *Marco Polo*, vol. ii. pp. 338–340.

[2] Among them was Caonabo, who died on the voyage.

[3] The curate thus heard the story of the second voyage from Columbus himself while it was fresh in his mind. Columbus also left with him written memoranda, so that for the events of this expedition the *Historia de los Reyes Católicos* is of the highest authority.

interfered with this enterprise. One was the marriage of the son and daughter of Ferdinand and Isabella to the daughter and son of the Emperor Maximilian. The war with France was at the same time fast draining the treasury. Indeed, for more than twenty years, Castile had been at war nearly all the time, first with Portugal, next with Granada, then with France; and the Crown never found it easy to provide money for maritime enterprises. Accordingly, at the earnest solicitation of Vicente Yañez Pinzon and other enterprising mariners, the sovereigns

Edicts of 1495 and 1497

had issued a proclamation, April 10, 1495, granting to all native Spaniards the privilege of making, at their own risk and expense, voyages of discovery or traffic to the newly found coasts. As the Crown was to take a pretty heavy tariff out of the profits of these expeditions, while all losses were to be borne by the adventurers, a fairly certain source of revenue, be it great or small, seemed likely to be opened.[1] Columbus protested against this

[1] " All vessels were to sail exclusively from the port of Cadiz, and under the inspection of officers appointed by the Crown. Those who embarked for Hispaniola without pay, and at their own expense, were to have lands assigned to them, and to be provisioned for one year, with a right to retain such lands and all houses they might erect upon them. Of all gold which they might collect, they were to retain one third for themselves, and pay two thirds to the Crown. Of all other articles of merchandise, the produce of the island, they were

edit, inasmuch as he deemed himself entitled
to a patent or monopoly in the work of conducting expeditions to Cathay. The sovereigns
evaded the difficulty by an edict of June 2,
1497, declaring that it was never their intention
" in any way to affect the rights of the said Don
Christopher Columbus." This declaration was,
doubtless, intended simply to pacify the admiral.
It did not prevent the authorization of voyages
conducted by other persons a couple of years
later; and, as I shall show in the next chapter,
there are strong reasons for believing that on
May 10, 1497, three weeks before this edict, an
expedition sailed from Cadiz under the especial
auspices of King Ferdinand, with Vicente Yañez
Pinzon for its chief commander and Americus
Vespucius for one of its pilots.

It was not until late in the spring of 1498

to pay merely one tenth to the Crown. Their purchases were
to be made in the presence of officers appointed by the sovereigns, and the royal duties paid into the hands of the king's
receiver. Each ship sailing on private enterprise was to take
one or two persons named by the royal officers at Cadiz.
One tenth of the tonnage of the ship was to be at the service
of the Crown, free of charge. One tenth of whatever such
ships should procure in the newly discovered countries was
to be paid to the Crown on their return. These regulations
included private ships trading to Hispaniola with provisions.
For every vessel thus fitted out on private adventure, Columbus, in consideration of his privilege of an eighth of tonnage,
was to have the right to freight one on his own account."
Irving's *Columbus*, vol. ii. p. 76.

that the ships were ready for Columbus. Every-thing that Fonseca could do to vex and delay him was done. One of the bishop's minions, a converted Moor or Jew named Ximeno Breviesca, behaved with such outrageous insolence that on the day of sailing the admiral's indignation, so long re-strained, at last broke out, and he drove away the fellow with kicks and cuffs.[1] This impru-dent act gave Fonseca the opportunity to main-tain that what the admiral's accusers said about his tyrannical disposition must be true.

Columbus loses his tem-per

The expedition started on May 30, 1498, from the little port of San Lucar de Barrameda. There were six ships, carrying about 200 men besides the sailors. On June 21, at the Isle of Ferro, the admiral di-

The third voyage

[1] " Parece que uno debiera de, en estos reveses, y, por ventura, en palábras contra él y contra la negociacion destas Indias, mas que otro señalarse, y segun entendí, no debiera ser cristiano viejo, y creo que se llamaba Ximeno, contra el cual debió el Almirante gravemente sentirse y enojarse, y aguardó el dia que se hizo á la vela, y, ó en la nao que entró, por ventura, el dicho oficial, ó en tierra quando queria desem-barcarse, arrebatólo el Almirante, y dále muchas coces ó remesones, por manera que lo trató mal ; y á mi parecer, por esta causa principalmente, sobre otras quejas que fueron de acá, y cosas que murmuraron dél y contra él los que bien con él no estaban y le acumularon ; los Reyes indignados proveye-ron de quitarle la gobernacion." Las Casas, *Historia de las Indias,* tom. ii. p. 199.

vided his fleet, sending three ships directly to
Hispaniola, while with the other three he kept
on to the Cape Verde Islands, whence he steered
southwest on the 4th of July. A week later,
after a run of about 900 miles, his astrolabe
seemed to show that he was within five degrees
of the equator.[1] There were three reasons for
going so far to the south : 1, the natives of the
islands already visited always pointed in that
direction when gold was mentioned; 2, a
learned jeweller, who had travelled in the East,
had assured Columbus that gold and gems, as
well as spices and rare drugs, were to be found
for the most part among black people near the
equator; 3, if he should not find any rich
islands on the way, a sufficiently long voyage
would bring him to the coast of Champa (Cochin China) at a lower point than he had reached
on the preceding voyage, and nearer to the
Golden Chersonese (Malacca), by doubling
which he could enter the Indian Ocean. It will
be remembered that he supposed the south-

[1] The figure given by Columbus is equivalent only to 360
geographical miles (Navarrete, *Coleccion*, tom. i. p. 246),
but as Las Casas (*Hist.*, tom. ii. p. 226) already noticed,
there must be some mistake here, for on a S. W. course
from the Cape Verde Islands it would require a distance of
900 geographical miles to cut the fifth parallel. From the
weather that followed, it is clear that Columbus stated his
latitude pretty correctly ; he had come into the belt of calms.
Therefore his error must be in the distance run.

westerly curve in the Cuban coast, the farthest point reached in his second voyage, to be the beginning of the coast of Cochin China according to Marco Polo.

Once more through ignorance of the atmospheric conditions of the regions within the tropics Columbus encountered needless perils and hardships. If he had steered from Ferro straight across the ocean a trifle south of west-southwest, he might have made a quick and comfortable voyage, with the trade-wind filling his sails, to the spot where he actually struck land.[1] As it was, however, he naturally followed the custom then so common, of first running to the parallel upon which he intended to sail. This

The belt of calms

long southerly run brought him into the belt of calms or neutral zone between the northern and southern trade-winds, a little north of the equator.[2] No words can describe what followed so well as those of

[1] Humboldt in 1799 did just this thing, starting from Teneriffe and reaching Trinidad in nineteen days. See Bruhn's *Life of Humboldt*, vol. i. p. 263.

[2] "The strength of the trade-winds depends entirely upon the difference in temperature between the equator and the pole; the greater the difference, the stronger the wind. Now, at the present time, the south pole is much colder than the north pole, and the southern trades are consequently much stronger than the northern, so that the neutral zone in which they meet lies some five degrees north of the equator." *Excursions of an Evolutionist*, p. 54.

Irving: " The wind suddenly fell, and a dead sultry calm commenced, which lasted for eight days. The air was like a furnace; the tar melted, the seams of the ship yawned; the salt meat became putrid; the wheat was parched as if with fire; the hoops shrank from the wine and water casks, some of which leaked and others burst, while the heat in the holds of the vessels was so suffocating that no one could remain below a sufficient time to prevent t damage that was taking place. The mariners lost all strength and spirits, and sank under the oppressive heat. It seemed as if the old fable of the torrid zone was about to be realized; and that they were approaching a fiery region where it would be impossible to exist." [1]

Fortunately, they were in a region where the ocean is comparatively narrow. The longitude reached by Columbus on July 13, when the wind died away, must have been about 36° or 37° W., and a run of only 800 miles west from

[1] Irving's *Columbus*, vol. ii. p. 137. One is reminded of a scene in the *Rime of the Ancient Mariner* : —

> " All in a hot and copper sky
> The bloody sun, at noon,
> Right up above the mast did stand,
> No bigger than the moon.

> " Day after day, day after day,
> We stuck, — nor breath nor motion ;
> As idle as a painted ship
> Upon a painted ocean."

that point would have brought him to Cayenne. His course between the 13th and 21st of July must have intersected the thermal equator, or line of greatest mean annual heat on the globe, —an irregular curve which is here deflected as much as five degrees north of the equinoctial line. But although there was not a breath of wind, the powerful equatorial current was quietly driving the ships, much faster than the admiral uld have suspected, to the northwest and ard land. By the end of that stifling week ey were in latitude 7° N., and caught the trade-wind on the starboard quarter. Thence after a brisk run of ten days, in sorry plight, with ugly leaks and scarcely a cask of fresh water left, they arrived within sight of land. Three mountain peaks loomed up in the offing before them, and as they drew nearer it appeared that those peaks belonged to one great mountain; wherefore the pious admiral named the island Trinidad.

Here some surprises were in store for Columbus. Instead of finding black and woolly-haired natives, he found men of cinnamon hue, like those in Hispaniola, only — strange to say — lighter in colour. Then in coasting Trinidad he caught a glimpse of land at the delta of the Orinoco, and called it Isla Santa, or Holy Island.[1] But, on passing

Trinidad and the Orinoco

[1] He "gave it the name of Isla Santa," says Irving (vol.

into the Gulf of Paria, through the strait which he named Serpent's Mouth, his ships were in sore danger of being swamped by the raging surge that poured from three or four of the lesser mouths of that stupendous river. Presently, finding that the water in the gulf was fresh to the taste, he gradually reasoned his way to the correct conclusion, that the billows which had so nearly overwhelmed him must have come out from a river greater than any he had ever known or dreamed of, and that so vast a stream of running water could be produced only upon land of continental dimensions.[1] This

ii. p. 140), " little imagining that he now, for the first time, beheld that continent, that Terra Firma, which had been the object of his earnest search." The reader of this passage should bear in mind that the continent of South America, which nobody had ever heard of, was *not* the object of Columbus's search. The Terra Firma which was the object of his search was the mainland of Asia, and that he never beheld, though he felt positively sure that he had already set foot upon it in 1492 and 1494.

[1] A modern traveller thus describes this river : " Right and left of us lay, at some distance off, the low banks of the Apuré, at this point quite a broad stream. But before us the waters spread out like a wide dark flood, limited on the horizon only by a low black streak, and here and there showing a few distant hills. This was the Orinoco, rolling with irrepressible power and majesty sea-wards, and often upheaving its billows like the ocean when lashed to fury by the wind. . . . The Orinoco sends a current of fresh water far into the ocean, its waters — generally green, but in the shallows milk-white

coast to the south of him was, therefore, the coast of a continent, with indefinite extension toward the south, a land not laid down upon Toscanelli's or any other map, and of which no one had until that time known anything.[1]

In spite of the correctness of this surmise, Columbus was still as far from a true interpretation of the whole situation as when he supposed Hispaniola to be Ophir. He entered upon a series of speculations which forcibly remind us how empirical was the notion of the earth's rotundity before the inauguration of physical astronomy by Galileo, Kepler, and Newton. We now know that our planet has the only shape possible for such a rotating mass that once was fluid or nebulous, the shape of a spheroid slightly protuberant at the equator and flattened at the poles; but this

Speculations as to the earth's shape

— contrasting sharply with the indigo blue of the surrounding sea." Bates, *Central America, the West Indies, and South America*, 2d ed., London, 1882, pp. 234, 235. The island of Trinidad forms an obstacle to the escape of this huge volume of fresh water, and hence the furious commotion at the two outlets, the Serpent's Mouth and Dragon's Mouth, especially in July and August, when the Orinoco is swollen with tropical rains.

[1] In Columbus's own words, in his letter to the sovereigns describing this third voyage, " Y digo que . . . viene este rio y procede de tierra infinita, pues al austro, de la cual fasta agora no se ha habido noticia." Navarrete, *Coleccion*, tom. i. p. 262.

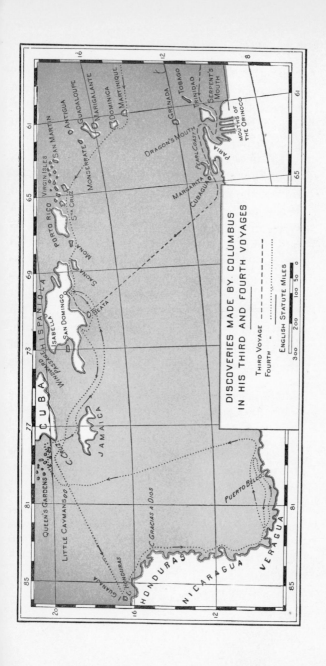

DISCOVERIES MADE BY COLUMBUS
IN HIS THIRD AND FOURTH VOYAGES

THIRD VOYAGE
FOURTH "

ENGLISH STATUTE MILES
300   200   100 50   0

knowledge is the outcome of mechanical prin-
ciples utterly unknown and unsuspected in the
days of Columbus. He understood that the
earth is a round body, but saw no necessity for
its being strictly spherical or spheroidal. He
now suggested that it was probably shaped like
a pear, rather a blunt and corpulent pear, nearly
spherical in its lower part, but with a short,
stubby apex in the equatorial region somewhere
beyond the point which he had just reached.
He fancied he had been sailing up a gentle slope
from the burning glassy sea where his ships had
been becalmed to this strange and beautiful
coast where he found the climate en- The moun-
chanting. If he were to follow up tain of Para-
the mighty river just now revealed, it dise
might lead him to the summit of this apex of
the world, the place where the terrestrial paradise, the Garden which the Lord planted eastward in Eden, was in all probability situated![1]

As Columbus still held to the opinion that
by keeping to the west from that point he should
soon reach the coast of Cochin China, his conception of the position of Eden is thus pretty

[1] Thus would be explained the astounding force with which
the water was poured down. It was common in the Middle
Ages to imagine the terrestrial paradise at the top of a mountain. See Dante, *Purgatorio*, canto xxviii. Columbus quotes
many authorities in favour of his opinion. The whole letter is
worth reading. See Navarrete, tom. i. pp. 242–264.

clearly indicated. He imagined it as situated about on the equator, upon a continental mass till then unknown, but evidently closely connected with the continent of Asia if not a part of it. If he had lived long enough to hear of Quito and its immense elevation, I should suppose that might very well have suited his idea of the position of Eden. The coast of this continent, upon which he had now arrived, was either continuous with the coast of Cochin China (Cuba) and Malacca, or would be found to be divided from it by a strait through which one might pass directly into the Indian Ocean.

Relation of the "Eden continent" to "Cochin China"

It took some little time for this theory to come to maturity in the mind of Columbus. Not expecting to find any mainland in that quarter, he began by calling different points of the coast different islands. Coming out through the passage which he named Dragon's Mouth, he caught distant glimpses of Tobago and Grenada to starboard, and turning westward followed the Pearl Coast as far as the islands of Margarita and Cubagua. The fine pearls which he found there in abundance confirmed him in the good opinion he had formed of that country. By this time, the 15th of August, he had so far put facts together as to become convinced of the continental character of that coast, and would have been glad

The Pearl Coast

to pursue it westward. But now his strength gave out. During most of the voyage he had suffered acute torments with gout, his temperature had been very feverish, and his eyes were at length so exhausted with perpetual watching that he could no longer make observations. So he left the coast a little beyond Cubagua, and steered straight for Hispaniola, aiming Arrival at at San Domingo, but hitting the San Domingo island of Beata because he did not make allowance for the westerly flow of the currents. He arrived at San Domingo on the 30th of August, and found his brother Bartholomew, whom he intended to send at once on a further cruise along the Pearl Coast, while he himself should be resting and recovering strength.

But alas! there was to be no cruising now for the younger brother nor rest for the elder. It was a sad story that Bartholomew Roldan's had to tell. War with the Indians had rebellion broken out afresh, and while the Adelantado was engaged in this business a scoundrel named Roldan had taken advantage of his absence to stir up civil strife. Roldan's rebellion was a result of the ill-advised mission of Aguado. The malcontents in the colony interpreted the admiral's long stay in Spain as an indication that he had lost favour with the sovereigns and was not coming back to the island. Gathering together a strong body of rebels, Roldan retired to Xaragua and formed an alliance with the brother of the late chieftain Caonabo. By the time the admiral arrived the combination of mutiny with barbaric warfare had brought about a frightful state of things. A party of soldiers, sent by him to suppress Roldan, straightway deserted and joined that rebel. It thus became necessary to come to terms with Roldan, and this revelation of the weakness of the government only made matters worse. Two wretched years were passed in attempts to restore order in Hispaniola, while the work of discovery and exploration was postponed. Meanwhile the items of information that found their way to Spain were skilfully Fonseca's employed by Fonseca in poisoning machinations the minds of the sovereigns, until at last they decided to send out a judge to the island, armed with plenary authority to make investigations and settle disputes. The glory which Columbus had won by the first news of the discovery of the Indies had now to some extent faded away. The enterprise yielded as yet no revenue and entailed great expense ; and whenever some reprobate found his way back to Spain, the malicious Fonseca prompted him to go to the treasury with a claim for pay alleged to have been wrongfully withheld by the admiral. Ferdinand Columbus tells how some fifty such scamps were gathered one day in the courtyard of the Alhambra, cursing his father and catching hold of the king's robe, crying, " Pay us ! pay us !" and as he and his brother Diego, who were pages in the queen's service, happened to pass by, they were greeted with hoots : "There go the sons of the Admiral of Mosquitoland, the man who has discovered a land of vanity and deceit, the grave of Spanish gentlemen !"[1]

An added sting was given to such taunts by a great event that happened about this time. In the summer of 1497, Vasco da Gama started from Lisbon for the Cape of Good Hope, and in the summer of 1499 he returned, after having doubled the cape and crossed the Indian Ocean to Calicut on the Malabar coast of Hindustan. His voyage was the next Portuguese step sequent upon that of Bartholomew Dias. There was nothing questionable or dubious about Gama's triumph. He had seen splendid cities, talked with a powerful Rajah, and met with Arab vessels, their crews madly jealous at the unprecedented sight of Christian ships in those waters ; and he brought back with him to Lisbon nutmegs and cloves, pepper and ginger, rubies and emeralds, damask

Gama's voyage to Hindustan, 1497

---

[1] " Ecco i figliuoli dell' Ammiraglio de' Mosciolini, di colui che ha trovate terre di vanitá e d' inganno, per sepoltura e miseria de' gentiluomini castigliani." *Vita dell' Ammiraglio*, cap. lxxxiv.

robes with satin linings, bronze chairs with cush-
ions, trumpets of carved ivory, a sunshade of
crimson satin, a sword in a silver scabbard, and
no end of such gear.[1] An old civilization had
been found and a route of commerce discovered,
and a factory was to be set up at once on that
Indian coast. What a contrast to the miserable
performance of Columbus, who had started with
the flower of Spain's chivalry for rich Cipango,
and had only led them to a land where they
must either starve or do work fit for peasants,
while he spent his time in cruising among wild
islands! The king of Portugal could now snap
his fingers at Ferdinand and Isabella, and if a
doubt should have sometimes crossed the minds
of those chagrined sovereigns, as to whether this
plausible Genoese mariner might not, after all,
be a humbug or a crazy enthusiast, we can
hardly wonder at it.

The person sent to investigate the affairs of
Hispaniola was Francisco de Bobadilla, a knight
commander of the order of Calatrava.

Fonseca's
creature,
Bobadilla

He carried several documents, one of
them directing him to make inquiries
and punish offenders, another containing his
appointment as governor, a third commanding
Columbus and his brothers to surrender to him
all fortresses and other public property.[2] The

[1] Major, *Prince Henry the Navigator*, pp. 398–401.

[2] The documents are given in Navarrete, *Coleccion de*

two latter papers were to be used only in case
of such grave misconduct proved against Columbus as to justify his removal from the government. These papers were made out in the
spring of 1499, but Bobadilla was not sent out
until July, 1500. When he arrived at San
Domingo on the 23d of August, the insurrec-
tion had been suppressed ; the admiral and Bartholomew were bringing things into order in
distant parts of the island, while Diego was left
in command at San Domingo. Seven ringleaders had just been hanged, and five more were
in prison under sentence of death. If Bobadilla
had not come upon the scene this wholesome
lesson might have worked some improvement
in affairs.[1] He destroyed its moral in a twin-
kling. The first day after landing, he read aloud,
at the church door, the paper directing him to
make inquiries and punish offenders ; and forthwith demanded of Diego Columbus that the
condemned prisoners should be delivered up to
him. Diego declined to take so important a step
until he could get orders from the admiral.
viages, tom. ii. pp. 235–240 ; and, with accompanying narrative, in Las Casas, *Hist. de las Indias*, tom. ii. pp. 472–
487.

[1] No better justification for the government of the brothers
Columbus can be found than to contrast it with the infinitely
worse state of affairs that ensued under the administrations
of Bobadilla and Ovando. See below, vol. iii. pp. 256–
269.

Next day Bobadilla read his second and third papers, proclaimed himself governor, called on Diego to surrender the fortress and public buildings, and renewed his demand for the prisoners. As Diego still hesitated to act before news of these proceedings could be sent to his brother, Bobadilla broke into the fortress, took the prisoners out, and presently set them free. All the rebellious spirits in the colony were thus drawn to the side of Bobadilla, whose royal commission, under such circumstances, gave him irresistible power. He threw Diego into prison and loaded him with fetters. He seized the admiral's house, and confiscated all his personal property, even including his business papers and private letters. When the admiral arrived in San Domingo, Bobadilla, without even waiting to see him, sent Columbus in chains an officer to put him in irons and take him to prison. When Bartholomew arrived, he received the same treatment. The three brothers were confined in different places, nobody was allowed to visit them, and they were not informed of the offences with which they were charged. While they lay in prison, Bobadilla busied himself with inventing an excuse for this violent behaviour. Finally he hit upon one at which Satan from the depths of his bottomless pit must have grimly smiled. He said that he had arrested and imprisoned the brothers only because he had reason to believe

they were inciting the Indians to aid them in
resisting the commands of Ferdinand and Isabella ! ! In short, from the day of his landing
Bobadilla made common cause with the insur-
gent rabble, and when they had furnished him
with a ream or so of charges against the admiral and his brothers, it seemed safe to send
these gentlemen to Spain. They were put on
board ship, with their fetters upon them, and
the officer in charge was instructed by Bobadilla
to deliver them into the hands of Bishop Fonseca, who was thus to have the privilege of glut-
ting to the full his revengeful spite.

The master of the ship, shocked at the sight
of fetters upon such a man as the admiral,
would have taken them off, but Co- Return to
lumbus would not let it be done. No, Spain
indeed ! they should never come off except
by order of the sovereigns, and then he would
keep them for the rest of his life, to show how
his labours had been rewarded.[1] The event —
which always justifies true manliness — proved
the sagacity of this proud demeanour. Fonseca
was baulked of his gratification. The clumsy
Bobadilla had overdone the business. The sight
of the admiral's stately and venerable figure in

[1] Las Casas, *Hist. de las Indias,* tom. ii. p. 501 ; F. Columbus, *Vita dell' Ammiraglio,* cap. lxxxv. Ferdinand adds
that he had often seen these fetters hanging in his father's
room.

chains, as he passed through the streets of Cadiz, on a December day of that year 1500, awakened a popular outburst of sympathy for him and indignation at his persecutors. While on the ship he had written or dictated a beautiful and touching letter[1] to a lady of whom the queen was fond, the former nurse of the Infante, whose untimely death, three years since, his mother was still mourning. This letter reached the court at Granada, and was read to the queen before she had heard of Bobadilla's performances from any other quarter. A courier was sent in all haste to Cadiz, with orders that the brothers should at once be released, and with a letter to the admiral, inviting him to court and enclosing an order for money to cover his expenses. The

Release of Columbus

scene in the Alhambra, when Columbus arrived, is one of the most touching in history. Isabella received him with tears in her eyes, and then this much-enduring old man, whose proud and masterful spirit had so long been proof against all wrongs and insults, broke down. He threw himself at the feet of the sovereigns in an agony of tears and sobs.[2]

How far the sovereigns should be held responsible for the behaviour of their agent is not altogether easy to determine. The appointment

---

[1] It is given in full in Las Casas, *op. cit.* tom. ii. pp. 502-510.

[2] Herrera, *Historia*, dec. i. lib. iv. cap. 10.

of such a creature as Bobadilla was a sad blunder, but one such as is liable to be made under any government. Fonseca was very powerful at court, and Bobadilla never would have dared to proceed as he did if he had not known that the bishop would support him. Indeed, from the indecent haste with which he went about his work, without even the pretence of a judicial inquiry, it is probable that he started with private instructions from that quarter. But, while Fonseca had some of the wisdom along with the venom of the serpent, Bobadilla was simply a jackass, and behaved so that in common decency the sovereigns were obliged to disown him. They took no formal or public notice of his written charges against the admiral, and they assured the latter that he should be reimbursed for his losses and restored to his viceroyalty and other dignities.

How far were the sovereigns responsible for Bobadilla?

This last promise, however, was not fulfilled; partly, perhaps, because Fonseca's influence was still strong enough to prevent it, partly because the sovereigns may have come to the sound and reasonable conclusion that for the present there was no use in committing the government of that disorderly rabble in Hispaniola to a foreigner. What was wanted was a Spanish priest, and a military priest withal, of the sort that Spain then had in plenty. Obedience to priests

came natural to Spaniards. The man now selected was Nicolas de Ovando, a knight commander of the order of Alcántara,
of whom we shall have more to say
hereafter.[1] Suffice it now to observe
that he proved himself a famous disci-
plinarian, and that he was a great favourite with Fonseca, to whom he seems to have
owed his appointment. He went out in February,
1502, with a fleet of thirty ships carrying 2500
persons, for the pendulum of public opinion
had taken another swing, and faith in the Indies was renewed. Some great discoveries, to
be related in the next chapter, had been made
since 1498 ; and, moreover, the gold mines of
Hispaniola were beginning to yield rich treasures.

*Ovando, an-
other creature
of Fonseca,
appointed
governor of
Hispaniola*

But, while the sovereigns were not disposed
to restore Columbus to his viceroyalty, they
were quite ready to send him on another voyage of discovery which was
directly suggested by the recent Portuguese voyage of Gama. Since nothing was
yet known about the discovery of a New World,
the achievement of Gama seemed to have
eclipsed that of Columbus. Spain must make a
response to Portugal. As already observed, the
admiral supposed the coast of his " Eden continent " (South America) either to be continuous

*Purpose of
Columbus's
fourth voyage*

[1] See below, vol. iii. pp. 256-269.

with the coast of Cochin China (Cuba) and
Malacca, or else to be divided from that coast
by a strait. The latter opinion was the more
probable, since Marco Polo and a few other
Europeans had sailed from China into the Indian
Ocean without encountering any great continent
that had to be circumnavigated. The recent
expedition of Vespucius and Ojeda (1499–1500)
had followed the northern coast of South America for a long distance to the west of Cubagua,
as far as the Gulf of Maracaibo. Columbus now
decided to return to the coast of Cochin China
(Cuba) and follow the coast southwestward until
he should find the passage between his Eden
continent and the Golden Chersonese (Malacca)
into the Indian Ocean. He would thus be able
to reach by this western route the same shores
of Hindustan which Gama had lately reached
by sailing eastward. So confident did he feel
of the success of this enterprise, that he wrote
a letter to Pope Alexander VI., renewing his
vow to furnish troops for the rescue of the
Holy Sepulchre.[1] It was no doubt the symptom
of a reaction against his misfortunes that he grew
more and more mystical in these days, consol-
ing himself with the belief that he was a chosen
instrument in the hands of Providence for enlarging the bounds of Christendom. In this
mood he made some studies on the prophecies,

[1] Navarrete, *Coleccion*, tom. ii. pp. 280–282.

after the fantastic fashion of his time,[1] and a habit grew upon him of attributing his discoveries to miraculous inspiration rather than to the good use to which his poetical and scientific mind had put the data furnished by Marco Polo and the ancient geographers.

The armament for the admiral's fourth and last voyage consisted of four small caravels, Crossing the Atlantic of from fifty to seventy tons burthen, with crews numbering, all told, 150 men. His brother Bartholomew, and his younger son Ferdinand, then a boy of fourteen, accompanied him. They sailed from Cadiz on the 11th of May, 1502, and finally left the Canaries behind on the 26th of the same month. The course chosen was the same as on the second voyage, and the unfailing trade-winds brought the ships on the 15th of June to an island called Mantinino, probably Martinique, not more than ten leagues distant from Dominica. The admiral had been instructed not to touch at Hispaniola upon his way out, probably for fear of further commotions there until Ovando should have succeeded in bringing order out of the confusion ten times worse confounded into which Bobadilla's misgovernment had thrown that island. Columbus might stop there on his

[1] The MS. volume of notes on the prophecies is in the Colombina. There is a description of it in Navarrete, tom. ii. pp. 260–273.

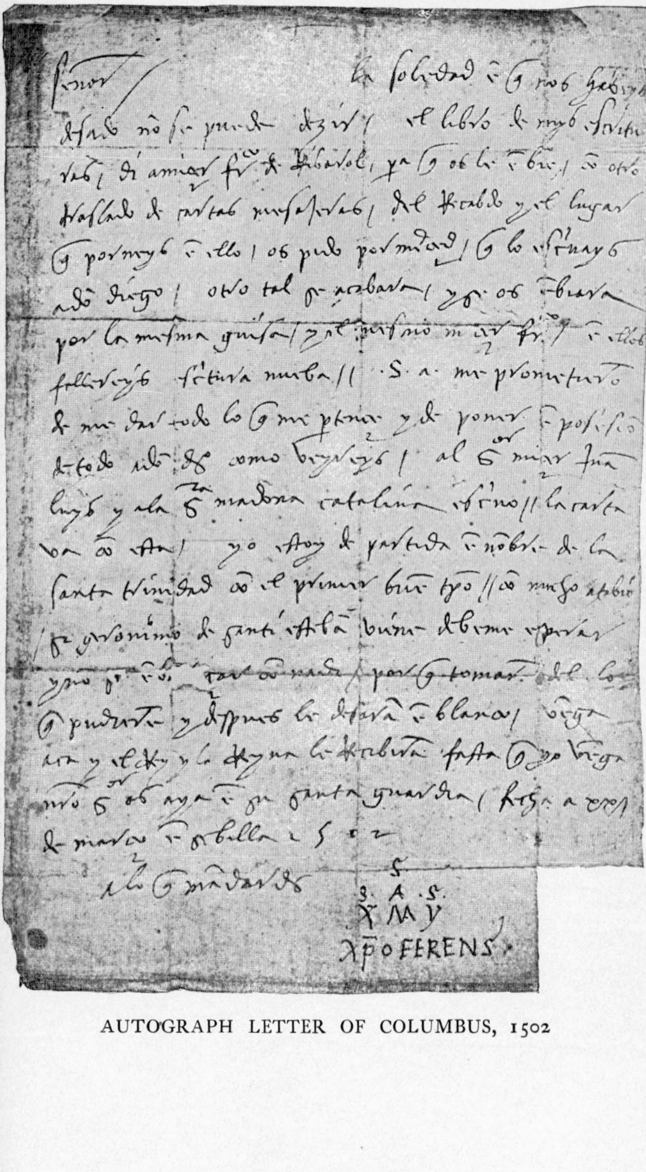

.S.
.S. A .S.
X M Y
Xpo FERENS.

AUTOGRAPH LETTER OF COLUMBUS, 1502

return, but not on his outward voyage. His intention had, therefore, been, on reaching the cannibal islands, to steer for Jamaica, thence make the short run to " Cochin China," and then turn southwards. But as one of his caravels threatened soon to become unmanageable, he thought himself justified in touching at San Domingo long enough to hire a sound vessel in place of her. Ovando had assumed the government there in April, and a squadron of 26 or 28 ships, containing Roldan and Bobadilla, with huge quantities of gold wrung from the enslaved Indians, was ready to start for Spain about the end of June. In one of these ships were 4000 pieces of gold destined for Columbus, probably a part of the reimbursement that had been promised him. On the 29th of June the admiral arrived in the harbour and stated the nature of his errand. At the same time, as his practised eye had detected the symptoms of an approaching hurricane, he requested permission to stay in the harbour until it should be over, and he furthermore sent to the commander of the fleet a friendly warning not to venture out to sea at present. His requests and his warnings were alike treated with contumely. Columbus not allowed to stop at San Domingo He was ordered to leave the harbour, and did so in great indignation. As his first care was for the approaching tempest, he did not go far, but found safe anchorage in a sheltered and secluded cove, where his vessels rode the storm with difficulty but without serious damage. Meanwhile the governor's great fleet had rashly put out to sea, and was struck with fatal fury by wind and wave. Twenty or more ships went to the bottom, with Bobadilla, Roldan, and most of the admiral's principal enemies, besides all the ill-gotten treasure; five or six shattered caravels, unable to proceed, found their way back to San Domingo; of all the fleet, only one ship arrived safe and sound in Spain, and that, says Ferdinand, was the one that had on board his father's gold. Truly it was such an instance of poetical justice as one does not often witness in this world. "We will not inquire now," says Las Casas, who witnessed the affair, "into this remarkable divine judgment, for at the last day of the world it will be made quite clear to us."[1] If such judgments were more often visited upon the right persons, perhaps the ways of Providence would not have so generally come to be regarded as inscrutable.

The hurricane was followed by a dead calm, during which the admiral's ships were carried

---

[1] "Aqueste tan gran juicio de Dios no curemos de escudriñallo, pues en el dia final deste mundo nos será bien claro." *Hist. de las Indias*, tom. iii. p. 32; cf. *Vita dell' Ammiraglio*, cap. lxxxvii. As Las Casas was then in San Domingo, having come out in Ovando's fleet, and as Ferdinand Columbus was with his father, the testimony is very direct.

by the currents into the group of tiny islands called the Queen's Gardens, on the south side of Cuba. With the first favourable breeze he took a southwesterly course, in order to strike that Cochin-Chinese coast farther down toward the Malay Peninsula. This brought him directly to the island of Guanaja and to Cape Honduras, which he thus reached without approaching the Yucatan Channel.[1]

Arrival at Cape Honduras

Upon the Honduras coast the admiral found evidences of semi-civilization with which he was much elated, — such as copper knives and hatchets, pottery of skilled and artistic workmanship, and cotton garments finely woven and beautifully dyed. Here the Spaniards first tasted the *chicha*, or maize beer, and marvelled at the heavy clubs, armed with sharp blades of obsidian, with which the soldiers of Cortes were by and by to become unpleasantly acquainted. The people here wore cotton clothes, and, according to Ferdinand, the women covered themselves as carefully as the Moorish women of Granada.[2] On inquiring as to the sources of gold and other

---

[1] In the next chapter I shall give some reasons for supposing that the admiral had learned the existence of the Yucatan Channel from the pilot Ledesma, coupled with information which made it unlikely that a passage into the Indian Ocean would be found that way. See below, p. 318.

[2] *Vita dell' Ammiraglio*, cap. lxxxviii.

wealth, the admiral was now referred to the west, evidently to Yucatan and Guatemala, or, as he supposed, to the neighbourhood of the Ganges. Evidently the way to reach these countries was to keep the land on the starboard and search for the passage between the Eden continent and the Malay Peninsula.[1] This course at first led Columbus eastward for a greater number of leagues than he could have relished. Wind and current were dead against him, too; and when, after forty days of wretched weather, he succeeded in doubling the cape which marks Cape Gracias a Dios on that coast the end of Honduras and the beginning of Nicaragua, and found it turning square to the south, it was doubtless joy at this auspicious change of direction, as well as the sudden relief from headwinds, that prompted him to name that bold prominence Cape Gracias a Dios, or Thanks to God.

As the ships proceeded southward in the

[1] Irving (vol. ii. pp. 386, 387) seems to think it strange that Columbus did not at once turn westward and circumnavigate Yucatan. But if — as Irving supposed — Columbus had not seen the Yucatan Channel, and regarded the Honduras coast as continuous with that of Cuba, he could only expect by turning westward to be carried back to Cape Alpha and Omega, where he had already been twice before ! In the next chapter, however, I shall show that Columbus may have shaped his course in accordance with the advice of the pilot Ledesma.

direction of Veragua, evidences of the kind of semi-civilization which we recognize as characteristic of that part of aboriginal America grew more and more numerous. Great houses were seen, built of " stone and lime," or perhaps of rubble stone with adobe-mortar. Walls were adorned with carvings and pictographs. Mummies were found in a good state of The coast of Veragua preservation. There were signs of abundant gold ; the natives wore plates of it hung by cotton cords about their necks, and were ready to exchange pieces worth a hundred ducats for tawdry European trinkets. From these people Columbus heard what we should call the first " news of the Pacific Ocean," though it had no such meaning to his mind. From what he heard he understood that he was on the east side of a peninsula, and that there was another sea on the other side, by gaining which he might in ten days reach the mouth of the Ganges.[1] By proceeding on his present course he would soon come to a " narrow place " between the two seas. There was a curious equivocation here. No doubt the Indians were honest and correct in what they tried to tell Columbus. But by the "narrow place" Fruitless search for the Strait of Malacca they meant narrow land, not narrow water ; not a strait which connected but an isthmus which divided the two seas, not

[1] Navarrete, *Coleccion de viages,* tom. i. p. 299.

the Strait of Malacca, but the Isthmus of Darien![1] Columbus, of course, understood them to mean the strait for which he was looking, and in his excitement at approaching the long-expected goal he pressed on without waiting to verify the reports of gold mines in the neighbourhood, a thing that could be done at any time.[2] By the 5th of December, however, having reached a point on the isthmus, a few leagues east of Puerto Bello, without finding the strait, he yielded to the remonstrances of the crews, and retraced his course to Veragua. If the strait could not be found, the next best tidings to carry home to Spain would be the certain information of the discovery of gold mines, and it was decided to make a settlement here which might serve as a base for future operations.

[1] *Vita dell' Ammiraglio,* cap. lxxxix. ; Humboldt, *Examen critique,* tom. i. p. 350.

[2] " Nothing could evince more clearly his generous ambition than hurrying in this brief manner along a coast where wealth was to be gathered at every step, for the purpose of seeking a strait which, however it might produce vast benefit to mankind, could yield little else to himself than the glory of the discovery." Irving's *Columbus,* vol. ii. p. 406. In this voyage, however, the express purpose from the start was to find the Strait of Malacca as a passage to the very same regions which had been visited by Gama, and Columbus expected thus to get wealth enough to equip an army of Crusaders. Irving's statement does not correctly describe the admiral's purpose, and as savouring of misplaced eulogy, is sure to provoke a reaction on the part of captious critics.

Three months of misery followed. Many of the party were massacred by the Indians, the stock of food was nearly exhausted, and the ships were pierced by worms until it was feared there would be no means left for going home. Accordingly, it was decided to abandon the enterprise and return to Hispaniola.[1] In order to allow for the strong westerly currents in the Caribbean Sea, the admiral first sailed eastward almost to the Gulf of Darien, and then turned to the north. The allowance was not enough, however. The ships were again carried into the Queen's Gardens, where they were caught in a storm and nearly beaten to pieces. At length, on St. John's eve, June 23, 1503, the crazy wrecks — now full of water and unable to sail another league — were beached on the coast of Jamaica and converted into a sort of rude fortress; and while two trusty men were sent over to San Domingo in a canoe, to obtain relief, Columbus and his party remained shipwrecked in Jamaica. They waited there a whole year before it proved possible to get any relief from Ovando. He was a slippery knave, who knew how to deal out promises without taking the first step toward fulfilment.

Futile attempt to make a settlement

Columbus shipwrecked

[1] A graphic account of these scenes, in which he took part, is given by Ferdinand Columbus, *Vita dell' Ammiraglio*, cap. xciii.–cvi.

It was a terrible year that Columbus spent upon the wild coast of Jamaica. To all the horrors inseparable from such a situation there was added the horror of mutiny. The year did not end until there had been a pitched battle, in which the doughty Bartholomew was, as usual, victorious. The ringleader was captured, and of the other mutineers such as were not slain in the fight were humbled and pardoned. At length Ovando's conduct began to arouse indignation in San Domingo, and was openly condemned from the pulpit; so that, late in June, 1504, he sent over to Jamaica a couple of ships which brought away the admiral and his starving party. Ovando greeted the brothers Columbus with his customary hypocritical courtesy, which they well understood. During the past year the island of Hispaniola had been the scene of atrocities such as have scarcely been surpassed in history. I shall give a brief account of them in a future chapter. Columbus was not cheered by what he saw and heard, and lost no time in starting for Spain. On the 7th of November, 1504, after a tempestuous voyage and narrow escape from shipwreck, he landed at San Lucar de Barrameda and made his way to Seville. Queen Isabella was then on her deathbed, and breathed her last just nineteen days later.

A year of misery

Last return to Spain

The death of the queen deprived Columbus of the only protector who could stand between him and Fonseca. The reimbursement for the wrongs which he had suffered at that man's hands was never made. The last eighteen months of the admiral's life were spent in sickness and poverty. Accumulated hardship and disappointment had broken him down, and he died on Ascension Day, May 20, 1506, at Valladolid. So little heed was taken of his passing away that the local annals of that city, " which give almost every insignificant event from 1333 to 1539, day by day, do not mention it." [1] His remains were buried in the Franciscan monastery at Valladolid, whence they were removed in 1513 to the monastery of Las Cuevas, at Seville, where the body of his son Diego, second Admiral and Viceroy of the Indies, was buried in 1526. Ten years after this date, the bones of father and son were removed to Hispaniola, to the cathedral of San Domingo ; whence they have since been transferred to Havana. The result of so many removals has been to raise doubts as to whether the ashes now reposing at Havana are really those of Columbus and his son ; and over this question there has been much critical discussion, of a sort that we may cheerfully leave to those who like to spend their time over such trivialities.

Death of Columbus

[1] Harrisse, *Notes on Columbus*, New York, 1866, p. 73.

There is a tradition that Ferdinand and Isabella, at some date unspecified, had granted to Columbus, as a legend for his coat of arms, the noble motto : —

> Á Castilla y á Leon
> Nuevo mundo dió Colon,

i. e. "To Castile-and-Leon Columbus gave a New World;" and we are further told that, when the admiral's bones were removed to Seville, this motto was, by order of King Ferdinand, inscribed upon his tomb.[1] This tradition crumbles under the touch of historical criticism. The admiral's coat of arms, as finally emblazoned under his own inspection at Seville in 1502, quarters the royal Castle-and-Lion of the kingdom of Castile with his own devices of five anchors, and a group of golden islands with a bit of Terra Firma, upon a blue sea. But there is no legend of any sort, nor is anything of the kind mentioned by Las Casas or Bernaldez or Peter Martyr. The first allusion to such a motto is by Oviedo, in 1535, who gives it a somewhat different turn : —

> Por Castilla y por Leon
> Nuevo mundo halló Colon,

i. e. "For Castile-and-Leon Columbus found a New World." But the other form is no doubt

---

[1] *Vita dell' Ammiraglio,* cap. cvii. This is unquestionably a gloss of the translator Ulloa. Cf. Harrisse, *Christophe Colomb,* tom. ii. pp. 177–179.

the better, for Ferdinand Columbus, at some time not later than 1537, had adopted it, and it may be read to-day upon his tomb in the cathedral at Seville. The time-honoured tradition has evidently transferred to the father the legend adopted, if not originally devised, by his son.

But why is this mere question of heraldry a matter of importance for the historian? Simply because it furnishes one of the most striking among many illustrations of the fact that at no time during the life of Columbus, nor for some years after his death, did anybody use the phrase " New World " with conscious reference to *his* discoveries. At the time of his death their true significance had not yet begun to dawn upon the mind of any voyager or any writer. It was supposed that he had found a new route to the Indies by sailing west, and that in the course of this achievement he had discovered some new islands and a bit or bits of Terra Firma of more or less doubtful commercial value. To group these items of discovery into an organic whole, and to ascertain that they belonged to a whole quite distinct from the Old World, required the work of many other discoverers, companions and successors to Columbus. In the following chapter I shall endeavour to show how the conception of the New World was thus originated and at length became developed into the form with which we are now familiar.

VII

MUNDUS NOVUS

SOMETIMES in Wagner's musical dramas the introduction of a few notes from some leading melody foretells the inevitable catastrophe toward which the action is moving; as when in Lohengrin's bridal chamber the well-known sound of the distant Grail motive steals suddenly upon the ear, and the heart of the rapt listener is smitten with a sense of impending doom. So in the drama of maritime discovery, as glimpses of new worlds were beginning to reward the enterprising crowns of Spain and Portugal, for a moment there came from the north a few brief notes fraught with ominous portent. The power for whom destiny had reserved the world empire of which these southern nations — so noble in aim, so mistaken in policy — were dreaming stretched forth her hand, in quiet disregard of papal bulls, and laid it upon the western shore of the ocean. It was only for a moment, and long years were to pass before the consequences were developed. But in truth the first fateful note that heralded the coming English supremacy was sounded when John Cabot's tiny craft sailed out from the Bristol Channel on a bright May morning of 1497.

The story of the Cabots can be briefly told. Less is known about them and their voyages than one could wish.[1] John Cabot, a native of Genoa, moved thence to Venice, where, after a residence of fifteen years, he was admitted to full rights of citizenship in 1476. He married a Venetian lady and had three sons, the second of whom, Sebastian, was born in Venice some time before March, 1474. Nothing is known about the life of John Cabot at Venice, except that he seems to have been a merchant and mariner, and that once in Arabia, meeting a caravan laden with spices, he made particular inquiries regarding the remote countries where such goods were obtained. It is not impossible that he may have reasoned his way, independently of Columbus, to the conclusion that those countries might be reached by sailing westward;[2] but there is no evidence

John Cabot (margin note)

[1] The best critical discussion of the subject is that of M. Harrisse, *Jean et Sébastien Cabot*, Paris, 1882. Most of the author's conclusions seem to me very strongly supported.

[2] This seems to be implied by the words of the late Dr. Charles Deane : "Accepting the new views as to 'the roundness of the earth,' as Columbus had done, he was quite disposed to put them to a practical test." Winsor, *Narr. and Crit. Hist.*, vol. iii. p. 1. But is it not strange to find so

that such was the case. About 1490 Cabot moved to England with his family and made his home in Bristol,[1] and he may have been one of the persons who were convinced at that time by the arguments of Bartholomew Columbus.

Bristol was then the principal seaport of England, and the centre of trade for the Iceland fisheries.[2] The merchants of that town were fond of maritime enterprise, and their ships had already ventured some distance out upon the Atlantic. William of Worcester informs us that in the summer of 1480 the wealthy merchant John Jay and another sent out a couple of ships, one of them of eighty tons burthen, commanded by Thomas Lloyd, "the most scientific mariner in all England," in order to find "the island of Brazil to the west of Ireland," but after sailing the sea for nine weeks without making any discovery foul weather sent them back to Ireland.[3] From

The merchants of Bristol

learned a writer alluding to the ancient doctrine of the earth's globular form as " new " in the time of Columbus !

[1] M. d'Avezac's suggestion (*Bulletin de la Société de Géographie*, Paris, 1872, 6e série, tom. iv. p. 44) that Columbus may have consulted with Cabot at Bristol in 1477 seems, therefore, quite improbable.

[2] See Hunt's *Bristol*, pp. 44, 137 ; Magnusson, *Om de Engelskes Handel paa Island*, Copenhagen, 1833, p. 147.

[3] " 1480 die jullij navis . . . et Joh[ann]is Jay junioris ponderis 80 doliorum inceperunt viagium apud portum Bristolliæ de Kyngrode usque ad insulam de Brasylle in occiden-

a letter of Pedro de Ayala, one of the Spanish embassy in London in 1498, it would appear that several expeditions, beginning perhaps as early as 1491, may have sailed from Bristol, at the instigation of John Cabot, in search of the imaginary islands of Brazil and Antilia.[1]

We are told that the news of the first voyage of Columbus was received by the Cabots and their English friends with much admiration. To have reached the coast of China by sailing westward was declared a wonderful achievement, and it was resolved to go and do likewise. On the 21st of January, 1496, the Spanish ambassador Puebla informed his sovereigns that "a person had

Effects of the news from Columbus

tali parte Hiberniæ, sulcando maria per . . . et . . . Thlyde [*i. e.* Th. Lyde = Lloyd] est magister scientificus marinarius tocius Angliæ, et noua venerunt Bristolliæ die lune 18 die septembris, quod dicta navis velaverunt maria per circa 9 menses nec invenerunt insulam sed per tempestas maris reversi sunt usque portum . . . in Hibernia pro reposicione navis et mariniorum." *Itinerarium Willelmi de Wyrcestre*, MS. in library of Corpus Christi College, Cambridge, No. 210, p. 195, apud Harrisse, *op. cit.* p. 44. See also Fox-Bourne, *English Merchants*, vol. i. p. 105. Though the Latin says nine *months*, it is evident that only nine *weeks* are meant to be included between "a day of July" and the 18th day of September.

[1] Ayala to Ferdinand and Isabella, July 25, 1498; Harrisse, p. 329. The reader has doubtless already observed these fabulous islands on the Toscanelli map; see above, p. 28.

come, like Columbus, to propose to the king of England an enterprise like that of the Indies." On the 28th of March the sovereigns instructed Puebla to warn Henry VII. that such an enterprise could not be put into execution by him without prejudice to Spain and Portugal.[1] But before this remonstrance arrived, the king had already issued letters patent, authorizing John Cabot and his three sons " to sail to the east, west, or north, with five ships carrying the English flag, to seek and discover all the islands, countries, regions, or provinces of pagans in whatever part of the world." [2] The expedition must return to the port of Bristol, and the king was to have one fifth of the profits. By implicitly excluding southerly courses it was probably intended, as far as possible, to avoid occasions for conflict with Spain or Portugal.

The voyage seems to have been made with a single ship, named the Matthew, or Matthews, after the evangelist, or perhaps after some English patron.[3] The crew numbered eighteen men. Sebastian Cabot may quite probably have ac-

John Cabot finds land supposed to be Cathay, June 24, 1497

[1] Ferdinand and Isabella to Puebla, March 28, 1496; Harrisse, p. 315.

[2] " Pro Johanne Cabot et filiis suis super Terra Incognita investiganda," March 5, 1496; Harrisse, p. 313.

[3] Barrett, *History and Antiquities of Bristol*, 1789, p. 172. A contemporary MS., preserved in the British Museum, says that besides the flagship equipped by the king there were

companied his father. They sailed from Bristol early in May, 1497,[1] and discovered what was supposed to be the Chinese coast, "in the territory of the Grand Cham," on the 24th of June. By the end of July they had returned to Bristol, and on the 10th of August we find thrifty Henry VII. giving "to hym that founde the new isle" the munificent largess of £10 with which to celebrate the achievement.[2]

three or four others, apparently equipped by private enterprise : " In anno 13 Henr. VII. This yere the Kyng at the besy request and supplicacion of a Straunger venisian, which [i. e. who] by a Cœart [i. e. chart] made hymself expert in knowyng of the world caused the Kynge to manne a ship wᵗ vytaill and other necessairies for to seche an Iland wherein the said Straunger surmysed to be grete commodities : wᵗ which ship by the Kynges grace so Rygged went 3 or 4 moo oute of Bristowe, the said Straunger beyng Conditor of the saide Flete, wheryn dyuers merchauntes as well of London as Bristow aventured goodes and sleight merchaundises, which departed from the West Cuntrey in the begynnyng of Somer, but to this present moneth came nevir Knowlege of their exployt." See Harrisse, p. 316. On page 50 M. Harrisse seems disposed to adopt this statement, but its authority is fatally impaired by the last sentence, which shows that already the writer had mixed up the first voyage with the second, as was afterwards commonly done.

[1] The date is often incorrectly given as 1494, owing to an old misreading of M. CCCC. XCIIII instead of M. CCCC. XCVII.

[2] Harrisse, pp. 51, 59. " Fazi bona ziera," says Pasqualigo ; "pour s'amuser," says Harrisse, or, as one might put it, " to go on a spree." It must be remembered that £10 then was equivalent to at least £100 of to-day. The

The news in England seems to have taken the form that Cabot had discovered the isles of Brazil and the Seven Cities, and the kingdom of the Great Khan. A Venetian gentleman, Lorenzo Pasqualigo, writing from London August 23, 1497, says that "honours are heaped upon Cabot, he is called Grand Admiral, he is dressed in silk, and the English run after him like madmen."[1] It seemed to Cabot that by returning to the point where he had found land, and then proceeding somewhat to the southward, he could find the wealthy island of Cipango, and this time we do not hear that any dread of collision with Spain prevailed upon the king to discountenance such an undertaking. A second expedition, consisting of five or six ships, sailed from Bristol in April, 1498, and explored a part of the coast of North America. In a despatch dated July 25, Ayala told his sovereigns that its return was expected in September. One of the vessels, much damaged by stress of weather, took refuge in an Irish port. When the others returned we do not know, nor do we hear anything more of John Cabot. It is probable that he sailed as commander of the expedition, and it has been supposed that he may

John Cabot and his son Sebastian go in search of Cipango, April, 1498

king also granted to Cabot a yearly pension of £20, to be paid out of the receipts of the Bristol custom-house.

[1] The letter is given in Harrisse, p. 322.

have died upon the voyage, leaving the command to his son Sebastian. It has further been supposed, on extremely slight evidence, that Sebastian may have conducted a third voyage in 1501 or 1503.

Sebastian Cabot married a Spanish lady, and seems to have gone to Spain soon after the death of Henry VII.[1] He entered the service of Ferdinand of Aragon October 20, 1512. In 1518 Charles V. appointed him Pilot Major of Spain; we shall presently find him at the congress of Badajoz in 1524; from 1526 to 1530 he was engaged in a disastrous expedition to the river La Plata, and on his return he was thrown into prison because of complaints urged against him by his mutinous crews. The Council of the Indies condemned him to two years of exile at Oran in Africa,[2] but the emperor seems to have remitted the sentence as unjust, and presently he returned to the discharge of his duties as Pilot Major. In 1548 he left the service of Spain and went back to England, where he was appointed governor of a company of merchants, organized for the purpose of discovering a northeast passage to China.[3] This enterprise opened a trade between England and Russia by way

Later career of Sebastian Cabot

---

[1] Peter Martyr, dec. iii. lib. vi. fol. 55.
[2] Navarrete, *Biblioteca maritima*, tom. ii. p. 699.
[3] Winsor, *Narr. and Crit. Hist.*, vol. iii. p. 6.

of the White Sea; and in 1556 the Muscovy Company received its charter, and Sebastian Cabot was appointed its governor. He seems to have died in London in 1557, or soon afterwards.

The life of the younger Cabot thus extended over the whole of the period during which Europeans were gradually awakening to the astounding fact that the western coasts of the Atlantic were not the coasts of Asia, but of a new continent, the existence of which had never been suspected by any human being, except in the unheeded guess of Strabo cited in a previous chapter.[1] The sixty years following 1497 saw new geographical facts accumulate much faster than geographical theory could interpret them, as the series of old maps reproduced in the present volume will abundantly show. By the end of that time the revolution in knowledge had become so tremendous, and men were carried so far away from the old point of view, that their minds grew confused as to the earlier stages by which the change had been effected. Hence the views and purposes ascribed to the Cabots by writers in the middle of the sixteenth century have served only to perplex the subject in the minds of later historians. In Ramusio's collection of voyages an anonymous

Perplexities caused by the rapid accumulation of geographical facts in the sixteenth century

[1] See above, p. 44.

writer puts into the mouth of Sebastian Cabot
more or less autobiographical narrative, in which
there are almost as many blunders as lines.[1] In
this narrative the death of John Cabot is placed
before 1496, and Sebastian is said to have conducted the first voyage in that year. It thus
happened that until quite recently the discovery
of the continent of North America was attributed to the son, while the father was well-nigh
forgotten. It is to Ramusio's narrator, moreover, that we owe the ridiculous statement —
repeated by almost every historian from that
day to this — that the purpose of the voyage
of 1498 was the discovery of a " northwest passage " to the coast of Asia ! As I shall hereafter
show, the idea of a northwest passage through
or around what we call America to the coast of
Asia did not spring up in men's minds until
after 1522, and it was one of the consequences
of the voyage of Magellan.[2] There is no reason for supposing that Sebastian Cabot in 1498
suspected that the coast before him was anything but that of Asia, and it does not appear
that he contributed anything toward the discovery of the fact that the newly found lands
were part of a new continent, though he lived
long enough to become familiar with that fact,

[1] Ramusio, *Raccolta di Navigationi e Viaggi*, Venice,
1550, tom. 1.

[2] See below, vol. iii. pp. 317–320.

as gradually revealed through the voyages of other navigators.

The slight contemporary mention, which is all that we have of the voyages of the Cabots in 1497 and 1498, does not enable us to determine with precision the parts of the North American coast that were visited. We know that a chart of the first voyage was made, for both the Spanish envoys, Puebla and Ayala, writing between August 24, 1497, and July 25, 1498, mentioned having seen such a chart, and from an inspection of it they concluded that the distance run did not exceed 400 leagues. The Venetian merchant, Pasqualigo, gave the distance more correctly as 700 leagues, and added that Cabot followed the coast of the " territory of the Grand Khan " for 300 leagues, and in returning saw two islands to starboard. An early tradition fixed upon the coast of Labrador as the region first visited, and until lately this has been the prevailing opinion.

What part of North America did the Cabots visit?

The chart seen by the Spanish ministers in London is unfortunately lost. But a map engraved in Germany or Flanders in 1544 or later, and said to be after a drawing by Sebastian Cabot,[1] has at the

Map of 1544, attributed to Sebastian Cabot

---

[1] It was discovered in 1843 in the house of a clergyman in Bavaria, and is now in the National Library at Paris. There is a beautiful facsimile of it in colours in Harrisse's *Jean et Sébastien Cabot,* and it is described by M. d'Avezac, *Bulletin*

north of what we call the island of Cape Breton the legend "*prima tierra vista*," i. e. "*first land seen;*" and in this connection there is a marginal inscription, Spanish and Latin, saying: "This country was discovered by John Cabot, a Venetian, and Sebastian Cabot, his son, in the year of our Saviour Jesus Christ M. CCCC. XCIIII [1] on the 24th of June in the morning, which country they called *prima tierra vista*, and a large island near by they named St. John because they discovered it on the same day." Starting from this information it has been supposed that the navigators, passing this St. John, which we call Prince Edward Island, coasted around the Gulf of St. Lawrence and passed out through the Strait of Belle Isle. The two islands seen on the starboard would then be points on the northern coast of Newfoundland, and a considerable part of Pasqualigo's 300 leagues of coasting would thus be accounted for. But inasmuch as the Matthew had returned to Bristol by the first of August, it may be doubted whether so long a route could have been traversed within five weeks.

If we could be sure that the map of 1544 in its present shape and with all its legends ema-

de la Société de Géographie, 1857, 4ᵉ série, tom. xiv. pp 268–270.

[1] This date is wrong. The first two letters after xc should be joined together at the bottom, making a v.

nated from Sebastian Cabot, and was drawn with
the aid of charts made at the time of discovery,
its authority would be very high indeed. But
there are some reasons for supposing it to have
been amended or "touched up" by the en-
graver, and it is evidently compiled from charts
made later than 1536, for it shows the results
of Jacques Cartier's explorations in the Gulf of
St. Lawrence. Its statement as to the first landfall is, moreover, in conflict with the   Testimony
testimony of the merchant Robert of Robert
Thorne, of Bristol, in 1527,[1] and with Thorne
that of two maps made at Seville in 1527 and
1529, according to which the "prima tierra vista"
was somewhere on the coast of Labrador. It must
be remembered, too, that John Cabot was instructed to take northerly and westerly courses,
not southerly, and an important despatch from
Raimondo de Soncino, in London, to the Duke
of Milan, dated December 18, 1497, describes
his course in accordance with these instructions.
It is perfectly definite and altogether probable.
According to this account Cabot sailed from
Bristol in a small ship, manned by eighteen
persons, and having cleared the western shores
of Ireland, turned northward, after a Cabot's
few days headed for Asia, and stood course, as
 described by
mainly west till he reached " Terra Soncino
Firma," where he planted the royal standard,

[1] Hakluyt, *Principall Navigations*, vol. i. p. 216.

and forthwith returned to England.[1] In other words, he followed the common custom in those days of first running to a chosen parallel, and then following that parallel to the point of destination. Such a course could hardly have landed him anywhere save on the coast of Labrador. Supposing his return voyage simply to have reversed this course, running southeasterly to the latitude of the English Channel and then sailing due east, he may easily have coasted 300 leagues with land to starboard before finally bearing away from Cape Race. This view is in harmony with the fact that on the desolate coasts passed he saw no Indians or other human beings. He noticed the abundance of codfish, however, in the waters about Newfoundland, and declared that the English would no longer need to go to Iceland for their fish. Our in-

[1] " Cum uno piccolo naviglio e xviii persone se pose ala fortuna, et partitosi da Bristo porto occidentale de questo regno et passato Ibernia più occidentale, e poi alzatosi verso il septentrione, comenció ad navigare ale parte orientale [*i. e.* toward eastern Asia], lassandosi (fra qualche giorni) la tramontana ad mano drita, et havendo assai errato, infine capitoe in terra ferma, dove posto la bandera regia, et tolto la possessione per questa Alteza, et preso certi segnali, se ne retornato." See Harrisse, p. 324. The phrase " havendo assai errato " is rendered by Dr. Deane " having wandered about considerably " (Winsor, *Narr. and Crit. Hist.*, iii. 54), but in this context it seems to me rather to mean " having wandered sufficiently far [from Europe]," *i. e.* having gone far enough he found Terra Firma.

formant adds that Master John, being foreign-born and poor, would have been set down as a liar had not his crew, who were mostly Bristol men, confirmed everything he said.

With regard to the coasts visited in the expedition of 1498 our sole contemporary authority is the remarkable map made in 1500 by the Biscayan pilot, Juan de La Cosa, who had sailed with Columbus on his first and second voyages. So far as is known, this is the earliest map in existence made since 1492, and its importance is very great.[1] Las

La Cosa's map, 1500

[1] The original was found and identified by Humboldt in the library of Baron Walckenaer in 1832, and after the death of the latter it was bought April 21, 1853, at an auction sale in Paris, for the queen of Spain against Henry Stevens, for 4020 francs. It is now to be seen at the Naval Museum in Madrid. It was made by La Cosa at Puerto Santa Maria, near Cadiz, at some time between June and October, in the year 1500 (see Leguina, *Juan de La Cosa*, Madrid, 1877, p. 70). It is superbly illuminated with colours and gold. Its scale of proportions, remarkably correct in some places, is notably defective in others. The Newfoundland region is properly brought near to the papal meridian of demarcation, and what we call Brazil is cut by it; which may possibly indicate that La Cosa had heard the news of Cabral's discovery, presently to be noticed, which reached Lisbon late in June. The Azores and Cape Verde Islands are much too far west. The voyages of which the results are distinctly indicated upon the map are the first three of Columbus, the two of the Cabots, that of Ojeda (1498–99), and that of Pinzon (1499–1500), and, as we shall presently see, the map gives very important and striking testimony regarding the first voyage of Vespucius. The coast-

Casas calls La Cosa the best pilot of his day.

The Cabot voyages probably ranged from Labrador, through the Gulf of St. Lawrence, and perhaps as far as Cape Cod

His reputation as a cartographer was also high, and his maps were much admired. The map before us was evidently drawn with honesty and care. It represents the discoveries of the Cabots as extending over 360 leagues of coast, or about as far as from the Strait of Belle Isle to Cape Cod, and the

lines and islands marked by La Cosa with names and flags represent results of actual exploration so far as known to La Cosa or exhibited to him by means of charts or log-books. The coast-lines and islands without names represent in general his unverified theory of the situation. Of the northern island " Frislanda " he must probably have been told by Columbus, for he could not have known anything of the Zeno narrative, first made public in 1558. In the middle of the west side of the map is a vignette representing Christopher (the Christ-bearer) wading through the waters, carrying upon his shoulders the infant Christ or Sun of Righteousness, to shine upon the heathen. At the bottom of the vignette is the legend " Juan de la cosa la fizo en el puerto desta mra en año de 1500." The original is five feet nine inches long by three feet two inches wide, and is a map of the world. The full-sized facsimile published by M. Jomard (in his *Monuments de la géographie*, pl. xvi.) is in three elephant folio sheets. The hypothetical coast-line of Brazil, at the bottom of the third or western sheet, is cut off square, so that the map may be there attached to a roller ; and beyond the cut-off this same coast-line is continued on the first, or eastern sheet, as the coast of Asia east of the Ganges. In the opinion of most geographers of that time, the situation of Quinsay (Hang-chow) in China would come a little to the west of the westernmost English flagstaff.

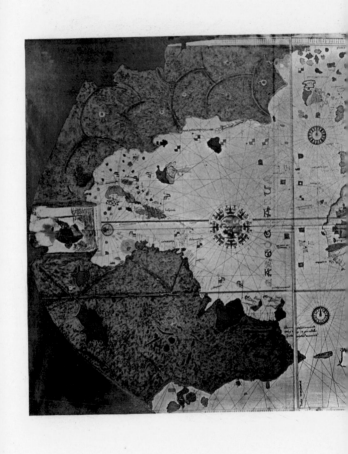

Juan de la Cosa's Map of the World, 1500

Map of the World
made by Columbus's pilot
Juan de la Cosa in the year 1500

names from "Cabo de Ynglaterra" to "Cabo Descubierto" are probably taken from English sources. But whether the coast exhibited is that of the continent within the Gulf of St. Lawrence, or the southern coast of Newfoundland with that of Nova Scotia, is by no means clear.[1] The names end near the mouth of a large river, which may very probably be meant for the St.

---

[1] The former view, which is that of Humboldt, is perhaps the more probable. See Ghillany, *Geschichte des Seefahrers Ritter Martin Behaim*, Nuremberg, 1853, p. 2. The latter view is held by Dr. Kohl (*Documentary History of Maine*, vol. i. p. 154), who identifies "Cabo de Ynglaterra" with Cape Race. To me it seems more likely that Cabo de Ynglaterra is the promontory just north of Invuktoke Inlet on the coast of Labrador, and that the island to the right of it (Ysla Verde) is meant for Greenland. If, then, Isla de la Trinidad is the northern extremity of Newfoundland and the river by Cabo Descubierto is the St. Lawrence, we have a consistent and not improbable view. In spite of the two additional flags, the coast to the left of the St. Lawrence is evidently hypothetical ; the next river is probably meant for the Hoang-ho in China (called by Polo the Caramoran ; see Yule's *Marco Polo*, ii. 104–106), and the "sea discovered by the English" was probably supposed to be the Yellow Sea.

There is no good ground for the statement that Sebastian Cabot sailed as far south as Florida. "The remark of Peter Martyr, in 1515, about Cabot's reaching on the American coast the latitude of Gibraltar, and finding himself then on a meridian of longitude far enough west to leave Cuba on his left, is simply absurd, dilemmatize it as you will. Such a voyage would have landed him near Cincinnati." Stevens, *Historical and Geographical Notes*, p. 35.

Lawrence, and beyond the names we see two more English flags with the legend, " Sea discovered by Englishmen." Inasmuch as it would be eminently possible to sail through the Gulf of St. Lawrence without becoming aware of the existence of Newfoundland, except at the Strait of Belle Isle (which at its narrowest is about ten miles wide), one is inclined to suspect that the " Isla de la Trinidad " may represent all that the voyagers saw of that large island. It is worthy of note that on the so-called Sebastian Cabot map of 1544 Newfoundland does not yet appear as a single mass of land, but as an archipelago of not less than eleven large islands with more than thirty small ones. By this time the reader is doubtless beginning to have " a realizing sense " of the fact that the work of discovering America was not such a simple and instantaneous affair as is often tacitly assumed.

The second voyage of the Cabots was regarded in England as a failure, for the same
Why the Cabot voyages were not followed up
reason that the later voyages of Columbus were regarded with diminishing interest in Spain, because there was much outlay and little profit. Whatever there was to be found on these tantalizing coasts, it surely was not golden Cathay. The inhospi-

mar oceanũ

Cuba

hábana

laespañola

Circulocanern

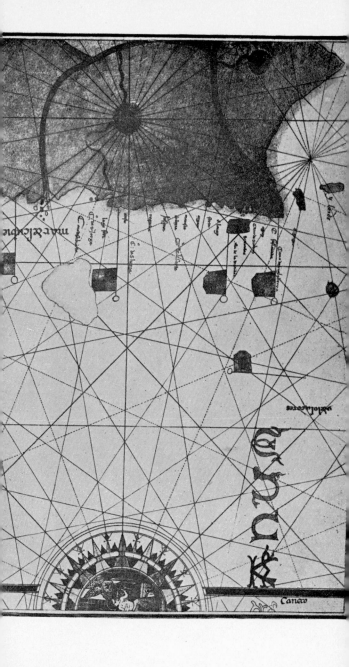

table shores of Labrador offered much less that
was enticing than the balmy valleys of Hispaniola. Furs do not seem as yet to have attracted attention, and although the unrivalled
fisheries were duly observed and reported, it
was some time before the Bristol merchants
availed themselves of this information, for they
considered the Iceland fisheries safer.[1] There
was thus little to encourage the cautious Henry
VII. in further exploration. In 1505 he made a
contract with some sailors from the Azores for a
voyage to " the New-found-land," and one item
of the result may be read in an account-book of
the treasury : " To Portyngales that brought
popyngais and catts of the mountaigne with
other Stuf to the Kinges grace, 5 l." [2]

In the reign of Henry VIII., and in
one and the same year, 1527, we find
mention of two voyages from Portsmouth, the
one conducted by John Rut, in the Samson and
the Mary of Guilford, the other by a certain
Master Grube, in the Dominus Vobiscum, the
latter being perhaps the most obscure of all the
voyages of that century. I suspect that the two
voyages were identical and the reports multi-
farious.[3] Rut's expedition was undertaken, at

*Voyage of
John Rut,
1527*

---

[1] Hunt's *Bristol*, p. 137.

[2] Harrisse, *Jean et Sébastien Cabot*, pp. 142, 272.

[3] See Harrisse, *op. cit.* p. 294.

the instance of Robert Thorne, of Bristol, for the purpose of finding a route to Cathay. It encountered vast icebergs; the Samson was lost with all its crew, and the Mary "durst not go no further to the northward for fear of more ice;" so after reaching Cape Race and the bay of St. John's she returned to England.[1]

We hear of no further enterprises of this sort during the reign of Henry VIII. The lack of interest in maritime discovery is shown by the very small number of books on such matters published in England, — only twelve before 1576.[2] We may suppose that public attention was for the time monopolized by the struggles of the Reformation, and, even had the incentives to western voyages been much stronger than they seem to have been, there was serious risk of their leading to diplomatic complications with Spain. The government of Charles V. kept a lynx-eyed watch upon all trespassers to the west of Borgia's meridian.[3] It was not until the Protestant England of Elizabeth had come to a life and death grapple with Spain,

Change in the situation between the reign of Henry VIII. and that of Elizabeth

[1] Hakluyt, *Principall Navigations*, vol. iii. p. 129; *Purchas his Pilgrimes*, vol. iii. p. 809; Fox-Bourne, *English Merchants*, vol. i. p. 159; De Costa, *Northmen in Maine*, pp. 43–62.

[2] Winsor, *Narr. and Crit. Hist.*, vol. iii. pp. 199–208.

[3] See Harrisse, *op. cit.* p. 146.

and not until the discovery of America had advanced much nearer to completion, so that its value began to be more correctly understood, that political and commercial motives combined in determining England to attack Spain through America, and to deprive her of supremacy in the colonial and maritime world. Then the voyages of the Cabots assumed an importance entirely new, and could be quoted as the basis of a prior claim, on the part of the English Crown, to lands which it had discovered. In view of all that has since happened, as we see these navigators coming upon the scene for a moment in the very lifetime of Columbus, and setting up the royal standard of England upon a bit of the American coast, we may well be reminded of the phrase of prophetic song that heralds a distant but inevitable doom.

La Cosa's map shows that definite information of the Cabot voyages and their results had been sent to Spain before the summer of 1500. Similar information was possessed in Portugal, and the enterprising King Emanuel (who had succeeded John II. in 1495) was led to try what could be accomplished by a voyage to the northwest. Some of the land visited by the Cabots seemed to lie very near Borgia's meridian; perhaps on closer inspection it might be

Portuguese voyages to Labrador; the brothers Cortereal, 1500–1502

233

found to lie to the east of it. There can be little doubt that this was one of the leading motives which prompted the voyages of the brothers Cortereal. Into the somewhat vexed details of these expeditions it is not necessary for our purposes to enter. The brothers Gaspar and Miguel Cortereal were gentlemen of high consideration in Portugal. Two or three voyages were made by Gaspar in the course of the years 1500 and 1501; and from the last voyage two of his ships returned to Lisbon without him, and he was never heard of again. On May 10, 1502, Miguel sailed with three caravels in search of his brother; and again it happened that two of the ships returned in safety, but the commander and his flagship never returned. The incidents of the various voyages are sadly confused; but it seems clear that the coasts visited by Gaspar Cortereal were mainly within the region already explored by the Cabots, from Labrador perhaps as far south as the Bay of Fundy. He probably followed the eastern shores of Newfoundland, and crossed over to Greenland. He brought home wild men (*homines silvestres*) and white bears, as well as a gilded sword-hilt and some silver trinkets of Venetian manufacture which the natives had evidently obtained from the Cabots.[1] The coast

[1] These voyages are ably discussed by M. Harrisse, *Les Corte-Real et leurs voyages au Nouveau Monde*, Paris, 1883;

ich he had followed, or part of it, was deed to lie to the east of the papal meridian
l to belong to Portugal. A despatch dated
ctober 17, 1501, recounting these facts, was
sent to Ercole d' Este, Duke of Ferrara, by his
agent or envoy, Alberto Cantino, then resident
in Lisbon. An elaborate map, concerning which
we shall presently have more to say, was made
for Cantino at a cost of twelve golden ducats,
and carried by him to Italy in the The Cantino
autumn of 1502. This map is now map, 1502
preserved in the Biblioteca Estense at Modena.[1]

see also the accounts in Peschel's *Geschichte des Zeitalters
der Entdeckungen*, 2ᵉ aufl., Stuttgart, 1877; Kunstmann,
Die Entdeckung Amerikas, Münich, 1859; Lafitau, *Histoire
des déouvertes des Portugais dans le Nouveau Monde*, Paris,
1733, 2 vols. 4to; Winsor, *Narr. and Crit. Hist.*, vol. iv.
pp. 1–4, 12–16.

[1] The reproduction here presented gives no idea whatever
of the fulness of detail and the gorgeous beauty of this remarkable map. A full-sized facsimile of the western portion, 3 feet
5¾ inches in width by 3 feet 2½ inches in height, in the
original colours, is to be found in the portfolio accompanying
M. Harrisse's work on the Cortereals. The continents are
given in a soft green, the islands in rich blues and reds. Flags
in their proper colours mark the different sovereignties, from
that of the Turks at Constantinople to that of the Spaniards
near Maracaibo. The two tropics are in red, the equator in
gold, and the papal line of demarcation in a brilliant blue.
Africa is characterized by a hilly landscape in pale blues and
greens, a castellated Portuguese fortress, native huts, negroes
in jet black, birds of various hue, and a huge lion-headed figure in brown and gold. A circular structure called " Tower

On it we see the papal meridian cutting throu[gh] Brazil, and we see the outer coast of Newfou[nd]land laid down to the east of the meridian a[nd] labelled " Land of the King of Portugal." Th[e] southern extremity of Greenland is also depicted with remarkable clearness. The islands afterwards known as West Indies, heretofore known simply as Indies, here appear for the first time as Antilles (*has Antilhas*).

Portuguese sailors were prompt in availing themselves of the treasures of the Newfoundland fisheries. By 1525 a short-lived Portuguese colony had been established on Cape Breton Island.[1] But, as the name of that island reminds of Babilonja '' appears in Egypt, while Russia is marked by a pile of characteristic architecture suggestive of Moscow. Newfoundland, placed to the east of the papal meridian and labelled '' Terra del Rey de Portugall,'' is decked out with trees in green and gold. The Brazilian coast — the southern part of which is given from hearsay, chiefly from the third voyage of Vespucius, who returned to Lisbon September 7, 1502 (as is proved, among other things, by its giving the name of the Bay of All Saints, discovered in that voyage) — is adorned with tall trees in green, gold, and brown, among which are interspersed smaller trees and shrubs in various shades of blue, and three enormous paroquets intensely red, with white beaks and claws, and divers wing and tail feathers in blue, buff, and gold. The ocean is of an ivory tint, and the lettering, sometimes gothic sometimes cursive, is in black and red. Every detail speaks for the intense and loving interest felt in this kind of work.

[1] Souza, *Tratado das Ilhas Novas*, p. 5 ; Harrisse, *Jean et Sébastien Cabot*, p. 76.

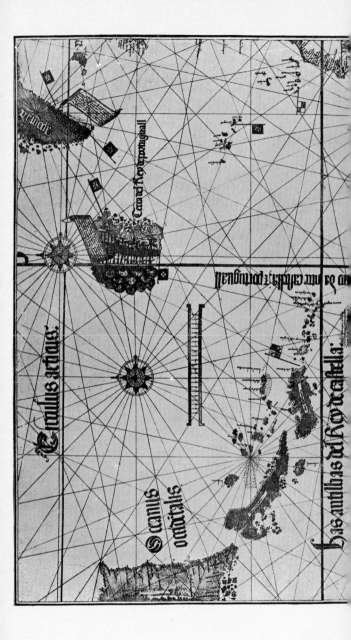

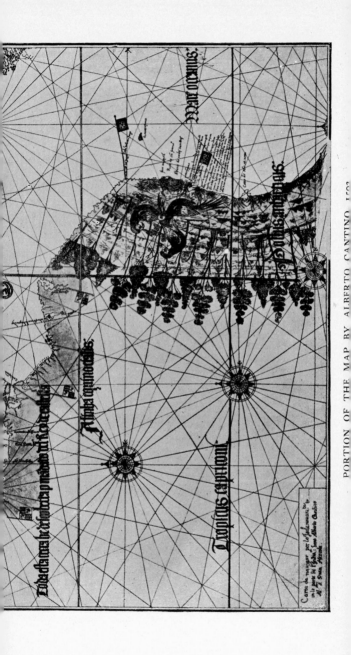

PORTION OF THE MAP BY ALBERTO CANTINO, 1502

us, the Portuguese had sturdy rivals in this work.
As early as 1504 that spot was visited by Breton,
Norman, and Basque sailors, and from that time
forth the fisheries were frequented by all these
people, as well as the Portuguese.[1] The name
" Baccalaos," applied on most of the The New-
early maps to Newfoundland or the foundland
adjacent regions, is the Basque name Baccalaos
for codfish.[2] The English came later upon the

[1] When John Rut reached the bay of St. John's, August 3,
1527, he found two Portuguese, one Breton, and eleven Norman ships fishing there. *Purchas his Pilgrimes*, vol. v. p.
822 ; Harrisse, *Jean et Sébastien Cabot*, p. 75 ; Brown, *History of the Island of Cape Breton*, p. 13.

[2] See the book of the Jesuit father, Georges Fournier, *Hy-
drographie*, 2e éd., Paris, 1667. Peter Martyr is mistaken in
saying that the land was named Baccalaos (by Sebastian Cabot)
because it was the native name for codfish. Gomara's account,
as rendered by Richard Eden, in 1555, is entertaining :
" The newe lande of Baccalaos is a coulde region, whose in-
habitantes are Idolatours and praye to the sonne and moone
and dyuers Idoles. They are whyte people and very rustical,
for they eate flesshe and fysshe and all other things rawe. Sum-
tymes also they eate man's flesshe priuily, so that their Cacique
have no knowledge thereof [!]. The apparell, both of men
and women, is made of beares skynnes, although they have
sables and marternes, not greatly estemed because they are
lyttle. Sum of them go naked in sommer and weare apparell
only in wynter. The Brytons and Frenche men are accus-
tomed to take fysshe in the coastes of these lands, where is
found great plenty of Tunnies which the inhabitauntes caul
Baccalaos, whereof the land was so named. . . . In all this
newe lande is neyther citie nor castell, but they lyue in com-

237

scene. Had England been more prompt in following up the Cabot voyages, there would probably have been a serious dispute, for Portugal did not cease to claim the sovereignty of Newfoundland, on the ground that it lay to the east of the papal meridian, and in those days it was not easy to disprove this assumption.[1] But the question was swallowed up in the events of 1580, when Spain conquered and annexed Portugal; and it was not long after that time that the inability of the Spaniards to maintain their mastery of the sea left the wealth of these fisheries to be shared between France and England.

While these northern voyages are highly interesting in their relations to the subsequent work of English colonization, nevertheless in the history of the discovery of the New World they occupy but a subordinate place. John Cabot was probably the first commander since the days of the Vikings to set foot upon the continent of North America, yet it would be ridiculous to

panies lyke heardes of beastes." *The First Three English Books on America*, Birmingham, 1885, p. 345.

[1] The reader will observe the name of Cortereal upon Newfoundland as an island on Sebastian Münster's map of 1540; as an archipelago on Mercator's map of 1541; and as part of the mainland on Lok's map of 1582. See below, p. 386, and vol. iii. pp. 330, 356.

compare his achievement with that of Columbus. The latter, in spite of its admixture of error with truth, was a scientific triumph of the first order. It was Columbus who showed the way across the Sea of Darkness, and when once he had stood that egg upon its end it was easy enough for others to follow.[1] On the other hand, in so far as the discovery of America was com-pleted when it was made known to Europeans that what Columbus had found was not Asia, but a New World, the northern voyages had absolutely nothing to do with its completion. The causal sequence of events, from Columbus to Magellan, which brought out the fact that a New World had been discovered, would not have been altered if the voyages of the Cabots had never been made. It was only by voyages to the south that the eyes of Europeans could be opened to the real significance of what was going on. Our attention is thus directed to the famous navigator who, without himself under-standing the true state of the case, nevertheless

As links in the chain of discovery, the northern voyages were far less impor-tant than the southern

[1] The anecdote of Columbus and the egg is told by Ben-zoni, *Historia del Mondo Nuovo*, Venice, 1572, p. 12. It belongs to the class of migratory myths, having already been told of Brunelleschi, the great architect who built the dome of the cathedral at Florence about 1420. As Voltaire says, in this connection, "La plupart des bons mots sont des redites." *Essai sur les Mœurs*, tom. iii. p. 351.

went far toward revealing it. The later voyages of Vespucius began to give a new meaning to the work of Columbus, and prepared the way for the grand consummation by Magellan.

Amerigo Vespucci[1] was born at Florence on the 18th of March, 1452 (N. S.). He was the third son of Anastasio Vespucci and Lisabetta Mini. The family was old and respectable, and had been wealthy. Anastasio was a notary public. His brother Giorgio Antonio was a Dominican monk, an accomplished Hellenist in those days of the Renaissance, and a friend of the martyr Savonarola. One of Amerigo's brothers, Antonio, studied at the University of Pisa. The second, Jerome, engaged in some business which took him to Palestine, where he suffered many hardships. Amerigo was educated by his uncle, the

Early life of Americus Vespucius

[1] Amerigo, Amerrigo, Merigo, Morigo, Almerico, Alberico, Alberigo ; Vespucci, Vespucy, Vespuchy, Vespuche, Vesputio, Vespulsius, Espuchi, Despuchi ; latinized Americus Vespucius. *Amerigo* is an italianized form of the old German *Amalrich* (not Emmerich), which in mediæval French became *Amaury*. It means "the steadfast" ("celui qui endure des labeurs"). See Humboldt, *Examen critique*, tom. iv. pp. 52–57. This derivation would naturally make the accent fall upon the penult, *Amerígo, Americus ;* and thus light seems to be thrown upon the scanning of George Herbert's verses, written in 1631, during the Puritan exodus : —

> "Religion stands on tip-toe in our land,
> Readie to passe to the American strand."
> *The Church Militant*, 235.

Dominican, who seems to have had several youth under his care ; among these fellow-students was the famous Piero Soderini, afterward gonfaloniere of Florence from 1502 to 1512.[1] Amerigo acquired some knowledge of Latin and was sufficiently affected by the spirit of the age to be fond of making classical quotations, but his scholarship did not go very far. At some time, however, if not in his early years, he acquired an excellent practical knowledge of astronomy, and in the art of calculating latitudes and longitudes he became an expert unsurpassed by any of his contemporaries.[2] After his school-days were over, he was taken into the great commercial house of the Medici, and seems to have led an uneventful life at Florence until he was nearly forty years of age.[3] He devoted his lei-

[1] See Guicciardini, *Storia Fiorentina*, cap. xxv. ; Trollope's *History of the Commonwealth of Florence*, vol. iv. pp. 294, 337.

[2] See the testimony of Sebastian Cabot and Peter Martyr, and Humboldt's remarks in connection therewith, in *Examen critique*, tom. iv. pp. 144, 183, 191 ; tom. v. p. 36. Considering his strong inclination for astronomical studies, one is inclined to wonder whether Vespucius may not have profited by the instruction or conversation of his fellow-townsman Toscanelli. How could he fail to have done so ?

[3] What little is known of the early life of Vespucius is summed up in Bandini, *Vita e lettere di Amerigo Vespucci*, Florence, 1745. The only intelligent modern treatise on the life and voyages of this navigator is Varnhagen's collection of monographs — *Amerigo Vespucci: son caractère, ses écrits*

sure hours to the study of geography, and was an eager collector of maps, charts, and globes. On one occasion he paid 130 golden ducats for a map made in 1439 by Gabriel de Valsequa.[1] He also became an expert map-maker himself,[2]

(*même les moins authentiques*), *sa vie et ses navigations*, Lima, 1865 ; *Le premier voyage de Amerigo Vespucci définitivement expliqué dans ses détails*, Vienna, 1869 ; *Nouvelles recherches sur les derniers voyages du navigateur florentin, et le reste des documents et éclaircissements sur lui*, Vienna, 1869 ; *Postface aux trois livraisons sur Amerigo Vespucci*, Vienna, 1870 ; *Ainda Amerigo Vespucci : novos estudos e achegas especialmente em favor da interpretacão dada á sua la viagem em 1497–98*, Vienna, 1874. These are usually bound together in one small folio volume. Sometimes the French monographs are found together without the Portuguese monograph. Varnhagen's book has made everything else antiquated, and no one who has not mastered it in all its details is entitled to speak about Vespucius. In the English language there is no good book on the subject. The defence by Lester and Foster (*Life and Voyages of Americus Vespucius*, New York, 1846) had some good points for its time, but is now utterly antiquated and worse than useless. The chapter by the late Sydney Howard Gay, in Winsor's *Narrative and Critical History*, vol. ii. chap. ii., is quite unworthy of its place in that excellent work ; but its defects are to some extent atoned for by the editor's critical notes.

[1] In 1848 this map " was still in the library of Count de Montenegro at Palma, in the island of Majorca." Harrisse, *Bibliotheca Americana Vetustissima, Additions*, p. xxiii. It is the only relic of Vespucius to which we can point as existing in the present century.

[2] " I repayred to the byshoppe of Burges [Fonseca] beinge the chiefe refuge of this nauigation. As wee were therefore

and along with such tastes one can easily see
how there was a latent love of adventure which
it only required circumstances to bring out. He
seems in these earlier years, as throughout his
life, to have won and retained the respect of
all who knew him, as a man of integrity and
modesty, quiet, but somewhat playful in manner, mild and placable in temper, and endowed
with keen intelligence. He seems to have been
of middle height, and somewhat brawny, with
aquiline features and olive complexion, black
eyes and hair, and a mouth at once firm and refined.

The Medici had important business interests
in Spain, and at some time between the midsummer of 1489 and the end of 1491   Vespucius
they sent Vespucius to Barcelona as   goes to Spain
their confidential agent. He took with him
several young Florentines who had been placed
under his care, and among them his own nephew,
Giovanni (afterwards spanished into Juan) Ves-

secretly togyther in one chamber, we had many instrumentes
perteynynge to these affayres, as globes and many of those
mappes which are commonly cauled the shipmans cardes, or
cardes of the sea. Of the which, one was drawen by the Por-
tugales, whereunto Americus Vesputius is sayde to have put
his hande, beinge a man moste experte in this facultie and a
Florentyne borne ; who also vnder the stipende of the Portu-
gales hadde sayled towarde the south pole.'' Peter Martyr,
Decades of the Newe Worlde, Eden's translation, 1555, dec.
ii. lib. x.

pucci, a very capable youth who accompanied
him in some if not all his voyages, and lived to
be regarded as one of the most accomplished
navigators and cosmographers of the age.[1] Early
in 1493 Americus seems to have formed some
sort of connection with the Florentine commercial house of Juanoto Berardi, at Seville.[2] This
Berardi, who had been domiciled in Spain for
more than nine years and was a friend of Columbus, was employed by the Crown in fitting out
ships for the Atlantic voyages. On the 9th of
April, 1495, we find him signing a contract en-

[1] " The younge Vesputius is one to whom Americus Vesputius his vncle left the exact knowledge of the mariners facultie, as it were by inheritance after his death, for he was a
very expert maister in the knowledge of his carde, his com-
passe, and the eleuation of the pole starre with all that per-
teineth therto. . . . Vesputius is my verye familyar frende,
and a wyttie younge man in whose coompany I take great
pleasure, and therefore vse hym oftentymes for my geste."
Peter Martyr, *Decades of the Newe Worlde*, Eden's translation, 1555, dec. iii. lib. v.

[2] " Vostra Mag. sapra, come el motiuo della venuta mia in
questo regno di Spagna fu p' tractare mercatantie : & come
seguissi in q'sto proposito circa di quattro anni : nequalli uiddi
& connobbi edisuariati mouime'ti della fortuna ; . . . delib-
erai *lasciarmi della mercantia* & porre elmio fine in cosa piu
laudabile & ferma : che fu che midisposi dandare a uedere
parte del mondo, & le sue marauiglie." *Lettera di Amerigo Vespucci delle isole nuouamente trouate in quattro suoi
viaggi*, — written to Soderini from Lisbon, September 4,
1504 ; primitive text reprinted in Varnhagen, Lima, 1865,
p. 35.

gaging to furnish twelve vessels with an aggregate burthen of 900 tons, and to have four of them ready that same month, four more in June, and the rest in September.[1] We shall presently find this contract quite interesting and its date eloquent. In December of that same year Berardi died, and we find Vespucius taking his place and fulfilling what remained to be fulfilled of the contract and sundry obligations growing out of it. From the above facts the statement, often made, that Vespucius took part in fitting out the second voyage of Columbus is quite probable. He can hardly have failed to become acquainted with Columbus in the summer of 1493, if he had not known him before. The relations between the two seem always to have been most cordial;[2] and after the admiral's death his sons seem to have continued to hold the Florentine navigator in high esteem.

Our information concerning Americus Vespucius, from the early part of the year 1496 until after his return from the Portuguese to the Spanish service in the latter part of 1504, rests primarily upon his two famous letters: the one addressed to his

His letters to Medici and Soderini

---

[1] See the document in Varnhagen, p. 93 ; Navarrete, tom. ii. pp. 159–162.

[2] See the admiral's letter to his son Diego, dated February 5, 1505, in Navarrete, tom. i. p. 351.

old patron Lorenzo di Pier Francesco de' Medici (a cousin of Lorenzo the Magnificent) and written in March or April, 1503, giving an account of his third voyage;[1] the other addressed to his old school-fellow Piero Soderini and dated from Lisbon, September 4, 1504, giving a brief account of four voyages which he had made under various commanders in the capacity of astronomer or pilot.[2] These letters, for reasons presently to be set forth, became speedily

---

[1] The earliest Latin and Italian texts are given in Varnhagen, pp. 9–26.

[2] The primitive Italian text and the famous Latin version presently to be noticed are given in Varnhagen, pp. 33–64.

Varnhagen prints three other letters, attributed to Vespucius, which have been often quoted. They are all addressed to Lorenzo di Pier Francesco de' Medici: 1. relating to the second voyage, and dated July 18, 1500, first published in 1745 by Bandini; it is unquestionably a forgery, not older than the seventeenth century, and has done much to bemuddle the story of Vespucius; 2. dated from Cape Verde, June 4, 1501, while starting on the third voyage, first published in 1827 by Baldelli; the document itself is not original, but I am inclined to think it may perhaps be made up from genuine notes or memoranda; 3. relating to the third voyage, and dated 1502, first published in 1789 by Bartolozzi. I do not regard it as genuine, but as it adds nothing to what is contained in the genuine letters, the point is of no great importance.

A Spanish letter from Vespucius to Cardinal Ximenes is published by Augusto Zeri, in his *Tre Lettere di Colombo e Vespucci*, Rome, 1881; but it has no reference to the questions discussed in the present chapter.

popular, and many editions were published, more especially in France, Germany, and Italy. It is extremely improbable that proof-sheets of any of these editions could ever have been read by the author, and it is perfectly clear that if his eye ever rested at any time upon the few strange errors of editing and proof-reading which were destined to embroil and perplex his story in the minds of future generations, he could not possibly have foreseen or dimly surmised what wretched complications were going to flow from the slight admixtures of error in the printed text. For Americus died, as Columbus had died, without ever having suspected the real significance of the discoveries in which he had been concerned.

The letter to Soderini gives an account of four voyages in which the writer took part, the first two in the service of Spain, the other two in the service of Portugal. The first expedition sailed from Cadiz May 10, 1497, and returned October 15, 1498, after having explored a coast so long as to seem unquestionably that of a continent. This voyage, as we shall see, was concerned with parts of America not visited again until 1513 and 1517. It discovered nothing that was calculated to invest it with much importance in Spain, though it by no means passed without notice there, as has often been wrongly asserted.

The four voyages described in the letters: First voyage

Outside of Spain it came to attract more attention, but in an unfortunate way, for a slight but very serious error in proof-reading or editing in the most important of the Latin versions caused it after a while to be practically identified with the second voyage, made two years later. This confusion eventually led to most outrageous imputations upon the good name of Americus, which it has been left for the present century to remove.

The second voyage of Vespucius was that in which he accompanied Alonso de Ojeda and Second voyage Juan de La Cosa, from May 20, 1499, to June, 1500. They explored the northern coast of South America from some point on what we would now call the north coast of Brazil, as far as the Pearl Coast visited by Columbus in the preceding year; and they went beyond, as far as the Gulf of Maracaibo. Here the squadron seems to have become divided, Ojeda going over to Hispaniola in September, while Vespucius remained cruising till February.

In the autumn of 1500, or early in 1501, at the invitation of King Emanuel of Portugal, Third voyage Vespucius transferred his services to that country. His third voyage was from Lisbon, May 14, 1501, to September 7, 1502. He pursued the Brazilian coast as far as latitude 34° S., and ran thence S. E., as far as the island of South Georgia. I shall presently show why it was that such a voyage, into this wholly new part of the world, excited public curiosity even more keenly than those of Columbus and Gama, and how curiously but naturally it led to the placing of the name "America" upon the map.

In a fourth voyage, from June 10, 1503, to June 18, 1504, Vespucius, with Gonzalo Coelho, undertook to follow the Brazilian coast Fourth to its end or until they should find voyage some passage into the Indian Ocean. This expedition met with disasters, and after reaching latitude 23° S., Vespucius returned to Lisbon without accomplishing anything.

In the autumn of 1504 Americus returned to the service of Spain with the rank of captain and a salary of 30,000 maravedis. He Later voyages went on two more voyages, in company with La Cosa, in 1505 and 1507, for the exploration of the Gulf of Urabá and the coasts adjoining. It seems to have been early in 1505 that he married a Spanish lady, Maria Cerezo, and became legally domiciled at Seville. On the 22d of March, 1508, because of the growing interest in voyages to the Indies and the increasing number of squadrons equipped for such a purpose, the government created the highly responsible office of Pilot Major of Spain. It was to be the duty of this officer to institute

249

and superintend examinations for all candidates for the position of pilot, to judge of their proficiency in practical astronomy and navigation, and to issue certificates of competence to the successful candidates. Such work involved the establishment and supervision of regular methods of training in nautical science. The pilot major was also general inspector of maps, globes, and sailing charts, and he was expected to provide for the compilation of a "Carta Padron Real," or authoritative government map, which was to be revised and amended with reference to new information brought home by pilots from the Indies year after year.[1] On the 6th of August, 1508, this important office was conferred upon Vespucius, with a salary of 75,000 maravedis. It was but a short time that Americus lived to discharge the duties of pilot major. After his death, which occurred at Seville, February 22, 1512, he was succeeded in that office by Juan Diaz de Solis, who in turn was succeeded by Sebastian Cabot.

Vespucius appointed Pilot Major of Spain

His death

In view of the Egyptian darkness that has heretofore enveloped, and in the popular mind still surrounds, the subject of Americus Vespu-

[1] The official document describing the duties and powers of the pilot major is given in Navarrete, *Coleccion de viages,* tom. iii. pp. 299–302.

cius and his voyages, it has seemed advisable to complete the mere outline of the events of his life before entering into discussion, in the hope of showing where the truth is to be found and how the mistakes have been made. The reader will find it convenient to bear in mind this simple outline sketch while I now return to the consideration of the first and second voyages, and point out how the mystery that has so long surrounded them has been in great part cleared away and seems likely erelong to be completely dispelled.

First we must note the character of our primary and only detailed authority for the events of all four voyages, the letter from Vespucius to Soderini, dated Lisbon, September 4, 1504. Observe that this is not a formal or official document; it is not a report from a naval commander or the conductor of a scientific expedition to the head of his department. It is the business of such official reports to give names and incidents, dates and distances, and all relevant statistical information, with the greatest possible fulness and precision ; and if there is any noticeable deficiency in this regard, we are entitled to blame the writer. With informal letters written to one's friends the case is very different. If Vespucius, in sending to his old schoolmate a cursory account of his adventures during seven years past,

The letter from Vespucius to Soderini

failed to mention sundry details which it annoys and puzzles us not to know, we have no business to find fault with him. He had a perfect right to tell his story in his own way. He was writing to a friend, not posing for posterity. Some querulous critics have blamed him for not mentioning the names of his commanders, as if he were intending to convey a false impression of having commanded in these voyages himself. No such impression is conveyed to the reader, however, but quite the contrary. On the first voyage Americus describes himself as invited by King Ferdinand to "assist" in the enterprise; as to his position in the second voyage there is no implication whatever; as to the third and fourth he expressly mentions that he served under other captains. His whole letter shows plainly enough that on his most important voyages he went in the capacity of "astronomer." During the latter half of the fifteenth century, as voyages were extending farther and farther into unknown stretches of sea, it became customary to sail with such an officer on board. Each ship had its captain, its "master" (or mate), and its pilot; and for the squadron, besides its captain-general, and its chief pilot, expert in the knack and mystery of navigation, there was apt to be (whenever it was possible to find one) a person well skilled in the astrolabe,

He went on his earlier voyages in the capacity of astronomer

fertile in expedients for determining longitude, and familiar with the history of voyages and with the maps and speculations of learned geographers. Sometimes there was a commander, like Columbus, who combined all these accomplishments in himself; but in the case of many captains, even of such superb navigators as Pinzon and La Cosa, much more in the case of land-lubbers like Bastidas and Ojeda, it was felt desirable to have the assistance of a specialist in cosmography. Such was evidently the position occupied by Vespucius; and occasions might and did arise in which it gave him the control of the situation, and made the voyage, for all historical purposes, his voyage.

It is certainly much to be regretted that in the narrative of his first expedition Vespucius did not happen to mention the name of the chief commander. If he had realized what a world of trouble one little name, such as Pinzon, would have saved us he would doubtless have obliged us by doing so. However, as already observed, he was writing not for us, but for his friend, and he told Soderini only what he thought would interest him. In his preface Americus somewhat playfully apologizes for presuming to intrude upon that magistrate's arduous cares of state with so long a letter. He accordingly refrains from giving professional details, except in stating latitudes and longitudes and distances run, and even here he leaves gaps and contents himself with general statements that to us are sometimes far from satisfactory. He also gives very few proper names of places, either those supposed to be current among the natives, or those applied by the discoverers. But of such facts as would be likely to interest Soderini he gives plenty. He de-

Character of his descrip-tions

scribes, with the keen zest of a natu-ralist, the beasts, birds, and fishes, the trees, herbs, and fruits, of the countries visited; their climates, the stars in their firmament, the personal appearance and habits of the natives, their food and weapons, their houses and canoes, their ceremonies and their diversity of tongues. Such details as these proved intensely interest-ing, not only to Soderini, but to many another reader, as was shown by the wide circulation obtained by the letter when once it had found its way into print. In an age when Pope Leo X. sat up all night reading the " Decades " of Peter Martyr, curiosity and the vague sense of wonder were aroused to the highest degree, and the facts observed by Vespucius — although told in the hurried and rambling style of an offhand epistle — were well adapted to satisfy and further to stimulate these cravings. But for the modern investigator, engaged upon the problem of determining precise localities in tropical America, these descriptions are too general. They may sometimes be made to apply to more than one region, and we are again reminded of the difficulty which one finds in describing a walk or drive over country roads and making it intelligible to others without the aid of *recognized proper names*. The reader will please note these italics, for it is an error in proper names that has been chiefly responsible for the complicated misunderstandings that have done such injustice to Vespucius.

In the letter to Lorenzo de' Medici, written about April, 1503, reference is made to a book, or group of three pamphlets, which Vespucius had already written, giving a definite and detailed account of his voyages. He tells Lorenzo that the pamphlet describing the third voyage is now in the hands of the king of Portugal, and he hopes it will soon be returned to him. He hopes at some future day, when more at leisure, to utilize these materials in writing a treatise on cosmography, in order that posterity may remember him and that God's creative work in a region unknown to the ancients may be made known. If God shall spare his life until he can settle down quietly at Florence, he hopes then, with the aid and counsel of learned men, to be able to complete such a book.[1] But just now he is

The Quattro Giornate, the lost book of Vespucius

---

[1] " Vt si quando mihi ocium dabitur possim omnia hec singularia atque mirabilia colligere, et vel geographie vel cosmo-

about to start on a fourth voyage, the results of which will probably need to be added to the book. In the letter to Soderini, written seventeen months later, after the return from the fourth voyage, Americus refers more than once to this book, under the title "Four Journeys" (*Quattro Giornate*). It is not yet published, he says, because he needs more time to revise it; in this narrative everything will be minutely described.[1] It is thus quite clear why Vespucius was not more explicit in his letters; and we can also well understand how his arduous duties as Pilot Major of Spain would delay the publication of his book until discourteous death [2] overtook him. Unfortunately, while versions of the hastily written letters, intended only for the mo-

graphie librum conscribere : ut mei recordatio apud posteros vivat, & omnipotentis dei cognoscatur tam immensum artificium in parte priscis ignotum, nobis autem cognitum. . . . Patriam & quietem repetere conabor, vbi & cum peritis conferre : & ab amicis id opus proficiendum confortari et adjuvari valeam." Varnhagen, p. 25.

[1] " In questa gente, & in loro terra conobbi & uiddi tanti de loro costumi & lor modi di uiuere, che no' curo di allargharmi in epsi : perche sapra V. M. come in ciascuno delli miei uiaggi ho notate le cose piu marauigliose : & tutto ho ridocto in un uolume in stilo di geografia : & le intitulo Le Quattro Giornate : nella quale opera sicontiene le cose p, minuto & per anchora no' sene data fuora copia, perche me necessario conferirla." Varnhagen, p. 45.

[2] " Morte villana ;" see Dante, *Vita Nuova*, viii., and Professor Norton's charming version.

ment, have survived, the manuscript of the carefully written book, so conscientiously withheld
until it could be perfected, has perished.[1]

As for the letters themselves, the manuscripts
are nowhere forthcoming, and until lately it has
been maintained that none of the printed texts
are originals, but that all are reprints
from a primitive text that has been
lost. Of the letter to Soderini the version which has played the most important part in history is the Latin one first
published at the press of the little college at
Saint-Dié in Lorraine, April 25 (vij Kl' Maij),
1507. We shall presently have more to say
about the remarkable book in which this version appears; suffice it here to observe that it
was translated, not from an original text, but
from an intermediate French version, which is
lost. Of late years, however, we have detected,
in an excessively rare Italian text, the original

*The Latin
version
(1507) of
the letter to
Soderini*

---

[1] One hesitates to say too positively about any book that it
has perished. Things have such queer ways of turning up,
as for instance Aristotle's treatise on the government of Athens,
after its Rip Van Winkle slumber of two thousand years. Of
a certain copy of Oviedo's first folio (Toledo, 1526) M.
Harrisse observes : " The only other copy which we know of
this extremely rare book is in Havana, and was found in a
Madrid butcher's stall, as the illiterate dealer in meat was
tearing it to wrap a sirloin of beef which a pretty *manola*
had just purchased." *Notes on Columbus*, New York, 1866,
p. 13.

from which the famous Lorraine version was ultimately derived. Of this little book M. Har-

Recent discovery of the primitive Italian text, 1505–06

risse was able in 1872 to mention four copies as still existing,—one in the Palatine Library at Florence, one in the library of the Marquis Gino Capponi in that city, one in the British Museum, and one purchased at Havana in 1863 by the eminent Brazilian historian, Francisco Adolpho de Varnhagen, Viscount de Porto Seguro. This last-named copy had once been in the Cartuja at Seville, and it was bound in vellum together with a tract of St. Basil, printed at Florence by the printer Gian Stefano di Carlo di Pavia, for the publisher Pietro Pacini, of Pescia, in 1506. From the manner in which the edges of the leaves were gnawed it was evident that the two tracts had been within the same cover for a great length of time. Closer examination showed that they were printed from the same font of type; and a passage in Girolamo Priuli's diary, dated July 9, 1506, says that the voyages of Vespucius have already been printed.[1] If we were absolutely sure that this statement refers to this edition, it would settle its date beyond all question; but as there is no other edition ever heard

---

[1] "Questa navigazione, e la natura delle persone, e li viaggi, e li venti, e tutto sono in stampa notati con gran intelligenza." Foscarini, *Letteratura veneziana,* Padua, 1752, p. 179.

TITLE-PAGE OF THE LETTER FROM VESPUCIUS TO
SODERINI, 1505–1506

of or known to have existed to which it can
possibly refer, the circumstantial evidence becomes exceedingly strong. Moreover the language of this text is a corrupt Italian, abounding
in such Spanish and Portuguese words and turns
of expression as Vespucius would have been
likely, during fourteen years of residence in the
Iberian peninsula and of association with its
sailors, to incorporate into his every-day speech.
This fact is very significant, for if a book thus
printed in Florence were a translation from anything else, its language would be likely to be
the ordinary Italian of the time, not a jargon
salted with Atlantic brine. Altogether it seems
in the highest degree probable that we have
here the primitive text, long given up for lost,
of the ever memorable letter from Vespucius to
his former schoolmate Soderini.[1]

[1] The title of this edition is *Lettera di Amerigo Vespucci
delle isole nuouamente trouate in quattro suoi viaggi*, sixteen
unnumbered leaves in quarto. It is No. 87 in Harrisse's *Bibliotheca Americana Vetustissima*, New York, 1866, where
the date 1516 is conjecturally assigned it ; but that date is
clearly wrong, as M. Harrisse has since recognized. In the
Additions (Paris, 1872) to his great work he is inclined to
adopt Varnhagen's date, 1505–1506, and considers it "almost certain" that this text was the original source of the
Lorraine Latin version published April 25, 1507. M. d'Avezac is of the same opinion ; see his *Martin Waltzemüller*,
p. 46. For the whole argument, see Varnhagen, *Amerigo Vespucci*, pp. 27–31. This primitive text is reproduced, page
for page and line for line, with all its typographical peculiari-

If now we compare this primitive text with the Latin of the Lorraine version of 1507, we observe that in the latter one proper name — the Indian name of a place visited by Americus on his first voyage — has been altered. In the original it is *Lariab*; in the Latin it has become *Parias*. This looks like an instance of injudicious editing on the part of the Latin translator, although, of course, it may be a case of careless proof-reading. Lariab is a queer-looking word. It is no wonder that a scholar in his study among the mountains of Lorraine could make nothing of it. If he had happened to be acquainted with the language of the Huastecas, who dwelt at that time about the river Panuco, — fierce and dreaded enemies of their southern neighbours, the Aztecs, — he would have known that names

Change of the Indian name *Lariab* into the Indian name *Parias* in the Latin version of 1507; original source of all the calumny against Americus

ties and its few quaint wood cuts, by Varnhagen. Mr. Quaritch (*Rough List*, No. 111, April 16, 1891, p. 52) says there are five copies extant. He bought one for £524 at the sale of the late Dr. Court's library at Paris in 1884; and it is now, I believe, in the library of Mr. C. H. Kalbfleisch, of New York. From this original Mr. Quaritch published in 1885 a facsimile reproduction, which may be bought for five guineas, and an English translation, price two guineas and a half; so that now for the first time since the discovery of America an English reader not thoroughly at home in Italian thickly interlarded with Spanish and Portuguese can see for himself what Vespucius really said.

of places in that region were apt to end in *ab*
(Tanlajab, Tancuayalab, Tancuallalab),[1] very
much as English names of towns are apt to end
in *ham* and Persian names of countries in *stan*.
But as such facts were quite beyond our worthy
translator's ken, we cannot much blame him if
he felt that such a word as Lariab needed doc-
toring. Parias (Paria) was known to be the native name of a region on the western shores of
the Atlantic, and so Lariab became Parias. As
the distance from the one place to the other is
more than two thousand miles, this little emendation shifted the scene of the first voyage beyond all recognition, and cast the whole subject
into an outer darkness where there has since
been much groaning and gnashing of teeth.

Another curious circumstance came in to con-
firm this error. On his first voyage, shortly
before arriving at Lariab, Vespucius
saw an Indian town built over the
water, "like Venice." He counted
forty-four large wooden houses, "like
barracks," supported on huge tree-
trunks and communicating with each other by
bridges that could be drawn up in case of danger. This may well have been a village of
communal houses of the Chontals on the coast

How the " little wooden Venice " aided and abetted the error

[1] Orozco y Berra, *Geografía de lengoas y carta etnográfica
de México*, p. 289 ; Varnhagen, *Le premier voyage de Vespucci*, p. 20.

of Tabasco; but such villages were afterwards seen on the Gulf of Maracaibo, and one of them was called Venezuela,[1] or "Little Venice," a name since spread over a territory nearly twice as large as France. So the amphibious town described by Vespucius was incontinently moved to Maracaibo, as if there could be only one such place, as if that style of defensive building had not been common enough in many ages and in many parts of the earth, from ancient Switzerland to modern Siam. Such "little Venices" might once have been seen near the mouth of the Amazon, and there is now, or has lately been, a similar town named Bodegas, on the coast of Ecuador, near Guayaquil.[2]

Thus *in spite of the latitudes and longitudes distinctly stated by Vespucius in his letter* did Lariab and the little wooden Venice get shifted from the Gulf of Mexico to the northern coast of South America. Now there is no question that Vespucius in his second voyage, with Ojeda for captain, did sail along that coast, visit-

The charge that Vespucius feigned to have discovered the coast of Paria in 1497

---

[1] The name occurs in this place on La Cosa's map, which thus confirms the common statement that Ojeda found such a village on his first voyage (Vespucius's second) in 1499. Ojeda at first called the gulf "the lake of St. Bartholomew," because he discovered it on the 24th of August; some years afterward he spoke of it as "gulf of Venice" (*golfo de Venecia*). See Navarrete, *Coleccion*, tom. iii. p. 8.

[2] Varnhagen, *Le premier voyage de Vespucci*, p. 13.

ing the gulfs of Paria and Maracaibo. This was
in the summer of 1499, one year after a part of
the same coast had been visited by Columbus.
Hence in a later period, long after the actors in
these scenes had been gathered unto their fathers,
and when people had begun to wonder how the
New World could ever have come to be called
America instead of Columbia, it was suggested
that the first voyage described by Vespucius
must be merely a clumsy and fictitious duplicate
of the second, and that he invented it and thrust
it back from 1499 to 1497, in order
that he might be accredited with the
"discovery of the continent" one year
in advance of his friend Columbus.
It was assumed that he must have
written his letter to Soderini with the base intention of supplanting his friend, and that the
shabby device was successful. This explanation
seemed so simple and intelligible that it became
quite generally adopted, and it held its ground
until the subject began to be *critically* studied
and Alexander von Humboldt showed, about
sixty years ago, that the first naming of America occurred in no such way as had been supposed.

As soon as we refrain from projecting our
modern knowledge of geography into the past,
as soon as we pause to consider how these great
events appeared to the actors themselves, the

263

absurdity of this accusation against Americus
becomes evident. We are told that he falsely
pretended to have visited Paria and Maracaibo
in 1497, in order to claim priority over Columbus in the discovery of " the continent." What
continent? When Vespucius wrote that letter
to Soderini, in 1504, neither he nor
anybody else suspected that what we
now call America had been discovered.

Absurdity inherent in the charge

The only continent of which there could be
any question, so far as supplanting Columbus
was concerned, was Asia. But in 1504 Columbus was generally supposed to have discovered
the continent of Asia, by his new route, in 1492.
In that year and in 1494, taking the two voyages together, he had sailed more than a thousand miles along the coast of Cuba without
detecting its insular character. As the history
of that time has always, until very lately, been
written, we have been told that the insularity
of Cuba was first revealed by Sebastian de
Ocampo, who circumnavigated it in 1508. If
this opinion were correct, Americus could not
possibly have undertaken to antedate Columbus
with his figure 1497; it would have been necessary for him to feign a voyage earlier than
the autumn of 1492. As I shall presently show,
however, Americus probably did know, in 1504,
that Cuba was an island, inasmuch as in 1497–98
he had passed to the west of it himself, touch-

ing the coasts of both Yucatan and Florida! If this view is correct, then he did visit what we now know to have been the continent of America, but which he supposed to be the continent of Asia, a year in advance of Columbus, and of course the accusation against him falls to the ground. From this dilemma there seems to be no escape.

The perplexity surrounding the account of the first voyage of Vespucius is therefore chiefly due to the lack of intelligence with which it has been read. There is no reason whatever for imagining dishonesty in his narrative, and no reason for not admitting it as evidence on the same terms as those upon which we admit other contemporary documents. The court presumes the witness to be truthful until adequate reason has been alleged for a contrary presumption. What, then, are we to conclude in the case of this voyage of 1497?

The evidence that no such voyage was made in that year *along the Pearl Coast* is as strong as it is possible for negative evidence to be; indeed it seems unanswerable. We have seen how Columbus, owing to his troubles with rebellious Spaniards and the machinations of his enemy Fonseca, was deprived of his government of Hispaniola, and how he ended his days in poverty and neglect, vainly urging King Ferdinand (as acting regent of Castile) to reinstate him in the dignities and emoluments which had been secured to him by solemn compact under the royal seal in April, 1492. The right to these dignities and emoluments was inherited by his eldest son, Don Diego Columbus, and that young man was earnest in pressing his claims. He urged that Ovando should be recalled from Hispaniola and himself duly installed as viceroy of the Indies, with his percentage of the revenues accruing from Hispaniola, the Pearl Coast, and such other regions as his father had discovered. Whether these claims of Diego would ever have received any recognition, except for one fortunate circumstance, may be doubted. Diego seems to have inherited his father's good fortune in winning the hearts of aristocratic ladies. He had lived in the royal household since he was taken there as a page in 1492, and in 1508 he married a princess, Maria de Toledo, whose paternal grandmother was sister to the mother of Ferdinand the Catholic.[1] The next year Ovando was recalled from Hispaniola, and Diego, accompanied by his bride and many people from the court, went out and assumed the government of the Indies.[2] The king, however, was not prepared to admit the full claims of Diego

Claims of Diego Columbus

---

[1] See Harrisse, *Christophe Colomb*, tom. ii. p. 247.

[2] Herrera, dec. i. cap. vii. p. 189; Oviedo, *Historia general de las Indias*, tom. i. p. 97.

Ojeda himself, who made the voyage along
that coast in 1499, when he had with him Juan
de La Cosa, Americus Vespucius, and other
pilots.[1] Ojeda was a friend of Fonseca and an
enemy of Columbus. In his voyage of 1499 he
used a copy of a chart, furnished him
by Fonseca, which had been made by
Columbus the year before and sent by
him to the sovereigns. At the time
of the *Probanzas*, Vespucius and La
Cosa were both in their graves and could not
be summoned as witnesses, but Ojeda's testimony was positive and explicit that Columbus
was the discoverer of the Pearl Coast. Now if
his own pilot, Vespucius, had visited that coast
in 1497, Ojeda could not have failed to know
the fact, and he would have been only too glad
to proclaim it. If such a fact could have been
established, it would at once have settled the
question as to the Pearl Coast in favour of the
king, and there would have been no need of the
elaborate but weak and unsuccessful arguments
to which the Crown lawyers had recourse. The
result of the inquiry was overwhelmingly in favour of Columbus; and from beginning to end
not an interrogatory nor an answer, either on
the part of Diego or on the part of the Crown,

It proves that Vespucius did not discover the Pearl Coast in 1497

---

[1] "En este viage que este dicho testigo trujo consigo á Juan
de la Cosa, piloto, e Morigo Vespuche, e otros pilotos."
Navarrete, tom. iii. p. 544.

betrayed the faintest glimmering of a conscious-
ness that anybody had ever made, *or that anybody had ever professed to have made*, a voyage
along the Pearl Coast before 1498.

This fact has been commonly and rightly regarded as decisive. It makes it morally certain
that Vespucius did not visit Paria or Maracaibo
or the coast between them in 1497. But it contains another implication which seems
to have passed without notice. *It
makes it equally certain that Vespucius
had never professed to have made such
a voyage.* At the beginning of the
Probanzas, in 1513, the Italian letter from Vespucius to Soderini had been in print at least
seven years; the Latin version, which made it
accessible to educated men all over Europe, had
been in print six years, and was so popular that
it had gone through at least six editions. We
can hardly suppose the letter to have been unknown in Spain; indeed we know that one copy
of the Italian original was in Spain in 1513 in
the possession of Ferdinand Columbus, who
bought it in Rome in September, 1512, for five
cuattrini.[1] From 1508 until his death in February, 1512, Americus held one of the highest
positions in the Spanish marine. Now if the
Pilot Major of Spain had ever made any public
pretensions which in any way tended to invali-

It proves,
with equal
force, that he
never pro-
fessed to have
done so

[1] Harrisse, *Fernand Colomb*, p. 11.

date the claim of Diego Columbus, that his father had first discovered the Pearl Coast, can we for a moment suppose that at just that time, with such a lawsuit impending, the king would not have heard of those pretensions and used them for all they were worth? It is not supposable. The fact that neither party to the suit knew of such claims on the part of Americus proves *not only that they were unfounded, but that they had never been made.* It shows that contemporary Spaniards, familiar with the facts and reading the narrative of his voyages, did not understand the first one as referring to the Pearl Coast, but to an entirely different region.

It was M. Varnhagen who first turned inquiry on this subject in the right direction. Where does Vespucius *say* that he went on his first voyage? He says that he started May 10, 1497, from Cadiz and ran to the Grand Canary, the distance of which from Lisbon he calls 280 leagues. We thus find the length of the league used by Vespucius and get a scale wherewith to measure his distances. That run is not likely to have been made in less than seven days, and as he staid eight days more at the Grand Canary, he must have started thence about May 25. After a run of 37 (or 27) days[1] he made land in a direction about west-southwest from the

The landfall on the first voyage of Vespucius was near Cape Honduras

[1] See below, p. 312, note.

Canaries and distant 1000 leagues, in latitude
16° N. and longitude 75° W. from the meridian
of the Grand Canary. If we suppose this land
to have been Cape Honduras, the latitude, about
which Vespucius was least likely to be mistaken,
is exactly right; his distance by dead reckoning
is somewhat too small, probably because he
failed to allow for the acceleration due to the
westward current in the Caribbean Sea; and his
longitude is scarcely 5° in excess, a very moderate
error for those days. The northern coast of
Honduras not only thus suits the conditions of
the case,[1] but makes the subsequent details of
the voyage consistent and intelligible. Having
taken a correct start by simply following the
words of Vespucius himself, from a primitive
text, without reference to any preconceived theories or traditions, M. Varnhagen finds, from
further analysis of the narrative, that he sailed
around Yucatan, and found his aquatic village
of communal houses,[2] his little wooden Venice,
on the shore of Tabasco. Thence, after a fight

[1] The entrance to the Gulf of Maracaibo is about 12° N.
by 52° W. from Canaries; Paria, at the other end of the
Pearl Coast, is about 11° N. by 44° W. from Canaries; so
that no point on that coast can by any possibility be intended
by Vespucius.

[2] In a single house Vespucius found 600 people, and in
one place he estimated the population of 13 houses as about
4000, or rather more than 300 to a house. These figures are
eminently probable.

with the natives in which a few tawny prisoners[1] were captured and carried on board the caravels, Vespucius seems to have taken a straight

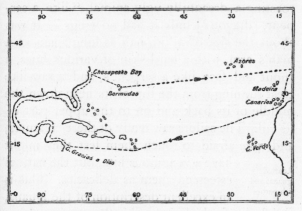

First voyage of Vespucius (with Pinzon and Solis, 1497–98).

course to the Huasteca country by Tampico,
without touching at points in the region subject or tributary to the Aztec
confederacy. This Tampico country
was what Vespucius understood to be called

The "pro-
vince of La-
riab "

---

[1] They were of medium stature, and well proportioned,
with reddish skin like a lion's : "Sono di mediana statura,
molto ben proportionati : le lor carni sono di colore che pende
in rosso come pelle di lione." *Lettera* (ed. 1505–1506), fol.
a. iii. recto. Varnhagen, p. 37. He notes their ornaments
of gorgeous feathers, their hammocks, and their "paterno-
strini che fanno dossi di peschi," *i. e.* "paternosters made of
fish-bones" (fol. a. iv. verso), meaning strings analogous to
quipus and to wampum-belts. See below, vol. iii. p. 97.

Lariab. He again gives the latitude definitely
and correctly as 23° N.,[1] and he mentions a few
interesting circumstances. He saw the natives
roasting a dreadfully ugly animal, " like a serpent, [dragon?] only it had no wings." It was
about the size of a kid, half as long again as a
man's arm, with a hard skin of various hues, a
snout and face like a serpent's, and a saw-like
crest running from the top of its head down the
middle of its back and on to the upper part of
its tail. The sailors saw many of these creatures,
and were afraid to touch them lest they might
have a venomous bite, but the natives
esteemed them as delicacies. This is
an excellent description of the iguana,
the flesh of which is to this day an important
article of food in tropical America.[2] These

Roasted
iguanas and
fish patties

[1] It is just 2400 miles distant, as the crow flies, from Paria,
the region with which it has so long been stupidly identified.
This has been preëminently one of the cases mentioned by
Bishop Berkeley, in which commentators first kick up a dust
and then wonder why they cannot see through it !

[2] " Doue uede'mo che arrostiuano un certo animale ch'
pareua un serpe'te, saluo ch' no' teneua alia, & nella appa-
renza ta'to brutto, che molto cimarauiglia'mo della sua fiereza :
Anda'mo cosi p͏ le lor case, o uero tra bacche & haua'mo
molti di questi serpe'te uiui, & eron legati pe piedi . . . :
eron di tanto fiero aspecto, che nessuno di noi no' ardiua di
torne uno, pensando, ch' eron uenenosi : sono di grandeza di
uno cauretto & di lu'gheza braccia uno & mezo : te' gono
epiedi lunghi & grossi & armati co' grosse unghie : tengono la
pelle dura, & sono di uarii colori : elmuso & faccia tengon di

274

Huastecas also made cakes or patties out of small fish, which they kneaded up with a sort

serpe'te : & dal naso simuoue loro una cresta come una segha, che passa loro p͏ elmezo delle schiene infino alla sommita della coda : in co'clusione gligiudica'mo serpi & uenenosi, segli ma'giauano." *Lettera*, fol. a. v. recto. Varnhagen, p. 43. Compare the description in the *Century Dictionary:* "It attains a length of five feet or more, and presents a rather formidable appearance, but is inoffensive unless molested ; . . . its flesh is much used for food. The tail is very long, compressed, and tapering ; a row of scales along the back is developed into a serrate crest or dorsal ridge ; the head is covered with scaly plates ; . . . its coloration is variegated with brownish, greenish, and yellowish tints." Yet this well-known animal has sorely puzzled the commentators. It is not easy to imagine, says Navarrete (tom. iii. p. 225), what kind of a serpent this could have been, as big as a kid, and with wings and feet (*y que tenian alas y pies*), and he is inclined to set it down as "one of Vespucio's many absurdities" (*uno de los muchos absurdos de Vespucio en sus relaciones*). Apparently Navarrete could not read his own text correctly when a chance was offered for a fling at poor old Vespucius, for that text (on the very same page ! !) reads "only it did NOT have wings" (*solo que no tenia alas*) ! Why should Vespucius have taken the pains to say that it had no wings ? It probably indicates that he had only a literary acquaintance with serpents, and dimly confused them with dragons.

Navarrete's remark is a fair specimen of the mingled dulness and flippancy with which commentators have been wont to treat the great Florentine sailor, — finding it easier to charge him with absurdities than patiently to ascertain his meaning. Even Mr. Lester, in a different temper from Navarrete, thinks that "the navigator has perhaps drawn somewhat upon his imagination in his description of this animal" (*Life of*

of pastry and baked upon red-hot coals. The Spaniards tasted them and found them good.[1] The people were enemies of those whom the Spaniards had found in the " little Venice " over on the Tabasco shore, and when it was observed that some of the latter were shackled prisoners on board the caravels,[2] the white men were forthwith greeted as friends. The Indians received them most hospitably, and under their escort twenty-three of the mariners, among whom Vespucius was one, made a journey some eighteen leagues inland, to see what could be found in that country. They visited several villages, composed of communal houses. In one of these villages, described as well peopled, the number

Americus Vespucius, p. 129). Yet, as we have here seen, his description is strictly accurate, and I cite it in illustration of the general faithfulness of his narrative. — As for the flesh of the ugly reptile, I do not find any mention of it among the 1394 dishes described by Alessandro Filippini, of Delmonico's, in his interesting book, *The Table*, New York, 1889 ; but one fancies that it might be so treated as to commend itself to epicures, even as the peerless terrapin, of which one of our British cousins is said to have declared, " Upon my word, it 's not so nasty as it looks ! " I have been told that the flavour of the iguana reminds one of spring chicken.

[1] " Proua'molo, & troua'mo che era buono." Compare some of the Mexican dishes mentioned below, vol. iii. p. 62.

[2] They were expert swimmers and thought nothing of jumping overboard and striking out for the shore, even when it was several leagues distant and out of sight ; so that all those whom the Spaniards had not put in irons had escaped.

of such houses was but nine. Lions and panthers (*i. e.* probably pumas and ocelots) were seen, but neither horse, ass, nor cow, nor any kind of domesticated animal.[1] It was a populous country, with no end of rivers,[2] and an astonishing quantity of birds of most brilliant plumages. The people were struck dumb with amazement at the sight of the white strangers, and when they had so far recovered themselves as to ask the latter whence they came, the Spaniards gave them to understand that they came from beyond the sky.

After leaving this country of Lariab the ships kept still to the northwest for a short distance, and then followed the windings of the coast for 870 leagues,[3] frequently landing and doing petty traffic with the

Coasting to Florida and around it

---

[1] "No te'ghono caualli ne muli, ne co' reuerentia asini, ne cani, ne di sorte alcuna bestiame peculioso, ne uaccino : ma sono ta'ti li altri animali che te'ghono & tucti sono saluatichi, & di nessuno siseruono per loro seruitio, che no' siposson contare." *Lettera*, fol. b. i. recto. Varnhagen, p. 45.

[2] "Questa terra e populatissima, & di gente piena, & dinfiniti fiumi." *Id.* The whole description agrees with Tampico.

[3] According to the most obvious reading of the text they sailed N. W. for 870 leagues, but this would be impossible upon any theory of the voyage : "Partimo di questo porto : la prouincia sidice Lariab : & nauiga'mo allungo della costa sempre a uista della terra, tanto che corre'mo dessa 870 leghe tutta uia uerso el maestrale," etc. *Lettera*, fol. b. i.

natives. They bought a little gold, but not much. Here the letter hurries over the scene somewhat abruptly. It was not likely that Soderini would be particularly interested in the shape of these strange coasts, and as for red Indians, much had already been said about them in the earlier part of the letter. So we are brought quickly to the end of the journey. After traversing the 870 leagues of crooked coast the ships found themselves in "the finest harbour in the world." It was in June, 1498, thirteen months since they had started from Spain. The ships were leaky and otherwise dilapidated, no discoveries of abundant gold or

verso. Varnhagen, p. 46. Does *tuttavia* here mean "always," or "still"? For the equivalent Spanish *todavia* the latter meaning is the more primary and usual. M. Varnhagen supposes that the words " tutta uia uerso el maestrale " belong in the writer's mind with " partimo di questo porto ; " so that the sense would be, " we sailed from this port still to the N. W., and we followed the coast always in sight of land until we had run 870 leagues " (*Le premier voyage de Vespucci*, p. 22). If the style of Vespucius were that of a correct and elegant writer, such a reading would be hardly admissible, but as his style was anything but correct and elegant, perhaps it may pass. Or perhaps N. W. may have been carelessly substituted for N. E., as would have been easy if signs were used in the manuscript instead of words like *maestrale* and *greco*. Then it would mean that the *general* direction after leaving Lariab was N. E. Upon any possible supposition there is a blunder in the statement as it appears in the printed text.

spices or jewels, calculated to awaken enthusiasm, had been made, and the men were tired
of the voyage. It was therefore unanimously
agreed [1] to beach and repair the ships, and then
return home. They spent seven and thirty days
in this unrivalled harbour, preparing for the
home voyage, and found the natives very hospitable. These red men courted the aid of the
white strangers. On some islands a hundred
leagues or more out at sea there lived a fierce
race of cannibals, who from time to time in
fleets of canoes invaded the coasts of the mainland and carried off human victims by the score.
Here a source of profit for the Spaniards was
suggested ; for Columbus, as we shall hereafter
see,[2] had already set the example of kidnapping
cannibals, and it was coming to be a recognized
doctrine, on the part of the Spanish government, that it was right for people " guilty of
that unnatural crime " to be sold into slavery.
The expedition with which Vespucius was sailing weighed anchor late in August, The Bermu-
taking seven of the friendly Indians ^{das}
for guides, on condition that they should return to the mainland in their own canoes. The
Indians were glad to go on these terms and

---

[1] " Acchorda'mo di comune consiglio porre le nostre naui
amonte, & ricorrerle per stancharle, che faceuano molta ac-
qua," etc. fol. b. i. verso.

[2] See below, vol. iii. p. 254.

witness the discomfiture of their enemies. After a week's voyage they fell in with the islands, some peopled, others uninhabited, evidently the Bermudas,[1] 600 miles from Cape Hatteras as the crow flies. The Spaniards landed on an island called Iti, and had a brisk fight with a large body of cannibals, who defended themselves manfully, but could not withstand fire-arms. More than 200 prisoners were taken, seven of whom were presented to the seven Indian guides. Taking a large canoe from the island, these friendly barbarians paddled away westward, "right merry and marvelling at our power."[2] "We also set sail for Spain, with 222 prisoners, slaves; and arrived in the port of Cadiz on the 15th day of October, 1498, where we were well received and sold our slaves. This is what happened to me in this my first voyage that may be most worth telling."[3]

[1] When these islands were rediscovered in 1522 they were entirely depopulated, — an instance, no doubt, of the frightful thoroughness with which the Spanish kidnappers from Hispaniola had done their work during the interval.

[2] "Sene tornarono allor terra molto allegri, marauiglia'dosi delle nostre forze." If they ever succeeded in getting home, one does not need to be told of the lurid fate of the captives.

[3] "Noi alsi facemo uela p̄ Spagna con 222 prigioni schiaui : & giugnemo nel porto di Calis adi 15 doctobre 1498 doue fumo ben riceuuti & uende'mo nostri schiaui. Questo e, quello che miacchadde in questo mio primo uiaggio di piu notabile." Fol. b. ii. verso. It was a dreadful number of

The words of Vespucius are too vague to enable us, without help from other sources, to determine the situation of that " finest harbour in the world," where the expedition made its last halt before striking eastward into the Atlantic. So much depends upon the quantity of allowance to be made for tacking and for the sinuosities of the coast-line, that it is impossible to say with any confidence to what point a run of 870 leagues from Tampico would have brought the ships. It is clear that they must have sailed between Cuba and Florida, and must have taken their final start from some point on the Atlantic coast of what is now the United States. The conditions of the case seemed at first to M. Varnhagen to point to the waters of the Chesapeake, but he was afterward inclined to designate Cape Cañaveral on the Florida coast as the final point of departure for the cannibal islands which apparently must have been the Bermudas.[1] But, as Mr. Hubert Ban-

slaves to pack away in four caravels, and 22 has been suggested as a more probable figure. Perhaps so ; mistakes in numerals are easy and frequent. The annals of the slave trade, however, give gruesome instances of what human greed can do. " De nos jours encore," observes Varnhagen, " que la traite des nègres est presque entièrement supprimée, nous avons vu aborder au Callao, venant de Chine, dans un seul navire, quelques cents Coolies : plus de la dixième partie de ces Coolies avait péri à bord, pendant le traversée."

[1] Varnhagen, *Amerigo Vespucci*, Lima, 1865, p. 99, and

croft suggests, it is hard to imagine what port near Cape Cañaveral could have been called the best harbour in the world, except " by a navigator little familiar with good harbours." I shall presently point to some reasons for believing that capes Charles and Cañaveral were probably the northern and southern limits between which the final departure was taken. Meanwhile another and more important question claims our attention.

We have hitherto been considering only the statements of Vespucius himself in an informal letter. It has been urged, with reference to the credibility of these statements, that there is no contemporary allusion whatever to such a voyage, either in books of history or in archives.[1]

Why critics have found no contemporary allusions to this voyage There is strong reason for believing that this sweeping assertion is far from correct, and that contemporary allusions have not been found simply because scholars have sought them in the wrong

chart at the end ; *Le premier voyage de Vespucci*, Vienna, 1869, p. 30.

[1] " It should first of all be noted that the sole authority for a voyage made by Vespucci in 1497 is Vespucci himself. All contemporary history, other than his own letters [it should be *letter*], is absolutely silent in regard to such a voyage, whether it be history in printed books, or in the archives of those kingdoms of Europe where the precious documents touching the earlier expeditions to the New World were deposited." S. H. Gay, in Winsor, *Narr. and Crit. Hist.*, ii. 137.

quarter. With their backs turned upon Lariab they have been staring at Paria, and might have gone on staring to eternity without seeing what was all the time behind them. So, too, one might look long into narratives and archives, and look in vain for a " voyage of Vespucius," for it was customary to speak of a voyage by the name of the commanding officer, and the language of Vespucius distinctly implies that in this voyage of 1497 he was not the commander; he was chosen by King Ferdinand " to go with the ships and *assist* in the work of discovery." [1] Let us, then, turn our faces toward Lariab, and see if contemporary documents know anything about a voyage into the Gulf of Mexico earlier than those of Ocampo in 1508 and Ponce de Leon in 1513. We find at once a remarkable and significant group of allusions, both in narratives and in archives, to such a voyage, undertaken by no less a person than Vicente Yañez Pinzon, captain of the little ship Niña in the first voyage of Columbus. Associated with Pinzon, and probably second in command, was another consummate sailor, Juan Diaz de

There are such contemporary allusions

[1] " Che fu, chel Re don Ferrando di Castiglia haue'do a mandare quattro naui a discoprire nuoue terre uerso loccidente fuelecto per sua alteza che io fussi in essa flocta per adiutare a discoprire." *Lettera*, fol. a. ii. recto. Varnhagen, p. 35.

PRINCIPAL SPANISH AND PORTUGUESE VOYAGES SOUTH OF TROPIC OF CANCER.

N. B. — *Portuguese in Italics.*

NO.	NAME.	DATE.	PLACE.
1	Columbus I.	Aug. 3, 1492 — March 15, 1493.	Several Bahamas ; Cuba and Hayti, north coasts.
2	Columbus II.	Sept. 25, 1493 — June 11, 1496.	Several lesser Antilles ; Jamaica ; Cuba and Hayti, south coasts.
3	Pinzon and Solis, Vespucius I.	May 10, 1497 — Oct. 15, 1498.	North coast of Honduras, Gulf of Mexico, Florida, Bermudas.
4	*Gama.*	*July 8, 1497 — July 10, 1499.*	*West coast of Hindustan via Cape of Good Hope.*
5	Columbus III.	May 30, 1498 — Nov. 25, 1500.	Trinidad, Paria, and Pearl Coast as far west as Cubagua.
6	Ojeda, La Cosa, Vespucius II.	May 16, 1499 — June, 1500.	From some point on north coast of Brazil to Paria and westward to Maracaibo, and to Cape de la Vela.
7	Pinzon.	Dec., 1499 — Sept., 1500.	Brazilian coast at about 8° S., and thence northwestward.
8	Lepe.	Jan. — June, 1500.	Brazilian coast to about 10° S.
9	*Cabral.*	*March 9, 1500 — July, 1501.*	*Brazilian coast from about 12° to 16° 30′ S., thence via Cape of Good Hope to Hindustan.*
10	Bastidas, La Cosa.	Oct., 1500 — Sept., 1502.	From Pearl Coast westward to Puerto Bello on Isthmus of Darien.
11	*Nuno Manuel ? Vespucius III.*	*May 14, 1501 — Sept. 7, 1502.*	*Brazilian coast from 5° to 34° S., thence to South Georgia Island, 54° S.*
12	Columbus IV.	May 11, 1502 — Nov. 7, 1504.	From Cape Honduras eastward and southward to Gulf of Darien.

13	*Coelho, Vespucius IV.*	*June 10, 1503 — June 18, 1504.*	*Brazilian coast, Vespucius to about 23° S., Coelho to about 40° S.*
14	*Christovão Jaques.*	*1503.*	*Brazilian and Patagonian coasts to about 52° S.*
15	La Cosa, Vespucius V.	May — Dec., 1505.	Search for a strait in Gulf of Darien and Atrato River.
16	Almeida.	1506.	Ceylon.
17	La Cosa, Vespucius VI.	March — Nov., 1507.	Further explorations about Darien.
18	Pinzon and Solis.	June 29, 1508 — Oct., 1509.	Brazilian coast, etc., to about 40° S.
19	Ocampo.	1508.	From Hayti circumnavigated Cuba.
20	*Sequeira.*	*1509.*	*Malacca.*
21	*Abreu and Serrano.*	*1512.*	*The Spice Islands (Moluccas) by eastward route.*
22	Ponce de Leon.	1513.	Florida.
23	Solis.	1516.	Search for a strait at river La Plata.
24	*Andrade.*	*1517.*	*First voyage of European ships to China.*
25	Córdova.	1517.	Rediscovery and circumnavigation of Yucatan.
26	Grijalva.	1518.	Exploration of Gulf of Mexico.
27	Cortes.	1519.	March into Mexico.
28	Magellan, Elcano.	Sept. 20, 1519 — Sept. 8, 1522.	The Spice Islands (Moluccas) by westward route, circumnavigating the globe.

Solis, who in 1512 succeeded Vespucius as Pilot Major of Spain.

The date commonly assigned to this voyage of Pinzon and Solis is 1506. The figure rests upon the single unsupported statement of Antonio de Herrera, whose great work was published in 1601.[1] For events that happened in the time of Ferdinand and Isabella, this book cannot be cited as of original authority. It is a compilation of priceless value, but not without grave defects. Mr. Hubert Bancroft is quite right in saying that we find in it " evidences everywhere of inexperience and incompetent assistance. Now that we have before us many of the sources of Herrera's material, we can see that his notes were badly extracted and compiled in a bungling manner; so much so that in addition to the ordinary errors, from which to some extent the most carefully executed work cannot be expected to be wholly free, there are many and serious discrepancies and contradictions for which there is no excuse, the cause being simply carelessness." [2]

Now Herrera tells us that when it had been made known in Castile what the admiral had

Antonio de Herrera

---

[1] Herrera, *Historia general de los hechos de los Castellanos en las islas i tierra firme del Mar Oceano*, Madrid, 1601, 4 vols. in quarto.

[2] *History of Central America*, San Francisco, 1882, vol. i. p. 317.

discovered afresh, Pinzon and Solis made up their minds to go and further pursue the route which he had taken; and from the Guanajos Islands on the northern coast of Honduras they sailed westward and passed the Golfo Dulce [1] without seeing it, but they gave the name of Navidad to what is now known as the Bay of Honduras. Thence they discovered the mountains (or lands) of *Caria* and a considerable part of Yucatan. But *as there was nobody who followed up that discovery*, nothing more was known about those coasts until the whole of New Spain was discovered [in 1517–19] from Cuba. The principal object of these navigators, Pinzon and Solis, adds Herrera, was, through a spirit of rivalry with the admiral, to discover land and to pass beyond what he had discovered.[2]

His account of the first voyage of Pinzon and Solis

---

[1] For the position of the Golfo Dulce, see the map of the region around Tuzulutlan, below, vol. iii. p. 292. It is simply the deep inlet at the head of the Bay of Honduras.

[2] The passage in Herrera is somewhat confused and involved, from the wrong connection in which he conceived it ; but when once we have fathomed the confusion under which he laboured, it is remarkable how nearly right he was in the principal items of his statement : " Sabido en Castilla lo que havia descubierto de nuevo el Almirante, Juan Diaz de Solis i Vincente Yañez Pinzon determinaron de ir à proseguir el camino que dejaba hecho, i fueron à tomar el hilo desde las islas de los Guanajos i volver de ellas à levante ; pero navegaron desde las dichas islas hácia el poniente hasta el parage de

In this statement Herrera understands the voyage of Pinzon and Solis to have been consequent upon the news of what Columbus had

el Golfo Dulce, aunque no lo vieron, porque está escondido ; reconocieron la entrada que hace la mar entre la tierra que contiene el Golfo, i la de Yucatan que es como una grande ensenada, ó baia, que asi llaman los marineros. . . . Y como vieron aquel rincon grande que hace la Mar entre dos Tierras, la una que está à la mano esquierda teniendo las espaldas al Oriente, que es la costa que contiene el Puerto de Caballos, i adelante de él el Golfo Dulce : i la otra de mano derecha, la costa del reino de Iucatan, parecióles gran baia, i por esto la llamaron la gran Baia de Navidad, desde donde descubrieron las sierras [tierras ?] de Caria ; bolvieron al Norte, i descubrieron mucha parte de el reino de Yucatan, pero como despues no huvo nadie, que prosiguiese aquel Descubrimiento, no se supo mas, hasta que se descobrió todo lo de Nueva España desde la isla de Cuba, i estos Descubridores principalmente pretendian descubrir tierra por emulacion del Almirante, i pasar adelante de lo que él habia descubierto '' (dec. i. lib. vi. cap. 17). *Pretendian* here does not mean " pretended," but " undertook " or " attempted." The allusion to *sierras de Caria* has always been felt to be puzzling, as no mountain-chains are known which it seems to fit. The expression is evidently taken by Herrera from Pinzon's testimony in the *Probanzas*, in which occur several other names now unintelligible, such as the countries of *Camarona*, *Chabaca*, and *Pintigron*, which Pinzon says he visited after turning northward from Honduras, but to which we have no further clue. The lapse into oblivion of so many names known to the first navigators is just what we might expect in the case of a voyage which was not followed up for twenty years (cf. Nos. 3, 25, 26 in my table of voyages). We shall presently have a similar illustration in the names upon a part of the Cantino map.

discovered in his fourth voyage (1502–1504);
and this opinion is evidently based upon his
interpretation of the testimony of Pinzon himself and other sailors in the *Probanzas*. It is a very natural way in which to read that testimony if we have nothing but the text itself to guide us; and if Herrera made a mischievous mistake we cannot blame him. There are the strongest reasons for believing that he did make such a mistake, and that this voyage of Pinzon and Solis was made, not in consequence of the fourth voyage of Columbus, but in consequence of the news of what he had discovered in 1494 in the course of his second voyage.

Herrera got the date wrong — 1506 instead of 1497

In the first place the evidence collected by Navarrete seems to prove conclusively that Pinzon did not go upon any voyage of discovery between the end of the year 1504 and June 29, 1508. A voyage for him was indeed contemplated as early as February or April, 1505, but it was not a voyage in the direction of Honduras, nor had it any reference to the fourth voyage of Columbus. On the contrary, as we shall hereafter see, it was a direct consequence of the fourth voyage of Vespucius. Its object was the further exploration of the Brazilian coast south of the tropic of Capricorn, and while it was planned early in 1505, the fear of complications with Portugal

Pinzon did not go on any voyage in 1506

prevented such an expedition from sailing until the summer of 1508. During that interval we keep coming upon documents that prove the presence of Pinzon in Spain; and it is not for a moment to be supposed that while thus concerned in this enterprise he could have been at the same time engaged in a long voyage into the Gulf of Mexico.[1] We have no alternative but to suppose that Herrera's date of 1506 for Pinzon's Honduras voyage is a mistake, and that he ought to have made it consequent, not upon the fourth, but upon the second, voyage of Columbus.

It was all the more easy to make such a mistake since the farthest point reached by Colum-

[1] We find Pinzon in Spain receiving a payment of 10,000 maravedis, February 28, 1505 (Navarrete, *Coleccion*, iii. 112) ; he is appointed to command a fortress in San Juan de Porto Rico, March 14, 1505 (iii. 112) ; the king wishes to consult with Pinzon and Vespucius about a projected voyage, May 17, 1505 (iii. 302) ; Pinzon wants a lawsuit settled, as it is hindering his departure on a voyage, September 28, 1505 (iii. 113) ; he is in Spain, busy on work on which he has evidently been engaged for a good while, August 23, 1506 (iii. 294) ; on September 15, 1506, the officers of the Casa de la Contratacion inform the king that the expedition will not be able to sail before February, 1507 (iii. 321) ; by that time the growl from Portugal has become so audible that the expedition is for the time abandoned and the ships used for other purposes (*id.*). These documents evidently relate to one and the same voyage, and they leave no place for a voyage to Honduras and the Gulf of Mexico.

bus upon the southern coast of Cuba in June,
1494, was not far from the point whence he
crossed from Cuba to Honduras in July, 1503.
If he had kept straight ahead in the former
voyage and left the coast of Cuba, he would
have crossed to Honduras very much as in the
latter voyage. It is not strange, then, that in
the mind of Herrera, as perhaps even in the
report of the *Probanzas* upon which Herrera
seems to have relied, the two voyages should
have got more or less mixed together.

Assuming, then, that Pinzon's first voyage
was consequent upon news received from Columbus in 1494, and that it was the voyage
upon which Vespucius describes himself as having sailed in May, 1497, we can understand
sundry statements in early historians of the Discovery, that have heretofore been un-   Testimony of
intelligible. Peter Martyr, in a pas-   Peter Martyr
sage written before 1508, says: "For there
are many which affirme that they haue sayled
rownd abowt Cuba. But whether it bee so or
not, or whether enuyinge the good fortune of
this man [Columbus] they seeke occasions of
querelinge ageynste hym, I cannot judge. But
tyme shall speake, which in tyme appoynted,
reuealeth both truth and falsehod." [1] In another

---

[1] "Neque enim desunt qui se circuisse Cubam audeant
dicere. An hæc ita sint, an invidia tanti inventi occasiones
quærant in hunc virum, non dijudico : tempus loquetur, in

place Martyr says that Vicente Yañez sailed about Cuba, which had hitherto, because of its great size, been regarded as continent; and having found that this is an island, he went on and struck upon other lands to the west of it.[1] Again Gomara says that three years before Co-

Testimony of Gomara and Oviedo

lumbus visited the coast of Honduras that coast had been discovered by Pinzon and Solis.[2] Gomara's three years should be five, but the main fact is the fact of priority, which is again expressly affirmed by Oviedo (in 1526–35): " Some persons have attributed the discovery of the Bay of Honduras to Don Christopher Columbus, the first admiral, saying that he discovered it. But that is not true; for it was discovered by the pilots Vicente Yañez Pinzon, Juan Diaz de Solis, and

quo verus judex invigilat." Martyr, dec. i. lib. vi. As Humboldt says, this last clause shows conclusively that the passage was written before Ocampo's voyage in 1508.

[1] " Vicentius Annez . . . Cubam, a multis ad ea usque tempora ob suam magnitudinem continentem putatam, circuivit. . . . Vicentius Annez cognito jam experimento patenti Cubam esse insulam, processit ulterius et terras alias ad occidentem Cubæ offendit." *Id.*, dec. ii. lib. vii.

[2] " Descubrió Christoual Colon treziẽtas y setẽta leguas de costa, que ponen de rio grande de Higueras al Nõbre de Dios, el año de mil y quinientos y dos; dizen empero algunos q̃ tres años ante lo auian andado Vicente Yañez Pinzon y Juan Diaz de Solis, q̃ fueron grandíssimos descubridores." Gomara, *Historia general de las Indias*, Antwerp, 1554, cap. lv. fol. 63 recto.

Pedro de Ledesma, with three caravels, and that was before Vicente Yañez had discovered the river Amazon,"[1] in other words, before January, 1500. This explicit and definite testimony from a contemporary first-hand authority is not lightly to be set aside.

There can be little doubt that Oviedo, Gomara, Martyr, Herrera, and the witnesses in the tenth section of the *Probanzas*, in their various references to the voyage of Pinzon and Solis, are all referring to the first voyage described by Vespucius in his letter to Soderini, — a voyage which achieved the first discovery of Honduras, with parts of the coasts of Mexico and Florida, and which first revealed to some persons the insularity of Cuba. Here the map made in 1500 by La Cosa becomes quite interesting. It will be remembered that this able navigator was with Columbus on that memorable occasion in June, 1494, when all hands solemnly subscribed to the belief that Cuba was part of the Asiatic continent.[2] On that occasion,

[1] " Algunos atribuyen al Almirante primero, Don Christoval Colon, diciendo que él lo descubrió. Y no es así ; porque el golfo de Higueras lo descubrieron los pilotos Vicente Yañez Pinzon é Johan Diaz de Solis é Pedro de Ledesma, con tres caravelas, antes que el Vicente Yañez descubriese el rio Marañon." Oviedo, *Historia general de las Indias*, Madrid, 1851, tom. ii. p. 140.

[2] This affair, so grotesque according to modern notions, is usually misrepresented ; *e. g.* "Columbus voyaged for

La Cosa declared that he had never heard of an island with 335 leagues length of coast from east to west, and that from the contour of this

India, thought his first landing was there, and forced his crew to swear they thought so too by threatening to cut out their tongues." (Prof. J. D. Butler, in a very meritorious paper on " The Naming of America," in *Transactions of Wisconsin Academy of Sciences*, 1874, vol. ii. pp. 203–219.) The passage in Henry Stevens's *Hist. and Geog. Notes*, p. 12, to which the writer refers, does not justify such a statement. Stevens simply says " caused his captains, his pilots, his master of charts [La Cosa], and all his sailors to sign a declaration under oath, that they believed Cuba to be part of the continent of Asia near Mangi." The notary's original document, preserved in the Archives of the Indies at Seville (printed in Navarrete, tom. ii. pp. 143–149), does not indicate that in this " causing " there was either any force or any threat used. The officers and men were asked to state their dissenting views if they had any. Nobody seems to have had any, and there is no reason for supposing that anybody signed the declaration reluctantly. The formal provision, that if any one should afterward deny that on this occasion he had expressed the opinion written down in the document he should have the tip of his tongue slit (as was often done to liars), was simply a bit of genuine mediævalism, about equivalent to the solemn imprecations of modern children : " Huck Finn and Tom Sawyer wishes they may drop down dead in their tracks if they ever tell of this and rot," as Mark Twain so faithfully puts it. For the owlish gravity with which some modern writers use this incident in evidence of the admiral's alleged " deceitfulness " and weakness of character, the proper answer is a peal of Homeric laughter. I have described the affair above, pp. 166, 167, with as much seriousness as I think it deserves.

coast, as well as its apparently interminable length, he had no sort of doubt that it was the mainland. We have no reason for supposing that La Cosa did not mean precisely what he said. Yet upon his famous map, of which a sketch is given at page 228 of this volume, Cuba is distinctly represented as an island. On the north of it the left-hand flagstaff marks the westernmost point reached by Columbus and La Cosa in 1492 ; on the south we read *C. Bien Espera,* the " Cape of Good Hope " where in 1494 La Cosa and his comrades all testified that to the best of their knowledge and belief they were on the coast of Asia ; and just to the south of this cape we see a few small islands whereunto the map-maker's fancy has added a goodly archipelago of bigger ones. The shore on the west of these islands Columbus called Evangelista, deeming it " fraught with good tidings " for him when he should come that way again. On the map we see " Abangelista," albeit written too far to the west. Then Cuba is terminated by a western coast-line all the way around from the archipelago to the flagstaff, — a coast-line which, as even an unpractised eye may see, is drawn not from exploration, but from theory or from hearsay. On the original map this western coast-line is abruptly cut off with a dash of

Cuba represented as an island on La Cosa's map, 1500

green paint.[1] This means to my mind that when La Cosa drew the map, between June and October, 1500, he had been informed of, or brought to believe in, the insularity of Cuba, but had not seen a chart of its western extremity. Where did he get his information? The answer is obvious. He had just returned from that voyage on the Pearl Coast with Ojeda (the second voyage of Vespucius) in which he and Vespucius were associated as pilots. Evidently the latter had told him of the discovery of a passage between Cuba and the mainland two years before, but had not shown him his charts,

---

[1] Hence the late Henry Stevens suggested that La Cosa did not intend to be understood as representing Cuba as an island, but only meant to show that his own definite knowledge did not go beyond the archipelago on the south and the flagstaff on the north. (*Historical and Geographical Notes*, London, 1869, p. 13.) But if that was all that he meant to show, why did he separate Cuba from the mainland at all? The mere fact of the separation indicates a knowledge of something to the west of "Abangelista," though confessedly a dim knowledge. At least it indicates a decided change of opinion since 1494; otherwise La Cosa would not only have made the western end of Cuba flare like the outline of a trumpet, but beyond the flagstaff it would have trended strongly to the northward and become continuous with the mainland. At the archipelago it would have been prolonged indefinitely to the southwest, and there would have been nothing of that vague but unmistakable suggestion of the Gulf of Mexico which La Cosa cannot have got from any other source than the first voyage of Vespucius.

which very likely were then in the hands of Bishop Fonseca. Hence it appears that the continental coast-line opposite Cuba was drawn not wholly from theory, but partly from hearsay. The protruding land at the words " Mar Oceanuz " and below may indicate that La Cosa had heard something about Florida, but having no drawings to guide him, had pictured it to himself as a big promontory rather than a peninsula.

The striking suggestion thus afforded by the map of La Cosa is confirmed with overwhelming force by that of Alberto Cantino The Cantino already mentioned in connection with map, 1502 the voyages of the brothers Cortereal. This map was made in Portugal by some cartographer unknown, at the order of Alberto Cantino, who carried it to Italy in the autumn of 1502, and sent it to Ercole d' Este, Duke of Ferrara. It had reached the duke, or was on its way to him, November 19, 1502, as we know from Cantino's letter of that date written at Rome. It has been carefully preserved, and since 1868 has been accessible in the Biblioteca Estense at Modena; but it is only within the past ten years that scholars have begun to wake up to its importance.

The Cantino map,[1] which gives both Hayti

[1] A sketch showing the relative positions was given above on page 236. This sketch of the Florida coasts I have copied

and Cuba, not only represents the latter as an
island, terminated on the west by a *hypotheti-*
cal coast, but goes on to depict a
considerable portion of the coast-line
of the United States, including both
sides of the peninsula of Florida, and all this is
depicted as a *visited* coast, with sundry details
of bay and headland, upon which are placed
twenty-two local names. A few of these names
have been distorted beyond recognition by the
Portuguese draughtsman, but their original form
is unquestionably Spanish and not Portuguese.
The names furnish absolute proof that this part
of the map was copied from a Spanish map [1] by
a person not familiar with Spanish, and furthermore that this copyist was a Portuguese. These
names, like fossils from an age extinct, are elo-

from the full-sized facsimile published in 1883 by M. Harrisse, and have taken pains to reproduce with accuracy the
details of the coast-line. Off the southwestern coast the original has a group of islands which I have omitted in order to
get room for the names. One cannot do all that one would
like on so small a page. These islands may be seen on the
other sketch just mentioned. On the original map the coasts
end abruptly just where they touch my border, at " Rio de
las Palmas " and " Costa del Mar Vaano."

[1] The mistakes are mistakes of the eye, not of the ear ; they
stand for misread letters, not for misheard sounds. M. Harrisse, in his work on the Cortereals, demonstrates that no
Portuguese voyages, nor any *recorded* voyage whatever, except that of Vespucius in 1497–98, will account for this
delineation of Florida upon the Cantino map.

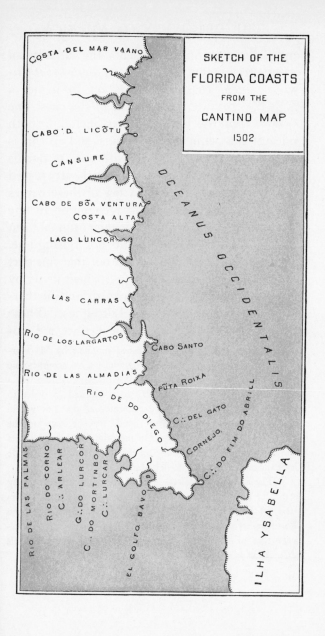

SKETCH OF THE
FLORIDA COASTS
FROM THE
CANTINO MAP
1502

COSTA DEL MAR VAANO

CABO D. LICOTU

CANSURE

CABO DE BOA VENTURA

COSTA ALTA

LAGO LUNCOR

LAS CABRAS

RIO DE LOS LARGARTOS

CABO SANTO

RIO DE LAS ALMADIAS

PUTA ROIXA

RIO DE DO DIEGO

C: DEL GATO

CORNEJO

C: DO FIM DO ABRILL

OCEANUS OCCIDENTALIS

RIO DE LAS PALMAS

RIO DO CORNO

C: ARLEAR

G: DO LURCOR

C: DO MORTINBO

C: LURCAR

EL GOLFO BAVO

ILHA YSABELLA

quent in their silence. As I shall presently show, they had ceased to be understood before the rediscovery of Florida by Ponce de Leon in 1513; the continuity of tradition was broken off short. All this means that THIS PORTION OF THE UNITED STATES COAST WAS VISITED AND MAPPED BY SPANISH MARINERS BEFORE NOVEMBER, 1502, AND THAT THE VOYAGE IN WHICH THIS WAS DONE WAS NOT FOLLOWED UP.

It is not only clear that the Cantino map was copied or compiled from an older Spanish map or maps; it is also clear that it was not based upon the map of La Cosa, but upon some entirely different authority. For upon the northern coast of South America, where La Cosa has forty-five names [1] and Cantino twenty-nine, only three of these names agree on the two maps. It therefore appears that the Cantino map, while it represents knowledge gained at some length of time before the autumn of 1502, also gives testimony that is independent, and not a mere repetition of the testimony of La Cosa.

It is worth our while here to follow out a little further some of the relations of this map to the cartography of that time. The original from which it was made exercised much more influence than that of La Cosa, which does not seem to have been engraved or extensively copied. In

Waldseemül-ler's map, the Tabula Terre Nove, made before 1508

[1] They are not all given in my reduced sketch.

the edition of Ptolemy published at Strasburg in 1513 there is a remarkable map, made before 1508[1] by Martin Waldseemüller, a geographer of whom we shall have more to say

---

[1] " Charta autem Marina, quam Hydrographiam vocant, per Admiralem quondam serenissimi Portugaliæ [Castellæ ?] regis Ferdinandi, cæteros denique lustratores verissimis peragrationibus lustrata : ministerio Renati dum vixit, nunc pie mortui Ducis illustrissimi Lotharingiæ liberius prælographationi tradita est," etc., *anglicè*, " The sailing chart, or Hydrography, as it is called, rectified by means of very exact navigations made by a former Admiral of the most gracious King Ferdinand of Portugal [Castile ?], and thereafter by other explorers, was liberally given to be engraved by the care of the most illustrious René, in his lifetime Duke of Lorraine, now deceased," etc. Avezac, *Martin Waltzemüller*, p. 153 ; cf. Lelewel, *Géographie du Moyen Age*, tom. ii. pp. 157–160 ; Humboldt, *Examen critique*, tom. iv. p. 109. As René died in 1508, this is perhaps the earliest *engraved* map now extant showing portions of America, though the map made by Johann Ruysch and published in the edition of Ptolemy issued at Rome, August 13, 1508 (see below, p. 346), may have been engraved earlier. The Waldseemüller map, known by its title *Tabula Terre Nove*, seems to have been made after an original chart obtained from Portugal by Duke René in 1504 (see Harrisse, *Bibliotheca Americana Vetustissima*, p. 108). The " former Admiral " above mentioned is probably Columbus, and calling Ferdinand " king of Portugal " was a mere slip of the pen. It has often been called " The Admiral's Map," but that phrase is misleading. It represents, as the editors say, the results of voyages made by Columbus, " and thereafter by other explorers ; " but it is not likely that it emanated from Columbus. It leads us much more directly back to Vespucius.

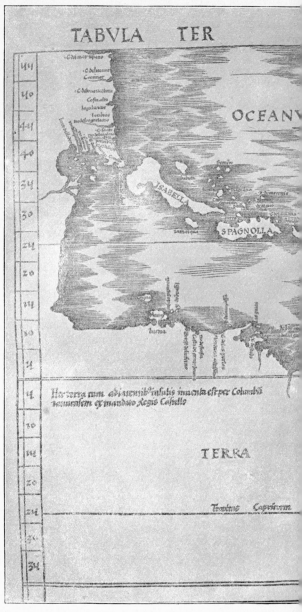

OCEANV

44
40
44
40
34
30
24
20
14
10

ISABELLA

SPAGNOLLA

Hæc terra tum adiacentib9 insulis inuenta est per Columbū
ianuensem ex mandato Regis Castello

TERRA

Tropicus Capricorni

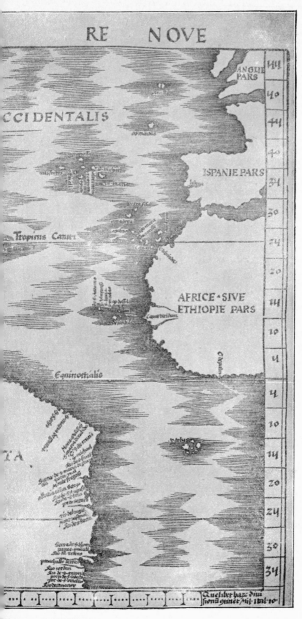

ANGLIE
PARS

44

40

41

40

34

30

CCIDENTALIS

ISPANIE PARS

Tropicus Cancri

24

20

14

AFRICE•SIVE
ETHIOPIE PARS

Capus Viridum

10

4

Equinoctialis

4

TA

10

14

20

24

30

34

Quellver haze dini
sionū gtiner/til·1000·10·

E 1513 PTOLEMY

before 1508

hereafter. This map, known as *Tabula Terre Nove*, has been a puzzle to scholars, but a long step is taken toward understanding it when we learn that it was made from an original chart which found its way from Portugal into Lorraine in 1504, and when we furthermore see that this original must have been the same that was followed by Cantino's draughtsman. This is proved by the identity in names, of which the list on page 302, containing all the names upon the Florida coasts, is sufficiently striking.

Of the twenty-two names on Cantino's coasts of Florida, nineteen are thus repeated in the later map. Originally Spanish, these names have on the Portuguese map in a few instances been deformed beyond recognition; on the Lorraine map the deformity is generally carried a little farther, as we might expect. There can be no doubt that, so far as the delineation of Florida is concerned, the two maps are drawn from the same source. Observe the conclusions to which this fact carries us. As the history of the Discovery of America has usually been written, Florida was first visited by Ponce de Leon on Easter Sunday, 1512; and a superficial observer might not be surprised at seeing the Florida coasts laid down on a map first published in 1513; perhaps, too, it might not occur to him that the peculiar names on these coasts are not

The Florida coasts were visited by Spaniards before 1502

301

CANTINO.	TABULA TERRE NOVE.	MEANINGS.
	lago de loro,	parrot lake.
Rio de las palmas,	Rio de la parmas,	river of palms.
rio do corno,	rio de como,	{ dogwood river ? { r. *corvo*, crow river ? }
C. arlear,	C. arlear,	?
G. do lurcor,	G. dolivor,	?
C. do mortinbo,		?
C. lurcar,	C. lurcar,	?
el golfo bavo,		?
C. do fim do abrill,	C. doffim de abril,	cape of the end of April.
cornejo,	comello,	dogwood ?
Rio de do diego,		river of Don Diego.
C. del gato,	C. de lago,	cape of the cat.
puta Roixa,	ponta royal,	{ red point ? { p. *Bayxa*,[1] low point ? }
Rio de las almadias,	rio de las amadias,	river of canoes.
Cabo Santo,	C. Santo,	holy cape.
Rio de los largartos,	rio de los garlartos,	river of lizards, or alligators.
las cabras,	la cablas ?	?
lago luncor,	lago luncor,	l. *luengo*, long lagoon ?
Costa alta,	Costa alta,	high coast.
Cabo de boa ventura,	C. de bonauentura,	cape of good fortune.
Cansure,	Camnor,	?
Cabo d. licotu,	C. del itontir,	*C. del encontro*,[1] cape of meeting ?
Costa del mar vạano,	C. del mar usiano,	{ coast } { cape ? } of the ocean sea.

derived from the explorations that began with
Ponce de Leon. But now, while on the one
hand it has lately been proved that Ponce de
Leon did not see Florida until Easter Sunday,
1513,[2] on the other hand the map of the 1513

[1] I am indebted for these two suggestions to M. Harrisse,
Les Corte-Real, pp. 89, 90.

[2] See Peschel, *Geschichte des Zeitalters der Entdeckungen*,
p. 521; Kohl, in *Documentary History of Maine*, vol. i. p.
240; Winsor, *Narr. and Crit. Hist.*, ii. 233.

Ptolemy was certainly made before 1508, and the comparison with the Cantino map proves it to have been drawn from an original as old as 1502, and probably older. It follows, therefore, with the force of absolute demonstration, that the coasts of Florida were explored and the insularity of Cuba detected before 1502. There is no possible escape from this conclusion.

But this is not the whole story. Our facts show that while Florida was visited at that early date, and while for the moment the discovery attracted enough attention, among cartographers at least, to leave its indelible impression upon more than one map, nevertheless it soon ceased to occupy attention and became forgotten, so that the names it left behind became a source of worry and confusion for map-makers. Because Florida (as yet without a name) purported to be a piece of continent, and because until after 1508 most people believed Cuba to be a piece of continent, the old maps used to mix them together without rhyme or reason; and the perplexity was increased by the fact that the true Cuba was often called Isabella. Sometimes the island appeared under the latter designation, while the name Cuba was placed upon the Florida peninsula; sometimes the two were fused into one, because while geographers found both countries mentioned or drawn upon maps, they knew only

How the old map-makers were puzzled

of the one as being actually visited, and hence tried to correct the apparent error. For example, in Johann Ruysch's map, 1508, to the west of Hispaniola we see an island abruptly cut off with the scroll marked C, upon which is the legend, " the ships of Ferdinand, king of Spain, have come as far as here."[1] Now this might be meant for Cuba, and the two ends of the scroll might be intended to mark the two farthest points reached by Columbus in 1492 and 1494; or it may be meant for Florida, partially capsized, — an accident not uncommon in early maps, — and the scroll may simply show what Ruysch was able to gather from the original of the Cantino map. That the latter is probably the true explanation is indicated by the names :[2] at the eastern point we have *C. de Fundabril*, and, going thence to the right, *Corveo* (for *Cornejo*) and *C. Elicontii* (for *C. de licontu*) ; going to the left, we have *Culcar* (for *C. arlear*) and then *Lago del Oro*. This seems to show what Ruysch had in mind. On the other hand, on Stobnicza's map, 1512, which was in part derived from the Cantino source, we see the islands of " Spagnolla " and " Isabella " rudely drawn in much the same outline as in the *Tabula Terre Nove*, but the name

---

[1] See below, p. 346.

[2] There is not room enough for them on my reduced sketch of this map.

" Isabella " has taken refuge upon the mainland.[1]

These examples show that the geographers
of that time had more facts set before them
than they were able to assimilate. In some
directions a steady succession of voy-   Why they
ages served to correct imperfections   were thus
in theory and to attach certain names   puzzled
permanently to certain localities. But the facts
relating to the Gulf of Mexico and Florida
remained indigestible because from fifteen to
twenty years elapsed before the earliest voyage
in those waters was followed up and the first
crude impressions made definite. The names
applied to those coasts soon sank into oblivion,
and when the actors in that generation had all
passed from the scene, the very memory of the
voyage itself was lost, the maps which it inspired
slept unheeded in the gloom of great libraries,
the only literary document describing it was
wrongly referred to a very different voyage, and
the illustrious writer of that document became
the target for all manner of ignorant abuse.

There is little room for doubt that the first
voyage of Vespucius was made just as he describes it in his own sea-faring dialect. No other
source is known from which those Florida coasts,
depicted with their long-forgotten names upon
the Cantino and Waldseemüller maps, can pos-

[1] See below, p. 414.

sibly have come. We must either admit that Americus Vespucius circumnavigated the Florida peninsula before 1502, or we must *invent* some voyage, never heard of and never mentioned by anybody, in which that thing was done; and as the latter alternative is not likely to commend itself to sensible minds, we are driven to the former.[1] But if Ves-

The voyage of Vespucius in 1497–98 is the only voyage on record that explains the Cantino map

---

[1] "De toutes les expéditions maritimes du xv siècle, celle-ci [the first voyage of Vespucius] est la seule qui cadre avec les configurations géographiques que l'on relève sur la carte de Cantino." Harrisse, *Les Corte-Real,* p. 107. In a footnote to this passage M. Harrisse is strongly tempted to believe that the Portuguese map which Peter Martyr saw in Bishop Fonseca's office, "whereunto Americus Vesputius is sayde to have put his hande," was the very prototype of the map made in Lisbon for Cantino. Yet M. Harrisse finds a difficulty in supposing that the voyage which inspired the Cantino map was made before 1500. If it had been, he thinks the Florida coasts would have been delineated and studded with names on La Cosa's map. Since La Cosa, when he made his map, had just been for a year in company with Vespucius, why had not the latter put him in possession of all the facts recorded upon the Cantino map, if he knew them? To M. Harrisse this difficulty seems so formidable that he is actually disposed to *invent* a voyage between 1500 and 1502 in order to account for the Cantino map! *Les Corte-Real,* p. 151. To my mind the difficulty does not exist. La Cosa's map seems to me — as I have already observed — to show just the knowledge which he must have gained from conversation with Vespucius without seeing a chart of the Florida coast; and I see no reason why Vespucius must necessarily have carried such a chart

pucius made this voyage before November, 1502, then he must have made it exactly when he says he did, in 1497–98, for we can trace him through the whole intervening period and know that he was all the time busy with other things.

To return, then, to the beginning, and sum up the case, it seems to me that things must have happened about as follows : —

It was in the course of the year 1494 that Ferdinand and Isabella began to feel somewhat disappointed at the meagre results obtained by Columbus. The wealth of Cathay and Cipango had not been found, the colonists, who had expected to meet with pearls and gold growing on bushes, were sick and angry, Friar Boyle was preaching that the admiral was a humbug, and the expensive work of discovery was going on at a snail's pace. Meanwhile Vicente Yañez Pinzon and other bold spirits were grumbling at the monopoly granted to Columbus and begging to be allowed to make ventures for themselves. Now in this connection several documents preserved in the Archives of the Indies at Seville are very significant. On the 9th of April, 1495, the sovereigns issued their letter of credentials to Juan Aguado, whom they were

How it came about that Vespucius and Pinzon made this voyage in 1497

with him on a voyage to the Pearl Coast, or why he should have been anxious to impart all the details of his professional experience to a brother pilot.

307

about sending to Hispaniola to inquire into the charges against Columbus.[1] On that very same day they signed the contract with Berardi, whereby the latter bound himself to furnish twelve vessels, four to be ready at once, four in June, and four in September. On the next day they issued the decree throwing open the navigation to the Indies and granting to all native Spaniards, on certain prescribed conditions, the privilege of making voyages to the

[1] The reader may like to see the form of this sort of letter, which so often carried dismay to explorers, worthy and unworthy, in the New World : " El Rey é la Reina : Caballeros y Escuderos y otras personas que por nuestro mandado estais en las Indias, allá vos enviamos á Juan Aguado, nuestro Repostero, el cual de nuestra parte vos hablará. Nos vos mandamos que le dedes fe y creencia. De Madrid á nveve de Abril de mil y cuatrocientos y noventa y cinco años. — Yo EL REY. — Yo LA REINA. — Por mandado del Rey é de la Reina nuestros Señores — HERNAND ALVAREZ." Las Casas, *Hist. de las Indias*, tom. ii. p. 110 ; *anglicè* : —

THE KING AND THE QUEEN :

Cavaliers, Esquires, and other persons, who by our command are in the Indies, we send you thither Juan Aguado, our Gentleman of the Chamber, who will speak to you on our part. We command that you give him faith and credence. From Madrid the ninth of April, one thousand four hundred and ninety-five.

I THE KING : I THE QUEEN.

By command of the King and Queen, our Lords,

HERNAND ALVAREZ.

Brief but comprehensive !

newly found coasts. On the 12th they instructed
Fonseca to put Aguado in command of the
first four caravels.[1] All these acts were coherent
parts of a settled policy which the sovereigns
were then pursuing. Under the permission of
April 10, says Gomara, quite a number of navigators sailed, some at their own expense, others
at the expense of the king; all hoped to acquire
fame and wealth, but since for the most part they
only succeeded in ruining themselves with their
discovering, their voyages were forgotten.[2]

The delays in fitting out such expeditions
were apt to be many and vexatious. Of the
twelve caravels which Berardi was to furnish,
the first four started off in August,   The three
with Agaudo in command. The sec-   Berardi
ond squadron of four, which was to   squadrons
have been ready in June, was not yet fully
equipped in December, when Berardi died.
Then Vespucius, representing the house of
Berardi, took up the work and sent the four
caravels to sea February 3, 1496. They were

[1] Navarrete, *Coleccion*, tom. ii. pp. 159–169.

[2] " Entendiendo quan grandissimas tierras eran las que
Christoval Colon descubria, fueron muchos á continuar el
descubrimiento de todas ; unos á su costa, otros á la del Rey,
y todos pensando enriquecer, ganar fama y medrar con los
Reyes. Pero como los mas dellos no hizieron sino descubrir y
gastarse, no quedó memoria de todos, que yo sepa," etc.
Gomara, *Historia general de las Indias*, Saragossa, 1553,
fol. 50.

only two days out when a frightful storm overtook and wrecked them, though most of the
crews were saved.[1] The third squadron of four
caravels was, I believe, that which finally sailed
May 10, 1497. While it was getting ready
Vicente Yañez Pinzon returned from the Le-
vant, whither he had been sent on important
business by the sovereigns in December, 1495.[2]
Columbus, who had returned to Spain in June,
1496, protested against what he considered an
invasion of his monopoly, and on June 2, 1497,
the sovereigns issued a decree which for the
moment was practically equivalent to a revocation of the general license accorded to navigators by the decree of April 10, 1495.[3] Observe that this revocation was not issued until

[1] These particulars are from memoranda in MS., extracted
by Muñoz from account-books in the Casa de Contratacion
at Seville. See Irving's *Columbus*, vol. iii. p. 397. Irving
and Navarrete had access to the documents of Muñoz, and
Navarrete (tom. iii. p. 317), in speaking of a payment made
from the treasury on January 12, 1496, observes that Vespucius " went on attending to everything until the armada was
despatched from San Lucar," *i. e.* February 3, 1496. Humboldt strangely interpreted this statement as meaning that
Vespucius fitted out the third expedition of Columbus, and
was thus kept in Spain till May 30, 1498 (*Examen critique*,
tom. iv. p. 268). This ingenious *alibi*, often quoted as
proving the impossibility of a voyage anywhere by Vespucius
in 1497, is not sustained.

[2] Navarrete, tom. iii. p. 75.

[3] Navarrete, tom. ii. p. 201.

after the third squadron had sailed! The sovereigns were not going to be baulked in the little scheme which they had set on foot two years before, and for which they had paid out, through Vespucius, so many thousands of maravedis.[1] So the expedition sailed, with Pinzon in chief command and Solis second, with Ledesma for one of the pilots, and Vespucius as pilot and cosmographer.

The course taken and the coasts visited have already been sufficiently indicated. The landfall was undoubtedly upon the northern coast of Honduras,[2] points on the coasts of Yucatan

[1] Vespucius speaks of the expedition as sailing in the service of King Ferdinand. He does not say " their highnesses," or " Los Reyes," the sovereigns, but mentions only the king, and this agrees with Gomara's expression above quoted, "some at their own expense, others at the expense of the king," and also with the expression of the pilot Ledesma in his testimony in the *Probanzas*, "por mandado de S. A." (Navarrete, tom. iii. p. 558). On the other hand Pinzon, in his testimony, says " por mandado de SS. AA." (which he would not have been likely to say, by the way, if he had been referring to events of the year 1506, after the queen's death). On the whole it seems not unlikely that this was especially Ferdinand's venture.

[2] It was a very common custom to name newly discovered places after the saint upon whose day they were discovered. When you see a saint's name on a cape or bay, it is good ground for a presumption that the name was given by some explorer who first visited it on that saint's day. When you see *Navidad* it generally means Christmas, but not unfrequently June 24, the Nativity of John the Baptist. When

and Tabasco were visited, then a straight run
was made to Tampico, and thence the coast
was followed to some point on the Atlantic

Herrera tells us that Pinzon and Solis discovered the Bay of
Honduras and named it " Baia de Navidad," it affords a
strong presumption that it was discovered on St. John's day.
The ships, as we have seen, probably started May 25 from
the Grand Canary, whence a run of 27 days would bring
their landfall at or near Cape Honduras on June 21. Three
more days would enable them to recognize the water to the
west of that point as a great bay. But the primitive text of
Vespucius says the landfall occurred after 37 days. As the
figure is given in Arabic numerals there is a good chance for
error. Curiously enough, the Latin version of 1507 says
" viginti septem vix elapsis diebus," *i. e.* " after barely
twenty-seven days." Is this a mistake, or an emendation
suggested to the Latin translator by some outside source of
information ? The latter, I suspect. With the trade-wind
nearly dead astern, and with the powerful westward current
in the Caribbean Sea, the quicker run is the more probable,
and it fits the name *Navidad*. The reader will remember
that this same June 24, 1497, was the date of John Cabot's
landfall on the northeastern coast of North America. If the
Latin figure is correct, Vespucius probably saw " the continent " two or three days before Cabot. The question may
have interest for readers fond of such trifles. It is really of
no consequence what navigator — after the genius of Columbus had opened the way — happened to be the first to see
land which we have since come to know as part of the coast-
line of a continental system distinct from the Old World.
Nor has the question a historic interest of any sort ; for, as
we shall see, considerations of " priority " connected with
this voyage of 1497 had nothing whatever to do with the
naming of America.

coast of the United States which may perhaps be determined if any one can succeed in interpreting the details of the Cantino map. How far north did Vespucius follow the coast of the United States? If the latitudes on the *Tabula Terre Nove* were given with any approach to correctness, it would be helpful in deciding this point; but they are hopelessly wrong. Though Vespucius was in all probability the original source of this part of the map, it is impossible that he should ever have given such latitudes. It is pretty clear that the data must have been "amended" by Waldseemüller to suit some fancy of his own. The Pearl Coast is not far out of place, but Hispaniola is more than five degrees too far north and above the tropic of Cancer; the tip of Florida comes in 35°, which is ten degrees too far north; and for aught we know the error may go on increasing to the top of the map. The latitude assigned to " C. del mar usiano " is 55°, the latitude of Hopedale on the coast of Labrador! That is of course absurd. But if we turn back to the Cantino sketch of Florida and suppose the *proportions* of the sailing chart from which it was taken to have been fairly preserved, we may give a sort of definiteness to our guessing. As a starting-point, what is the " River of Palms " ? M. Varnhagen thinks it is the Mississippi,[1] and if we were to

[1] Varnhagen, *Amerigo Vespucci*, p. 98.

adopt that scale it would throw the "Costa del mar vạano" as far north as Long Island. But I suspect that M. Varnhagen is mistaken. This "River of Palms" may be seen in the same place upon the *Tabula Terre Nove*, and farther to the left, a little above the 30th parallel, we see the delta-like mouth of a much larger river, which strongly suggests the Mississippi. Although it is tilted too far to the left and the coast-line is incorrectly drawn, such things are what we expect to find in these old maps. It seems to me that this is the Mississippi, and that the river of the palms or palmettos is the Appalachicola, while the lake of the parrots may be St. Andrew's bay or Santa Rosa bay. Perhaps as far as the Chesapeake With the scale thus reduced the "Costa del mar vạano" (which should probably be "Cabo del mar oceano") may very probably represent Cape Hatteras. If this was the point reached by Vespucius, as he says, in June, 1498, we can easily understand the significance of the name "Cape of the end of April,"[1] applied to the extremity of Florida.

---

[1] On St. Bernard's day, August 20, Vespucius was very likely at the Bermudas, and Mr. Hubert Bancroft (*Central America*, vol. i. p. 106) suggests that "the Bermudas may have been the archipelago of San Bernardo, famous for its fierce Carib population, but generally located off the Gulf of Urabá." This seems not unlikely.

The reader must not attach to these suggestions an importance which I am far from claim-
ing for them. The subject is a difficult one, and
stands much in need of further clues, which
perhaps may yet be found. The obscurity in
which this voyage has so long been enveloped
is due chiefly to the fact that it was not followed
up till many years had elapsed, and Why the
the reason for this neglect impresses voyage was
not followed
upon us forcibly the impossibility of up
understanding the history of the Discovery of
America unless we bear in mind all the atten-
dant circumstances. One might at first suppose
that a voyage which revealed some 4000 miles
of the coast of North America would have
attracted much attention in Spain and have become altogether too famous to be soon forgotten. Such an argument, however, loses sight of
the fact that these early voyagers were not trying
to "discover America." There was nothing to
astonish them in the existence of 4000 miles of
coast-line on this side of the Atlantic. To their
minds it was simply the coast of Asia, about
which they knew nothing except from Marco
Polo, and the natural effect of such a voyage as
this would be simply to throw discredit upon
that traveller. So long a stretch of coast without any great and wealthy cities did not answer
at all to his descriptions. It may seem strange
that Pinzon and Solis did not come upon pyram-

idal temples and other evidences of semi-civil-ization on the coast of Yucatan, as Hernandez de Cordova did in 1517; but any one who has sailed along coasts in various weathers knows well how easy it is for things to escape notice at one time which at another time fairly jump at your eyes. As will be shown in the next chap-ter, it was such sights in 1517, after Cuba had been colonized by Spaniards, that turned the drift of exploration into the Gulf of Mexico. Not happening to catch sight of such things in 1497, and nowhere finding an abun-dance of gold or jewels or spices, the voyagers did not regard their expedi-tion as much of a success, and there is no reason why people in Spain should have so regarded it. If King Ferdinand made an especial venture on this occasion, he probably took no pleasure in recollecting the fact or having it recalled to him. Indeed, the tone of Vespucius, in this part of his letter to Soderini, is not at all that of a man exulting in the consciousness of having taken part in a great discovery. He says that they did not find anything of profit in that country, ex-cept some slight indications of gold; but he suggests that perhaps they might have done better if they had understood the languages of the natives. The general impression left by the letter is that but for the capture of as many slaves as they could crowd into their four cara-

It was not a commercial success

vels, they would have returned home without much to show for their labours.

It is plain, then, that the 1497 voyage of Pinzon and Solis was not followed up for precisely the same reason that prevented the voyages of the Cabots from being followed up. There was no prospect of immediate profit, and, moreover, public attention was absorbed in another direction. All eyes were turned to the south, and for a good reason, as I had occasion to observe in the preceding chapter, in connection with the declining reputation of Columbus. In July, 1499, Vasco da Gama returned to Lisbon from Hindustan, with ships laden with the riches of the East. The fame of this achievement for the time threw Columbus quite into the shade. The glories of Cipango and Cathay seemed unsubstantial, like promissory notes thrice renewed, when Portugal stepped blithely into the foreground jingling the hard cash. Interest in the eastern coast of Asia for the moment died away. The great object was to get into the Indian Ocean, and come as nearly as possible to the rich countries visited by Gama. Spain could not go east of the papal meridian; she must go to the west and seek the vaguely rumoured Strait of Malacca, which was supposed to be somewhere to the south of Honduras. Nothing more was done in the Gulf of Mexico for twenty years, and the first voyage

All eyes were turned toward the Indian Ocean

made by Spaniards in those waters was probably seldom talked of.

We have already seen that the fourth voyage of Columbus was a direct response to the voyage of Gama. It was an attempt to get from the Atlantic into the Indian Ocean. If the view here taken of the first voyage of Vespucius be correct, Columbus must have known its results in 1502, for he took with him Pedro Ledesma, who had been one of the pilots in that voyage. Perhaps the admiral may have selected him for that very reason. Ledesma would naturally tell Columbus that he had sailed through the passage between Cuba and Yucatan, and found a continental coast which led him ultimately far to the north of the tropic of Cancer. Columbus would thus see that Cuba, though not a part of the continent as he had supposed, was nevertheless close by it; that a voyage upon the coast of that continent would, as he had supposed, only lead him northward; and that he was not likely in the latitude of Cuba to find a channel westward through Asia into the Indian Ocean. With his general view of the situation thus confirmed in spite of the insularity of Cuba, Columbus had no motive for steering west; and the prompt decisiveness with which from the Queen's Gardens he steered across open sea straight for Cape Honduras and there turned

Probable influence of the first voyage of Vespucius upon the fourth of Columbus

eastward is to my mind a strong indication that
he was well informed as to what his friend
Americus had seen to the west of that cape.
But for such definite information would he not
have hugged the coast of Cuba? and when he
had thus passed his "Cape of Good Hope"
and reached the end of the island, with no land
in sight before him in any direction, would not
a natural impulse have carried him westward
into the Gulf of Mexico?

The fourth voyage of Columbus was not the
first response made by Spain to the voyage of
Gama. The first response was entrusted to
Vicente Yañez Pinzon, the way hav- Second voy-
ing been indicated by the second voy- age of Ves-
age of Vespucius, in company with pucius
Ojeda and La Cosa, in the summer of 1499.
The voyage of Ojeda was instigated by Bishop
Fonseca, with some intention of taking out of
the hands of Columbus the further exploration
of the coast upon which valuable pearls had
been found. The expedition sailed May 16,
1499, from Cadiz, ran down to the Cape Verde
Islands, crossed the equator, and sighted land
on the coast of Brazil in latitude 4° or 5° S.,
somewhere near Aracati. Vespucius gives a good
account of this half-drowned coast.[1]   Thence

[1] The landfall on this voyage has been commonly placed
on the coast of Surinam, about 600 miles eastward from Trin-

the ships ran a few leagues to the southeast, probably to see whether the shore seemed to

idad. This is because Ojeda, in his testimony in the *Probanzas*, did not allude to any place farther east than Surinam. But this negative evidence is here of small value. In a second voyage, in 1502, Ojeda had trespassed upon Portuguese territory, and had been censured and heavily fined for so doing (Navarrete, tom. ii. p. 430). Evidently in giving his testimony, in 1513, Ojeda thought it prudent to give the Portuguese a wide berth, and as there was no occasion for his saying that he had been on the coast of Brazil, he said nothing about it. The account of Vespucius is clear and straightforward. It is true that Mr. Hubert Bancroft says, " his account in the different forms in which it exists is so full of blunders that it could throw but little light upon the subject " (*Central America*, vol. i. p. 113). When Mr. Bancroft says this, he of course has in mind the spurious letter published in 1745 by Bandini, in which Vespucius is supposed to give to his friend Lorenzo di Pier Francesco de' Medici an account of his second voyage. The MS. of this letter which professes to be an original, and by which Bandini was deceived, is at Florence, in the Biblioteca Riccardiana, MS. No. 2112. Neither the paper nor the ink is older than the seventeenth century, the handwriting is not that of Vespucius, the language is a very different Italian from that which he used, and the pages swarm with absurdities. (See Varnhagen's paper in *Bulletin de la société de géographie*, avril, 1858.) Nothing except the blundering change of *Lariab* to *Parias* has done so much to bemuddle the story of Vespucius as this letter which some clever scamp was kind enough to write for him after he had been more than a hundred years under the sod. It is curious to see the elaborate arguments to which Humboldt was driven, in his *Examen critique*, tom. v., because he did not begin at the beginning, with textual criticism

be that of an island or a continent. Finding progress difficult against the equatorial current, they turned about and ran northwest as far as Cayenne, thence to Paria, and so on to Maracaibo and to Cape de la Vela. From this point Ojeda, with part of the little squadron, went over to Hispaniola, and arrived there on the 5th of September. Ojeda's visit to that island was made in no friendly spirit toward Columbus, but there is good reason for believing that the admiral or some of his people learned the particulars of Ojeda's route across the ocean and his landfall. Early in October two caravels were sent from San Domingo to Spain, and probably carried such information as to determine the route to be taken by Pinzon. That gallant captain started in December, and followed in the track of Vespucius and Ojeda, but went a little farther to the south, *Second voyage of Pinzon* losing sight of the pole-star, and finally striking the coast of Brazil near the site of Pernambuco, in latitude 8° S. Our accounts of this voyage[1] are meagre, and it does not

of sources, and so accepted this epistle as genuine. The account of Ojeda's voyage in the third volume of Irving's *Columbus*, from its mixing the first and second voyages of Vespucius, is so full of blunders as to be worse than worthless to the general reader.

[1] Manuel de Valdovinos, one of the witnesses in the *Probanzas*, says that he went on this voyage with Pinzon *the* SECOND *time that he* (Pinzon) *went to make discoveries* (" la

appear just why Pinzon turned northward from that point. While crossing the equator from south to north, with no land in sight, he found the sea-water fresh enough to drink. Full of wonder at so strange a thing, he turned in toward the coast and entered the mouth of the greatest river upon the earth, the Amazon, nearly a hundred miles wide and sending huge volumes of fresh water more than a hundred miles out into the sea. After proceeding as far as the Pearl Coast and Hispaniola, and losing two of his ships in a hurricane, Pinzon returned to Spain in September, 1500. When he arrived he found that his fellow-townsman Diego de Lepe had set sail just after him, in January, with two caravels, and had returned in June, after having doubled Cape San Roque and followed the Brazilian coast to latitude 10° S., or thereabouts, far enough to begin to recognize its southwesterly trend.[1]

segunda vez que fué á descubrir,'' Navarrete, tom. iii. p. 552). This might mean that his first voyage was the one with Columbus in 1492, but in accordance with the general usage of these speakers, the phrase refers to him as for the second time in command, so that his first voyage must have been that of 1497–98.

[1] From June, 1499, to April, 1500, Pero Alonso Niño and Cristoval Guerra made a voyage to the Pearl Coast and acquired much wealth, but as it contributed nothing to the progress of discovery I have not included it in my list.

The voyage of Rodrigo de Bastidas, with La Cosa for

Affairs now became curiously complicated.
King Emanuel of Portugal entrusted to Pedro
Alvarez de Cabral the command of a fleet for
Hindustan, to follow up the work of Cabral crosses
Gama and establish a Portuguese cen- the Atlantic
tre of trade on the Malabar coast. accidentally
This fleet of thirteen vessels, carrying about
1200 men, sailed from Lisbon March 9, 1500.
After passing the Cape Verde Islands, March
22, for some reason not clearly known, whether
driven by stormy weather or seeking to avoid
the calms that were apt to be troublesome on
the Guinea coast, Cabral took a somewhat more
westerly course than he realized, and on April
22, after a weary progress averaging less than
60 miles per day, he found himself on the coast
of Brazil not far beyond the limit reached by
Lepe.   It was easy enough thus to cross the
ocean unintentionally, for in that latitude the
Brazilian coast lies only ten degrees west of
the meridian of the Cape Verde Islands, and
the southern equatorial current, unknown to Cabral, sets strongly toward the very spot whither
he was driven.   Approaching it in such a way
Cabral felt sure that this coast must fall to the

pilot, from October, 1500, to September, 1502, was also in
its main intent a voyage for pearls and gold, but it completed
the discovery of the northern coast of what we now know to
be South America, from Cape de la Vela to Puerto Bello on
the Isthmus of Darien.

east of the papal meridian. Accordingly on
May day, at Porto Seguro in latitude 16° 30′ S.,
he took formal possession of the country for
Portugal, and sent Gaspar de Lemos in one of
his ships back to Lisbon with the news.[1] On
May 22 Cabral weighed anchor and stood for
the Cape of Good Hope. As the fleet passed
that famous headland the angry Genius of the
Cape at last wreaked his vengeance upon the
audacious captain who had dared to reveal his
secret. In a frightful typhoon four ships were
sunk, and in one of them the gallant Bartholomew Dias found a watery grave.

Cabral called the land he had found Vera
Cruz, a name which presently became Santa
Cruz ; but when Lemos arrived in Lisbon with
the news he had with him some gorgeous paro-
quets, and among the earliest names on old
maps of the Brazilian coast we find " Land of
Paroquets " and " Land of the Holy Cross."
The land lay obviously so far to the east that
Spain could not deny that at last there was
something for Portugal out in the " ocean sea."
Much interest was felt at Lisbon. King Eman-

---

[1] See Gandavo, *Historia da provincia Santa Cruz a vul-
garmente chamamos Brazil*, Lisbon, 1576, cap. i. ; Riccioli,
Geographia et Hydrographia, Venice, 1671, lib. iii. cap. 22 ;
Barros, *Asia*, dec. i. lib. v. cap. 2 ; Macedo, *Noções de Co-
rographia do Brasil*, Rio de Janeiro, 1873 ; Machado, *Memoria sobre o descobrimento do Brasil*, Rio de Janeiro, 1855.

uel began to prepare an expedition for exploring this new coast, and wished to secure the services of some eminent pilot and cosmographer familiar with the western waters. Overtures were made to Americus, a fact which proves that he had already won a high reputation. The overtures were accepted, for what reason we do not know, and soon after his return from the voyage with Ojeda, probably in the autumn of 1500, Americus passed from the service of Spain into that of Portugal.

Vespucius passes into the service of Portugal

The remark was made long ago by Dr. Robertson, that if Columbus had never lived, and the chain of causes and effects at work independently of him had remained unchanged, the discovery of America would not long have been postponed.[1] It would have been discovered by accident on April 22, 1500, the day when Cabral first saw the coast of Brazil. All other navigators to the western shores of the Atlantic since 1492 were successors of Columbus ; not so Cabral. In the line of causal sequence he was the successor of Gama and Dias, of Lançarote and Gil Eannes, and the freak of wind and wave that carried him to Porto Seguro had no connection with the scientific triumph of the great Genoese.

America would have been discovered without Columbus

[1] Robertson, *History of America*, book ii. Harrisse makes a similar remark in the preface to his *Christophe Colomb*.

This adventure of Cabral's had interesting consequences. It set in motion the train of events which ended after some years in placing the name "America" upon the map. On May 14, 1501, Vespucius, who was evidently principal pilot and guiding spirit in this voyage under unknown skies, set sail from Lisbon with three caravels. It is not quite clear who was chief captain, but M. Varnhagen has found reasons for believing that it was a certain Don Nuno Manuel.[1] The first halt was made on the African coast at Cape Verde, the first week in June; and there the explorers met Cabral on his way back from Hindustan. According to the letter attributed to Vespucius and published in 1827 by Baldelli,[2] the wealth stowed away in Cabral's ships was quite startling. "He says there was an immense quantity of cinnamon, green and dry ginger, pepper, cloves, nutmegs, mace, musk, civet, storax, benzoin, porcelain, cassia, mastic, incense, myrrh, red and white sandalwood, aloes, camphor, amber," Indian hemp and cypress, as well as opium and other drugs too numerous to mention. "Of jewels he saw many diamonds, rubies, and pearls, and one ruby of a most beau-

Vespucius meets Cabral at Cape Verde

[1] Varnhagen, *Nouvelles recherches sur les derniers voyages du Navigateur Florentin*, Vienna, 1869, p. 9.

[2] If not itself genuine, it is very likely based on genuine memoranda.

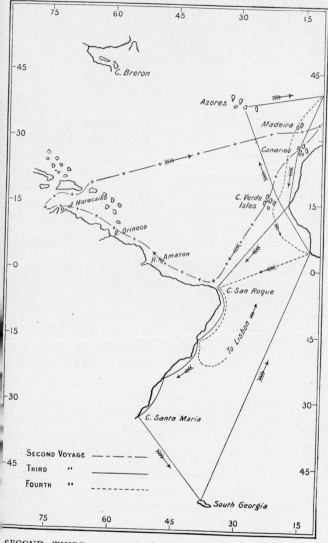

SECOND, THIRD, AND FOURTH VOYAGES OF VESPUCIUS

tiful colour weighed seven carats and a half, but he did not see all."[1] Verily, he says, God has prospered King Emanuel.

After leaving Cape Verde the little fleet had to struggle through the belt of calms, amid a perpetual sultry drizzle with fierce thunder and lightning. After sixty-seven days of "the vilest weather ever seen by man" they reached the coast of Brazil in latitude about 5° S., on the evening of the 16th of August, the festival-day of San Roque, whose name was accordingly given to the cape before which they dropped anchor. From this point they slowly followed the coast to the southward, stopping now and then to examine the country. In some places the inhabitants were ferocious Indians, who received them with showers of arrows, but fled in terror from firearms.[2] In other places they found the

On his third voyage Vespucius explores the coast of Brazil,

---

[1] Major, *Prince Henry the Navigator*, p. 412 ; see the document in Varnhagen, *Amerigo Vespucci*, p. 81.

[2] "There were two in the shippe which toke vpon them to vewe the lande, and learne what spyces and other commodities might be had therein. They were appoynted to returne within the space of fiue daies at the vttermost. But when eyght dayes were now paste, they whiche remayned in the shippes heard yet nothing of theyr returne : wher as in the meane time great multitudes of other people of the same lande resorted to the Sea syde, but could by no meanes be allured to communicacion. Yet at the length they broughte certaine women, which shewed themselues familier towarde the Span-

natives disposed to be friendly, but "wicked and licentious in their manner of living, more like the style of the Epicureans than that of the Stoics. All their women are in common, and they have neither kings nor temples nor idols. Neither have they commerce or money; but they have strife among them and fight most cruelly and without any order. They also feed on human flesh. I saw one very wicked wretch who boasted, as if it were no small honour to himself, that he had eaten three hundred men. I saw also a certain town, in which I staid about

and meets with cannibals

iardes [*i. e.* Portuguese]. Wherupon they sent forth a young man, beyng very strong and quicke, at whom as the women wondered, and stode gazing on him and feling his apparell, there came sodenynly a woman downe from a mountayne, bringing with her secretely a great stake, with which she gaue him such a stroke behynde that he fell dead on the earth. The other womenne foorthwith toke hym by the legges, and drewe him to the mountayne, whyle in the mean tyme the men of the countreye came foorth with bowes and arrowes, and shot at oure men. But the [Portuguese] dischargeing foure pieces of ordenaunce agaynst them, droue them to flighte. The women also which had slayne the yong man, cut hym in pieces euen in the sight of the [Portuguese], shewing them the pieces, and rosting them at a greate fyre. The men also made certayn tokens, wherby they declared that not past viii. daies before they had in lyke maner serued other christian men. Wherfore ye [Portuguese] hauinge thus sustayned so greuous iniuries vnreuenged, departed with euil wyl." Eden's *Treatise of the Newe India*, London, 1553.

twenty-seven days, where salted human flesh was suspended from the roofs of the houses, even as we suspend the flesh of the wild boar from the beams of the kitchen, after drying and smoking it, or as we hang up strings of sausages. They were astonished to hear that we did not eat our enemies, whose flesh they say is very appetizing, with dainty flavour and wondrous relish." [1] The climate and landscape pleased Americus much better than the people. He marvelled at the temperate and balmy atmosphere, the brilliant plumage of the birds, the enormous trees, and the aromatic herbs, endowed by fancy with such hygienic virtues that the people, as he understood them to say, lived to be a hundred and fifty years old. His thoughts were of Eden, like those of Columbus on the Pearl Coast. If the terrestrial paradise is anywhere to be found on the earth, said Vespucius, it cannot be far from this region.

So much time was given to inspecting the country and its inhabitants that the progress of the ships was slow. It was not until The Bay of All Saints day, the first of November, All Saints that they reached the bay in latitude 13° S., which is still known by the name which they gave it, Bahia de Todos Santos.[2] On New

[1] See the letter to Medici, in Varnhagen, *Amerigo Vespucci*, p. 19.

[2] The misreading of this name, in which the *h* was changed

Year's day, 1502, they arrived at the noble bay where fifty-four years later the chief city of Brazil was founded. They would seem to have mis-

Change of direction near the mouth of La Plata

taken it for the mouth of another huge river, like some that had already been seen in this strange world ; for they called it Rio de Janeiro (river of January).[1] Thence by February 15 they had passed Cape Santa Maria, when they left the coast and took a southeasterly course out into the ocean. Americus gives no satisfactory reason for this change of direction ; such points were probably reserved for his book. Perhaps he may have looked into the mouth of the river La Plata, which is a bay more than a hundred miles wide;

into *d*, gave rise to one of the funniest absurdities known to geography. *A Bahia de Todos Santos* became *La Badia de Todos Santos* (Latin, *Abbatia Omnium Sanctorum*) ; so the *Bay* became an *Abbey*, supposed to exist on that barbarous coast ! ! The reader may see this name, given very distinctly, upon the Ruysch map, and also (if his eyes are sharp) on the *Tabula Terre Nove*.

Mr. Winsor (*Narr. and Crit. Hist.*, viii. 373) attributes the discovery of the Bahia de Todos Santos to Christovão Jaques in 1503. But that is impossible, for the name occurs in that place on the Cantino map. Vespucius arrived in Lisbon September 7, 1502 ; so that I believe we can fix the date of that map at between September 7 and November 19, 1502.

[1] Varnhagen, p. 110 ; the name is sometimes attributed to Martino de Sousa, 1531, but that is improbable. See Winsor, *Narr. and Crit. Hist.*, viii. 390.

and the sudden westward trend of the shore may have led him to suppose that he had reached the end of the continent. At any rate, he was now in longitude more than twenty degrees west of the meridian of Cape San Roque, and therefore unquestionably out of Portuguese waters. Clearly there was no use in going on and discovering lands which could belong only to Spain. This may account, I think, for the change of direction. New lands revealed toward the southeast might perhaps come on the Portuguese side of the line. Americus was already somewhat farther south than the Cape of Good Hope, and nearer the antarctic pole than any civilized man had ever been before, except Bartholomew Dias. Possibly he may also have had some private notion of putting Ptolemy's theory of antarctic land to the test. On the part of officers and crews there seems to have been ready acquiescence in the change of course. It was voted that for the rest of the voyage Americus should assume the full responsibility and exercise the chief command ; and so, after laying in food and fresh water enough to last six months, they started for realms unknown.

The nights grew longer and longer until by April 3 they covered fifteen hours. On that day the astrolabe showed a southern latitude of 52°. Before night a frightful storm overtook our navigators, and after four days of scudding under bare poles, land hove in sight, but no words of welcome greeted it. In that rough sea Discovery of South Georgia, April 7, 1502 the danger on such a coast was appalling, all the more so because of the fog and sleet. It was the island of South Georgia, in latitude 54° S., and about 1200 miles east from Tierra del Fuego. Captain Cook, who rediscovered it in January (midsummer), 1775, called it the most wretched place he had ever seen on the globe. In comparison with this scarped and craggy island, covered down to the water's edge with glaciers, Cook called the savage wastes of Tierra del Fuego balmy and hospitable. Struggling gusts lash the waves into perpetual fury, and at intervals in the blinding snow-flurries, alternated with freezing rains, one catches ominous glimpses of tumbling ice-floes and deadly ledges of rock. For a day and a night while the Portuguese ships were driven along within sight of this dreadful coast, the sailors, with blood half frozen in their veins, prayed to their patron saints and made vows of pilgrimage. As soon as the three ships succeeded in exchanging signals, it was decided to make for home. Vespucius then Return to Lisbon, Sept. 7, 1502 headed straight N. N. E., through the huge ocean, for Sierra Leone, and the distance of more than 4000 miles was made — with wonderful accuracy, though Vespucius says nothing about that — in thirty-three days.

MUNDUS NOVUS

At Sierra Leone one of the caravels, no longer
seaworthy, was abandoned and burned ; after a
fortnight's rest ashore, the party went on in the
other two ships to the Azores, and thence after
some further delay to Lisbon, where they arrived on the 7th of September, 1502.

When we remember how only sixty-seven
years before this date the dauntless Gil Eannes
sailed into the harbour of Lisbon *Historical
amid deafening plaudits over the *importance
proud news that in a coasting voy- *of this voyage*
age he had passed beyond Cape Bojador, there
is something positively startling in the progress
that had been achieved. Among all the voyages
made during that eventful period there was none
that as a feat of navigation surpassed this third
of Vespucius, and there was none, except the
first of Columbus, that outranked it in historical importance. For it was not only a voyage
into the remotest stretches of the Sea of Darkness, but it was preëminently an incursion into
the antipodal world of the southern hemisphere.
Antarctic cold was now a matter of positive
experience, no less than arctic cold.[1] Still more

[1] Vespucius might well have said, in the words of the great
Spanish epic : —

> Climas passé, mudé constelaciones,
> Golfos inavegables navigando,
> Estendiendo, Señor, vuestra corona
> Hasta la austral frigida zona.

Ercilla, *Araucana*, xxxvii.

333

remarkable was the change in the aspect of the starry heavens. Voyages upon the African coast had indeed already familiarized Portuguese sailors with the disappearance of the pole-star below the northern horizon, and some time before reaching the equator one could see the majestic Southern Cross.[1] But in this course from Lisbon to South Georgia Vespucius sailed over an arc of 93°, or more than one fourth the circumference of the globe. Not only the pole-star, but the Great Bear, the Swan, and the larger part of the constellations visible from Lisbon An Antarctic World sank out of sight; Castor and Pollux, Arcturus and the Pleiades, were still visible, but in strange places, while over all the sky ahead twinkled unknown stars, the Milky Way changed its shape, and the mysterious Coalsacks seemed to beckon the voyager onward into realms of eternal sleet and frost. Our Florentine navigator was powerfully affected by these sights. The strange coast, too, which he

[1] In Ptolemy's time the Southern Cross passed the meridian of Alexandria at an altitude of 6° 54' above the horizon; to-day, owing to the precession of the equinoxes, it is 3° below the horizon in that place. See Humboldt, *Examen critique*, tom. iv. p. 321. The sight of it was familiar to Christian anchorites in Egypt in the days of St. Athanasius, and to Arab sailors in the Red Sea in the Middle Ages, whence Dante may have got his knowledge of it. It finally passed out of sight at Alexandria about A. D. 1340. Cadamosto observed it in 1454 from the river Gambia.

had proved to extend at least as far south as the
Cape of Good Hope, arrested his attention in
a very different way from the coasts of Honduras and Florida. In these there was nothing to
startle one out of the natural belief that they
must be parts of Asia, but with the Brazilian
shore it was otherwise. A coast of continental
extent, beginning so near the meridian of the
Cape Verde Islands and running southwesterly
to latitude 35° S. and perhaps beyond, did not
fit into anybody's scheme of things. None of
the ancient geographers had alluded to such a
coast, unless it might be supposed to be connected with the Taprobane end of _Why Vespu-_
Mela's Antichthones, or with Ptole- _cius thought_
my's Terra Incognita far to the east _it was a_
"new
and southeast of Cattigara. In any _world"_
case it was land unknown to the ancients, and
Vespucius was right in saying that he had beheld there things by the thousand which Pliny
had never mentioned.[1] It was not strange that

---

[1] " Et certe credo quod Plinius noster millesimam partem
non attigerit generis psitacorum reliquarumque auium, necnon
& animalium que in iisdem regionibus sunt, cum tanta facie-
rum atque colorum diuersitate quod consumate picture artifex
Policletus in pingendis illis deficeret. Omnes arbores ibi sunt
odorate : et singule ex se ginnum vel oleum vel liquorem ali-
quem emittunt. Quorum proprietates si nobis note essent non
dubito quin humanis corporis saluti forent, & certe si paradisus
terrestris in aliqua sit terre parte, non longe ab illis regionibus
distare existimo." Varnhagen, p. 21. In this charming pas-

he should call it a New World, and in meeting with this phrase, on this first occasion in which it appears in any document with reference to any part of what we now call America, the reader must be careful not to clothe it with the meaning which it wears in our modern eyes. In using the expression "New World" Vespucius was not thinking of the Florida coast which he had visited on a former voyage, nor of the "islands of India" discovered by Columbus, nor even of the Pearl Coast which he had followed after the admiral in exploring. The expression occurs in his letter to Lorenzo de' Medici, written from Lisbon in March or April, 1503, relating solely to this third voyage. The letter begins as follows : —

"I have formerly written to you at sufficient length [1] about my return from those new coun-

---

sage the great sailor, by a slip of the memory, got one of his names wrong. It was not the sculptor Polycletus, but the painter Polygnotus that he really had in mind.

[1] Several allusions in the letter indicate that Vespucius had written to Lorenzo soon after his return, announcing that fact and promising to send him his journal of the voyage. He was unable to fulfil this promise because the king of Portugal kept the journal and Vespucius felt delicate about asking him for it. At last, in the spring of 1503, before starting on another long voyage, our navigator wrote this brief letter to his old friend, giving him "just the main points," though he had not yet recovered his journal.

tries which in the ships and at the expense and command of the most gracious king of Portugal we have sought and found. It is proper to call them a new world." His letter to Lorenzo

Observe that it is only the new countries visited on this third voyage, the countries from Cape San Roque southward, that Vespucius thinks it proper to call a new world, and here is his reason for so calling them : —

" Since among our ancestors there was no knowledge of them, and to all who hear of the affair it is most novel. For it transcends the ideas of the ancients ; since most of them say that beyond the equator to the south there is no continent, but only the sea which they called Atlantic, and if any of them asserted the existence of a continent there, they found many reasons for refusing to consider it a habitable country. But this last voyage of mine has proved that this opinion of theirs was erroneous and in every way contrary to the facts, since in those southern regions I have found a continent more thickly inhabited by peoples and animals than our Europe, or Asia, or Africa, and moreover a climate more temperate and agreeable than in any other region known to us ; as you will understand below when I write you briefly just the main points, and [describe] the most remarkable things that were seen or heard by

me in this new world, — as will appear below."[1]

[1] I give here in parallel columns two of the earliest texts of
this very interesting and important paragraph : —

Latin text of 1504.

"Superioribus diebus satis
ample tibi scripsi de reditu
meo ab novis illis regionibus
quas et classe et impensis et
mandato istius serenissimi Por-
tugalio Regis perquisivimus
& invenimus. Quasque no-
vum mundum appelare licet.
Quando apud maiores nostros
nulla de ipsis fuerit habita
cognitio & audientibus omnibus sit nouissima res. Et enim
hec opinionem nostrorum an-
tiquorum excedit : cum illorum maior pars dicat vltra
lineam equinotialem et versus
meridiem non esse continentem, sed mare tantum quod
Atlanticum vocauere et si qui
eorum continentem ibi esse
affirmauerunt, eam esse terram
habitabilem multis rationibus
negaverunt. Sed hanc eorum
opinionem esse falsam et veri-
tati omnino contrariam, hec
mea ultima navigatio declara-
uit, cum in partibus illis meri-
dianis continentem invenerim

*Italian version in Venetian
dialect, Vicenza,* 1507.

"Li passati zorni assai am-
plame'te te scrissi de la mia
retornata de q̗lli noui paese :
iquali & cu' larmata & cu'
lespese & coma'dame'to de
q̗sto Serenissimo Re de portogallo hauemo cercato & retrouato : i q̗li nouo mondo
chiamare ne sta licito p̗ ch'
ap̗sso dei mazori n̗ri niuna
de q̗lli estata hauta cognitio'e : & a tuti q̗lli che al-
dira'no sera nouissime cose :
imperoche q̗sto la oppinione
de li n̗ri antiq̗ excede : co'-
cio sia che d' q̗lli la mazor
p̗te dica ultra lalinea eq̗-
notiale : & uerso el mezo zorno
no' esser co'tinente : Ma el
mare solame'te : el qual Ata-
la'tico ha'no chiamato : E si
qual che uno de q̗lle co'tinente li esser ha'no affirmato :
q̗lla esser terra habitabile per
molte rasione ha'no negato.
Ma questa sie oppinione esser
falsa & alauerita ogni modo
co'traria : Questa mia ultima

This expression "Novus Mundus," thus occurring in a private letter, had a remarkable career. Early in June, 1503, about the time when Americus was starting on his fourth voyage, Lorenzo died. By the beginning of 1504, a Latin version of the letter was printed and published, with the title "Mundus Novus." It is a small quarto of only four leaves, with no indication of place or date; but on the verso of the last leaf we are informed that "The interpreter Giocondo translated this letter from the Italian into the Latin language, that all who are

The letter translated into Latin and published by the architect Giocondo

frequentioribus populis & animalibus habitatam quam nostram Europam, seu Asiam, vel Africam, et insuper aerem magis temperatum et amenum quam in quauis alia regione a nobis cognita : prout inferius intelliges vbi succincte tantum rerum capita scribemus, et res digniores annotatione et memoria que a me vel vise vel audite in hoc nouo mundo fuere : vt infra patebit."

nauigatione he dechiarato : co' ciosia che in quelle parte meridionale el co'tinente io habia retrouato : de piu frequenti populi & a'i'ali habitata de la n ra Europa : o uero Asia : o uero Affrica : & ancora laere piu temperato & ameno : che in que banda altra regione de nui cognosciute : come de sotto intenderai : Doue breuamente solamente de la cose icapi scriueamo : & le cose piu degne de annotatio'e & de memoria : le qual da mi : o uero uiste : o uero audite in questo nouo mo'do foreno : como de sotto sera'no manifeste."

versed in the Latin may learn how many wonderful things are being discovered every day, and
that the temerity of those who want to probe
the Heavens and their Majesty, and to know
more than is allowed to know, be confounded;
as notwithstanding the long time since the world
began to exist, the vastness of the earth and
what it contains is still unknown." [1] This re-
buke to some of the audacious speculators of
the time is quite in the clerical vein, and we are
not surprised to learn that "the interpreter
Giocondo" [2] was a Dominican friar. He was
Giovanni Giocondo, of Verona, the eminent
mathematician, the scholar who first edited Vi-
truvius, and himself an architect famous enough
to be entrusted with the building of the dome
of St. Peter's during part of the interval between
Bramante and Michael Angelo. [3] From 1499 to
1507 Giocondo was living in Paris, engaged in
building the bridge of Notre Dame, which is
still standing. [4] Of all the thousands who pass

[1] For an account of this and the other early editions of
Mundus Novus, see Harrisse, *Bibliotheca Americana Vetustissima*, pp. 55–88, and *Additions*, pp. 16–21, 26.

[2] "Iocūdus interpres" becomes, in the hands of the Venetian translator of 1507, "el iocondo interprete," *anglicè*
"the jocund interpreter"!!

[3] Symonds, *Renaissance in Italy*, vol. ii. p. 429, vol. iii.
p. 91.

[4] Sauval, *Histoire et recherches des antiquités de Paris*,
Paris, 1724, tom. i. p. 230; Tiraboschi, *Letteratura*

over it from day to day, how many have ever
dreamed of associating it with the naming of
America? This Giocondo, who is now positively
known to have been the one that translated the
letter of Vespucius,[1] was on terms of intimacy
with the Medici family at Florence and also with
Soderini. There would be nothing strange,
therefore, in a manuscript copy of a brief but
intensely interesting letter finding its way into
his hands from this quarter. I can find no indication that any *printed* Italian text preceded
this Latin version, and am disposed to believe
that Giocondo made it directly from a manuscript copy of the original letter. The first edition of Giocondo's version was clearly one of

italiana, Florence, 1809, tom. vi. pp. 128, 203, 1144–
1150.

[1] Walter Lud, *Speculum Orbis,* Strasburg, 1507, fol. iii.
This little tract, of only four leaves folio, has been of priceless
value in clearing up many of the unjust and absurd aspersions
against Vespucius. One of the only two copies known to be
now in existence was discovered in 1862 by my old and much
esteemed friend Henry Stevens, who was the first to point out
its importance. After trying in vain to place it in some American library, Mr. Stevens showed it to Mr. Major, and it
found a place in that greatest of all treasure-houses for the
materials of American history, the British Museum. It is one
of the most precious documents in the world. See Stevens,
Historical and Geographical Notes, p. 35 ; Avezac, *Martin
Waltzemüller,* pp. 60–67 ; Harrisse, *Bibliotheca Americana
Vetustissima,* No. 49. The other copy is in the Imperial
Library at Vienna.

those that were published in Paris late in 1503 or early in 1504. At that time Vespucius, on the coast of Brazil, and Columbus, on the coast of Jamaica, were alike contending against the buffets of adverse fortune. People in Europe, except the few persons directly concerned with their enterprises, took little heed of either of these mariners. The learned Giocondo, if interrogated about their doings, would probably have replied that Columbus had arrived at the eastern coast of Asia by sailing westward, and that Vespucius had disclosed the existence of an Inhabited World in the south temperate zone and in a new and untried direction. It surely would not have occurred to Giocondo that the latter achievement came into competition with the former or tended in any way to discredit it.

The little four-leaved tract, " Mundus Novus," turned out to be the great literary success of the day. M. Harrisse has described at least

Great interest felt in " Mundus Novus " eleven Latin editions probably published in the course of 1504, and by 1506 not less than eight editions of German versions had been issued. Intense curiosity was aroused by this announcement of the existence of a populous land beyond the equator and UNKNOWN (could such a thing be possible?) TO THE ANCIENTS!! One of the early Latin editions calls for especial mention, by reason of its title and its editor. Instead of the ordinary

"Mundus Novus" we find, as an equivalent, the significant title "De Ora Antarctica," concerning the Antarctic Coast lately discovered by the king of Portugal. This edition, published at Strasburg in 1505, was edited by "Master Ringmann Philesius," a somewhat pale and slender youth of two and twenty, who is a personage of much importance in our narrative. He was a young man of remarkable promise, a native of Schlestadt, a little town on ^{Matthias Ringmann} the eastern slope of the Vosges Mountains in Alsace. His name was Matthias Ringmann, but in accordance with the prevailing fashion he was more commonly known by a dog-Latin epithet, Philesius Vogesigena, in allusion to his birthplace. He acquired an early reputation by his graceful Latin verses, which sparkled with wit and could sting if the occasion required it. In 1504 Ringmann was in Paris, studying at the college of Cardinal Lemoine, and there he seems to have become acquainted with Fra Giocondo and with the letter of Vespucius, a new edition of which he presently brought out at Strasburg. Thus in its zigzag career the Italian letter sent by its writer from Lisbon to Florence was first turned into Latin and printed at Paris, with its phrase "New World" lifted up from the text and turned into a catching title, by the friar Giocondo, and thereupon a friend of this accomplished friar sent it into Alsace, and into a neighbourhood where the affair was soon to enter into a new stage of development.

We shall the better understand that further stage if we pause to illustrate, by means of two or three early maps, just what the phrase "New World" meant to the men who first used it. A glance at my sketch of Martin Behaim's globe [1] will assure the reader that in the old scheme of things there was no place for such a

What did the phrase "New World" originally mean?

---

[1] See above, p. 104. Martin Behaim was born at Nuremberg in 1436, and is said to have been a pupil of the celebrated astronomer, Regiomontanus, author of the first almanac published in Europe, and of Ephemerides, of priceless value to navigators. He visited Portugal about 1480, invented a new kind of astrolabe, and sailed with it in 1484 as cosmographer in Diego Cam's voyage to the Congo. On his return to Lisbon he was knighted, and presently went to live on the island of Fayal, of which his wife's father was governor. He was a friend of Columbus. Toward 1492 he visited Nuremberg, to look after some family affairs, and while there "he gratified some of his townspeople by embodying in a globe the geographical views which prevailed in the maritime countries; and the globe was finished before Columbus had yet accomplished his voyage. The next year (1493) Behaim returned to Portugal; and after having been sent to the Low Countries on a diplomatic mission, he was captured by English cruisers and carried to England. Escaping finally, and reaching the Continent, he passes from our view in 1494, and is scarcely heard of again." (Winsor, *Narr. and Crit. Hist.*, ii. 104.) He died in May, 1506. A ridiculous story that he anticipated Columbus in the discovery of America originated in the misunderstanding of an interpolated passage in

344

coast as that which Americus had lately explored.
Such a coast would start to the east of Behaim's
330th meridian, a little below the equator, and
would run at least as far south as the southern
extremity of Behaim's island of "Candyn." Nobody had ever dreamed of inhabited
land in such a place. What could it   Oceanic and
be? What could be said of its rela-   theories
tions to Asia? Two contrasted opinions are
revealed by the old maps. As in the days of
Ptolemy and Mela, we again see a dry theory
confronted by a wet theory. Some supposed
the "Land of the Holy Cross" to be a southeasterly projection from the vast continental
mass of Asia; others conceived it as an island
of quasi-continental dimensions lying to the

the Latin text of Schedel's *Registrum*, Nuremberg, 1493,
p. 290 (the so-called *Nuremberg Chronicle*). See Winsor,
op. cit. ii. 34 ; Major's *Prince Henry*, p. 326 ; Humboldt,
Examen critique, tom. i. p. 256; Murr, *Diplomatische Geschichte des Ritters Behaim*, Nuremberg, 1778 ; Cladera, *In-
vestigaciones históricas*, Madrid, 1794; Harrisse, *Bibliotheca
Americana Vetustissima*, pp. 37–43. — The globe made by
Behaim may now be seen in the city hall at Nuremberg. It
"is made of *papier-maché*, covered with gypsum, and over
this a parchment surface received the drawing ; it is twenty
inches in diameter." (Winsor, *op. cit.* ii. 105.) The
portion west of the 330th meridian is evidently copied from
Toscanelli's map. I give above (p. 111) a sketch (from
Winsor, after Ruge's *Geschichte des Zeitalters der Entdeckungen*, p. 230) of Behaim's ocean, with the outline of the
American continent superimposed in the proper place.

southeast of Asia, somewhat in the position actually occupied by Australia. This theory is most vividly presented on the map of the world

Ruysch's map, 1508

by Johann Ruysch, in the edition of Ptolemy published at Rome in 1508.[1] This is the earliest *published* map that shows

---

[1] A reduction of a part of the original map, in Ruysch's conical projection, may be seen in Winsor, *Narr. and Crit. Hist.*, iii. 8. As that projection would be puzzling to most readers, I have reduced it to Mercator's. An English translation of the various legends upon the map is here subjoined : —

A. "Here the ship's compass loses its property, and no vessel with iron on board is able to get away."

B. "This island was entirely burnt in 1456." [See above, vol. i. p. 279.]

C. "The ships of Ferdinand, king of Spain, have come as far as here." [See above, p. 304.]

D. "Marco Polo says that 1400 miles eastward from the port of Zaiton there is a very large island called Cipango, whose inhabitants are idolaters, and have their own king, and are tributary to no one. Here is a great abundance of gold and all sorts of gems. But as the islands discovered by the Spaniards occupy this spot, we have not ventured to place this island here, thinking that what the Spaniards call Spagnola [Hispaniola, Hayti] is the same as Cipango, since the things which are described as in Cipango are found in Spagnola, besides the idolatry."

E. "Spanish sailors have come as far as here, and they call this country a New World because of its magnitude, for in truth they have not seen it all nor up to the present time have they gone beyond this point.

UNIVERSALIOR
Johann Ruysch's Map of the World, publ

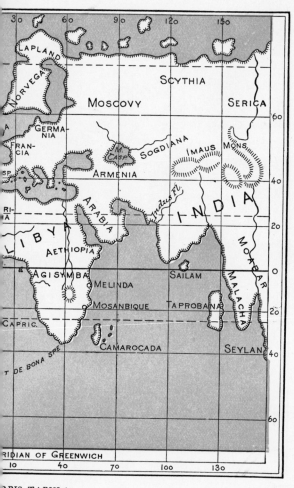

any parts of America, and it is the first such
map that was engraved, except perhaps the *Tabula Terre Nove*. It exhibits a study of many
and various sources of information, and is a
very interesting sketch of the earth's surface as
conceived at that time by a truly learned geographer. In the eastern half of his map Ruysch
is on a pretty firm ground of knowledge as far
east as the Ganges. The relative position of
Sailam (Ceylon) is indicated with a fair approach
to correctness. Taprobana (Ptolemy's Ceylon)
has now become a different island, apparently

> Wherefore it is here left incomplete, especially as we
> do not know in what direction it goes.''

F. " This region, which by many people is believed to
be another world (*alter terrarum orbis*), is inhabited
at different points by men and women who go about
either quite naked or clad in interwoven twigs adorned
with feathers of various hues. They live for the most
part in common, with no religion, no king ; they carry
on wars among themselves perpetually and devour the
flesh of human captives. They enjoy a wholesome
climate, however, and live to be more than 140 years
old. They are seldom sick, and then are cured merely
by the roots of herbs. There are lions here, and
serpents, and other horrid wild beasts. There are
mountains and rivers, and there is the greatest abundance of gold and pearls. The Portuguese have
brought from here brazil-wood and quassia.''

G. " Portuguese mariners have examined this part of this
country, and have gone as far as the 50th degree of
south latitude without reaching its southern extremity.''

Sumatra ; and both this island and Malacca are carried more than a thousand miles too far to the south, probably from associations with Ptolemy's Cattigara land. Curiously enough, Ceylon (Seylan) reappears in latitude 40° S. as the very tip end of Asia. Coming now to the western half of the map, we find Sumatra reappearing as " Iava Minor," and Java itself as " Iava Major " wildly out of place. Ciamba (Cochin China), Mangi and Cathay (southern and northern China) are given, after Marco Polo, with tolerable correctness ; but Bangala (Bengal) is mixed up with them on the coast of the Plisacus Sinus (Yellow Sea). Gog and Magog, from the Catalan map of 1375, are separated only by a great desert from Greenland, which is depicted with striking correctness in its relations to Gunnbjörn's Skerries (at B) and Iceland, as well as to Terra Nova (probably Labrador) and I. Baccalauras (Newfoundland). The voyages of the Cortereals are recognized in the name *C. de Portogesi*. In rather startling proximity comes the Barbadoes. The island which terminates with the scroll C probably represents the Florida of the Cantino map, with which this of Ruysch is demonstrably connected by the droll blunder " Abatia ōniū sāctorū " on the Brazilian coast. There is no mistaking Spagnola (Hayti), which Ruysch is still inclined (in legend D) to identify with Cipango. The fabulous Antilia is

in the same longitude as upon Behaim's globe.
If now, contrasting Ruysch with Behaim, we observe the emergence of the " Land of the Holy
Cross, or New World" from the Atlantic Ocean,
in place of the fabulous St. Brandan's Isle, we
cannot fail to see in a moment what was the most
huge and startling feature that had been added
to the map of the world during the interval
between 1492 and 1507. And this emergence
of land from an unknown deep was due chiefly
to the third voyage of Vespucius, for the short
extent of Pearl Coast explored by Columbus in
1498 was not enough to impress men's minds
with the idea of a great continent detached from
Asia.

So far as " Mundus Novus " is concerned, I
have called Ruysch's map an exponent of the
wet or oceanic theory. In its northern portion, however, where Green- The Lenox
globe, cir.
land and Labrador are joined to China, 1510
we have the continental or dry style of theorizing, very much after the fashion of Claudius
Ptolemy. For an extreme illustration of the
oceanic style of interpretation we must look to
the Lenox globe, which was discovered in Paris
about forty years ago, and afterward found its
way into the library of Mr. James Lenox, of
New York. This is a copper globe, about five
inches in diameter, made in two sections which
accurately fit together, making a spherical box;

the line of junction forms the equator. The maker's name is unknown, but it is generally agreed that it must have been made in 1510 or early in 1511.[1] It is one of the earliest records of a reaction against the theory that it would be possible to walk westward from Cuba to Spain dry-shod. Here the new discoveries are all placed in the ocean at a good distance from the continent of Asia, and all except South America are islands. The land discovered by the Cabots appears, without a name, just below the Arctic circle, with a small vessel approaching it on the east. Just above the fortieth parallel a big sea monster is sturdily swimming toward Portugal. The sixtieth meridian west from Lisbon cuts through Isabel (Cuba) and Hayti, which are placed too far north, as on most of the early maps. If we compare the position of these islands here with the imaginary Antilia on Ruysch's map, we shall have no difficulty in understanding how they came to be called Antilles. A voyage of about 1000 miles westward, from Isabel, on this Lenox globe, brings us to Zipangri (Japan), which occupies the position actually belonging to Lower California. Immediately southeast of Japan begins a vast island or quasi-continent, with the name " Terra

[1] There is a description of the Lenox globe by Dr. De Costa, in *Magazine of American History*, September, 1879, vol. iii. pp. 529–540.

do Brazil " at its northwestern extremity. The
general name of this whole portion of the earth
is " Mundus Novus " or " Terra Sanctæ Crucis." The purely hypothetical character of the
western coast-line is confessed by the dots. The
maker knew nothing of the existence of the Pacific Ocean and nothing of South America except the northern and eastern coasts; he had no
means of proving that it did not extend as solid
land all the way to Asia; but his general adher-
ence to the wet theory, *i. e.* his general disposition to imagine water rather than land in the
unknown regions, led him to give it a western
boundary. He would probably have called it a
vast island in the Atlantic Ocean. Observe that
the eastern coast seems to be known as far as
latitude 50° S. and beyond, and a notable eastward twist at the extremity seems intended to
include the ice-bound coast where Vespucius
turned back in 1502.

The Ruysch map and the Lenox globe illustrate sufficiently the various views of those who
were inclined to imagine the region we call
South America as separated from Asia by water.
In the globe we have an extreme instance of
oceanic theory, in Ruysch a kind of compromise. Now for an instance of the opposite or
continental theory we cannot do better than
cite a very remarkable globe, made, indeed, a
quarter of a century later than Ringmann's edi-

tion of the "Mundus Novus," but retaining
the earlier views in spite of more recent discoveries. This globe was made in 1531,
by Oronce Fine, better known as
Orontius Finæus, a native of Dau-
phiny, professor of mathematics in the Collège Royal de France. In his mathematics
Orontius, though clever, was decidedly un-
sound ; [1] but his knowledge of geography was
extensive and minute. One of the chief points
of interest in his globe is the conservatism with
which it presents a geographical theory derived
from Ptolemy, and dovetails into it the new
discoveries.[2] This makes it excellent testimony
to the views of the continentalists, if I may so
call them, in the time of Ruysch's map and the
Lenox globe. The reader must bear in mind
that before Orontius made his globe, Mexico

The globe of Orontius Finæus, 1531

---

[1] He believed that he had discovered how to square the
circle and trisect angles, " ce qui est un peu scandaleux de la
part d'un professeur du Collège Royal de France," says
Delambre, *Astronomie du Moyen Age*, p. 400.

[2] A double-hearted map representing this globe, with
northern and southern hemispheres each on a polar projection,
was published in Grynæus, *Novus Orbis*, Paris, 1531. It is
reproduced by Henry Stevens, in his *Historical and Geographical Notes*, London, 1869. Stevens also gives a reduction of it to Mercator's projection, after which I have made
my simplified sketch. For the sake of clearness I have omitted
many details which have nothing whatever to do with the
purpose for which it is here cited.

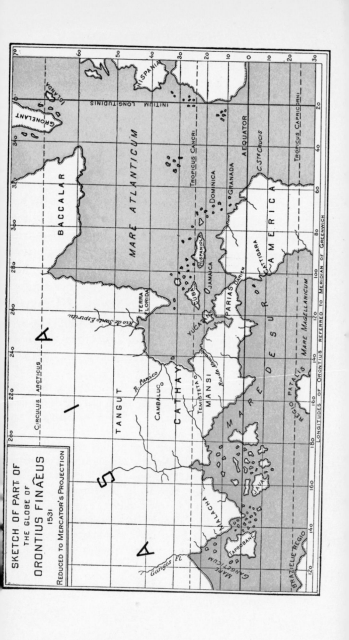

SKETCH OF PART OF
THE GLOBE OF
ORONTIUS FINÆUS
1531
Reduced to Mercator's Projection

CIRCULUS ARCTICUS

GROENLANT

GROENLANT ISLANDT

ISPANIA

BACCALAR

INITIUM LONGITUDINIS

MARE ATLANTICUM

TROPICUS CANCRI

DOMINICA

GRANADA

AEQUATOR

C. ST. CRUCIS

AMERICA

TROPICUS CAPRICORNI

TERRA
FLORIDA

Rio de Sta Espiritu

CUBA

HISPANIOLA

JAMACA

YUCATAN

FARIAS

CARTH

ANTIGARA

MARE DE SUR

TANGUT

CAMBALUC

CATHAY

TEMISTETA

MANSI

Rio de Rio

MARE MAGELLANICUM

REGIO PATALIS

LONGITUDES OF ORONTIUS REFERRED TO MERIDIAN OF GREENWICH

MALACHA

GANGES FL

Ganges Fl.

TAPROBANA

MARE
GANGETICUM

BRAZIELIE REGIO

had been discovered and conquered, the Pacific Ocean had been discovered and crossed, the Peruvian coast had been explored as far as latitude 10° S., the North American coast had been followed from Labrador to Florida, and Portuguese sailors had found their way around Malacca to the coast of China. Yet so far was Orontius from assimilating the unwieldy mass of facts so rapidly thrust before the mind, that we find him unable to surrender the preconceived theory — common to him with many other geographers — which made what we call South America a huge peninsula jutting out southeasterly from Asia. This, I say, was the dry or Ptolemaic way of conceiving the position of "Mundus Novus," as Ruysch's was the wet or Mela-like way of conceiving it.

Starting now from the prime meridian and from the top of the map, we may observe that Orontius has a fairly good idea of the relations between Greenland and Baccalar (Labrador-Newfoundland). Florida and the northern part of the Gulf of Mexico are quite well depicted. Observe the positions of the Rio de Santo Espiritu (the Mississippi), the R. Panuco, and the Rio de Alvarado, as well as of Temisteta (the city of Mexico); they are given with a fair approach to correctness. But observe also that these places are supposed to be in China, and there is Cambaluc (Peking) about 1000 miles distant

from the city of Mexico, slightly to west of
north! As for Parias (*i. e.* Lariab), which the
early maps sometimes correctly place by the
river Panuco, but which is oftener confounded
with Paria and placed near the island of Grenada, the worthy Orontius makes a compromise,
and it stands here for what we call Central
America. And now we come to the most instructive feature of the map. The Mexican
peninsula being represented as part of Asia, the
" Mundus Novus," here called AMERICA, is represented as a further offshoot from
Asia. But this is not all. In the
theory of Orontius America is evidently a part of the Terra Incognita
by which Ptolemy imagined Asia to
be joined to Africa, enclosing the Indian Ocean. This is proved by the
position of the name CATTIGARA,
which occurs in the same latitude at the easternmost verge of Ptolemy's world ; and it is further illustrated by the bits of antarctic continent
labelled " Regio Patalis " and "Brazielie Regio "
(!) peeping up from the lower border. The
" Mare Magellanicum," or Pacific Ocean, was to
the mind of Orontius only a huge gulf in a land-
locked Indian Ocean ! This notion of an antarctic continent coming well up into the southern
temperate zone may be seen upon many maps,

*The name
Cattigara
shows that
" America "
was supposed
to be part of
Ptolemy's
Terra Incog-
nita in the
southern
hemisphere*

and it survived into the seventeenth century.[1]
It was probably a reminiscence of both Ptolemy
and Mela, of Ptolemy's Terra Incognita and
Mela's Antichthon or Opposite-Earth. Mela's
idea that Taprobane, or some such point eastward in Asia, formed an entrance to this antipodal world[2] was very nearly in harmony with
the suggestion, upon Ptolemy's map, that one
might go thither from Cattigara.[3] In this southern world, according to Mela's doctrine of the
zones, the course of things was quite contrary
to that with which we are familiar. Shadows fell
to the south, it was summer in December and
winter in June, and the cold increased as you
went southward. Mela had even heard Mela's anti-
that somewhere out in " India," on podal world
the way toward this mysterious region, the
Greater and Lesser Bears disappeared from the

[1] See for example the maps of Agnese, 1536, and Gastaldi, 1548, below, vol. iii. pp. 328, 329. On the great influence of Ptolemy and Mela in the sixteenth century, there
are some good remarks in Thomassy, *Les Papes géographes et
la cartographie du Vatican*, Paris, 1852.

[2] See above, vol. i. p. 354.

[3] Orontius was not alone in identifying the New World
with Ptolemy's Cattigara land. The name recurs upon old
maps, as *e. g.* the French mappemonde of about 1540, now
in the British Museum. It is given in Winsor, *Narr. and
Crit. Hist.*, viii. 389. In this map, made after the discovery
of Peru had had time to take effect, the name Cattigara is
simply pushed southward into Chilian territory.

sky.[1] In the Middle Ages there was more or less discussion as to the possible existence of such an antipodal world as Mela had described ; and among the clergy there was a strong disposition to condemn the theory on the ground that it implied the existence of a race of men cut off (by an impassable torrid zone) from the preaching of the gospel. The notion of this fiery zone was irretrievably damaged when the Portuguese circumnavigated Africa ; it was finally demolished by the third voyage of Vespucius. Many things seen upon that voyage must have recalled Mela's antipodal world with startling vividness. It is true that the characteristics of the southern temperate zone had been to some extent observed in Africa. But to encounter them in a still greater degree and in the western ocean on the way to Asia, upon the coast of a vast country which no one could call by name, was quite another affair. That it did not fail to suggest Ptolemy's Terra Incognita is proved by the position of Cattigara and the general conception of the Indian Ocean upon the globe of Orontius ; and for those who preferred Mela's wet theory it was fair to suppose that the " Mundus Novus " as given upon Ruysch's

---

[1] *De Situ Orbis*, lib. iii. cap. 7 ; probably a misunderstanding of the very different statement reported by Strabo (ii. 1, § 19), that in the southern part of India the Greater and Lesser Bears are seen to set.

map was the entrance to that geographer's antipodal world. From a passage interpolated in the Latin text of the Nuremberg Chronicle (1493) we learn that this supposed antipodal world in the southern hemisphere was sometimes called "Quarta Pars." [1] Europe, Asia, and Africa were the three parts of the earth, and so this opposite region, hitherto unknown, but mentioned by Mela and indicated by Ptolemy, was the Fourth Part. We can now begin to understand the intense and wildly absorbing interest with which people read the brief story of the third voyage of Vespucius,[2] and we can see that in the nature

It was sometimes called "Quarta Pars"

---

[1] " Extra tres ptes orb : qrta ē ps trãsoccĕanũ ĭteriore ĩ meridie q sol' arderib⁸ nob' incognita ē̃ : ĩ cui⁸ finib⁸ antipodes fabulose habitare dicuntur." Harrisse, *Bibliotheca Americana Vetustissima*, p. 40.

[2] When we remember how much theological discussion there had been with regard to an antipodal world beyond the equator, we can appreciate the startling effect of the simple right-angled triangle with which Americus illustrated the statement that he had sailed over an arc of 90° from Lisbon to a point where the zenith corresponded to Lisbon's horizon : " Igitur ut dixi ab Olysippo, unde digressi sumus, quod ab linea equinoctiali distat gradibus trigintanouem semis nauigauimus vltra lineam equinoctialem per quinquaginta gradus qui simul juncti efficiunt gradus circiter nonaginta, que summa eam quartam partem obteniat summi circuli, secundum veram mensure rationem ab antiquis nobis traditam, manifestum est nos nauigasse quartam mundi partem. Et hac ratione nos Olysippum habitantes citra lineam equinoctialem gradu trigesimo

of that interest there was nothing calculated to bring it into comparison with the work of Columbus. The two navigators were not regarded as rivals in doing the same thing, but as men who had done two very different things; and

nono semis in latitudine septentrionali sumus ad illos qui gradu quingentesimo habitant vltra eandem lineam in meridionali latitudine angulariter gradus quinque in linea transuersali : et vt clarius intelligas : Perpendicularis linea que dum recti stamus a puncto celi imminente vertici nostro dependet in caput nosrum : illis dependet in datus [*read* latus] vel in costas. Quo fit vt nos simus in linea recta : ipsi vero in linea transuersa, et species fiat trianguli orthogoni, cujus vicem linee tenemus cathete ipsi autem basis et hipotenusa a nostro ad illorum pretenditur verticem : vt in figura patet.

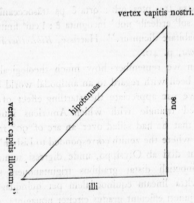

vertex capitis nostri.

hipotenusa

nos

vertex capitis illorum."

illi

Mundus Novus, 1504, apud Varnhagen, p. 24. The Venetian version introduces the above paragraph with the heading, ——

"Forma dela quarta parte de la terra retrouata."

358

to give credit to the one was by no means equivalent to withholding credit from the other.

The last point which we are called upon to observe in the Orontius globe is the occurrence of the name AMERICA in place of the *Mundus Novus* of the Ruysch map and the Lenox globe. Thus in about a quarter of a century the first stage in the development of the naming of America had been completed. That stage consisted of five distinct steps: 1. Americus called the regions visited by him beyond the equator a " new world " because they were unknown to the ancients; 2. Giocondo made this striking phrase *Mundus Novus* into a title for his translation of the letter, which he published at Paris while the writer was absent from Europe and probably without his knowledge;[1] 3. the name Mundus Novus got placed upon several maps as an equivalent for Terra Sanctæ Crucis, or what we call Brazil; 4. the suggestion was made that Mundus Novus was the Fourth Part of the earth, and might properly be named America, after its discoverer; 5. the name America thus got placed upon several maps as an equivalent for what we call Brazil, and sometimes came to

Successive steps in the naming of America

---

[1] Since Vespucius was so careful to withhold his book from the press until he could have leisure to revise it, I am inclined to believe that if he had known what Giocondo was doing he would not have been pleased.

stand alone as an equivalent for what we call South America, but still signified ONLY A PART OF THE DRY LAND BEYOND THE ATLANTIC TO WHICH COLUMBUS HAD LED THE WAY. We have described the first three of these steps, and it is now time to say something about the fourth and fifth.

René II. de Vaudemont, reigning Duke of Lorraine, and titular king of Sicily and Jerusalem — the "blue-eyed gentle René" who with the aid of stout Swiss halberds overthrew Charles the Bold at Nancy in 1477 — was an enthusiastic patron of literature and the arts, and at his little town of Saint-Dié, nestling in one of those quiet valleys in the Vosges Mountains which the beautiful tales of Erckmann-Chatrian have invested with imperishable charm, there was a college. The town had grown up about a Benedictine monastery founded in the seventh century by St. Deodatus, Bishop of Nevers. Toward the end of the tenth century this monastery was secularized and its government placed in the hands of a collegiate chapter of canons under the presidency of a mitred prelate whose title was Grand Provost. The chapter was feudal lord of the neighbouring demesnes, and thus as the population increased under its mild rule there grew up the small town in whose name

René II. of Lorraine

The town of Saint-Dié

Deodatus suffered contraction into *Dié*.[1] It is now a place of some 8000 inhabitants, the seat of a bishopric, and noted for its grain and cattle markets, its fine linen fabrics, and its note-paper. From the lofty peaks that tower above the town you can almost catch sight of Speyer, where Protestantism first took its name, while quite within the range of vision come Strasburg, associated with the invention of printing, Freiburg with that of gunpowder, and Vaucouleurs in the native country of the Maid of Orleans. The college of Saint-Dié was curiously associated with the discovery of America, for it was there that toward 1410 the Cardinal Pierre d'Ailly wrote his " Imago Mundi," the book which so powerfully influenced the thoughts of Columbus. At the end of that century there were several eminent men among the canons, as Pierre de Blarru, author of the local heroic poem the " Nancéide," Jean Basin de Sendacour, of whom we shall have ^{Walter Lud} more to say presently, and Duke René's secretary, Walter Lud. Under the auspices of the latter a printing press was set up at Saint-Dié about the year 1500, and so many learned men came to the college that Pico della Mirandola wondered how such a society could ever have been brought together in so obscure a town.

Avezac, *Martin Waltzemüller*, p. 12.

One of the lights of this little society was the brilliant and witty young Ringmann, who returned from Paris in 1505 and accepted a professorship of Latin at Saint-Dié. About the same time another young man of three and twenty or so, named Martin Waldseemüller,[1] a native of Freiburg in the Breisgau, was appointed professor of geography at Saint-Dié, and an intimate friendship sprang up between him and Ringmann. The latter had acquired while at Paris, and probably through his acquaintance with Fra Giocondo, a warm admiration for Vespucius, and published, as we have already seen, in 1505 a Latin version of the letter to Medici, under the title "De Ora Antarctica."

Martin Waldseemüller

Now Vespucius wrote his second epistle, the one to Soderini giving a brief account of his four voyages, at Lisbon, September 4, 1504, and Soderini had a certified MS. copy of it made February 10, 1505.[2] From that magistrate's hands it afterward passed into those of the publisher Pacini, for whom it was printed at Florence before July 9, 1506. From this Italian original, of which I have mentioned five copies

French version of the letter of Americus to Soderini

---

[1] The family name seems to have been Waltzemüller, but he always preferred to write it Waldseemüller. He was more commonly known by his literary name Hylacomylus.

[2] Varnhagen, *Amerigo Vespucci*, p. 30.

as still existing, somebody made a French version of which no copy is now to be found. Walter Lud tells us that a copy of this French version was obtained directly from Portugal for the little group of scholars at Saint-Dié. This copy could not have come from Vespucius himself, who before February 10, 1505, had left Portugal forever, and on the 5th of that month was making a friendly visit to Columbus at Seville. There is nothing to indicate the existence of any personal relations or acquaintanceship between Vespucius and any of the people at Saint-Dié.

The French version of the letter to Soderini arrived at Saint-Dié just as Lud and Ringmann and Waldseemüller had matured their plans for a new edition of Ptolemy, revised and amended so as to include the results of recent discovery. The strong interest felt in geographical studies during the latter half of the fifteenth century was shown in the publication of six Latin editions of Ptolemy between 1472 and 1490.[1] Before 1506 the rapid progress of discovery had made all these editions antiquated, and our friends at Saint-Dié proposed to issue one that should quite throw

The proposed new edition of Ptolemy

[1] At Bologna, 1472 ; Vicenza, 1475 ; Rome, 1478 and 1490; Ulm, 1482 and 1486; all except that of Vicenza provided with engraved maps. Avezac, *Martin Waltzemüller*, p. 23.

into the shade all that had gone before.[1] Walter Lud, who was blessed with a long purse, undertook to defray the expenses; Waldseemüller superintended the scientific part of the work and Ringmann the philological part, for the sake of which he made a journey to Italy and obtained from a nephew of the great Pico della Mirandola an important manuscript of the Greek text. Duke René, who was much interested in the scheme, gathered rare data from various quarters and seems to have paid for the engraving of Waldseemüller's map entitled *Tabula Terre Nove*, which was to accompany the new edition. Early in 1507 Waldseemüller had finished a small treatise intended as an introduction to the more elaborate work which he was embodying in the edition of Ptolemy, and it was decided to print this treatise at once on the college press. Just in the nick of time Duke René handed over to the professors the letter of Vespucius in its French version, which he had lately obtained from Portugal. It was forthwith turned into Latin by the worthy canon Jean Basin de Sendacour, who improved the situation by addressing his version to his enlightened sovereign René instead of Soderini, thus bemuddling the

The French version of the letter turned into Latin

---

[1] Just at the same time another little group of scholars at Vienna were similarly at work on a new edition of Pomponius Mela.

minds of posterity for ever so long by making Vespucius appear to address the Duke of Lorraine as his old schoolmate![1]

This Latin version, containing that innocent but baneful blunder of *Parias* instead of *Lariab*, the source of so much misunderstanding and so much unjust aspersion, was appended to Wald-seemüller's little treatise, along with some verses by Ringmann in praise of the great Florentine navigator. The book, entitled "Cosmographiæ Introductio," was first published at Saint-Dié on the 25th of April, 1507. The only copy of this edition known to exist at present was picked up for a franc on one of the Paris quays by the geographer Jean Baptiste Eyriès; upon his death in 1846, it was bought at auction for 160 francs by Nicolas Yéméniz, of Lyons; upon the death of Yéméniz in 1867, it was bought for 2000 francs; and it may now be seen in the Lenox Library at New York.[2] Three other editions

The Cosmographiæ Introductio

[1] The error has been furthered by the abbreviation *vostra Mag. i. e.* "your Magnificence," the proper form of address for the chief magistrate of Florence. It has been misread "your Majesty," a proper form of address for René, who was titular king of Sicily and Jerusalem. Now that we know how it happened, it is curious to see Humboldt struggle with the subject in his *Examen critique*, tom. iv. pp. 108, 113, 166.

[2] Winsor, *Narr. and Crit. Hist.*, ii. 166.

were published in 1507, concerning which there is no need of entering into particulars.[1] The copy in the library of Harvard University, which I have now before me, was published August 29, 1507, — a little quarto of fifty-two leaves.[2] Mr. Winsor mentions eighteen or twenty copies of it as still in existence, but in 1867 a copy was sold for 2000 francs, the same price paid that year for the first edition; in 1884 a copy in Munich was held at 3000 marks, equivalent to 750 dollars.

In this rare book occurs the first suggestion of the name AMERICA. After having treated of the division of the earth's inhabited surface into three parts— Europe, Asia, and Africa —Waldseemüller speaks of the discovery of a Fourth Part, and the passage is of so much historic interest that instead of a mere transcription the reader will doubtless prefer to see a photograph of that part of the page in our Harvard copy.[3] It is as follows :—

---

[1] They are described in Avezac, *Martin Waltzemüller*, pp. 28–59 ; Harrisse, *Bibl. Amer. Vetust.*, pp. 89–96; *Additions*, pp. 29–34 ; and more briefly mentioned in Winsor, *loc. cit.*

[2] It is No. 46 in Harrisse, *Bibl. Amer. Vetust.*

[3] It is somewhat reduced to fit my narrower page. The book contains another passage in which America is mentioned as part of Mela's antipodal world.

Nunc vero & heę partes ſunt latius luſtratæ/ &
alia quarta pars per Americū Veſputium(vt in ſeǫ
quentibus audietur)inuenta eſt:quā non video cur
quis iure vetet ab Americo inuentore ſagacis inge
nij viro Amerigen quaſi Americi terram/ſiuę Ame
ricam dicendam:cum & Europa & Aſia a mulieriǫ
bus ſua ſortita ſint nomina.Eius ſitū & gentis moǫ
res ex bis binis Americi nauigationibus quę ſequū
tur liquide intelligi datur.

Or, in English : " But now these parts have
been more extensively explored and another
fourth part has been discovered by   *The sugges-*
Americus Vespucius (as will appear in   *tion that*
what follows): wherefore I do not see   *Quarta Pars*
what is rightly to hinder us from call-   *should be*
                                          called Amer-
ing it Amerige or America, *i. e.* the   *ica*
land of Americus, after its discoverer Americus,
a man of sagacious mind, since both Europe and
Asia have got their names from women.[1] Its

[1] I suppose Waldseemüller was thinking of the passage
where Herodotus (iv. 45) speaks of Europe, Asia, and Libya
(*i. e.* the little known to him) as all one land, and cannot imagine why *three* names, *and women's names especially*, should
have been bestowed upon it. In this connection Herodotus
calls Asia the wife of Prometheus. Hesiod (*Theog.*, 359)
makes her a daughter of Oceanus and Tethys. Geographically
the name seems to have had an especial reference to a small
district about the Caÿster in Lydia (Æschylus, *Prometheus*,
411 ; Pindar, *Olymp.*, vii. 33). In its most common Greek
usage it meant Asia Minor, but by the time of Herodotus it
had already begun to be extended into the dim vastness of
continent behind that peninsula.

situation and the manners and customs of its people will be clearly understood from the twice two voyages of Americus which follow."

Much better known than the mythic personality of the female Asia is that of Europa, daughter of Agenor (Hegesippus, *Fragm.*, 6), or of Tityos (Pindar, *Pyth.*, iv.), or of Phoroneus (see Preller, *Griechische Mythologie*, ii. 37). This greater celebrity is due to her escapade with Zeus, about which so many verses have been written. Every reader remembers the exquisite picture in Tennyson's *Palace of Art*. Less generally known are the charming lines of Reynolds : —

> " We gathered wood flowers, — some blue as the vein
> O'er Hero's eyelid stealing, and some as white,
> In the clustering grass, as rich Europa's hand
> Nested amid the curls on Jupiter's forehead,
> What time he snatched her through the startled waves."
>
> *Garden of Florence*, London, 1821.

As for this Europa, Herodotus is sure that she never set foot in Europe ; and as for Libya he knows nothing except that she was a "native" woman. "However," he wisely concludes, "let us quit these matters. We shall ourselves continue to use the names which custom sanctions" (Rawlinson's *Herodotus*, vol. iii. p. 33). There was really nothing like uniformity of tradition in the mythical interpretations of these geographical names. Nor were they always feminine, for in Eustathius (*Comm. in Dionys. Perieg.*, 170) we read of Europus, Asius, and Libyus. Of course all these explanations got the cart before the horse ; the continents were not named after the persons, but the persons were eponymous myths invented to explain the names of the continents. Professor Rawlinson's opinion is highly probable, that both Europe and Asia are Semitic words which passed to the Greeks from the Phœnicians. *Europe* seems to be the Hebrew עֶרֶב, Assyrian *ereb*, Arabic *gharb* (whence *Arab*), meaning " the setting " and

Such were the winged words but for which, as M. Harrisse reminds us, the western hemisphere might have come to be known as Atlantis, or Hesperides, or Santa Cruz, or New India, or perhaps Columbia. There was not much likelihood, however, of its getting named after Columbus, because long before the distinct and separate existence of the western hemisphere

Why the
western hemi-
sphere was
not named
after Colum-
bus

" the west " (cf. Latin *occidens*, Italian *ponente*) ; while *Asia* seems to be a participial form of Hebrew אצי, Assyrian *Azu*, meaning " the rising " and " the east " (cf. Latin *oriens*, Italian *levante*). In the days when Phœnicia ruled the wave, the sailors of Tyre and Sidon probably called the opposite coasts of the Ægean Sea *Europe* and *Asia*= *west* and *east*, and the Greeks acquired the habit of using these names, just as they acquired so many other words and ideas from the Phœnicians. This seems to me downright common-sense. —As for the name *Libya*, it strongly suggests λύψ (*lips*) or λίβα (*liba*), the southwest wind (Aristotle, *Meteorol.*, ii. 6, 7; cf. Theocritus, ix. 11), which the Romans called *Africus* (Seneca, *Quæst. Nat.*, v. 16 ; Horat., *Epod.*, xvi. 22), and which Italian sailors still call *Affrico*. The Greeks called it λύψ (cf. λείβω) because it brought showers. According to this view Libya was simply " the southwest country." The meaning of the name *Africa* is very obscure. A conjecture, as plausible as any, connects it with Hebrew פֶּרֶךְ and supposes it to have been applied by the settlers of Carthage to the *nomadic* or barbarous tribes in the neighbourhood (Mövers, *Die Phönizier*, ii. 402). Originally confined to the region about Carthage, the name Africa gradually superseded Libya as a name for that continent.

was so much as suspected, the names had taken root in its soil, and before that time it would not have occurred to anybody to name it after Columbus, for the sufficient reason that it had two good names already, viz. " Asia " and " the Indies." Separate islands and stretches of coast received their local names, as Hispaniola or Veragua, but no one thought of proposing a new name for the whole western world.

Why, then, it may be asked, did Waldsee-müller propose America as a new name for the whole? The reply is, that he did nothing of the sort. We shall never understand what he had in mind until we follow Mr. Free-man's advice and free ourselves from the bondage of the modern map. Let us pursue for a moment the further fortunes of the work in which our friends of Saint-Dié were engaged. Upon the death of Duke René in 1508 the little coterie was broken up. Lud seems in some way to have become dissociated from the enterprise ; Ringmann in that year became professor of cosmography at Basel,[1] and his untimely death occurred in 1511. Waldseemüller was thus left comparatively alone. The next edition of the *Cosmographiæ Introductio* was published at Strasburg in 1509, the work upon the Ptolemy was kept up, or resumed, with the aid of two jurists

It was not the western hemisphere that was at first meant by America

[1] Avezac, *Martin Waltzemüller*, p. 105.

of that city, Jacob Aeszler and Georg Uebelin, and the book was at last published there in 1513. Among the twenty new maps in this folio volume is one to which we have had frequent occasion to refer, the *Tabula Terre Nove*, made for this edition of Ptolemy at the expense of Duke René and under the supervision of Waldseemüller, if not by his own hands, and engraved before 1508.[1] We must therefore regard this map and the text of the *Cosmographiæ Introductio* as expressions of opinion practically contemporaneous and emanating from the same man (or men, *i. e.* Waldseemüller and Ringmann). Now what do we find on this map? The Brazilian coast is marked with local names derived from the third voyage of Vespucius, but instead of the general name America, or even Mundus Novus, we have simply Terra Incognita; and over to the left, apparently referring to the Pearl Coast and perhaps also to Honduras, we read the inscription: "This land with the adjacent islands was discovered by Columbus of Genoa by order of the King of Castile."[2] The appearance of incompatibility between this statement and the assertion that Vespucius discovered the Fourth

The new Ptolemy published at Strasburg, 1513

The inscription upon Waldseemüller's map

[1] See above, p. 300.

[2] "Hec terra cùm adiacentib insulis inuenta est per Columbū ianuensem ex mandato Regis Castellæ."

Part has puzzled many learned geographers.[1] But I venture to think that this incompatibility is only apparent, not real. Suppose we could resuscitate those bright young men, Waldseemüller and Ringmann, and interrogate them! I presume they would say : " Bless you, dear modern scholars, you know many things that we did not, but you have clean forgotten some things that to us were quite obvious. When we let fall that little suggestion about naming the Fourth Part after Americus, perhaps we were not so fiercely in earnest as you seem to think. We were not born of Hyrcanian tigers, but sometimes enlivened our dry disquisitions with a wholesome laugh, and so neat a chance for quizzing Europa and the fair sex was not lost upon us. Seriously, however, what did we do that was inconsistent or unfair ? Did we not

What Ringmann and Waldseemüller really meant

give Columbus the credit for discovering exactly what he did discover, the Pearl and Honduras coasts and the adjacent islands ? And did we not say of Americus that he had found the Fourth Part, or Mundus Novus, *beyond the equator*, concerning which the ancients had no knowledge, but the existence of which was plainly indicated, in their different ways, by Ptolemy

[1] As for instance Humboldt, *Examen critique*, tom. iv. pp. 118–120 ; Avezac, *Martin Waltzemüller*, p. 154 ; Major, *Prince Henry the Navigator*, p. 386.

and Mela? But you go on to ask was it not
Columbus that first showed the way to the Indies? To be sure it was; we never denied it!
Again you ask if the Pearl Coast and the Mundus Novus were not alike parts of South America. Our answer is that when we were living on
the earth nobody had framed a conception of
the distinct and integral whole which you now
call South America. We knew that long
stretches of strange coast had been discovered
here and there; and some of them interested
us for one reason and some for another. It was
doubtless a thing more divine than human for
the Admiral Columbus to sail by the west to
Asia along the circumference of the Œcumene,
but he never supposed that he had thus found
a new part of the earth, nor did we. To sail
across the torrid zone and explore a new antipodal world that formed no part of the Œcumene was a very different thing, and it was this
deed for which we properly gave the credit to
Americus; for did not the learned and accurate
Master Ruysch testify that voyagers upon
this antarctic coast had beheld the southern
pole more than 50° above the horizon, and yet
had seen no end to that country? We therefore acted according to our best lights, empha-
sizing, as we admit, that which appealed to us
most forcibly. If we could have studied your
nineteenth century globes we should have

learned to express ourselves differently; but, bless you again, dear modern scholars, may not some of your own expressions run risk of being misunderstood after an equal lapse of time?"

If along with our two editors of Ptolemy we could also call back for a moment from the Un-

Significant silence of Ferdinand Columbus

discovered Country that learned geographer, accomplished scholar, and devoted son, Ferdinand Columbus, and let him hear their explanation, I feel sure that he would promptly and heartily recognize its substantial correctness. Upon the point in question we already have Ferdinand's testimony, clothed in a silence more eloquent than any conceivable words. I have already remarked upon Ferdinand's superb library, of which the remnant of four or five thousand volumes is still preserved, — the Biblioteca Colombina at Seville. It will be remembered that he had a habit of marking and annotating his books in a way that is sometimes quite helpful to the historian. Now the number 1773 of Ferdinand's library is a copy of the *Cosmographiæ Introductio* in the edition published at Strasburg in 1509. His autograph note informs us that he bought it at Venice in July, 1521, for five *sueldos*.[1] As his death occurred in 1539, he had this book in his possession for eighteen years, and during a part of this time he was engaged in preparing the

[1] Harrisse, *Christophe Colomb*, tom. ii. p. 370.

374

biography of his father. He was naturally very sensitive about everything that in any way great or small concerned his father's fame, and if any writer happened to make statements in the slightest degree derogatory to his father's importance or originality, Ferdinand would pause in his narrative and demolish the offender if it took a whole chapter to do it.[1] But his book makes no allusion whatever to Waldseemüller or his suggestion of the name America or his allusion to Vespucius as the discoverer of Quarta Pars. Not so much as a word had Ferdinand Columbus to say on this subject! Still more, the book of Waldseemüller did not sleep on the shelf during those eighteen years. Ferdinand read and annotated it with fulness and care, but made no comment upon the passage in question! This silence is absolutely decisive. Here was the son of Columbus and for some years the fellow-townsman of Americus at Seville, the familiar friend of the younger Vespucius who had gone with his uncle on most if not all his voyages, — can we for a moment suppose that

[1] See, for example, his refutation of Giustiniani's " thirteen lies " in *Vita dell' Ammiraglio*, cap. ii. ; and his attacks upon Martin Pinzon and Oviedo, cap. x., xvi., xli. As M. Harrisse observes, " Lorsqu'il rencontre sur son chemin un rival de Christophe Colomb, ou un écrivain dont le récit semble devoir diminuer l'importance du navigateur génois devant la posterité, il le vilipende sans pitié." *Fernand Colomb*, p. 141.

he did not know all that had been going on among these people since his boyhood? Of course he understood what voyages had been made and where, and interpreted them according to the best light of an age in which he was one of the foremost geographers. His annotations show him to have been eminently clear-headed, accurate, and precise. It would be impossible to find a contemporary witness more intelligent or more certain to utter a sharp and ringing protest against any attempt to glorify Americus at the expense of his father. Yet against Waldseemüller's suggestion Ferdinand Columbus uttered no protest. He saw nothing strange in the statement that it was Americus who discovered the Quarta Pars, or in the suggestion that it should bear his name. Under the circumstances there is but one possible explanation of this. It proves that Ferdinand shared Waldseemüller's opinion, and that to the former as to the latter this Fourth Part meant something very different from what we mean when we speak of America or of the New World.[1]

---

[1] M. Harrisse (in his *Fernand Colomb*, Paris, 1872, pp. 141–145) uses the silence of the *Vita dell' Ammiraglio*, as an argument in support of his crotchet that the book was not written by Ferdinand (see above, page 7, note). His argument suffers severely from " bondage to the modern map." Referring to Waldseemüller, he says : " On déclare d'abord

What that Fourth Part really meant I believe
I have now sufficiently explained. It is again
defined for us most clearly and expli- The Ptolemy
citly in the revised edition of Wald- of 1522
seemüller's Ptolemy published at Strasburg in
1522, three years after his death. This edition
was completed by Lorenz Fries, and is usually
known by his name. It uses the three names
America, Mundus Novus, and Quarta Pars as

que c'est Vespuce, *et non Christophe Colomb* [! ! the italicizing is mine : Waldseemüller says nothing of the sort], qui a
découvert le Nouveau Monde ; ensuite on promet de le prou-
ver ' ut in sequentibus audietur,' en publiant la relation de ses
quatre voyages ; enfin, pour l'en récompenser, l'auteur propose de donner et donne en effet d'une manière indélébile à
ces pays nouveaux le nom d'Amérique." It should be added
that M. Harrisse, while calling Waldseemüller's book " ce
méchant petit livre," does full justice to the integrity of Vespucius. In the argument just cited the reader will now be
able to see that all its force is lost by its failure to seize the
historical perspective ; it uses the phrase *Nouveau Monde* in
its nineteenth century sense. As regards Ferdinand Columbus, its force is destroyed by the fact that his silence extends
to his copy of Waldseemüller's book. But indeed Las Casas,
as will presently be shown, expressly declares that Ferdinand's book says nothing about the naming of America (*Historia de las Indias*, tom. ii. p. 396). — Among other books
belonging to Ferdinand, in which the name America was
adopted, or Vespucius mentioned as discoverer of Mundus
Novus, were Walter Lud's *Speculum*, the 1518 edition of
Pomponius Mela, the works of Johann Schöner, and the *Cosmographicus Liber* of Apianus (Harrisse, *op. cit.* p. 144).
There is nothing to show that anything in them disturbed him.

synonymous and interchangeable; and in its map corresponding to the *Tabula Terre Nove*, but variously amended, it substitutes America for Terra Incognita about where the name Brazil would come on a modern map; while at the same time in the Venezuelan region it repeats the inscription stating that this coast and the neighbouring islands were discovered by Columbus.

It is not to be supposed that all map-makers at that day took just the same view of this or
Different
conceptions
of Mundus
Novus of any other obscure subject. Some thought the Mundus Novus deserved its name because it was Ptolemy's unknown land beyond Cattigara, as the Orontius globe proves; some because it was of indefinite extent and reminded them of Mela's antipodal world, as we may gather from Ruysch's map;[1] some simply because it was an enormous mass of land in an unexpected quarter.[2] When care-

[1] "Terra etiam nova . . . a Vesputio nuper inventa, quam ob sui magnitudinem *Mundum novum* appellant, ultra æquatorem plus 35 gradibus, Vesputii observatione protendi cognita est, et *necdum finis inventus*." Alberto Pighi Campense in 1520, apud Humboldt, *Examen critique*, tom. iv. p. 145. Compare the inscriptions E and G on Ruysch's map.

[2] "Sic si ad austrum spectes, magna pars terræ nostra tempestate explorata est, aut salte circumnavigata, quam Ptolemæus ut incognitam reliquit : ab Hispanis uero quum in orientem nauigio contendunt, obambulatur & circuitur, ut

fully placed, with strict reference to its origin,
the name Mundus Novus, or its alternative
America, is always equivalent to Brazil ; but
sometimes where the southern continent appears
as a great island its position is so commanding
as to make it practically the name of that island.
This is the case with one of the earliest maps
upon which the name America appears. This
map was discovered about thirty years ago
in Queen Victoria's library at Wind- The map at-
sor Castle, in a volume of MS. notes tributed to
and drawings by Leonardo da Vinci. Leonardo da
Vinci, cir.
There is much reason for regarding 1514
the map as the work of Leonardo, but this has
been doubted.[1] It represents the oceanic theory
in its extreme form and has some points of
likeness to the Lenox globe. The northern

paulo post disseremus. Quin & in oceano occidentali fere
nouus orbis nostris tĕporibus ab Alberico Vesputio & Christo-
phoro Columbo, multisque aliis insignibus uiris inuentus est,
qui non abs re quarta orbis pars nuncupari potest, etiam terra
non sit tripartita, sed quadripartita, quum hæ Indianæ insulæ
sua magnitudine Europam excedant, presertim ea quā ab
Americo primo inuentore Americam uocat.'' Sebastian
Münster, *Tabulæ cosmographicæ*, apud Grynæus, *Novus
Orbis*, Paris, 1832.

[1] The subject is elaborately discussed by Major, '' Me-
moir on a Mappemonde by Leonardo da Vinci, being the
earliest Map hitherto known containing the name of America,''
Archæologia, London, 1866, vol. xl. pp. 1–40. The sketch
here given is reduced from Wieser's *Magalhães-Strasse*.

continent is represented by the islands of Bacalar and Terra Florida, and the latter name proves the date of the map to be subsequent to Ponce de Leon's discovery on Easter Sunday, 1513. Cipango, here spelled Zipugna, still hovers in the neighbourhood. The western coast of the southern continent is drawn at random ; and the antarctic land, the inevitable reminiscence of Ptolemy and Mela, protrudes as far as the parallel of 60° S.

In 1515 Johann Schöner, professor of mathematics at Nuremberg, made a globe upon which America is drawn very much as upon Leonardo's map, with an inscription stating that the western coast is unknown ; above, corresponding to Mexico, is "Parias" in the true position of Vespucius's Lariab, and this is joined to the Florida (with no name) taken from Cantino and ending with a scroll, as in Ruysch, saying that what is beyond is unknown. Leonardo's antarctic land here comes up so as almost to touch America, and it bears the name " Brazilie Regio," reminding us of Orontius.

America on Schöner's first globe ;

In 1520 Schöner made a second globe, which is still preserved at Nuremberg. Here the unnamed Florida has taken the name " Terra de Cuba," though both globes also give the island. " Paria " still denotes Mexico, while " Terra Parius " appears for the

and on his second globe

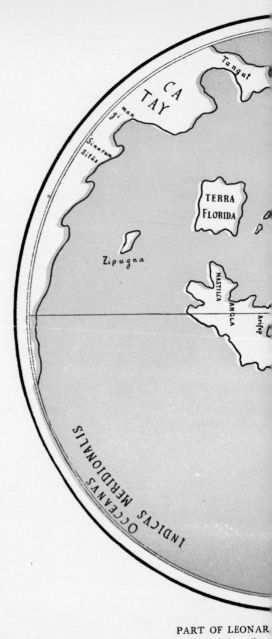

CATAY

Tangut

man
gi
Sinaram
Sita

TERRA
FLORIDA

Zipugna

MASTILCA
ANGLA

OCCEANVS INDICVS MERIDIONALIS

PART OF LEONAR
One of the earliest

OCCEANVS
OCCIDENTALIS

ISA
BELLA

PORIAN

ERICA

C·D·S·TVANI
C·D·S·agosto
Abatia
Brazill
C·FRIO
CANANEA

360
EQVINOTIALIS

I'S MAP, CIR. 1514
h the name America

true Paria on the Pearl Coast. America is expressly identified with the land discovered by Cabral; the legend between latitudes 10° and 20° S. is "America or Brasilia or Land of Paroquets." The antarctic land has here become "Brasilia Inferior."[1]

On the important map made by Baptista Agnese at Venice in 1536, the name America does not appear, but Mundus Novus and Brazil are placed close together and south of the equator.[2] And on the map made *Various maps* by Sebastian Münster for the 1540 Ptolemy, we read, a little below the equator, "Novus Orbis, the Atlantic island which they call Brazil and America." Below, to the west of the river La Plata, we read "Die Nüw Welt."[3] These are some of the examples which show that it was an essential part of *The "New World" was not the western, but the southern world* the conception of the "New World," in the minds of the men who first used the expression, that it was *a world lying south of the equator.* The opposition between Old World and New World was not, as now, between the eastern and western hemispheres; the opposition was between the north-

---

[1] Sketches of these two Schöner globes are given in Winsor, *Narr. and Crit. Hist.*, ii. 118, 119.

[2] This map is given below, vol. iii. p. 328.

[3] This map, upon which we see also Cattigara, is given below, vol. iii. p. 330.

ern hemisphere and the southern; and as Columbus had not crossed the equator in the course of his four voyages, he had never entered or seen what Waldseemüller and geographers generally during the first half of the sixteenth century called the New World.

But the course of time and the progress of discovery wrought queer changes in men's conception of Mundus Novus and in the application of the name America. It was not very difficult for such a euphonious name to supplant its unwieldy synonyms, Land of Paroquets and Land of the Holy Cross. Nor did it require much extension for it to cover the whole southern continent soon after the idea of that continent as an integral whole distinct from other wholes had once been conceived. The names of Paria and the Pearl Coast, Venezuela and Darien have remained upon the map to this day; but Terra Firma, the cumbrous name which covered the four, was easily swallowed up by America. Thus the name of the Florentine navigator came to be synonymous with what we call South America; and this wider meaning became all the more firmly established as its narrower meaning was usurped by the name Brazil. Three centuries before the time of Columbus the red dye-wood called brazil-wood was an article of commerce, under that same name, in

Extension of the name "America" from Brazil to South America

Italy and Spain.[1] It was one of the valuable things that were brought from the East, and when the Portuguese found the same dye-wood abundant in those tropical forests that had seemed so beautiful to Vespucius, the name Brazil soon became fastened upon the country[2] and helped to set free the name America from its local associations.

By 1540 South America had been completely circumnavigated, and it was possible to draw an outline map of its coast with a fair approach to

---

[1] Muratori, *Antichità italiane*, tom. ii. pp. 894–899; Capmany, *Memorias sobre la antigua marina de Barcelona*, tom. ii. pp. 4, 17, 20; Humboldt, *Examen critique*, tom. 216–225. The name of the fabulous island *Brazil* or *Bresylle* in the ocean west of Ireland seems to be a case of accidental resemblance. It is probably the Gaelic name of an island in Irish folk-lore. See Winsor, *Narr. and Crit. Hist.*, i. 50.

[2] The Portuguese historian Barros declares that the substitution of such a name as Brazil for such a name as Holy Cross must have been the work of some demon, for of what account is this miserable wood that dyes cloth red as compared with the blood shed for our eternal salvation! — "Porém como o demonio per o final da Cruz perdeo o dominio que tinha sobre nós, mediante a Pãixao de Christo Jesus consummada nella; tanto que daquella terra começou de vir o páo vermelho chamado Brazil, trabalhou que este nome ficasse na boca do povo, e que se perdesse o de Sancta Cruz, como que importava mais o nome de hum páo que tinge pannos, que daquelle páo que deo tintura a todolos Sacramentos per que somos salvos, por o sangue de Christo Jesus, que nelle foi derramado," etc. Barros, *Decadas da Asia*, Lisbon, 1778, tom. i. p. 391.

accuracy. It was thus beginning to be known as a distinct whole, and the name America had gone far toward taking exclusive possession of it. That continent was by far the most imposing result of discovery in the western waters, and the next step was for its name to spread beyond its natural limits so as to cover adjacent and less known regions.[1] Now by 1540 men were just beginning to grasp the fact that the regions called New Spain, Terra Florida, and Baccalaos were different parts of one continent that was distinct from Asia. There was as yet no steadiness of thought on the subject. The wet theory, as shown in Leonardo da Vinci's map, had long since separated North America from Asia, but only by reducing it to a few islands. The dry theory, as shown in the Orontius globe, made it continental, but only by attaching it to Asia. A combination of wet and dry theorizing was needed to bring out the

---

[1] Peter Bienewitz (called Apianus), in his celebrated book published in 1524, clearly distinguishes Cuba, Hispaniola, etc., from America. They are islands lying near America, and their inhabitants have customs and ceremonies like those of the people of America : " Habet autem America insulas udiacentes [adjacentes] q plurimas vt Parianã Insulam, Isabellam quo Cuba dicitur [sic] Spagnollam . . . Accolæ vero Spagnollæ insulæ loco panis vescuntur serpentibus maximis et radicibus. Ritus et cultus istarum circumiacentium Insularum par est Americæ accolarum cultui." *Cosmographicus Liber*, Landshut, 1524, fol. 69.

truth. This combination was for a moment realized in 1541 by a man who in such matters was in advance of his age. Gerard Kaufmann, better known by his latinized name Mercator, was a native of East Flanders, born in 1512, the year in which Vespucius died. Mercator was an able geographer and mathematician. He is now remembered chiefly for the important method of map projection called by his name, and for certain rules of navigation associated therewith and known as "Mercator's sailing." But he should also be remembered as the first person who indicated upon a map the existence of a distinct and integral western hemisphere and called the whole by the name America. Upon the gores for a globe which he made in 1541, Mercator represented the northern continent as distinct from Asia, and arranged the name America in large letters so as to cover both northern and southern continents, putting AME about on what we should call the site of the Great Lakes and RICA just west of the river La Plata.[1] This was a stride, nay a leap beyond what had gone before. We have only to contrast Mercator, 1541, with Agnese, 1536, and with Gastaldi, 1548, to realize what a startling innovation it

The name "America" first applied to the western hemisphere by Gerard Mercator, 1541

[1] The sketch is reduced from Winsor, *Narr. and Crit. Hist.*, ii. 177.

was.[1] It was some time yet before Mercator's ideas prevailed, but his map enables us to see how the recognition of a western hemisphere emerged and during the latter half of the sixteenth century became more and more distinct.[2] As this process went on and the ideas of the ancient geographers lapsed into oblivion, the old contrast between north and south became

Change of meaning in the names " New World " and " America " superseded by the new contrast between east and west. Thus the names America and New World came to awaken associations of ideas utterly different from those amid which they originated. If Waldseemüller had been told that a time would arrive when such places as Baccalaos and his Cape-of-the-end-of-April would be said to be in the New World, he would have asked, in great amazement, how could places in Asia and wholly within the bounds of the ancient Œcumene have anything whatever to do with the Quarta Pars! That time, however, did arrive, and when it came the name of America began to look like a standing denial of the just rights of Columbus. It looked as if at some time a question had arisen as to

[1] These two maps are given below, vol. iii. pp. 328, 329.

[2] See John Dee's map, 1580, below, vol. iii. p. 358; but Michael Lok's map, 1582, shows in this respect a less advanced stage of development than Mercator's. See below, vol. iii. p. 356.

AME

BACCALEARUM
REGIO

INS. CORTEREALIS

ISLAND
INS
OLIM
THYLE

HISPANIA MAJOR
CAPTA ANNO
1530

HEPTAPOLIS

CORBO
FLORES

GRACIOSA

FAIALO
TERCERA
VEL PICO
S. MICHAEL

BARMUDA
SIVE
GARÇA

ACORES INS

O S. MARIA

R. DEL
SPIRITU SANTO

FLORIDA

GUANAQ

PORTUS S?
MADERA

HISPANIA
NOVA

IUCATAN
COSUMELLA
JAMAICA

INS FORTUNATE
NUNC CANARIE

CAMERCANE
INSULE

S. DE
HESPERIDESO NUNC
INS DE ANTON

TRINITATIS INS

PARIA

S. PABLI

PERU
NOVA CASTILIA

C. S. CRUCIS

C. S. AUGUSTIN

COSCO

RICA
A MULTIS HODIE NOVA
INDIA DICTA

MARE PACIFICUM

7 4

FRETUM PATHAGONICUM
SIVE MAGELLANICUM

SKETCH FROM MERCATOR'S MAP, 1541

whose name should be given to the western hemisphere, and as if for some reason Americus was preferred to Columbus. When such a notion had got into men's heads Americus was sure to be attacked. No charge is easier to make than that of falsehood. The sin of lying is common enough, and geography is not the simplest of subjects. Hence most great travellers, from Herodotus down, have for one reason or another been ignorantly accused of lying. Never was such an accusation more completely the offspring of ignorance than in the case of Vespucius.

It was that precious blunder of " Parias " for " Lariab " that started the business, and it was aided by a slipshod expression of the Nuremberg professor, Johann Schöner. In a little tract published in 1515, probably as an accompaniment to his globe made in that year, Schöner alludes to " America, a new world and fourth part of the globe, named after its discoverer, Americus Vespucius, a man of sagacious mind, who found it in the year 1497." [1] This confusing the first voyage with the third was not ignorance, but

---

[1] " America siue Amerigen nouus mundus : & quarta orbis pars : dicta ab eius inuētore Americo Vesputio viro sagacis ingenii : qui eam reperit Anno domini. 1497. In ea sunt homines brutales," etc. Schöner, *Luculentissima quædā terræ totius descriptio*, Nuremberg, 1515. For an account of this very rare book see Harrisse, *Bibl. Amer. Vetust.*, No. 80.

downright carelessness, for inasmuch as on his globes Schöner placed " Parias " in Mexico and identified America with Brazil, he knew well enough that it was not in 1497, but in 1501 that Vespucius visited the Fourth Part. Eighteen years afterward Schöner made another bad slip when he said, though here again he knew better, that "Americus appointed a part of Upper India, which he supposed to be an island, to be called by his name." [1] There is nothing in the remark which implies censure,[2] but it was probably this that led Las Casas, after 1552, to say that Americus had been accused of putting his name on the map, " thus sinfully failing toward the admiral." Las Casas

Schöner's loose remarks

[1] " Americus Vesputius maritima loca Indiæ superioris ex Hispaniis navigio ad occidentem perlustrans, eam partem quæ superioris Indiæ est, credidit esse Insulam quam a suo nomine vocari instituit." Schöner, *Opusculum geographicum*, Nuremberg, 1533. Inasmuch as Schöner knew the *Cosmographiæ Introductio* he knew that it was Waldseemüller and not Vespucius who " instituit," etc. But he was evidently a man of slovenly speech.

[2] It is commonly spoken of as a " charge " against Vespucius. Harrisse calls it " the first attempt to tarnish the reputation of the Florentine cosmographer " (*Bibl. Amer. Vetust.*, p. 65). Here again comes the fallacy of reading our modern ideas into the old texts. There is nothing whatever in Schöner's context to suggest that he attached any blame to Vespucius or saw any impropriety in the name. Indeed he had himself put it on his globes in 1515 and 1520, and done as much as anybody to give it currency.

GERARD MERCATO

THE WORLD, 1538

had finally come back from America in 1547, and by 1552 had settled down quietly at Valladolid to work upon his great history. He was vexed at seeing the name America so commonly used,[1] since by that time it had come to cover much ground that belonged especially to Columbus. Indeed there can be no doubt that by 1550 the greater exploit of having sailed west in order to

The situation, as misunderstood by Las Casas after 1550

[1] The suggestion of Waldseemüller as to the name America seems to have been first adopted in the anonymous *Globus Mundi*, Strasburg, 1509. The name was used by Joachim Watt (called Vadianus) in his letter to Rudolphus Agricola, Vienna, 1515, reprinted in his edition of Mela, Vienna, 1518. I have already alluded to its adoption by Leonardo da Vinci and Schöner and Fries. Peter Bienewitz (called Apianus) put the name America on his map published in 1520 (given in Winsor, ii. 183) and adopted it in his *Cosmographicus Liber*, Landshut, 1524; an abridgment of this book was published by Gemma Frisius at Ingoldstadt, 1529. Heinrich Loritz (called Glareanus) used the name in his *De geographia liber unus*, Basel, 1527; Sebastian Münster gave it further currency in his essay in Grynæus, *Novus Orbis*, Paris, 1532; and so again did Honter in his *Rudimenta Cosmographica*, Zurich, 1542. All these were very popular books and were many times reprinted; being in Latin they reached educated people everywhere, and some of them were translated into Spanish, Italian, German, Bohemian, English, French, etc. Sir Thomas More in his *Utopia* speaks of the voyages of Vespucius as "nowe in printe and abrode in euery mannes handes." See Harrisse, *Bibl. Amer. Vetust.*, under the different years; Winsor, *Narr. and Crit. Hist.*, ii. 180–186; Varnhagen, *Nouvelles recherches*, pp. 19–24.

get to the east was somewhat overshadowed by
the lesser exploit of having revealed the continental dimensions of a mass of antipodal land
unknown to the ancients. Vespucius was more
talked about than Columbus. This aroused the
generous indignation of Las Casas. A wrong
seemed to have been done, and somebody must
have been to blame. Las Casas read
the Latin version of the letter to Soderini, appended to Waldseemüller's
book, and could not imagine why
Americus should write such a letter to
Duke René or why he should address him as an
old friend and schoolmate. But when he came
to the place where Vespucius seemed to be
speaking of Paria his wrath was kindled. Las
Casas quotes the guilty sentence, and exclaims,
" Americus tells us that he went to Paria on his
first voyage, saying: *And that province is called
by the people themselves Parias;* and then he
made his second voyage with Ojeda," also to
Paria.[1] The clause which I have italicized is the
very clause in which the Latin version ignorantly substitutes *Parias* for the *Lariab* of the
original text; and the passage in which Las

Effect upon Las Casas of the blundering substitution of " Parias " for " Lariab"

[1] " De haber llegado á Paria el Américo en este su primer
viaje, el mismo lo confiesa en su primera navegacion, diciendo :
Et provincia ipsa Parias ab ipsis nuncupata est. Despues hizo
tambien con el mismo Hojeda la segunda navegacion," etc.
Las Casas, *Historia de las Indias,* tom. ii. p. 273.

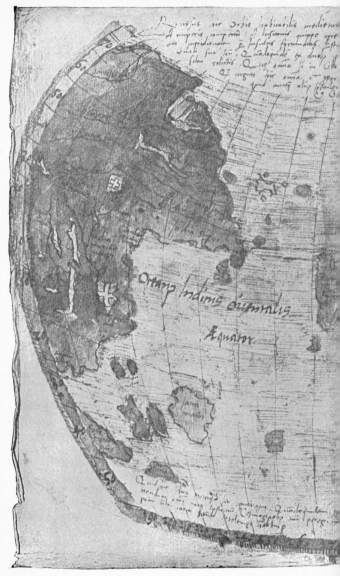

MANUSCRIPT MAP B

MUNICH CIR. 1510

Casas quotes it is the documentary evidence upon which I am content to rest the statement with which I opened this long discussion, that it was this miserable alteration that made all the trouble. It at once riveted the attention of Las Casas upon the Pearl Coast, in spite of the explicit statement, on the same page and only nine lines above the name " Parias," that it was "under the tropic of Cancer, in latitude 23° N." Las Casas understood Vespucius to say that he had been at Paria in 1497, and found no difficulty in proving that this could not be true. Could it be that Americus intended to usurp honours which he knew to belong to the admiral? If so, it was a great piece of wickedness, says Las Casas; still he admits that the fault may lie with the persons who printed the account of the four voyages.[1] For a while his strong love of fairness restrains the pen of Las Casas, but when at length he loses all patience with "these foreigners" who make maps and put the name America where they ought to put "Columba" [sic], he hastily includes Vespucius in his condemnation, and adds that he cannot conceive why Ferdinand Columbus, whom he

[1] " Y es bien aquí de considerar la injusticia y agravio que aquel Américo Vespucio parece haber hecho al Almirante, ó los que imprimieron sus cuatro navegaciones, atribuyendo á sí ó no nombrando sino á sí solo, el descubrimiento desta tierra firme," etc. *Op. cit.* tom. ii. p. 268.

knows to have had the book of the Vespucius voyages in his possession, did not take notice of this " theft and usurpation " by Americus of what belonged to his illustrious father.[1] If Las Casas had closely watched the gradual development of the affair he would have understood Ferdinand's silence, but as for half a century he had been mostly in America, absorbed in very different matters, the exaltation of Vespucius took him by surprise and he was unable to comprehend it.

As the history of Las Casas remained in manuscript, it produced no immediate effect upon the public mind. There were people still living between 1552 and 1561, as for example Ramusio and Benzoni,[2]

Herrera's charge against Vespucius, 1601

[1] " Y maravíllome yo de D. Hernando Colon, hijo del misma Almirante, que siendo persona de muy buen ingenio y prudencia, y teniendo en su poder las mismas nauegaciones de Américo, como lo sé yo, no advirtió en este hurto y usurpacion que Américo Vespucio hizo á su muy ilustre padre." *Op. cit.* tom. ii. p. 396. This reference to Ferdinand's book seems to prove that the remarks of Las Casas about Americus were written as late as 1552, or later. Las Casas seems to have begun work on his history at the Dominican monastery in San Domingo, somewhere between the dates 1522 and 1530. He took it up again at Valladolid in 1552 and worked on it until 1561. His allusion to Ferdinand Columbus was clearly made after the death of the latter in 1539, so that this part of the book was doubtless written somewhere between 1552 and 1561.

[2] At the end of the fifth chapter of his *Historia del Mondo*

who were probably competent to set Las Casas right. But in 1601 all such people had passed away, and then the charge against Vespucius was for the first time published by Herrera, the historiographer of Spain, who had used the manuscript of Las Casas.[1] Herrera flatly accused Vespucius of purposely antedating his voyage of 1499 with Ojeda to Paria, in order to make it appear that he had found Terra Firma before Columbus. Then Herrera assumed that Vespucius again accompanied Ojeda to Paria on the second voyage of that cavalier, which began in January, 1502. This assumption displaced the third voyage of Vespucius, who, it will be remembered, was in the harbour of Rio de Janeiro on that New Year's day. A doubt was thus raised as to whether the third voyage was not a lie, and so the tangle went on until one might well wonder whether any of these voyages ever were made at all! Surely no poor fellow was ever so victimized by editors and commentators as this honest Florentine sailor!

Nuovo, Venice, 1565, Benzoni enumerates various men for whom claims had been made that conflicted with the priority of Columbus in his discovery; he does not include Vespucius in the number. See the excellent remarks of Humboldt on Benzoni and Ramusio, in his *Examen critique*, tom. iv. pp. 146–152.

[1] Herrera, *Historia de las Indias Occidentales*, Madrid, 1601, tom. i. pp. 125–128, 131, 148, 224, 230.

From the dire confusion into which Herrera contrived to throw the subject it was no easy task for scholars to emerge. Where was the Ariadne who could furnish a clue to such a labyrinth? For two centuries and a half the assertion that Vespucius had somehow contrived to cheat people into the belief that he was the discoverer of the western hemisphere was re-

The charge of Herrera gave rise to the popular notion that Americus contrived to supplant Columbus

peated by historians, proclaimed in cyclopædias, preached about by moralists, and taught to children in their school-books. In the queer lumbergarret of half-formed notions which for the majority of mankind does duty as history this particular misty notion was, and is still, pretty sure to be found. Until the nineteenth century scarcely anybody had a good word for the great navigator except Bandini, Canovai, and other Florentine writers. But inasmuch as most of these defenders simply stood by their fellow-countryman from the same kind of so-called "patriotic" motives that impel Scandinavian writers to attack Columbus, their arguments produced little impression; and being quite as much in the dark as their adversaries, they were apt to overdo the business and hurt their case by trying to prove too much. Until the middle of the present century the renewal of assaults upon Vespucius used to come in

394

periodic spasms, like the cholera or the fashion
of poke bonnets.[1] Early in this century the

[1] The latest and fiercest of these assaults was the little
book of the Viscount de Santarem, *Recherches historiques,
critiques, et bibliographiques sur Améric Vespuce et ses voyages*, Paris, 1842. For perverse ingenuity in creating difficulties where none exist, this book is a curiosity in the literature of morbid psychology. From long staring into mare's
nests the author had acquired a chronic twist in his vision.
What else can be said of a man who wastes four pages (pp.
53–56) in proving that Vespucius could not have been a
schoolmate of the *first* René of Lorraine, who was born in
1410 ? and who is, or affects to be, so grossly ignorant of
Florentine history as to find it strange (p. 63) that Vespucius
should have been on friendly terms at once with Soderini and
with a Medici of the younger branch ? M. de Santarem's
methods would have been highly valued by such sharp prac-
titioners as Messrs. Dodson and Fogg : "Chops ! Gracious
heavens ! and tomato sauce ! ! Gentlemen, is the happiness
of a sensitive and confiding female to be trifled away by such
shallow artifices as these ? " With arguments of this character M. de Santarem contrived to abolish all the voyages of
Vespucius except the one with Ojeda. The only interest that
can be felt to-day in this worthless book lies in the fact that
an English translation of it was published in Boston in 1850,
and is to be held responsible for the following outburst, at
which no one would have been so shocked as the illustrious
author, if he had been properly informed : "Strange that
broad America must wear the name of a thief. Amerigo Vespucci, the pickle-dealer at Seville, who went out in 1499, a
subaltern with Hojeda, and whose highest naval rank was
boatswain's mate in an expedition that never sailed, managed
in this lying world to supplant Columbus and baptize half the

publication of many original documents seemed at first only to enhance the confusion, for it

earth with his own dishonest name." Emerson, *English Traits*, Boston, 1856 (p. 148 of the Riverside edition, 1883).

Closely connected with these recurrent assaults have been more or less serious proposals from time to time to change the name of America, or of North America, or of the United States. In point of euphony the names suggested would hardly be an improvement, and they have often been of dubious historical propriety ; *e. g. Cabotia ;* or even *Sebastiana,* which would be honouring the son at the expense of the father ; or *Alleghania,* but why should the Tallegwi monopolize it ? I suppose Mr. Lewis Morgan might have approved of *Ganowania,* or perhaps *Hodenosaunia,* "country of the Long House." Early in the seventeenth century Pizarro y Orellana (*Varones ilustres del Nuevo Mundo,* Madrid, 1639, p. 51) expressed his disgust at the name of America, not because it was an injustice to Columbus, but because it was not aristocratic enough ; the New World ought not to be named after anybody lower than royalty, and so he proposed to call it *Fer-Isabelica !* That would have been a nice name ! Gentle reader, how would you like to be a Fer-Isabelican ? Another sage Spaniard would have enshrined the memory of Charles V. in such an epithet as *Orbis Carolinus.* See Solórzano Pereyra, *De Indiarum Jure,* Leyden, 1672, lib. i. cap. 2. Late in the sixteenth century a learned Portuguese writer characterized the New World as Golden India, while he distinguished the eastern possessions of his nation as Aromatic India. See Gaspar Fructuoso, *Saudades da Terra,* Lisbon, 1590.

Speaking of *Alleghania* reminds me of the droll conceit of Professor Jules Marcou that the name America after all was not taken from Vespucius, but from a mountain range in Nicaragua, the Indian name of which was *Amerrique* or *Americ,*

took time and patient thinking to get so many new facts into the right connections.

At length the gigantic learning of Alexander von Humboldt was brought to bear on the subject, and enough was accomplished to vindicate forever the character of Americus. But owing to inadequate textual criticism, much still remained to be cleared up. Proceeding from the Latin text of 1507, and accepting the Bandini letter as genuine, Humboldt naturally failed to unravel the snarl of the first two voyages. Then came Varnhagen, who for the first time began at the very beginning by establishing the primitive and genuine texts from which to work. This

The charge partly refuted by Humboldt; fully by Varnhagen

and which he imagines (without a morsel of documentary evidence) that Columbus must have heard on his fourth voyage! (See *Atlantic Monthly*, March, 1875, vol. xxxv. pp. 291–296.) According to this fancy, the name America should have been first applied to Nicaragua, whereas it was really first applied to Brazil and had been used for many a year before it extended across the Isthmus of Darien. Speculation *a priori* is of little use in history, and a great many things that must have happened never did happen. If I were not afraid of starting off some venturesome spirit on a fresh wildgoose-chase, I would — well, I will take the risk and mention the elfish coincidence that, whereas Brazil, the original America, received its name from its dye-wood like that of the East Indies, there was a kind of this brazil-wood in Sumatra which the fourteenth century traveller Pegolotti calls AMERI, and along with it another and somewhat better kind which he calls COLOMBINO ! ! ! See Yule's *Marco Polo*, vol. ii. p. 315.

at once carried the first voyage far away from Paria, and then everything began to become intelligible. Though scholars are not as yet agreed as to all of Varnhagen's conclusions, yet no shade of doubt is left upon the integrity of Vespucius.[1] So truth is strong and prevails at last.

One thing more was needed, and that was to make a comprehensive statement of the case entirely freed from " bondage to the modern map," — a statement interpreting the facts as they appeared in the first half of the sixteenth century to students of Ptolemy and Mela, and rigorously avoiding the error of projecting our modern knowledge into the past. I sincerely hope that in the present chapter I have kept clear of that error.

It has not been merely through a desire to do justice to the memory of a great navigator and worthy man that I have devoted so much space to this subject and made such large demands upon the reader's patience. It will at once be recognized, I think, that through such a discussion, more than through any mere nar-

[1] No competent scholar anywhere will now be found to dissent from the emphatic statement of M. Harrisse : " After a diligent study of all the original documents, we feel constrained to say that there is not a particle of evidence, direct or indirect, implicating Americus Vespucius in an attempt to foist his name on this continent." *Bibliotheca Americana Vetustissima*, New York, 1866, p. 65.

rative, are we made to realize what a gradual process of evolution the Discovery of America really was. We have now to follow that process into its next stage of advancement, and see how men came to the knowledge of a vast ocean to the west of Mundus Novus. We have here fortunately arrived at a region where the air is comparatively clear of controversial mists, and although we have to describe the crowning achievement in the records of maritime discovery, the story need not long detain us.

We may properly start by indicating the purpose of the fourth voyage of Americus; and here we shall be helped by a tabular view showing its position in the group of voyages to which it belonged. The third voyage of Columbus, in which he skirted the Pearl Coast for a short distance, had revealed land which he had correctly interpreted as continental, and it was land in an unexpected position. His letter describing this voyage did not obtain a wide circulation, and there is no reason for supposing that it would have aroused public attention to any great extent if it had. People's ideas as to "continents" and "islands" in these remote parts were, as we have seen, very hazy; and there was nothing in this new land *north* of the equator to suggest the idea of Quarta Pars or Mundus Novus. But this voyage was followed up next

Causal sequence of voyages from the third of Columbus to that of Magellan

year by that of Ojeda with La Cosa and Vespucius, and it was proved that the Pearl Coast opposed quite a long barrier to voyages in this direction into the Indian Ocean. The triumphant return of Gama from Hindustan in midsummer of 1499 turned all eyes toward that country. Cathay and Cipango suffered temporary eclipse. The problem for Spain was to find a route into the Indian Ocean, either to the west or to the east of the Pearl Coast. Thus she might hope to find riches in the same quarter of the globe where Portugal had found them. As the Spanish search went on, it became in a new and unexpected way complicated with Portuguese interests through the discovery of a stretch of Brazilian coast lying east of the papal meridian. Bearing these points in mind, the reader will be helped by the following diagram

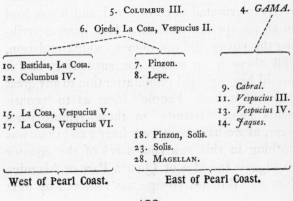

5. COLUMBUS III.   4. *GAMA.*

6. Ojeda, La Cosa, Vespucius II.

West of Pearl Coast.	East of Pearl Coast.
10. Bastidas, La Cosa. 12. Columbus IV.	7. Pinzon. 8. Lepe.
15. La Cosa, Vespucius V. 17. La Cosa, Vespucius VI.	9. *Cabral.* 11. *Vespucius III.* 13. *Vespucius IV.* 14. *Jaques.*
	18. Pinzon, Solis. 23. Solis. 28. MAGELLAN.

in which some of the voyages already discussed are grouped with those which we are now about to consider. The numbers refer back to the numbers in my fuller table of voyages on pages 284, 285 above, and here as there the Portuguese voyages are distinguished by italics.

While the voyages of Bastidas and Columbus between the Pearl Coast and Cape Honduras revealed no passage into the Indian Ocean, the voyages of Pinzon, Lepe, and Vespucius proved that from Paria to Cape San Roque, and thence southerly and southwesterly there extended a continuous coast as far as the latitude of the Cape of Good Hope. If this was Cattigara land, or part of Ptolemy's southern Terra Incognita, might it be possible to sail around it and enter the Indian Ocean? Or might some passage be found connecting the waters on its opposite sides? If such a passage should be found, of course much interest would attach to its position, whether east or west of the papal meridian. It was to determine such points as these that two expeditions sailed from Portugal in 1503, the one commanded by Gonçalo Coelho, the other by Christovão Jaques.[1]

Voyages of Coelho and Jaques

[1] The date 1503 for the Jaques voyage has been doubted (Varnhagen, *Primeiras negociaões diplomáticas respectivas ao Brazil*, Rio Janeiro, 1843). I here follow the more generally received opinion. For the French voyage of Gonneville in 1504 on the Brazilian coast as far as 26° S., see Avezac,

Coelho's fleet consisted of six ships, one of which was commanded by Vespucius. From Hindustan had come reports of the great wealth and commanding situation of the city of Malacca, a most important gateway and warehouse for the Gangetic sea, and much farther east and south than Calcutta. The purpose of Coelho and Jaques was to investigate the relations of the Brazilian coast to this rich gateway of the East. Of Jaques's voyage we know little except that he seems to have skirted the coast of Patagonia as far as 52° S., and may have caught a glimpse of the opening which Magellan afterward (by sailing through it) proved to be a strait. Why he should have turned and gone home, without verifying this point, is a question which will naturally occur to the reader who allows himself for a moment to forget the terrible hardships that were apt to beset these mariners and frustrate their plans. We shall have no difficulty in understanding it when we come to see how the crews of Magellan felt about entering this strait.

As for Coelho's expedition, starting from Lisbon June 10, 1503, its first stop was at the Cape Verde Islands, for a fresh supply of water and other provisions. From this point Vespucius

" Campagne du navire l'Espoir de Honfleur," in *Annales des voyages,* juin et juillet, 1869 ; Gaffarel, *Histoire du Brésil Français au seizième siècle,* Paris, 1878.

wished to take a direct course for Brazil, but Coelho insisted upon keeping on south-
erly to Sierra Leone, for no earthly
reason, says Americus rather tartly,
"unless to exhibit himself as the
captain of six ships;"[1] but I suspect that while

*Fourth voy-
age of Ves-
pucius, —
with Coelho,
1503*

Ships of the time of Vespucius.[2]

the scientific Italian would have steered boldly
across the trackless waste straight at his goal,

[1] "Et come elnostro capitano maggiore fusse huomo
p̥sumptuoso & molto cauezuto [*i. e.* Portuguese *cabeçudo*,
"headstrong"] uolle andare a riconoscere la Serra liona, . . .
senza tenere necessitá alcuna, se no' p̥ farsi uedere, ch' era
capitano di sei naui," etc. *Lettera*, etc., fol. c. iii. verso.

[2] From the original edition of the letter to Soderini, Florence, 1505–06, photographed from Varnhagen's facsimile
reproduction.

the Portuguese commander preferred the old-fashioned and more timid course of following two sides of a triangle and was not going to take advice from any of your confounded foreigners. But as several of the captains and pilots sustained Americus, the course actually followed, without much rhyme or reason, looks like the resultant of a conflict of opinions. Early in August, after much rough weather, they discovered a small uninhabited island near the Brazilian coast in latitude 3° S., since known as the island of Fernando Noronha; and there one of the ships, a carrack of 300 tons burthen, in which were most of the stores, staved in her bows against a rock and " nothing was saved but the crew." By the chief captain's orders Americus with his own ship sought a harbour on this island and found an excellent one about four leagues distant. His boat had been retained for general service by Coelho, who promised to send it after him with further instructions. We are not informed as to the weather, but it was probably bad, for after waiting a week in the harbour, Americus descried one of the ships on her way to him. She brought news that Coelho's ship had gone with him to the bottom and the other two had disappeared. So now the two ships of Vespucius and his consort, with one boat between them, were left alone at this little island. " It had plenty of fresh water," says Americus, " and a dense growth of trees filled with innumerable birds, which were so simple that they allowed us to catch them with our hands. We took so many that we loaded the boat with them." [1] After thus providing against famine, they sailed to the Bay of All Saints, which had been designated as a rendezvous in case of accidents, and there they faithfully waited two months in the vain hope of being overtaken by their comrades. Then giving up this hope, they weighed anchor again and followed the coast southward to Cape Frio, just under the tropic of Capricorn. Finding there a great quantity of brazil-wood, they decided to establish a colony there, and what follows we may let Vespucius tell in his own words : " In this port we staid five months, building a blockhouse and loading our ships with dye-wood. We could go no farther, for want of men and equipments. So after finishing this work we decided to return to Portugal, leaving twenty-four men

---

[1] This is another of the little observations which keep impressing us with the accuracy and fidelity of Vespucius in his descriptions. Modern naturalists are familiar with the fact that on desolate islands, where they have lived for many generations unmolested, birds become so tame that they can be caught by hand, and even the catching of a multitude of them will not frighten the others. For many instances of this, and the explanation, see Darwin's *Voyage of the Beagle*, new ed., London, 1870, p. 398 ; Spencer's *Essays*, 2d series, London, 1864, p. 134.

in the fortress, with twelve pieces of cannon, a good outfit of small arms, and provisions for six months.[1] We made peace with all the natives in the neighbourhood, whom I have not mentioned in this voyage, but not because we did not see and have dealings with great numbers of them. As many as thirty of us went forty leagues inland, where we saw so many things that I omit to relate them, reserving them for my book, the *Four Journeys*. . . . The bearer of this letter, Benvenuto di Domenico Benvenuti, will tell your Magnificence of . . . such things as have been omitted to avoid prolixity. . . . *I have made the letter as short as possible, and refrained from mentioning many things very natural to be told, through fear of seeming tedious.*"

Conclusion of the letter to Soderini

This passage, and especially the last sentence which I have italicized, affords abundant explanation of that reticence of Vespucius about many things which we should like to know; a reticence which the bats and moles of historical criticism, with these plain words staring them in the face, profess to regard as unaccountable!

When Americus arrived at Lisbon, June 18, 1504, the missing ships had not yet arrived, and were given up for lost, but after some time they

---

[1] This little colony or factory at Cape Frio was still kept up in 1511 and after. See Varnhagen, *Histoire générale du Brésil*, tom. i. p. 427.

returned, having extended their explorations perhaps as far as the mouth of the river La Plata.[1]

For some reason unknown Vespucius left the service of Portugal by the end of that year 1504, or somewhat earlier. This step may have been connected with his marriage, which seems to have occurred early in 1505; it may have been because he had become sufficiently impressed with the southwesterly trend of the Brazilian coast-line to realize that further discoveries in that direction would best be conducted under the Spanish flag; or it may have been simply because King Ferdinand outbid King Emanuel, whose policy was too often pennywise. At any rate, Americus made

Americus returns to Spain,

[1] This is the opinion of Varnhagen, who believes that Juan de Solis was then in the Portuguese service and in this fleet, and on this occasion made his first acquaintance with the river La Plata, which would almost surely be mistaken for a strait. If this opinion as to Solis be sustained, one can see a common feature in the shifting of two such captains as Vespucius and Solis from Spain to Portugal and back, coupled with the subsequent transfer of Magellan from the Portuguese service. The discovery of Brazil seemed to open an avenue for Portuguese enterprise in western waters, and so began to draw over navigators from Spain; but by 1504 it began to appear that the limit of achievement under the Portuguese flag in that direction had been reached, and so the tide of interest set back toward Spain. If Solis saw La Plata in 1504 and believed it to be a strait, he must have known that it was on the Spanish side of the line of demarcation. Its meridian is more than 20° west of Cape San Roque.

his way back to Spain. In February, 1505, just before starting from Seville on his journey to court, he called on his sick and harassed friend Columbus, to see what kind service he could render him. The letter which Vespucius carried from Columbus to his son Diego is very *and visits Co-* interesting.[1] The admiral speaks of *lumbus* Vespucius in terms of high respect, as a thoroughly good and honourable man, to whom Fortune had not rendered such rewards as his labours deserved; a staunch friend who had always done his best to serve him and was now going to court with the determination to set his affairs right if possible. There is something very pleasant in the relations thus disclosed between the persecuted Discoverer, then almost on his deathbed, and the younger navigator, to whom yet grosser injustice was to be done by a stupid and heedless world.[2]

The transactions of Vespucius at court, and the nature of the maritime enterprises that were set on foot or carried to completion during the

[1] The original is preserved in the family archives of the Duke of Veraguas, and a copy is printed in Navarrete, tom. i. p. 351.

[2] "If not among the greatest of the world's great men, he is among the happiest of those on whom good fortune has bestowed renown." S. H. Gay, apud Winsor, *Narr. and Crit. Hist.*, ii. 152. Is it, then, such a happy fortune to be unjustly stigmatized as a liar by ten generations of men?

next few years, are to be gathered chiefly from old account-books, contracts, and other business documents unearthed by the indefatigable Navarrete, and printed in his great collection. The four chief personages in the Spanish marine at that time, the experts to whom all difficult questions were referred and all arduous enterprises entrusted, were Vespucius and La Cosa, Pinzon and Solis. Unfortunately account-books and legal documents, having been written for other purposes than the gratification of the historian, are — like the "geological record" — imperfect. Too many links are missing to enable us to determine with certainty just how the work was shared among these mariners, or just how many voyages were undertaken. But it is clear that the first enterprise contemplated was a voyage by Pinzon, in company with either Solis or Vespucius or both, in the direction of the river La Plata, for the purpose of finding an end to the continent or a passage into the Indian Ocean. What Vespucius had failed to do in his last voyage for Portugal, he now proposed to do in a voyage for Spain. It was this expedition, planned for 1506, but never carried out, that Herrera a century later mistook for that voyage of Pinzon and Solis to Honduras and the Gulf of Mexico which the contemporary Oviedo (supported by Martyr and confirmed by Gomara)

The Pinzon expedition to La Plata; planned for 1506, but not carried out

positively declares to have been made before
1499. As I have already shown, Pinzon did not
leave Spain for any long voyage in 1506.[1] The
remonstrances of Portugal put a stop to the
enterprise, and the ships were used for other
purposes.

Meanwhile the search for a passage west of the
Pearl Coast was conducted by La Cosa and Vespucius. In this voyage, from May to
December, 1505, they visited the Gulf
of Darien and ascended the Atrato
River for some 200 miles. Of late
years it has been proposed to make an inter-
oceanic canal by connecting this river with the
San Juan, which flows into the Pacific. To
Vespucius and La Cosa it turned out not to be
the strait of which at first its general aspect had
given promise, but in its shallow upper stretches
they found its sandy bottom gleaming and glis-
tening with particles of gold. For three months
they explored the neighbouring country, and
found plenty of gold in the wild mountain
streams. On the way home they seemed to
have stopped on the Pearl Coast and gathered
a goodly store of pearls. The immediate profit
of the voyage was so great that it was repeated
two years later. During the year 1506 Vespucius was busy in Spain preparing the armament
for Pinzon, and when, in March, 1507, that ex-

Fifth and sixth voyages of Vespucius, — with La Cosa

1 See above, p. 290.

pedition was abandoned, Vespucius and La Cosa started at once for the Gulf of Darien, and returned in November, heavily freighted with gold. This, of course, was purely a commercial voyage. But during the summer the way for further discovery had been prepared, and in some way or other the Portuguese difficulty had been surmounted, for soon after New Year's, 1508, Americus told the Venetian ambassador at the court of Spain that a way to the lands of spice was to be sought, and that the ships would start in March without fail.[1]

[1] My brief mention of the doings of Vespucius, Pinzon, Solis, and La Cosa, between 1504 and 1509, is based upon the original documents relating to these four navigators scattered through the third volume of Navarrete's *Coleccion*, as illuminated by two precious bits of information sent to the Venetian senate by its diplomatic agents in Spain. The letter of Girolamo Vianello from Burgos, December 23, 1505 (dated 1506, according to an old Spanish usage which began the New Year at Christmas and sometimes even as early as the first of December), establishes the fact of the fifth voyage of Vespucius in 1505. This letter was found in Venice by the great historian Ranke, and a few lines of it were copied by him for Humboldt, who published the scrap in his *Examen critique*, tom. v. p. 157, but was puzzled by the date, because Americus was indisputably in Spain through 1506 (and Humboldt supposed through 1505 also, but a more attentive scrutiny of the documents shows him to have been mistaken). Varnhagen, delving in the Biblioteca di San Marco at Venice, again found the letter, and a copy of the whole is printed, with valuable notes, in his *Nouvelles recherches*, pp. 12–17. In 1867 Mr. Rawdon Brown discovered in Venice the two

They did not start, however, until June 29. In the interval La Cosa was appointed *alguazil mayor*, or high constable of the province about to be organized at the Gulf of Darien, and afterwards called Golden Castile (*Castilla del Oro*), so that, as we shall by and by see, these two voyages which he made with Vespucius were the first links in the chain of events that ended in the conquest of Peru. In March Vespucius received his appointment as pilot major, which

Voyage of Pinzon and Solis, 1508–09

kept him in Spain, and his place in the voyage with Pinzon was taken by Solis, who had probably visited the mouth of La Plata with Coelho in 1504. Pinzon and Solis sailed June 29, followed the Brazilian coast, passed the wide mouth of that river without finding it, and kept on, according to Herrera, as far as the river Colorado, in latitude 40° S. There was disagreement between the two captains, and they returned home, probably somewhat peevish with disappointment, in October, 1509. Nothing more was done in this direction for six years. After the death of Vespucius in 1513, he was succeeded by Solis as Pilot Major of Spain. Pinzon here disappears from our narrative, except as a witness in the

brief letters of the ambassador Francesco Cornaro, which have established the sixth voyage of Vespucius, in 1507. They are printed in Harrisse, *Bibl. Amer. Vetust., Additions*, Paris, 1872, p. xxvii.

Probanzas. He seems to have gone on no more voyages. He was ennobled in 1519.[1] Solis started on another search for the river La Plata in October, 1515. He entered that "fresh-water sea" (*mar dulce*) the following January, and while he was exploring its coast in a boat with eight companions the Indians suddenly swarmed upon the scene. Solis and his men were instantly captured, and their horrified comrades on shipboard, unable to save them, could only look on while they were deliberately roasted and devoured by the screaming and dancing demons.[2]

Last voyage and death of Solis, 1515-16

During these years events were gradually preparing the way for the emergence of the idea of a *separate* New World, a *western hemisphere* forming no part of the ancient Œcumene. There is nothing to indicate that any such idea was ever conceived by Vespucius. Its emergence was so gradual and so indefinite that it is not easy to trace it in literary documents or in maps.

Emergence of the idea of a western hemisphere; Stobnicza's map, 1512

---

[1] See the document in Navarrete, tom. iii. p. 145.

[2] The words of Peter Martyr in a different connection might well be applied here: "they came runninge owte of the wooddes with a terrible crye and most horrible aspect, much lyke vnto the people cauled *Picti Agathyrsi* of whom the poete virgile speaketh. . . . A man wold thinke them to bee deuylles incarnate newly broke owte of hell, they are soo lyke vnto helhoundes." Eden's translation, 1553, dec. i. bk. vii.

A hypothetical indication of an ocean corresponding in position to what we know as the Pacific may be seen upon the rude map of the Polish geographer Jan Stobnicza, published at Cracow in 1512, in an Introduction to Ptolemy. Like the *Tabula Terre Nove*, it is derived from a common original with the Cantino map. At the north is shown the land discovered by the Cabots. The name Isabella is transferred from Cuba to Florida, and the legend above seems to refer to the " C. de bonauentura" of the *Tabula Terre Nove*. Cape San Roque in Brazil is called " Caput S. Crucis." The rude indication of the Gulf of Mexico is repeated from the *Tabula Terre Nove* or its prototype. But the new and striking feature in this Stobnicza map is the combination of the northern and southern continents with an ocean behind them open all the way from north to south. As the existence of the Pacific was still unknown in 1512, this ocean was purely hypothetical, and so was the western coast-line of America, if it is proper to call coast-line this mere cut-off drawn in straight lines with a ruler. The interest of this crude map lies chiefly in its suggestion that in the maker's mind *the whole transatlantic coast already visited* (except the Cabot portion) *was conceived not as part of Asia, but as a barrier in the way of reaching Asia*. The vague adumbration of the truth appears in the position of the

STOBNICZA'

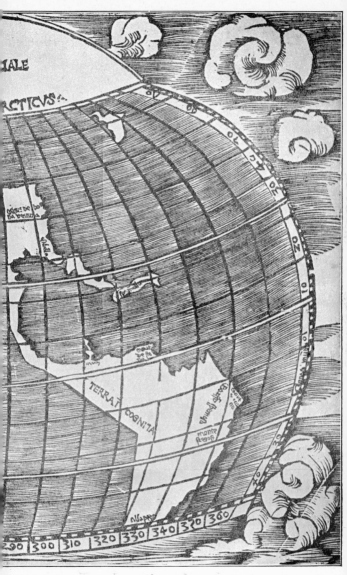

IALE

ACTICVS

OCEVS de bo...
na Brisila...

TERRA COGNITA

monte florido

290 300 310 320 330 340 350 360

WORLD, 1512

great island Cipango (*Zypangu insula*) in the ocean behind Mexico and some 600 miles distant. Before Stobnicza such maps as Ruysch's, which took full account of South America as a barrier, detached it from what little was known of North America, which was still reckoned as Asia. The peculiar combinations of land and water in Stobnicza's map make it dimly prefigure the result attained nearly thirty years afterward by Mercator. The suggestion was in advance of the knowledge of the time, and the map does not seem to have exerted any commanding influence; but in the next year after it was published an event occurred which, if correctly understood, would have seemed to justify it. In 1513 the Terra Firma was crossed at its narrowest place, and Vasco Nuñez de Balboa, from the summit of a peak in Darien, gazed upon an expanse of waters, which, as we have since learned, made part of the greatest ocean upon the globe.[1]

First sight of the Pacific by Balboa, 1513

[1] Colonel Higginson will pardon me for calling attention to an inadvertence of the kind which I have already so often characterized as projecting our modern knowledge into the past : "Columbus discovered what he thought was India [*i. e.* Asia], but Balboa proved that half the width of the globe still separated him from India." *Larger History of the United States*, p. 70. If Balboa could prove this by standing on a mountain in Darien and looking at the water before him, he must have had a truly marvellous pair of eyes ! Surely he had no positive means of knowing that this water stretched

It was not so much, however, the brief glimpse of Balboa as the steady eastward progress of

Eastward pro-
gress of the
Portuguese to
China and the
Moluccas,
1504–17

the Portuguese that began to reveal to practical navigators the character and extent of the waters west of Mundus Novus. The arrival of Portuguese traders in the Indian Ocean

was the signal for a tremendous struggle for commercial supremacy. In every seaport they found Arabs, or, as they called them, "Moors," their hereditary enemies. Arabs held nearly all the points of entrance and exit in that ocean, and

away for more than a hundred miles. Mere vision scarcely carried his discovery out into the open ocean beyond the Gulf of Panama, though, in accordance with information received from the Indians, he rightly interpreted it as a "South Sea" upon which one might hug the coast to the "Golden Kingdom," soon to be known as Peru. The first discoverer who proved the width of the Pacific was Magellan, who sailed across it. — Such little slips as the one here criticised are easy to make, and one cannot feel sure that one does not unwittingly do it oneself. The old poets were flagrant sinners in this respect. Lope de Vega, in a famous drama, makes Columbus know of "the New World" even before 1492. Why is it, asks Christopher in a talk with his brother Bartholomew, why is it that I, a poor pilot, a man with broken fortunes, yearn to add to this world another, and such a remote one? —

Un hombre pobre, y aun roto,
Que ansí lo puedo decir,
Y que vive de piloto,
Quiere á este mundo añadir
Otro mundo tan remoto !

El Nuevo Mundo Descubierto, Jorn. i.

the Portuguese at once perceived the necessity
of seizing these points. Blows were exchanged
from the start, and the ensuing warfare forms
one of the most romantic chapters in history.
It would not be easy to point out two commanders more swift in intelligence, more fertile
in resource, more unconquerable in action, than
Francisco de Almeida and Alfonso de Albuquerque. The result of their work was the
downfall of Arab power in the Indies, and the
founding of that great commercial empire which
remained in the hands of the Portuguese until
it was taken from them by the Dutch.[1] On the
African coast, from Sofala to the Strait of Bab-
el-Mandeb, the Portuguese held all the important trading stations. They seized the island
of Socotra, established themselves in force along
the coasts of Oman and Makran, and capturing
the wealthy Hormuz they gained secure control
of the outlet to the valley of the Euphrates.
They held the whole western coast of Hindustan
from above Bombay down to Cape Comorin,

[1] The story of the Portuguese empire in the East Indies is
told by Barros, *Decadas da Asia*, Lisbon, 1778–88, with
the continuation by Couto, in all 24 vols. ; Bras Affonso de
Albuquerque, *Commentarios do grande Afonso Dalboquerque*,
Lisbon, 1774, in 4 vols. I give the dates of my own copies,
which are, I think, the best editions. The great work of Barros
began to be published in 1552 ; that of Albuquerque, son of
the conqueror, was published in 1557. See also Faria y
Sousa, *Asia Portuguesa*, Lisbon, 1666, in 3 vols.

while on the Coromandel coast they had stations at Mylapur and Negapatam. In 1506 Almeida first visited Ceylon, which was afterward annexed to the Portuguese empire. In 1508 Sequeira advanced as far as Sumatra, and in 1511 the famous Malacca, the Gateway of the East, was conquered by Albuquerque. The way to the "lands where the spices grow" was thus at last laid open, and Albuquerque had no sooner riveted his clutch upon Malacca than he sent Antonio d'Abreu and Francisco Serrano, with three galleons, to make a friendly visit to the Spice Islands *par excellence*, the Moluccas. Sailing down by Java, and between Celebes and Flores, this little fleet visited Amboina and Banda, and brought away as heavy a load of nutmegs and cloves as it was safe to carry.[1] Six years afterward, in 1517, Fernam de Andrade conducted the first European ship that ever sailed to China. He reached Canton and entered into friendly commercial relations with that city.

Thus data were beginning to accumulate in evidence that the continent of Asia did not extend nearly so far to the east as Toscanelli and Columbus had supposed. A comparison of longitudes, moreover, between the Moluccas and the Brazilian coast could hardly fail to bring out

[1] For some account of the Spice Islands and their further history, see Argensola, *Conquista de las islas Molucas*, Madrid, 1609, folio.

the fact of a great distance between them. Still theory did not advance so surely and definitely as it might seem to us with the modern map in our minds. The multitude of unfamiliar facts was bewildering, and the breadth of the Pacific Ocean was too much for the mind to take in except by actual experience. We have now, in concluding this long chapter, to consider the heroic career of the man who finished what Columbus had begun, and furnished proof—though even this was not immediately understood—that the regions discovered by the admiral belonged to a separate world from Asia.

Dim rudimentary conception of a separate ocean between Mundus Novus and Asia

Ferdinand Magellan, as we call him in English,[1] was a Portuguese nobleman of the fourth

[1] The Portuguese name is Fernão da Magalhães; in Spanish it becomes Fernando de Magallanes, pronounced *Mahgah-lyáh-nays*. In English one often, perhaps commonly, hears it as *Ma-jel'-lan*. One does not like to be pedantic in such trifles, and I don't mind slaughtering a consonant or two when necessary, but to shift the accent of a word seems to destroy its identity, so that *Ma-jel-lan'*, which we sometimes hear, seems preferable.

The documentary sources of the life of Magellan are chiefly to be found in the fourth volume of Navarrete's *Coleccion de viages*. The early accounts of his voyage have been collected and translated by the late Lord Stanley of Alderley, *The First Voyage Round the World*, London, 1874 (Hakluyt Society). A good biography, almost the first in any language, has lately appeared in English : Guillemard, *The Life of Fer-*

grade, but of family as old and blood as blue as any in the peninsula. He was born at Sabrosa, Ferdinand near Chaves,[1] in one of the wild-Magellan est and gloomiest nooks of Tras-os-Montes, in or about the year 1480. The people of that province have always been distinguished for a rugged fidelity, combined with unconquerable toughness of fibre, that reminds one of the Scotch; and from those lonely mountains there never came forth a sturdier character than Ferdinand Magellan. Difficulty and danger fit to baffle the keenest mind and daunt the strongest heart only incited this man to efforts wellnigh superhuman. In his portrait, as given in Navarrete,[2] with the great arching brows, the fiery black eyes, the firm-set lips, and mastiff jaw, covered but not concealed by the shaggy beard, the strength is almost appalling. Yet in all this power there was nothing cruel. Magellan was kind-hearted and unselfish, and on more than one occasion we see him risking his life

dinand Magellan and the First Circumnavigation of the Globe, London, 1890.

[1] Various writers have given Lisbon, or Oporto, or some village in Estremadura as his birthplace; but Sabrosa seems clearly established. See the reference to his first will, in Guillemard, p. 23.

[2] *Coleccion de viages*, tom. iv. p. xxiv; it is reproduced in Lord Stanley's volume; in Winsor, *Narr. and Crit. Hist.*, ii. 593; and elsewhere; but one gets the effect most completely in Navarrete.

Ferdinand Magellan

FERDIN· MAGALLANUS·
SVPERATIS· ANTARCTICI· FRETI·
ANGVSTIIS· CLARISSIMVS·

in behalf of others with generosity worthy of a paladin.

Nothing is known of his childhood and youth except that at an early age he went to Lisbon and was brought up in the royal household. In 1505 he embarked as a volunteer in the armada which the brilliant and high-souled Almeida, first Portuguese viceroy of India, was taking to the East. There followed seven years of service under this commander and his successor Albuquerque. Seven years of anxious sailing over strange waters, checkered with wild fights against Arabs and Malays, trained Magellan for the supreme work that was to come. He was in Sequeira's expedition to Malacca, in 1508–09, the first time that European ships had ventured east of Ceylon. _Sequeira's expedition and the Malay plot, 1509_ While they were preparing to take in a cargo of pepper and ginger, the astute Malay king was plotting their destruction. His friendly overtures deceived the frank and somewhat too unsuspicious Sequeira. Malay sailors and traders were allowed to come on board the four ships, and all but one of the boats were sent to the beach, under command of Francisco Serrano, to hasten the bringing of the cargo. Upon the quarter-deck of his flagship Sequeira sat absorbed in a game of chess, with half a dozen dark faces intently watching him, their deadly purpose veiled with polite words and smiles.

Ashore the houses rose terrace-like upon the hillside, while in the foreground the tall tower of the citadel — square with pyramidal apex, like an Italian bell-tower — glistened in the September sunshine. The parties of Malays on the ships, and down on the bustling beach, cast furtive glances at this summit, from which a puff of smoke was presently to announce the fatal moment. The captains and principal officers on shipboard were at once to be stabbed and their vessels seized, while the white men ashore were to be massacred. But a Persian woman in love with one of the officers had given tardy warning, so that just before the firing of the signal the Portuguese sailors began chasing the squads of Malays from their decks, while Magellan, in the only boat, rowed for the flagship, and his stentorian shout of "Treason!" came just in time to save Sequeira. Then in wild confusion, as wreaths of white smoke curled about the fatal tower, Serrano and a few of his party sprang upon their boats and pushed out to sea. Most of their comrades, less fortunate, were surrounded and slaughtered on the beach. Nimble Malay skiffs pursued and engaged Serrano, and while he was struggling against overwhelming odds, Magellan rowed up and joined battle with such desperate fury that Serrano was saved. No sooner were all the surviving Portuguese brought to-

Sequeira and Serrano saved by Magellan

gether on shipboard than the Malays attacked in full force, but European guns were too much for them, and after several of their craft had been sent to the bottom they withdrew.

This affair was the beginning of a devoted friendship between Magellan and Serrano, sealed by many touching and romantic in-cidents, like the friendship between Gerard and Denys in "The Cloister and the Hearth;" and it was out of this friendship that in great measure grew the most wonderful voyage recorded in history. After Albuquerque had taken Malacca in 1511, Serrano commanded one of the ships that made the first voyage to the Moluccas. On its re-turn course his vessel, loaded with spices, was wrecked upon a lonely island which had long served as a lair for pirates. Fragments of wreckage strewn upon the beach lured ashore a passing gang of such ruffians, and while they were intent upon delving and searching, Ser-rano's men, who had hidden among the rocks, crept forth and seized the pirate ship. The nearest place of retreat was the island of Am-boina, and this accident led Serrano back to the Moluccas, where he established himself as an ally or quasi-protector of the king of Ternate, and remained for the rest of his short life. Letters from Serrano aroused in Magellan a strong de-sire to follow his friend to that "new world"

Serrano's shipwreck, and his stay at the Mo-luccas

423

in the Indian waves, the goal so long dreamed of, so eagerly sought, by Columbus and many another, but now for the first time actually reached and grasped. But circumstances came in to modify most curiously this aim of Magellan's. He had come to learn something about the great ocean intervening between the Malay seas and Mundus Novus, but failed to form any conception of its width at all approaching the reality. It therefore seemed to him that the line of demarcation antipodal to Borgia's meridian must fall to the west of the Moluccas, and that his friend Serrano had ventured into a region which must ultimately be resigned to Spain. In this opinion he was wrong, for the meridian which cuts through the site of Adelaide in Australia would have come near the line that on that side of the globe marked the end of the Portuguese half and the beginning of the Spanish half; but the mistake was easy to make and hard to correct.

The antipodal line of demarcation between Spanish and Portuguese waters

About this time some cause unknown took Magellan back to Lisbon, where we find him in the midsummer of 1512. His hope of a speedy return to India was disappointed. Whether on account of a slight disagreement he had once had with Albuquerque, or for some other reason, he found himself out of favour with the king. A year or more of service in Morocco followed, in the course of which a Moorish lance wounded Magellan in the knee and lamed him for life. After his return to Portugal in 1514, it became evident that King Emanuel had no further employment for him. He became absorbed in the study of navigation and cosmography, in which he had always felt an interest. It would have been strange if an inquiring mind, trained in the court of Lisbon in those days, had not been stirred by the fascination of such studies. How early in life Magellan had begun to breathe in the art of seamanship with the salt breezes from the Atlantic we do not know; but at some time the results of scientific study were combined with his long experience in East Indian waters to make him a consummate master. He conceived the vast scheme of circumnavigating the globe. Somewhere upon that long coast of Mundus Novus, explored by Vespucius and Coelho, Jaques and Solis, there was doubtless a passage through which he could sail westward and greet his friend Serrano in the Moluccas !

Magellan's return to Portugal; his scheme for sailing westward to the Moluccas

Upon both of Schöner's globes, of 1515 and 1520, such a strait is depicted, connecting the southern Atlantic with an ocean to the west of Mundus Novus. This has raised the question whether any one had ever discovered it before Magellan.[1] That there was in many minds a

[1] See the discussion in Wieser, *Magalhães-Strasse und*

425

belief in the existence of such a passage seems certain; whether because the wish was father *The strait on Schöner's globes* to the thought, or because the mouth of La Plata had been reported as the mouth of a strait, or because Jaques had perhaps looked into the Strait of Magellan, is by no means clear. But without threading that blind and tortuous labyrinth, as Magellan did, for more than 300 geographical miles, successfully avoiding its treacherous bays and channels with no outlet, no one could prove that there was a practicable passage there; and there is no good reason for supposing that any one had accomplished such a feat of navigation before Magellan.

The scheme of thus reaching the Moluccas by the westward voyage was first submitted to King Emanuel. To him was offered the first opportunity for ascertaining whether these islands lay within his half of the heathen world *Magellan's proposals are rejected by the king of Portugal;* or not. He did not smile upon the scheme, though he may have laughed at it. The papal bulls and the treaty of Tordesillas prohibited the Spaniards from sailing to the Indies by way of the

Austral-Continent auf den Globen des Johannes Schöner, Innsbruck, 1881; Kohl, *Geschichte der Entdeckungsreisen und Schiff-fahrten zur Magellans-Strasse,* Berlin, 1877; Winsor, *Narr. and Crit. Hist.,* viii. 375–387; Guillemard's *Magellan,* pp. 188–198.

Cape of Good Hope; and unless they could get through the barrier of Mundus Novus there was no danger of their coming by a westerly route. Why not let well enough alone? Apparently Emanuel did not put much faith in the strait. We are told by Gaspar Correa that Magellan then asked the royal permission to go and offer his services to some other master. "The King said he might do what he pleased. Upon this Magellan desired to kiss his hand at parting, but the King would not offer it."[1]

The alternative was thus offered to Magellan of abandoning his scheme of discovery or entering the service of Spain, and he *and accordingly he enters the service of Spain* chose the latter course. For this he has been roundly abused, not only by Portuguese writers from that day to this, but by others who seem to forget that a man has as clear a right to change his country and his allegiance as to move his home from one town to another. In the relations between state and individual the duty is not all on one side. As Faria y Sousa, more sensible than many of his countrymen, observes, the great navigator did all that honour demanded when by a special clause in his agreement with Spain he pledged himself to do nothing prejudicial to the interests of Portugal.[2]

[1] Guillemard, p. 82.

[2] Faria y Sousa, *Comentarios á la Lusiada de Camões,*

It was in October, 1517, that Magellan arrived in Seville and became the guest of Diego Barbosa, alcaide of the arsenal there, a Portuguese gentleman who had for several years been in the Spanish service. Before Christmas of that year he was married to his host's daughter Beatriz de Barbosa, who accompanied him to the court. Magellan found favour in the eyes of the boy king, Charles V., and even obtained active support from Bishop Fonseca, in spite of that prelate's ingrained hostility to noble schemes and honourable men. It was decided to fit out an expedition to pursue the search in which Solis had lately lost his life. More than a year was consumed in the needful preparations, and it was not until September 20, 1519, that the little fleet cleared the mouth of the Guadalquivir and stood out to sea.

Magellan's marriage

There were five small ships, commanded as follows : —

1. Trinidad, 110 tons, Captain-general Ferdinand Magellan ; pilot, Estevan Gomez.

2. San Antonio, 120 tons, Captain Juan de Cartagena.

3. Concepcion, 90 tons, Captain Gaspar Quesada.

4. Victoria, 85 tons, Captain Luis de Mendoza.

x. 140 ; Guillemard, p. 85. Cf. Lord Stanley of Alderley, *First Voyage Round the World,* pp. ii–xv.

5. Santiago, 75 tons, Captain Juan Serrano.

It is a striking illustration of the shiftlessness with which things were apt to be done by the government, and the difficulties under which great navigators accomplished their arduous work, that these five ships were all old and decidedly the worse for wear. All seem to have been decked, with castles at the stern and fore. About 280 men were on board, a motley crew of Spaniards and Portuguese, Genoese and Sicilians, Flemings and French, Germans and Greeks, with one Englishman from Bristol, and a few negroes and Malays. Of Portuguese there were at least seven and thirty, for the most part men attached to Magellan and who had left their country with him. It was fortunate that he had so many such, for the wiles of King Emanuel had pursued him into Spain and out upon the ocean. When that sovereign learned that the voyage was really to be made, he determined that it must not be allowed to succeed. Hired ruffians lurked about street corners in Seville, waiting for a chance that never came for rushing forth and stabbing the wary navigator; orders were sent to captains in the East Indies — among them the gallant Sequeira whom Magellan had saved — to intercept and arrest the fleet if it should ever reach those waters; and, worst of all, the seeds of mutiny were busily and

Ships and men of the great expedition

429

but too successfully sown in Magellan's own ships. Of the four subordinate captains only one was faithful. Upon Juan Serrano, the brother of his dearest friend, Magellan could absolutely rely. The others, Cartagena, Mendoza, and Quesada, sailed out from port with treason in their hearts. A few days after their start a small caravel overtook the Trinidad, with an anxious message to Magellan from his wife's father, Barbosa, begging him to be watchful, "since it had come to his knowledge that his captains had told their friends and relations that if they had any trouble with him they would kill him." For reply the commander counselled Barbosa to be of good cheer, for be they true men or false he feared them not, and would do his appointed work all the same.[1] For Beatriz, left with her little son, Rodrigo, six months old, the outlook must have been anxious enough.

Traitors in the fleet

Our chief source of information for the events of the voyage is the journal kept by a gentleman from Vicenza, the Chevalier Antonio Pigafetta, who obtained permission to accompany the expedition, "for to see the marvels of the ocean."[2] After leaving the

Pigafetta's journal

---

[1] Correa, *Lendas da India*, tom. ii. p. 627 ; Guillemard, p. 149.

[2] Pigafetta's journal is contained, with other documents, in the book of Lord Stanley of Alderley, already cited. There is

Canaries on the 3d of October the armada ran down toward Sierra Leone and was becalmed, making only three leagues in three weeks. Then "the upper air burst into life" and the frail ships were driven along under bare poles, now and then dipping their yard-arms. During a month of this dreadful weather, the food and water grew scarce, and the rations were diminished. The spirit of mutiny began to show itself. The Spanish captains whispered among the crews that this man from Portugal had not their interests at heart and was not loyal to the emperor. Toward the captain-general their demeanour grew more and more insubordinate, and Cartagena one day, having come on board the flagship, faced him with threats and insults. To his astonishment Magellan promptly collared him, and sent him, a prisoner in irons, on board the Victoria (whose captain was unfortunately also one of the traitors), while the command of the San Antonio was given to another officer. This example made things quiet for the moment.

On the 29th of November they reached the Brazilian coast near Pernambuco, and on the 11th of January they arrived at the mouth of La Plata, which they investigated sufficiently to convince them that it was a river's mouth and

also a French edition by Amoretti, *Premier Voyage autour du Monde*, Paris, 1800.

not a strait. Three weeks were consumed in this work. Their course through February and March along the coast of Patagonia was marked by incessant and violent storms, and the cold became so intense that, finding a sheltered harbour, with plenty of fish, at Port St. Julian, they chose it for winter quarters and anchored there on the last day of March. On the next day, which was Easter Sunday, the mutiny that so long had smouldered broke out in all its fury.

Winter quarters at Port St. Julian

The hardships of the voyage had thus far been what staunch seamen called unusually severe, and it was felt that they had done enough. No one except Vespucius and Jaques had ever approached so near to the south pole, and if they had not yet found a strait, it was doubtless because there was none to find. The rations of bread and wine were becoming very short, and common prudence demanded that they should return to Spain. If their voyage was practically a failure it was not their fault; there was ample excuse in the frightful storms they had suffered and the dangerous strains that had been put upon their worn-out ships. Such was the general feeling, but when expressed to Magellan it fell upon deaf ears. No excuses, nothing but performance, would serve his turn; for him hardships were made only to be despised and

Reasons for returning home; Magellan's refusal

dangers to be laughed at; and, in short, go on they must, until a strait was found or the end of that continent reached. Then they would doubtless find an open way to the Moluccas, and while he held out hopes of rich rewards for all, he appealed to their pride as Castilians. For the inflexible determination of this man was not embittered by harshness, and he could wield as well as any one the language that soothes and persuades.

So long as all were busy in the fight against wind and wave, the captain-general's arguments were of avail. But the deliberate halt to face the hardships of an antarctic winter, with no prospect of stirring until toward September, was too much. Patience under enforced inactivity was a virtue higher than these sailors had yet been called upon to exhibit. The treacherous captains had found their opportunity and sowed distrust broadcast by hinting that a Portuguese commander could not better serve his king than by leading a Spanish armada to destruction. They had evidently secured their men and prepared their blow before the fleet came to anchor. The ringleaders of the mutiny were the captains Quesada, The mutiny at Port St. Julian, April 1, 1520 of the Concepcion, and Mendoza, of the Victoria, with Juan de Cartagena, the deposed captain of the San Antonio, which was now commanded by Magellan's cousin, Alvaro de

Mesquita. On the night of Easter Sunday, Cartagena and Quesada, with thirty men, boarded the San Antonio, seized Mesquita and put him in irons; in the brief affray the mate of the San Antonio was mortally wounded. One of the mutineers, Sebastian Elcano, was put in command of the ship, such of the surprised and bewildered crew as were likely to be loyal were disarmed, and food and wine were handed about in token of the more generous policy now to be adopted. All was done so quickly and quietly that no suspicion of it reached the captain-general or anybody on board the Trinidad.

On Monday morning the traitor captains felt themselves masters of the situation. Three of the five ships were in their hands, and if they chose to go back to Spain, who could stop them? If they should decide to capture the flagship and murder their commander, they had a fair chance of success, for the faithful Serrano in his little ship Santiago was no match for any one of the three. Defiance seemed quite safe, and in the forenoon, when a boat from the flagship happened to approach the San Antonio she was insolently told to keep away, since Magellan no longer had command over that ship. When this challenge was carried to Magellan he sent the boat from ship to ship as a test, and soon learned that only the Santiago remained loyal. Presently Quesada sent a mes-

Desperate
situation of
Magellan

434

sage to the Trinidad requesting a conference between the chief commander and the revolted captains. Very well, said Magellan, only the conference must of course be held on board the Trinidad; but for Quesada and his accomplices thus to venture into the lion's jaws was out of the question, and they impudently insisted that the captain-general should come on board the San Antonio.

Little did they realize with what a man they were dealing. Magellan knew how to make them come to him. He had reason *His bold* to believe that the crew of the Vic- *stroke* toria was less disloyal than the others and selected that ship for the scene of his first *coup de main*. While he kept a boat in readiness, with a score of trusty men armed to the teeth and led by his wife's brother, Barbosa, he sent another boat ahead to the Victoria, with his alguazil, or constable, Espinosa, and five other men. Luis de Mendoza, captain of the Victoria, suffered this small party to come on board. Espinosa then served on Mendoza a formal summons to come to the flagship, and upon his refusal quick as lightning sprang upon him and plunged a dagger into his throat. As the corpse of the rebellious captain dropped upon the deck, Barbosa's party rushed over the ship's side with drawn cutlasses, the dazed crew at once surrendered, and Barbosa took command.

The tables were now turned, and with three ships in loyal hands Magellan blockaded the other two in the harbour. At night he opened fire upon the San Antonio, and strong parties The mutiny suppressed from the Trinidad and the Victoria boarding her on both sides at once, Quesada and his accomplices were captured. The Concepcion thereupon, overawed and crestfallen, lost no time in surrendering ; and so the formidable mutiny was completely quelled in less than four and twenty hours. Quesada was beheaded, Cartagena and a guilty priest, Pero Sanchez, were kept in irons until the fleet sailed, when they were set ashore and left to their fate ; all the rest were pardoned, and open defiance of the captain-general was no more dreamed of. In the course of the winter the Santiago was wrecked while on a reconnoissance, but her men were rescued after dreadful sufferings, and Serrano was placed in command of the Concepcion.

At length on the 24th of August, with the Discovery of the strait earliest symptoms of spring weather, the ships, which had been carefully overhauled and repaired, proceeded on their way.[1]

[1] While they were staying at Port St. Julian the explorers made the acquaintance of many Patagonians, — giants, as they called them. "Their height appears greater than it really is, from their large guanaco mantles, their long flowing hair, and general figure : on an average their height is about six feet, with some men taller and only a few shorter ; and the women are also tall." Darwin, *Voyage of the Beagle*, London, 1870,

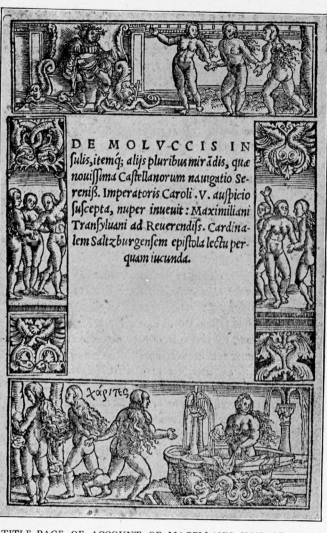

DE MOLVCCIS IN
ſulis, itemq́; alijs pluribus mirãdis, quæ
nouiſſima Caſtellanorum nauigatio Se-
reniß. Imperatoris Caroli . V. auſpicio
ſuſcepta, nuper inueuit : Maximiliani
Tranſyluani ad Reuerendiß. Cardina-
lem Saltzburgenſem epiſtola lectu per-
quam iucunda.

Χάριτες

TITLE–PAGE OF ACCOUNT OF MAGELLAN'S VOYAGE, 1523

Violent storms harassed them, and it was not until the 21st of October (St. Ursula's day) that they reached the headland still known as Cape Virgins. Passing beyond Dungeness they entered a large open bay, which some hailed as the long-sought strait, while others averred that no passage would be found there. It was, says Pigafetta, in Eden's version, "the straight now cauled the straight of Magellanus, beinge in sum place. C. x. leaques in length: and in breadth sumwhere very large and in other places lyttle more than halfe a leaque in bredth. On both the sydes of this strayght are great and hygh mountaynes couered with snowe, beyonde the whiche is the enteraunce into the sea of Sur. . . . Here one of the shyppes stole away priuilie and returned into Spayne." More than five weeks were consumed in passing through the strait, and among its labyrinthine twists and half-hidden bays there was ample opportunity for desertion. As advanced reconnoissances kept reporting the water as deep and salt, the conviction grew that the strait was found, and

p. 232. These Patagonians invoked a deity of theirs (or as Pigafetta puts it, "the chief of their devils") by the name of Setebos. Shakespeare makes Caliban use this name twice in the *Tempest*, act i. scene 2, and act v. scene 1 ; in all probability he had been reading Eden's translation of Pigafetta, published in London in 1555. Robert Browning has elaborately developed Shakespeare's suggestions in his *Caliban on Setebos*.

then the question once more arose whether it would not be best to go back to Spain, satisfied with this discovery, since with all these wretched delays the provisions were again running short. Magellan's answer, uttered in measured and quiet tones, was simply that he would go on and do his work "if he had to eat the leather off the ship's yards." Upon the San Antonio there had always been a large proportion of the malcontents, and the chief pilot, Estevan Gomez, having been detailed for duty on that ship, lent himself to their purposes. The captain Mesquita was again seized and put in irons, a new captain was chosen by the mutineers, and Gomez piloted the ship back to Spain, where they arrived after a voyage of six months, and screened themselves for a while by lying about Magellan.

Desertion of Gomez, with the San Antonio

As for that commander, in Richard Eden's words, "when the capitayne Magalianes was past the strayght and sawe the way open to the other mayne sea, he was so gladde thereof that for ioy the teares fell from his eyes, and named the poynt of the lande from whense he fyrst sawe that sea *Capo Desiderato*. Supposing that the shyp which stole away had byn loste, they erected a crosse upon the top of a hyghe hyll to direct their course in the straight yf it were theyr chaunce to coome that way." The broad expanse of waters before

Entering the Pacific

him seemed so pleasant to Magellan, after the
heavy storms through which he had passed, that
he called it by the name it still bears, Pacific.
But the worst hardships were still before him.
Once more a Sea of Darkness must be crossed
by brave hearts sickening with hope deferred.
If the mid-Atlantic waters had been strange to
Columbus and his men, here before Magellan's
people all was thrice unknown.

> "They were the first that ever burst
> Into that silent sea;"

and as they sailed month after month over the
waste of waters, the huge size of our planet began to make itself felt. Until after the middle
of December they kept a northward course, near
the coast of the continent, running away from
the antarctic cold. Then northwesterly and
westerly courses were taken, and on the 24th
of January, 1521, a small wooded islet was
found in water where the longest plummet-lines
failed to reach bottom. Already the voyage
since issuing from the strait was nearly twice as
long as that of Columbus in 1492 from the Canaries to Guanahani. From the useless island,
which they called San Pablo, a further run of
eleven days brought them to another uninhabited rock, which they called Tiburones, from
the quantity of sharks observed in the Famine and
neighbourhood. There was neither scurvy
food nor water to be had there, and a voy-

439

age of unknown duration, in reality not less than 5000 English miles, was yet to be accomplished before a trace of land was again to greet their yearning gaze. Their sufferings may best be told in the quaint and touching words in which Shakespeare read them: "And hauynge in this tyme consumed all theyr bysket and other vyttayles, they fell into such necessitie that they were inforced to eate the pouder that remayned thereof beinge now full of woormes. . . . Theyre freshe water was also putrifyed and become yelow. They dyd eate skynnes and pieces of lether which were foulded abowt certeyne great ropes of the shyps. [Thus did the captain-general's words come true.] But these skynnes being made verye harde by reason of the soonne, rayne, and wynde, they hunge them by a corde in the sea for the space of foure or fiue dayse to mollifie them, and sodde them, and eate them. By reason of this famen and vnclene feedynge, summe of theyr gummes grewe so ouer theyr teethe [a symptom of scurvy], that they dyed miserably for hunger. And by this occasion dyed. xix. men, and . . besyde these that dyed, xxv. or. xxx. were so sicke that they were not able to doo any seruice with theyr handes or arms for feeblenesse: So that was in maner none without sum disease. In three monethes and. xx. dayes, they sayled foure thousande leaques in one goulfe by the sayde

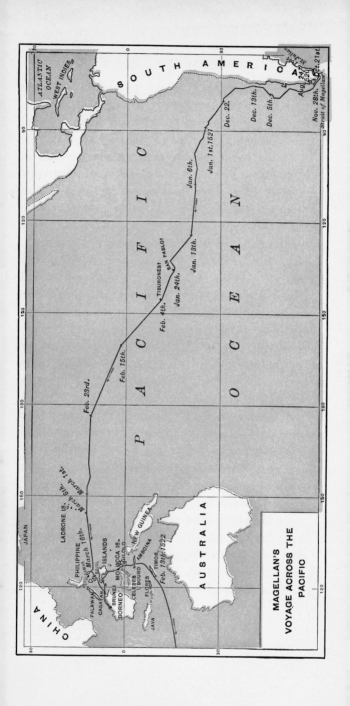

MAGELLAN'S VOYAGE ACROSS THE PACIFIC

sea cauled Pacificum (that is) peaceable, whiche may well bee so cauled forasmuch as in all this tyme hauyng no syght of any lande, they had no misfortune of wynde or any other tempest. . . . So that in fine, if god of his mercy had not gyuen them good wether, it was necessary that in this soo great a sea they shuld all haue dyed for hunger. Whiche neuertheless they escaped soo hardely, that it may bee doubted whether euer the like viage may be attempted with so goode successe." [1]

One would gladly know — albeit Pigafetta's journal and the still more laconic pilot's log-book leave us in the dark on this point — how the ignorant and suffering crews interpreted this everlasting stretch of sea, vaster, said Maximilian Transylvanus, "than the human mind could conceive." To them it may well have seemed that the theory of a round and limited earth was wrong after all, and that their infatuated commander was leading them out into the fathomless abysses of space, with no welcoming shore beyond. But that heart of triple bronze,[2] we may be sure, did not flinch. The situation had got beyond the point where mutiny could be suggested as a

Vastness beyond conception

---

[1] *The First Three English Books on America*, p. 253.

[2] Illi robur et æs triplex
Circa pectus erat, etc.

Horat., *Carm.*, i. 3 ; cf. Æschylus, *Prometh.*, 242.

remedy. The very desperateness of it was all in Magellan's favour; for so far away had they come from the known world that retreat meant certain death. The only chance of escape lay in pressing forward. At last, on the 6th of March, they came upon islands inhabited by The Ladrone savages ignorant of the bow and ar- Islands row, but expert in handling their peculiar light boats. Here the dreadful sufferings were ended, for they found plenty of fruit and fresh vegetables, besides meat. The people were such eager and pertinacious thieves that their islands received the name by which they are still known, the Islas de Ladrones, or isles of robbers.

On the 16th of March the three ships arrived at the islands which some years afterward were named Philippines, after Philip II. of Spain. Though these were islands unvisited by The Philip- Europeans, yet Asiatic traders from pines Siam and Sumatra, as well as from China, were to be met there, and it was thus not long before Magellan became aware of the greatness of his triumph. He had passed the meridian of the Moluccas, and knew that these islands lay to the southward within an easy sail. He had accomplished the circumnavigation of the earth through its unknown portion, and the remainder of his route lay through seas already traversed. An erroneous calculation of longitudes confirmed him in the belief that the Moluccas, as well as the Philippines, properly belonged to Spain. Meanwhile in these Philippines of themselves he had discovered a region of no small commercial importance. But his brief tarry in these interesting islands had fatal results, and in the very hour of victory the conqueror perished, slain in a fight with the natives, the reason of which we can understand only by considering the close complication of commercial and political interests with religious notions so common in that age.

As the typical Spaniard or Portuguese was then a persecutor of heresy at home, so he was always more or less of a missionary abroad, and the missionary spirit was in his case intimately allied with the crusading spirit. If the heathen resisted the gospel, it was quite right to slay and despoil them. Magellan's nature was devoutly religious, and exhibited itself in the points of strength and weakness most characteristic of his age. After he had made a treaty of alliance with the king of the island of Sebu, in which, among other things, the exclusive privilege of trading there was reserved to the Spaniards, Magellan made the unexpected discovery that the king and his people were ready and even eager to embrace Christianity! They had conceived an exalted idea of the powers and accomplishments of these

The mediæval spirit

443

white strangers, and apparently wished to imitate them in all things. So in less than a week's time a huge bonfire had been made of the idols, a cross was set up in the market, and all the people on the island were baptized! Now the king of Sebu claimed allegiance from chieftains on neighbouring islands who were slow to render it; and having adopted the white man's "medicine" he naturally wished to test its efficacy. What was Christianity good for if not to help you to humble your vassals? So the Christian king of Sebu demanded homage from the pagan king of Matan, and when the latter potentate scornfully refused, there was a clear case for a crusade! The steadfast commander, the ally and protector of his new convert, the peerless navigator, the knight without fear and without reproach, now turned crusader as quickly as he had turned missionary. Indeed there was no turning. These various aspects of life's work were all one to him; he would have summed up the whole thing as "serving God and doing his duty." So Magellan crossed over to the island of Matan, on the 27th of April, 1521, and was encountered by the natives in overwhelming force. After a desperate fight the Spaniards were obliged to retreat to their boats, and their commander, who years before had been the last man to leave a sinking ship, now lingered on the brink of danger, screening his men, till his helmet was knocked off and his right arm disabled by a spear thrust. A sudden Death of blow brought him to the ground, Magellan and then, says the Chevalier Pigafetta, " the Indians threw themselves upon him with iron-pointed bamboo spears and scimitars, and every weapon they had, and ran him through — our mirror, our light, our comforter, our true guide — until they killed him."[1]

In these scenes, as so often in life, the grotesque and the tragic were strangely mixed. The defeat of the white men convinced the king of Sebu that he had overestimated the blessings of Christianity, and so, by way of atonement for the slight he had cast upon the gods of his fathers, he invited some thirty of the leading Spaniards to a banquet, and massacred them. The massacre Among the men thus cruelly slain at Sebu were the faithful captains, Barbosa and Serrano. As the ships sailed hastily away the natives were seen chopping down the cross and conducting ceremonies in expiation of their brief apostasy. The blow was a sad one. Of the 280 men who had sailed out from the Guadalquivir only 115 remained. At the same time the Concepcion, being adjudged no longer seaworthy, was dismantled and burned to the water's edge. The constable Espinosa was elected captain of the

[1] Guillemard's *Magellan*, p. 252.

Victoria, and the pilot Carvalho was made captain-general, but proving incompetent, was presently superseded by that Sebastian Elcano who had been one of the mutineers at Port St. Julian. When the Trinidad and Victoria, after visiting Borneo, reached the Moluccas they found that Francisco Serrano had been murdered by order of the king of Tidor at about the same time that his friend Magellan had fallen at Matan. The Spaniards spent some time in these islands, trading. When they were ready to start, on the 18th of December, the Trinidad sprang a leak. It was thereupon decided that the Victoria should make for the Cape of Good Hope without delay, in order not to lose the favourable east monsoon. The Trinidad was to be thoroughly repaired, and then take advantage of the reversal of the monsoon to sail for Panama.[1] Apparently it was thought that the easterly breeze which had wafted them so steadily across the Pacific was a monsoon and would change like the Indian winds, — a most disastrous error. Of the 101 men still surviving, 54 were assigned to the Trinidad

Arrival at the Moluccas

---

[1] The circumstances of the founding of Panama will be mentioned below in volume iii., chapter x. In order to complete in a single picture the account of Mundus Novus, I tell the story of Magellan in the present chapter, somewhat in advance of its chronological position.

446

and 47 to the Victoria. The former ship was commanded by Espinosa, the latter by Elcano.

When the Trinidad set sail, April 6, 1522, she had the westerly monsoon in her favour, but as she worked up into the northern Pacific she encountered the northeast trade-wind, and in trying to escape it groped her way up to the fortieth parallel and beyond. By that time, overcome with famine and scurvy, she faced about and ran back to the Moluccas. When she arrived, it was without her mainmast. Of her 54 men all but 19 had found a watery grave; and now the survivors were seized by a party of Portuguese, and a new chapter of misery was begun. Only the captain Espinosa and three of the crew lived to see Spain again.

Fate of the Trinidad

Meanwhile on the 16th of May the little Victoria, with starvation and scurvy already thinning the ranks, with foretopmast gone by the board and foreyard badly sprung, cleared the Cape of Good Hope, and thence was borne on the strong and friendly current up to the equator, which she crossed on the 8th of June. Only fifty years since Santarem and Escobar, first of Europeans, had crept down that coast and crossed it ! Into that glorious half century what a world of suffering and achievement had been crowded ! Dire necessity compelled the Victoria to stop at the Cape Verde Islands. Her people sought safety in deceiving

Return of the Victoria

447

the Portuguese with the story that they were returning from a voyage in Atlantic waters only, and thus they succeeded in buying food. But while this was going on, as a boat-load of thirteen men had been sent ashore for rice, some silly tongue, loosened by wine in the head of a sailor who had cloves to sell, babbled the perilous secret of Magellan and the Moluccas. The thirteen were at once arrested and a boat called upon the Victoria, with direful threats, to surrender; but she quickly stretched every inch of her canvas and got away. This was on the 13th of July, and eight weeks of ocean remained. At last, on the 6th of September[1] — the thirtieth

[1] They were surprised to hear their friends at home calling it the 7th : "And amonge other notable thynges . . . wrytten as touchynge that vyage, this is one, that the Spanyardes hauinge sayled abowt three yeares and one moneth, and the most of them notynge the dayes, day by day (as is the maner of all them that sayle by the ocean), they founde when they were returned to Spayne that they had loste one daye. So that at theyr arryuall at the porte of Siuile, beinge the seuenth daye of September, was by theyr accompt but the sixth day. And where as Don Peter Martyr declared the strange effecte of this thynge to a certeyne excellente man, who, for his singular lernynge, was greately aduanced to honoure in his common welthe and made Themperour's ambassadoure, this worthy gentelman, who was also a greate Philosopher and Astronomer, answered that it coulde not otherwyse chaunce unto them, hauynge sayled three yeares continually, euer folowynge the soonne towarde the West." The First Three English Books on America, p. 246.

anniversary of the day when Columbus weighed anchor for Cipango — the Victoria sailed into the Guadalquivir, with eighteen gaunt and haggard survivors to tell the proud story of the first circumnavigation of the earth.[1]

The voyage thus ended was doubtless the greatest feat of navigation that has ever been performed, and nothing can be imagined that would surpass it except a journey to some other planet. It has not the unique historic position of the first voyage of Columbus, which brought together two streams of human life that had been disjoined since the Glacial period. But as an achievement in ocean navigation that voyage of Columbus sinks into insignificance by the side of it, and when the earth was a second time encompassed by the greatest English sailor of his age, the advance in knowledge, as well as the different route chosen, had much reduced the difficulty of the performance. When we consider the frailness of the ships, the immeasurable extent of the unknown, the mutinies that were prevented or quelled, and the hardships that were endured, we can have no hesitation in speaking of Magellan as the prince of navigators. Nor can we ever fail to admire the simplicity and purity of that devoted life in which there is nothing that seeks to be hidden or explained away.

An unparalleled voyage

[1] Their names are given below in vol. iii., Appendix D.

It would have been fitting that the proudest crest ever granted by a sovereign — a terrestrial globe belted with the legend *Primus circumdedisti me* (Thou first encompassed me) — should have been bestowed upon the son and representative of the hero ; but when the Victoria returned there was none to receive such recognition. In September, 1521, Magellan's son, the little Rodrigo, died, and by March, 1522, the gentle mother Beatriz had heard, by way of the Portuguese Indies, of the fate of her husband and her brother.[1] In that same month — " grievously sorrowing," as we are told — she died. The coat of arms with the crest just mentioned, along with a pension of 500 ducats, was granted to Elcano, a weak man who had ill deserved such honour. Espinosa was also, with more justice, pensioned and ennobled.

Elcano's crest

One might at first suppose that the revelation of such an immensity of water west of Mundus Novus would soon have resulted in the evolution of the conception of a distinct western hemisphere. This effect was, however, very slowly wrought in men's minds. The fact was too great and too strange to be easily taken in and assimilated with the mass of mingled fact and theory

How slowly the result was comprehended

[1] Guillemard, p. 90.